ARMENIAN APOCRYPHA

EARLY JUDAISM AND ITS LITERATURE

Ariel Feldman and Timothy J. Sandoval, General Editors

Editorial Board:
Atar Livneh
Daniel Machiela
Eshbal Ratzon
Elisa Uusimäki

Number 58

ARMENIAN APOCRYPHA

The Short Questionnaire from Adam to Moses

Michael E. Stone

SBL PRESS

Atlanta

Copyright © 2025 by SBL Press

All rights reserved. No part of this work may be reproduced or transmitted in any form or by any means, electronic or mechanical, including photocopying and recording, or by means of any information storage or retrieval system, except as may be expressly permitted by the 1976 Copyright Act or in writing from the publisher. Requests for permission should be addressed in writing to the Rights and Permissions Office, SBL Press, 825 Houston Mill Road, Atlanta, GA 30329 USA.

Library of Congress Control Number: 2023940933

Dedicated in gratitude to

"Matenadaran" Mesrop Mashtots Institute of Ancient Manuscripts

its directors and researchers

who, from 1986 to the present,

have always helped, encouraged, and supported my own research

into the remarkable heritage of the Armenian people.

Contents

List of Tables and Figures	xi
Preface	xiii
Abbreviations	xv
Armenian Apocryphal Works Mentioned	xxiii
Introductory Remarks	xxvii
M682, fols. 7r–9v	xxxvii

Texts, Translations, and Annotations

Parts 1–9. Questions Concerning Angels and the Garden of Eden

1. The Ranking of the Angels	5
Annotation 1. The Title	8
Annotation 2. Nine Classes of Angels	10
Annotation 3. The Seraphic Thrice Holy	18
2. Angels and Prophets' Praise	25
Annotation 4. Prayer and Angels	28
3. Nine Ranks of Angels and Human Leaders	33
4. Nine Ranks of Angels and Ecclesiastics	35
5. Another Ordering of Angels and Ecclesiastics	37
6. On Which Day Were the Angels Created?	39
Annotation 5. The Day on which the Angels Were Created	41
7. Where Did He Create Adam?	45
Annotation 6. The Place of the Protoplasts' Creation and Burial	46

8. On Which Day Did Sadayēl Fall from the Garden?	57
Annotation 7. The Name Sadayēl	59
Annotation 8. Why Did Satan Fall?	61
Annotation 9. Satan's Envy of and Enmity toward Humans	63
9. Adam and Eve in the Garden	69
Annotation 10. Stories of Paradise	73
Annotation 11. The Creation of Eden	78
Annotation 12. The Twelve Gifts that Adam Lost	82
Annotation 13. Luminous Garments	87

Parts 10–18. Noah to Exodus, the Oil of Anointing, and Prophets' Names

10. Expulsion from Eden up to the Flood	111
Exegetical Remarks	116
Annotation 14. Cain's Motive for Fratricide	120
Annotation 15. Abel's Sheep	128
11. The Sethites and the Cainites: Beginnings	131
Annotation 16. The Sons of God, the Sons of Seth, the Watchers, and the Giants	134
Annotation 17. Questionnaire's Position in the Armenian Tradition: Sethites and Cainites	156
12. Noah and the Building of the Ark	159
Annotation 18. Noah's Virginity	163
Annotation 19. The Raven	163
13. Peoples of the Sons of Noah	169
Annotation 20. Peoples of the Sons of Noah	176
Annotation 21. Maniton, Noah's Fourth Son	178
Annotation 22. Nimrod	185
14. Concerning the Construction of the Tower	193
Annotation 23. The Tower	195
Annotation 24. The Seventy-Two Languages and Nations	198
15. Concerning Abraham and His Sons	203
Annotation 25. The Death of Haran, Abraham's Brother	209

	Contents	ix
	Annotation 26. Ten Trials of Abraham	211
	Annotation 27. Isaac's Virginity and Fasting	212
16.	Egypt and Exodus	215
	Annotation 28. Jannes and Jambres in Armenian Texts	224
17.	The Oil of Anointing	227
18.	Names of the Twenty-Four Prophets	231
	Bibliography	235
	Ancient Sources Index	269
	General Index	287

List of Tables and Figures

Table 1. Overview of the Structure of the Questionnaire   xxxii
Table 2. The Twelve Gifts That Adam Lost   83

Figures 1–8. M682, fols. 7r–9v   xxxvii
Figure 9. J1925, fol. 414v (Ezekiel's Vision of the Divine Chariot)   29
Figure 10. M5523, 1414 (The Harrowing of Hell Showing Black Demon)   167

Preface

This book is the seventh of the series of Armenian apocrypha that has been published since 1982. Differently from the preceding volumes, this book presents only one, relatively short text. It is erotapocritic in character, using questions as keys for exposition of specific topics. The range of such question and answer (Q&A) texts in Armenian is large, both in subject matter and in literary character, from brief quizzes on points of biblical history to long expositions to which the question is just a formulaic introductory convention. This extensive genre is worthy of study in its own right, and these introductory remarks are not the appropriate place for that discussion.

This text, however, asks a series of questions about events that form the embroidered Bible story as it was told in Armenia in a developed form. It enquires about happenings from the fall of Satan and the creation of the angels down to the biblical patriarchs. I first edited and translated the text and then added textual and exegetical notes where needed. In addition, to many of the Q&As I have added longer or shorter studies in which I sought to do two things. The first was to draw together the varied Armenian traditions on these subjects, chiefly calling upon the Armenian parabiblical texts and traditions. Then, a second question was posed: How does this Armenian parabiblical material relate to treatments of the same subjects in Christian, particularly Greek and Syriac, Jewish, and to some extent other Abrahamic traditions—Islam, Manichean, Samaritan, and others.

The labor was large, and I was helped in it by some younger scholars. Dr. Shlomi Efrati read and commented on the whole manuscript. He wrote notes, some quite extensive, and has graciously agreed to publish several of them in the present volume. Such comments of his are placed within square brackets and conclude with his initials [–S.E.]. All material so marked is authored by him. In addition, my research assistants relieved me of much of the technical work as well as lightening the labor in many other ways: thank you Nathan Daniel, Yarden Siton, Matthew Wilson, and Roi Ziv. Your help and support were beyond value. Dr. Ani Arakelyan of the Matenadaran, painstakingly verified my collations and proofread all the Armenian text.

His Beatitude Archbishop Nourhan Manougian, the Armenian Patriarch of Jerusalem, has made the publication of figure 9 on fol. 414v of Jerusalem Armenian Patriarchate manuscript J1925 possible. Permission to publish this image was initially granted by the late Patriarch Torkom Manoogian.

Special thanks are due to the "Matenadaran" Mesrop Mashtots Institute of Ancient Manuscripts in Erevan, Armenia and its former and current directors, Vahan Ter-Ghevondyan and Ara Khzmalyan, both for the permission to publish this text from manuscript no. M286 (figs. 1–8) and for supplying me with the images of this text and also of M5523, fol. 1414 (fig. 10). The Matenadaran and its directors have encouraged my work and have made available to me the manuscript originals of many other texts cited in the present study. Most of all, however, I wish to express my appreciation for the collegial warmth, encouragement, and cooperation that have been extended to me over four decades and continue to this day.

The Israel Science Foundation supported my work in preparation of this seventh volume of the series of Armenian apocrypha by a Personal Research Grant, no. 1301/21, as they have supported the last four volumes of this undertaking. My thanks and appreciation are hereby expressed.

Abbreviations

General Abbreviations

a.m.	*anno mundi*, that is, the era starting with creation
bis	second occurrence of word in sentence, letter in word, etc.
fol(s).	folio(s)
l(l).	line(s)
n(n).	footnote(s)
p(p).	page(s)
[–S.E.]	comment by Shlomi Efrati

Critical Signs

< >	text introduced by the editor, either emendations, or manuscript readings drawn from another source
( )	words introduced into a translation for the sake of style or comprehensibility
[.]	lacuna in the manuscript text; "." indicates one letter
{ }	corruption in the manuscript text.

Procedures

- Each new segment or question is called a part, and parts are divided into sections indicated by §.
- Sigla for manuscript libraries follow the system Bernard Coulie developed for the Association internationale des études arméniennes. See Coulie 2021.
- Transliteration of Armenian always follows the method accepted by the *Revue des études arméniennes*, except for common biblical names, which normally appear in the ordinary English forms.
- Biblical citations are according to the RSV unless stated otherwise.

- Biblical and associated literature is cited according to the *SBL Handbook of Style*, 2nd edition. Where there is a difference of chapter and verse numbering between the Masoretic and Armenian versions of the Hebrew Bible, the Armenian number is given second and in round brackets.
- Armenian Apocrypha cited are presented in the list on pp. xxiii–xxvi, which includes the details of their place of publication; in the body of the book, they are referred to only by name and, as relevant, with chapter and verse or section (§) numbers.

Armenian Apocrypha Series edited by Michael E. Stone

Arm Apoc 1	Stone, Michael E. 1982. *Armenian Apocrypha Relating to Patriarchs and Prophets*. Jerusalem: Israel Academy of Sciences and Humanities.
Arm Apoc 2	Stone, Michael E. 1996. *Armenian Apocrypha Relating to Adam and Eve*. SVTP 14. Leiden: Brill.
Arm Apoc 3	Stone, Michael E. 2012. *Armenian Apocrypha Relating to Abraham*. EJL 37. Atlanta: Society of Biblical Literature.
Arm Apoc 4	Stone, Michael E. 2016. *Armenian Apocrypha Relating to Angels and Biblical Heroes*. EJL 45. Atlanta: SBL Press.
Arm Apoc 5	Stone, Michael E. 2019. *Armenian Apocrypha Relating to Biblical Heroes*. EJL 49. Atlanta: SBL Press.
Arm Apoc 6	Stone, Michael E. 2021. *Armenian Apocrypha from Adam to Daniel*. EJL 55. Atlanta: SBL Press.

Other Bibliographical Abbreviations

1 Clem.	1 Clement
1 En.	1 Enoch
1QH^a	1QHodayot
1QS	Rule of the Community
2 Bar.	2 Baruch
2 En.	2 Enoch
3 Bar.	3 Baruch (Greek Apocalypse of Baruch)
3 En.	3 Enoch
4 Bar.	4 Baruch (Paraleipomena Jeremiou)

4QGenApoc	4Q Genesis Apocryphon
ABD	Freedman, David Noel, ed. *Anchor Bible Dictionary*. 6 vols. New York: Doubleday, 1992.
A.J.	Josephus, *Antiquitates judaicae*
AJEC	Ancient Judaism and Early Christianity
a.m.	*anno mundi*
ANF	Roberts, Alexander, and James Donaldson, eds. 1885–1887. *The Ante-Nicene Fathers: Translations of the Writings of the Fathers Down to A.D. 325*. 10 vols. Buffalo, NY: Christian Literature. Repr. Grand Rapids: Eerdmans.
AOAT	Alter Orient und Altes Testament
Apoc. Abr.	Apocalypse of Abraham
Apoc. Paul	Apocalypse of Paul
Apoc. Zeph.	Apocalypse of Zephaniah
Apos. Cons.	Apostolic Constitutions
AS	*Aramaic Studies*
Ascen. Isa.	Ascension of Isaiah
Avod. Zar.	Avodah Zarah
Avot R. Nat.	Avot de Rabbi Nathan
AYBD	Freedman, David Noel, ed. 1992. *Anchor Yale Bible Dictionary*. New York: Doubleday.
b.	Babylonian Talmud
b. Bat.	Bava Batra
Barn.	Barnabas
Ber.	Berakhot
BETL	Bibliotheca Ephemeridum Theologicarum Lovaniensium
BibInt	Biblical Interpretation
BJS	Brown Judaic Studies
BN	*Biblische Notizen*
BSOAS	*Bulletin of the School of Oriental and African Studies*
CBET	Contributions to Biblical Exegesis and Theology
CBQM	Catholic Biblical Quarterly Monograph Series
CD	Damascus Document
CJA	Christianity and Judaism in Antiquity
CNS	*Cristianesimo nella storia*
Comm. Gen.	Commentary on Genesis
Comm. Matt.	Origen, *Commentarium in evangelium Matthaei*

ConBOT	Coniectanea Biblica Old Testament Series
CSCO	Corpus Scriptorum Christianorum Orientalium
CT	Cave of Treasures
Demonst.	Afrahat, *Demonstrations*
DOP	*Dumbarton Oaks Papers*
DSD	*Dead Sea Discoveries*
DSSSE	García Martínez, Florentino, and Eibert Tigchelaar. 1997. *The Dead Sea Scrolls: Study Edition.* 2 vols. Leiden: Brill.
ECCC	Eastern Christian Cultures in Contact
EJL	Early Judaism and Its Literature
EncJud	Skolnik, Fred, and Michael Berenbaum, eds. 2007. *Encyclopedia Judaica.* 2nd ed. 22 vols. Detroit: Macmillan Reference.
EncIslam	Fleet, Kate, Gudrun Krämer, Denis Matringe, John Nawas, Devin J. Steward, eds. 2023. *Encyclopedia of Islam.* 3rd ed. Online. https://referenceworks.brillonline.com/browse/encyclopaedia-of-islam-3.
Ep.	*Epistle*
ETL	*Ephemerides Theologicae Lovanienses*
Exod. Rab.	Exodus Rabbah
Exp.	Ephrem, *Exposition of the Gospels*
FC	Fathers of the Church
GCS	Die griechischen christlichen Schriftsteller der ersten [drei] Jahrhunderte
Gen.	Ephrem, *On Genesis*
Gen. Rab.	Genesis Rabbah
General Catalogue	*General Catalogue of the Matenadaran* (referred to by volume and column)
Gos. Barth.	Gospel of Bartholomew
Gos. Phil.	Gospel of Philip
Haer.	Irenaeus, *Adversus haereses*
Hag.	Hagigah
HdO	Handbuch der Orientalistik
Herm. Sim.	Shepherd of Hermas, Similitudes
Hist.	Agathangelos, *History of the Armenians*
Hom.	Pseudo-Clementines, *Homily*
Hom. Gen.	John Chrysostom, *Homily on Genesis*
HSS	Harvard Semitic Studies

HTR	*Harvard Theological Review*
HUAS	Hebrew University Armenian Series
Hul.	Hullin
IDB	Buttrick, George A., ed. 1962. *The Interpreter's Dictionary of the Bible.* 5 vols. New York: Abingdon.
IDBSup	*Interpreters Dictionary of the Bible Supplement*
Inan. glor.	John Chrysostom, *De inani gloria et de educandis liberis*
IOS	*Israel Oriental Studies*
JAS	*Journal of Armenian Studies*
JBL	*Journal of Biblical Literature*
JE	Singer, Isidore, ed. 1901–1906. *The Jewish Encyclopedia: A Descriptive Record of the History, Religion, Literature, and Customs of the Jewish People from the Earliest Times to the Present Day.* 12 vols. New York: Funk & Wagnalls.
JECS	*Journal of Eastern Christian Studies*
JSHRZ	Jüdische Schriften aus hellenistisch-römischer Zeit
JJS	*Journal of Jewish Studies*
JQR	*Jewish Quarterly Review*
JSAS	*Journal of the Society of Armenian Studies*
JSJ	*Journal for the Study of Judaism in the Persian, Hellenistic, and Roman Periods*
JSJSup	Journal for the Study of Judaism in the Persian, Hellenistic, and Roman Periods Supplement
JSOT	*Journal for the Study of the Old Testament*
JSOTSup	Journal for the Study of the Old Testament Supplement
JSP	*Journal for the Study of the Pseudepigrapha*
JSPSup	Journal for the Study of the Pseudepigrapha Supplement
JSQ	*Jewish Studies Quarterly*
JTS	*Journal of Theological Studies*
Jub.	Jubilees
LAB	Liber antiquitatum biblicarum
LAE	Life of Adam and Eve
LXX	The Septuagint Greek translation of the Hebrew Bible (Old Testament)

MEMAS	*Matenadaran: Medieval and Early Modern Armenian Studies*
Menah.	Menahot
Metaph.	Aristotle, *Metaphysics*
MH	Մատենագիրք Հայոց [*Armenian Classical Authors*], series referred to by volume and page.
Midr. Tanh.	Midrash Tanhuma
Midr. Teh.	Midrash Tehillim (Psalms)
MOTP	Richard Bauckham, James R. Davila, and Alexander Panayotov, eds. 2013. *Old Testament Pseudepigrapha: More Noncanonical Scriptures.* Vol. 1. Grand Rapids: Eerdmans.
MT	The Masoretic Hebrew Text of the Hebrew Bible (Old Testament)
NBHL	Awetikʻean, Gabriēl, Xačʻatur Siwrmēlean, and Mkrtičʻ Awkʻerean. 1837. Նոր Բառգիրք Հայկազեան Լեզուի [New Dictionary of the Armenian Language]. 2 vols. Venice: Saint Lazzaro.
Ned.	Nedarim
NPNF	Schaff, Philip, and Henry Wace, eds. 1886–1900. *Nicene and Post-Nicene Fathers of the Christian Church.* Edinburgh: T&T Clark.
NumenSup	Supplements to Numen
OCP	*Orientalia Christiana Periodica*
Odes Sol.	Odes of Solomon
OLA	Orientalia Lovaniensia Analecta
Opif.	Philo, *De opificio mundi*
OrChrAn	Orientalia Christiana Analecta
OTP	Charlesworth, James H., ed. 1983. *The Old Testament Pseudepigrapha.* 2 vols. Garden City, NY: Doubleday.
OtSt	Oudtestamentische Studien
PAAJR	*Proceedings of the American Academy of Jewish Research*
Pan.	Epiphanius, *Panarion* (*Adversus haerses*)
PEFQ	*Palestine Exploration Fund Quarterly*
Pesah.	Pesahim
Pesiq. Rab.	Pesiqta Rabbati
PH	Palaea Historica
PhA	Philosophia Antiqua

Pirqe R. El.	Pirqe de Rabbi Eliezer
Praep. ev.	Eusebius, *Praeparatio evangelica*
Princ.	Origen, *De principiis*
Q&A	Question and Answer texts, erotapokriseis
QE	Philo, *Quaestiones et solutiones in Exodum*
Qu. hebr. Gen.	Jerome, *Liber Quaestionum hebraicarum in Genesim*
RB	*Revue Biblique*
Rearm	*Revue des études arméniennes*
Recogn.	Pseudo-Clement, *Recognitiones*
REJ	*Revue des études juives*
RevQ	*Revue de Qumran*
RHPR	*Revue d'histoire et de philosophie religieuses*
ROC	*Revue de l'Orient chrétien*
RSO	*Rivista degli Studi Orientali*
RSV	Revised Standard Version
Sacr.	Philo, *De sacrificiis Abelis et Caini*
Sanh.	Sanhedrin
SBLDS	Society of Biblical Literature Dissertation Series
SBLMS	Society of Biblical Literature Monograph Series
SBLTT	Society of Biblical Literature Texts and Translations
SCS	Septuagint and Cognate Studies
SECA	Studies in Early Christian Apocrypha
Sib. Or.	Sibylline Oracles
Sifre Num.	Sifre Numbers
SJ	Studia Judaica
SNT	Studien zum Neuen Testament
SNTSMS	Society for New Testament Studies Monograph Series
Somn.	Philo, *De somniis*
Song Rab.	Songs Rabbah
SPCK	Society for the Promotion of Christian Knowledge
Spec.	Philo, *De specialibus legibus*
STDJ	Studies in the Texts of the Desert of Judea
SVTG	Septuaginta: Vetus Testamentum Graece
SVTP	Studia in Veteris Testamenti Pseudepigrapha
t.	Tosefta
T. Abr.	Testament of Abraham
T. Adam	Testament of Adam
T. Benj.	Testament of Benjamin
T. Isaac	Testament of Isaac

T. Iss.	Testament of Issachar
T. Levi	Testament of Levi
T. Reu.	Testament of Reuben
Tanh.	Tanhuma
TBN	Themes in Biblical Narrative
TDNT	Kittel, Gerhard, and Gerhard Friedrich. 1964–1976. *Theological Dictionary of the New Testament.* Translated by Geoffrey W. Bromiley. 10 vols. Grand Rapids: Eerdmans.
Theodor-Albeck	Theodor, Judah, and Chanoch Albeck. 1965. *Bereschit Rabba mit Kritischem Apparat und Kommentar* [Hebrew]. Repr., Jerusalem: Wahrmann.
Theog.	Hesiod, *Theogony*
TM	Tibat Marqe. See Tal, Abraham. 2019. *Tibat Marqe: The Ark of Marqe.* Studia Judaica 92; Studia Samaritana 9. Berlin: de Gruyter.
Trall.	Ignatius, *To the Trallians*
TSAJ	Texte und Studien zum antiken Judentum
TU	Texte und Untersuchungen
UPATS	University of Pennsylvania Armenian Texts and Studies
VC	*Vigiliae Christianae*
VCSup	Vigiliae Christianae Supplement
VT	*Vetus Testamentum*
VTSup	Vetus Testamentum Supplement
WUNT	Wissenschaftliche Untersuchungen zum Neuen Testament
y.	Jerusalem Talmud
Yevam.	Yevamot
ZAW	*Zeitschrift für die alttestamentliche Wissenschaft*
ZNW	*Zeitschrift für die neutestamentliche Wissenschaft und die Kunde der älteren Kirche*
ZRGG	*Zeitschrift für Religions- und Geistesgeschichte*

Armenian Apocryphal Works Mentioned

This list comprises those Armenian apocryphal or parabiblical works mentioned in the present volume, not all Armenian parabiblica. Most of these works are little known; therefore, it seemed wise to provide bibliographic information indicating their names and where they are published. It is hoped that this will facilitate future access to this rich literature.[1] Where they occur in the series Armenian Apocrypha (*Arm Apoc*), col. 2 gives the volume number and text number or, if there is none, page spans.

Text Name	Place of Publication
Abel and Cain, Abel, Sons of Adam, History of	Lipscomb 1990, 142–71, 249–54, 270–75; Yovsēpʻeancʻ 1896, 314–19; Issaverdens 1934, 53–58[2]
Abel and Other Pieces	*Arm Apoc* 2:141–57
Abraham and His Sons, Concerning	*Arm Apoc* 7 (forthcoming)
Abraham Text, Elenchic	*Arm Apoc* 3.10
Abraham, Concerning	*Arm Apoc* 5.4
Abraham, Father, Story of	*Arm Apoc* 3.2
Abraham, Genealogy of	*Arm Apoc* 3.5
Abraham, Hospitality, Concerning	*Arm Apoc* 3.11A
Abraham, Isaac, and Mamre	*Arm Apoc* 3.8
Abraham, Ten Trials of	*Arm Apoc* 3.13

---

    1. In certain instances, additional publications of texts, translations, or collations are also indicated.

    2. English translations of some of these Armenian apocryphal and parabiblical works are to be found in Issaverdens 1934. Translation of the Armenian Adam books into German may be found in Preuschen 1900.

Text Name	Place of Publication
Adam and Eve, Bones of	Stone 2000b
Adam and Eve, Creation and Transgression of	Yovsēpʻeancʻ 1896, 307–11; Issaverdens 1934, 43–48; Lipscomb 1990, 108–27, 241–45, 261–66
Adam and Eve, Repentance of	Yovsēpʻeancʻ 1896, 325–31; Issaverdens 1934, 43–48; Lipscomb 1990, 221–33
Adam and his Grandsons, History of	Arm Apoc 2:80–98
Adam, Book of	Yovsēpʻeancʻ 1896, 1–26; Issaverdens 1934, 21–42; Conybeare 1894
Adam, Death of	Arm Apoc 1:15–31, Arm Apoc 2:209–212
Adam, Descendants of	Arm Apoc 1:84–87
Adam, Eve and the Incarnation	Arm Apoc 2:8–79
Adam, Fragment 1	Arm Apoc 1:6–9; Stone 1992, 2–11
Adam, Fragment 2	Arm Apoc 1:10–11; Stone, 1992, 2–11
Adam, Story 1	Arm Apoc 2:101–08
Adam, Story 2	Arm Apoc 2:109–113
Adam, the Words of, to Seth	Arm Apoc 1:12–13; Yovsēpʻeancʻ 1896, 331–32; Issaverdens 1934, 43–48; Arm Apoc 1:12–13; Lipscomb 1990, 206–9
Adam, Penitence of	Stone 1981a
Biblical Paraphrases	Arm Apoc 1.2
Cycle of Four Works	Yovsēpʻeancʻ 1896, 307–24; Issaverdens 1934, 41–64; Lipscomb 1990, 102–205, 241–82
Daniel, Story of	Arm Apoc 5.18
Egypt, Ten Plagues of	Arm Apoc 4.4.9
Eleven Periods	Arm Apoc 2:139–40
Elijah, Short History of	Arm Apoc 5.14; Yovsēpʻeancʻ 1896, 333–42; Issaverdens 1934, 172–84
Eve, Creation and Disobedience of	Arm Apoc 6.7

Armenian Apocryphal Works Mentioned

Text Name	Place of Publication
Ezra, Fourth (Third)	Stone 1979
Flood, Sermon Concerning the	*Arm Apoc* 2:174–79
Forefathers, Adam and His Sons and Grandsons, History of the	*Arm Apoc* 2:180–200
Forefathers, History of the, to Abraham	*Arm Apoc* 4.2.7
Forefathers, Memorial of the	*Arm Apoc* 3.4
Forefathers, Short History of the Holy	*Arm Apoc* 4.4.5
History of the Discourse	*Arm Apoc* 4.3.9
Horarium (Testament of Adam)	*Arm Apoc* 1.1.4; *Arm Apoc* 2:167–73
Jannes and Mambres	*Arm Apoc* 4.4.10
Jeremiah, Susanna, and the Two Elders	*Arm Apoc* 5.16
Jonah 1	*Arm Apoc* 6.17.1
Jonah 2	*Arm Apoc* 6.17.2
Joseph, Third Story of	*Arm Apoc* 4.4.7
Joshua son of Nun, Short (Brief) History of	*Arm Apoc* 5.7
Millennia, Concerning the, 1	*Arm Apoc* 4.2.3.1
Millennia, Concerning the, 2	*Arm Apoc* 4.2.3.2
Millennia, Concerning the, 3	*Arm Apoc* 4.2.3.3
Moses and Aaron, Of	*Arm Apoc* 6.12
Patriarchs, Names of the Wives of	*Arm Apoc* 2.165
Noah, Story of	*Arm Apoc* 1:88–103
Noah's Ark, Construction of	*Arm Apoc* 5.3
Noah's Ark, Form and Structure of	*Arm Apoc* 6.8
Oil of Anointing of Israel, Concerning the	*Arm Apoc* 7 (227–30)
Patriarchs, Testaments of the Twelve	Stone and Hillel 2012
Peoples of the Sons of Noah	Stone 1981c, 224–28
Periods, Concerning the	*Arm Apoc* 4.2.4
Prophets, Twenty-Four, Names of the	*Arm Apoc* 7 (forthcoming)
Question	*Arm Apoc* 2:114–34

Text Name	Place of Publication
Question concerning the Archangels	*Arm Apoc* 4.3.3
Questionnaire (M682)	*Arm Apoc* 7 (the present volume)
Questions and Answers from the Holy Books (two versions)	*Arm Apoc* 4.3.8; *Arm Apoc* 6.23
Questions of Ezra	Yovsēpʻeancʻ 1896, 300–303; Issaverdens 1934, 504–09; Stone 1995; Leonhardt-Balzer 2005
Questions of St. Gregory	Stone 2018; Stone 2022
Questions of the Queen and Answers of King Solomon	Yovsēpʻeancʻ 1896, 229–31; Issaverdens 1934, 163–66; cf. Brock 1979b
Seth, Concerning the Good Tidings of	Yovsēpʻeancʻ 1896, 319–24; Issaverdens 1934, 59–64; Lipscomb 1990, 172–205
Sethites and Cainites	*Arm Apoc* 2:201–6
Sodomites and Gomorreans, Supplication about	*Arm Apoc* 5.6
Terah and Father Abraham, Story of	*Arm Apoc* 3.11
Tower Texts	*Arm Apoc* 6.9.1–5
Tower, Concerning the	*Arm Apoc* 4.4.1–4.2
Tree of Sabek	*Arm Apoc* 3.7

Introductory Remarks

Short Questionnaire Selected and Gathered from Written Sources is the title of a very interesting work preserved on fols. 7r–9v of Armenian manuscript M682, preserved at the Maštoc' Matenadaran Institute of Ancient Manuscripts in Erevan, Armenia. The codex is a miscellany copied in 1679.[1] Questionnaire, as I will refer to this work, is written in a cramped *notrgir* (late cursive) hand on large format paper, 23 x 18 cm in size, and in a single column. In the present book, I use the manuscript's foliation, which is marked in pencil on the recto sides of the folios. Its numbers are not quite sequential, since during the process of pagination, an additional folio was turned over simultaneously, apparently by error, while turning over folio 7. It seems that this mistake was discovered only after the folio numbers had been entered in the continuation of the manuscript. Instead of erasing all the folio numbers and renumbering all the folios from 7bis on, the unnumbered folio was paginated with the Armenian numerals 7c–7d. Thus, the folio numbers of the work being studied here run: 6v, 7a, 7b, 7c, 7d, 8r, 8v, 9r, 9v, and so on. In the present book, in referring to the manuscript original of the various parts into which I have divided the work, I give both the folio numbers and the line numbers on the manuscript page at their head. In addition to the biblical explanations being presented here in Questionnaire, the manuscript encompasses a variety of patristic works. On folios 95r–101v, the Armenian apocryphal Adam writing, Cycle of Four Works, with the embedded homilies occurs.[2]

---

1. See *General Catalogue* 3.310–316. Its provenance is unknown.
2. The edition by Lipscomb 1990 improves greatly on that of Yovsēpʻeancʻ 1896, both of which were printed without the homilies; see also Issaverdens 1934, 43–64. There are several still unpublished manuscripts of Cycle of Four Works mentioned in catalogues of manuscript collections, and it needs a full, critical edition. On this important Adam apocryphon, see Stone 1992, 102–4. An edition of one of the homilies that Cycle of Four Works intersperses between its blocks of narrative is given

Introductory Remarks

The work is written in ancient Armenian that poses few difficulties to the editor and translator. Its language, as is the case in many similar manuscript texts, exhibits some features of mediaeval style and orthography. The scribe regularly wrote only the initial letters of the tag words, Հ for Հարց ("question") and Պ for Պատասխանի ("answer") followed by a single dot, without any mark of abbreviation. This is often the case in such erotapokritic texts. I have chosen, however, to write both words out in full in the transcription.

Date of Questionnaire

Questionnaire itself presents no date, nor is its date ascertainable from external sources as far as I know. However, the author's practice of incorporating pieces of text that are drawn from other works sometimes enables its dating on comparative criteria. In the section on "Descent of Sethites from the Mountain," I have pointed out a certain point in which Questionnaire appears to depend on the Armenian translations of *The Chronography* of Michael the Syrian.[3] This would date it to after the middle of the thirteenth century. The same date is indicated by the author's apparent familiarity with *The Historical Compilation* of Vardan Arewelc'i.[4]

Format and Method of the Author

In §13.6 the author[5] feels the need to account for the fact that the existence and story of Maniton, Noah's fourth son, are not mentioned by Genesis. This shows that he regards his parabiblical narrative and exegetical tradi-

---

in Kazazian and Stone 2004. The work often retells biblical incidents and then treats them as paradigmatic in the hortatory addresses. This combination of narrative and homily contributes to my understanding of the creation and function of numerous pseudepigrapha extant in Armenian.

3. See part 11 at n. 44 and p. 139. See the discussion "*The Chronography* by Michael the Syrian (Twelfth Century)" in part 11 on this work.

4. See part 9, n. 51.

5. Throughout I use the masculine pronoun to designate the author and the copyist. Indeed, there are records of a few female copyists of mediaeval Armenian manuscripts, but the overwhelming number of the copyists and the theological authors whose gender is known were male. The reader should bear in mind that there is no decisive evidence as to the gender of the author and copyist of Questionnaire, and my usage is based on statistical probability.

tion as being authoritative, despite its content not having been drawn from Genesis. On the other hand, in §7.2 he invokes Scripture to determine a debated point, and, furthermore, in the next section he says of such a moot point, "But because Moses did not write (about this), it is knowable to God (alone)." This second type of argument clearly shows that the work was composed in a learned setting. This conclusion is also supported by the clear signs of scholastic learning that the author makes evident in the following instances: use of the tag "in other books" (introduction, n. 3)[6] to invoke an alternative tradition or view; lists (annotation 2, n. 47); "some say" or "they say" to mark a variant view (part 10, n. 76 and elsewhere). The very literary form of erotapokrisis, which is composed of questions posed to a text and answers to them, is itself nurtured in a scholarly context.

A method used by this author, again typical of a person trained in a scholastic environment, is to incorporate into the text both short extracts taken from other writings as well as varied short compositions and lists that are relevant to the subject being discussed. Those that I have identified in Questionnaire are set forth here. There may be others that have escaped my attention.

Part number	Source	Bibliography
13	Peoples of the Sons of Noah	Stone 1981c, 224–28
15	Ten Trials of Abraham	*Arm Apoc* 2:204–5
16	Ten Plagues of Egypt	*Arm Apoc* 4:254–57
11	The *Chronography* of Michael the Syrian	Sawalaneancʻ 1870 Sawalaneancʻ 1871
16	*The Historical Compilation* of Vardan Arewelcʻi	Thomson 1989

I have chosen to edit and annotate this composition not because of its own intrinsic value but because it touches, in the sequence of biblical chronology, on a great many subjects of the rewritten biblical history, the Embroidered Bible, of the Armenians.[7] It has thus provided me with the occasion to add to the edition of the text, and to my translation and commentaries

---

6. See further part 1, n. 4 below.
7. Concerning this term, see Stone 2019.

on Questionnaire itself, also twenty-eight more discursive annotations on these various themes and subjects. In these annotations, I have striven to assemble Armenian apocryphal witnesses to the various specific topics with which they deal and to indicate their connections with similar ideas and subjects that are preserved and developed in other cultural traditions. This tradition complex is then studied in its relation to more ancient para-biblical writings and traditions, chiefly Jewish and Christian.

Some Views Stressed by the Author of Questionnaire

In his presentation of the biblical story, the author takes opportunities to stress certain specific concepts. Here I shall list the chief among them. Further below, I shall give parallels to those concepts relating to the antediluvian period. Further consideration of these subjects may be found in Stone 2013. More discussions of these traditions and of lore known from later periods is to be found in the commentaries here, ad loc.

1. In part 8, On Which Day Did Sadayēl Fall from the Garden? §§1–2, the author emphasizes the notion that angels and humans have free will (անձնիշխանութիւն "autonomy") and in exercising that autonomy both angels and humans sometimes make a wrong choice.[8] Thus, angels as well as humans may sin.

2. In part 9, Adam and Eve in the Garden §2, the view is mentioned that Adam and Eve were in Eden only for one day and that they sinned on the very same day on which they were created. Questionnaire opposes this view rather energetically on the grounds that the serpent's persuasion of Eve and the protoplasts' eating of the fruit were too much activity to take place on the same Friday as Adam's creation. Equally, the author opposes the opinions that set their stay in Eden at forty days or one thousand years, on the grounds that the Enemy could not have waited so long.

3. In part 9 §3, our author, like other Armenian theological thinkers, combats the idea that the world was created from preexistent matter. In general, the issues of *creatio ex nihilo* and the denial of preexistent matter seem to have been of great import for the author. Moreover, he argues very strongly that God Himself created, and no other power was associ-

---

[8]. The corresponding rabbinic views are analyzed by Schäfer 1986, especially 76–77. Badalanova Geller 2021c, 21 says that according to 2 Enoch it is the view that angels did not have free will but were bound, like soldiers, to fulfill their commander's orders.

ated with Him in the creative acts. The present document, then, has as one of its polemical objects the attack on views holding preexistence of matter and that other beings were associated with God in creation.

4. In part 10, Expulsion from Eden up to the Flood §1, a reading of the Cain and Abel story is found that implicitly denies that God created evil or that evil was preexistent.[9]

This Edition

In this edition, I give the document Questionnaire in its entirety. In addition to those parts of the text being published for the first time here, it seemed wise to reprint in the present edition certain segments of the document that I had published previously in my thematic collections of writings relating to Abraham and to angels.[10] The texts and translations of such reprinted parts given here are drawn from those publications, with occasional slight revisions, and the notes written there are abbreviated to some extent in the present study. Thus, a full and overall picture of the document can be gained from the edition and translation that I am presenting here. However, my previous, partial editions, which are indicated clearly in the present work, should also be consulted. In addition to introductory remarks to each part and to the commented text and translation, I have introduced annotations on specific subjects, such as have been mentioned above, between the several parts.

A second, incomplete copy of an abbreviated and variant form of part of Questionnaire survives in Galata MS 154, on pp. 300–305.[11] I hope to publish this separately in the future. It also became evident during my investigation that parts of this work are closely allied with some other Armenian apocryphal writings and fragments, a subject discussed above. More such literary sources of Questionnaire may emerge as the labor of publication of the Armenian parabiblica progresses.

---

9. See Greatrex 2009, as discussed in part 8, nn. 36, 40 and the introduction there, pp. 63–64.

10. See *Arm Apoc* 4:83–91, no. 3.7.

11. See Kiwleserian 1961, 975–90. Galata MS 154 is now housed in the Armenian Patriarchate, Istanbul. Parts of the text are to be found in *Arm Apoc* 3:78–85. See also *Arm Apoc* 4:83–91, no. 3.7.

The Structure of the Questionnaire

Table 1. Overview of the Structure of the Questionnaire

Folio Number	Number and Title of Part	Literary Character
fol. 7a.5–12	1. The Ranking of the Angels	erotapokritic
fol. 7a.12–18	2. Angels and Prophets' Praise	list of praise of angels and prophets' dicta
fol. 7a.19–21	3. Nine Ranks of Angels and Human Leaders	list
fol. 7a.21–24	4. Nine Ranks of Angels and Ecclesiastics	list
fol. 7a.24–28	5. Another Ordering of Angels and Ecclesiastics	list
fol. 7a.28–fol. 7b.2	6. On Which Day Were the Angels Created?	hexaemeron
fol. 7b.2–5	7. Where Did He Create Adam?	erotapokritic
fol. 7b.6–7	8. On Which Day did Sadayēl Fall from the Garden?	erotapokritic
fol. 7b.7–19	9. Adam and Eve in the Garden	erotapokritic
fol. 7b.20–fol. 7g.10	10. Expulsion from Eden up to the Flood	extensive erotapokritic
fol. 7g.10–19	11. The Sethites and the Cainites: Beginnings	erotapokritic
fol. 7g.20–31	12. Noah and the Building of the Ark	narrative
fol. 7g.31–7d.24	13. Peoples of the Sons of Noah	erotapokritic
fol. 7d.24–32	14. Concerning the Construction of the Tower	prose
fol. 7d.33–fol. 8r.23	15. Concerning Abraham and His Sons	list
fol. 8v.1–fol. 9r.22	16. Egypt and Exodus	erotapokritic
fol. 9r.23–32	17. The Oil of Anointing	prose
fol. 9v.1–14	18. Names of the Twenty-Four Prophets	lists

As is evident from this table, all the parts from fol. 7a to fol. 9v form a single series of systematic, sequential, and predominantly erotapokritic discussions of events from the primordial age down to the exodus.

The first subjects raised are the enumeration and details of the angelic hierarchy and the correspondence of the nine angelic ranks to the ninefold structure of human ecclesiastical and other social institutions. The creation of the angels is next, followed by the narrative of the angelic fall before creation and the creation of Adam. These subjects are elements of the traditional *historia sacra* of the period preceding Adam's creation. The ensuing parts include elaborations on various biblical episodes: Adam's offspring down to Noah, Noah's children, the tower of Babel, Abraham and his descendants, and Egypt and the exodus. Questionnaire presents these in the sequence of their happening according to overall biblical chronology.

In greater detail, I may say that the work covers the following episodes: the times before the creation, the angelic ranks, Adam and Eve, the fall of the angels, Adam's offspring down to Noah, Noah's children, the tower of Babel, Abraham and his descendants, Egypt, and the exodus. Then, as noted in the table above, two further passages follow. The first is the recipe for the oil of anointing. This evokes the building and consecration of the tabernacle and the anointing of Aaron as priest, which events are related in Exod 29. The oil of anointing is also the type of the *miwṙon* (μύρον), the chrismatic oil.[12] The second passage lists the names of the prophets. Thus, by implication, Questionnaire traces the history of the world and of Israel from before creation down to the time of the Babylonian exile.

Overall, this document is not a narrative, neither was it composed as a verse-by-verse commentary on the Bible nor as a homily or series of homilies. Rather, it exhibits a learned character and is a sequential series of remarks about and expansions and explanations of specific points in the biblical narrative. Many of these remarks and expansions are formulated as answers to questions. As is made evident in full detail below, responding to the requirements of the composition's structure and, presumably, the information at his disposal, the author included several separate liter-

---

12. Exod 30:25 gives the biblical recipe for the oil. In the Armenian church, the chrismatic oil is called the *miwṙon* and is also a blend of aromatic spices and oils. See on the *miwṙon*, Sargsyan 2002. For the Armenian Canon of Blessing of the Holy Chrism, see Aznaworean 1996.

ary units as answers to some of the questions.[13] Indeed, this embedding of different literary units from diverse sources is a prime compositional characteristic of Questionnaire.

Before us, then, there lies a complex writing, many of the parts of which are in erotapokritic form.[14] However, differing from works such as *Questions and Answers from the Holy Books*, which are exclusively composed of questions with relatively short answers to them (see *Arm Apoc* 4:92–101), Questionnaire also includes narratives, lists, and other literary genres of documents, as well as the author's own ideas as answers. Moreover, since the author has incorporated into his composition some short works (mostly lists) that also occur as independent units of text in other manuscripts, we do not know whether these additions originate in a longer text(s) and were subsequently excerpted and then taken up by our author, or whether they were composed independently and incorporated over time into various longer writings. Likely, instances of both processes took place. Regardless, from the perspective of the author of Questionnaire, at least some of the lesser texts were preexistent, and he deliberately included them.[15] Such are a shortened form of The Peoples of the Sons of Noah (§10.6; see Stone 1981c, 224–28), The Ten Trials of Abraham (§12.1; see *Arm Apoc* 3:204–5), and The Ten Plagues of Egypt (§13.2; see *Arm Apoc* 4:254–57). Likewise, his sources apparently include *The Historical Compilation* of Vardan Arewelcʻi (lived 1200–1271) and another work of the thirteenth century, Vardan's Armenian translation of the *Chronography* of Michael the Syrian,[16] as well as other writings. Questionnaire is saturated with apocryphal stories and details resembling

---

13. See pp. 14 and 169 below. On the characterization of some of the literary genres used to retell or expound the biblical text in Armenian parabiblica, see Stone 2017.

14. See column 3 in the table above. On erotapokritic texts in Armenian apocryphal and parabiblical literature, see the remarks of *Arm Apoc* 6:255–58. Those observations constitute but an initial incursion into this fascinating material, which I hope to discuss in further detail.

15. This is, of course, a chicken-and-egg question. Moreover, their origin may well lie, at least partly, in the chronographic tradition, as some of the material in the *Chronography* of Philo of Tikor shows; see MH 5. This seventh-century chronography is being translated into English and annotated by Dr. Timothy Greenwood (personal communication).

16. See the discussion "*Chronography* by Michael the Syrian (Twelfth Century)" in part 11 below on this work.

those incorporated in the above-named writings, thus showing itself to be one type of literary embodiment of Embroidered Bible.[17] We may conclude, therefore, that this document belongs to a literarily distinct branch of the extensive Armenian literature of questions and answers, which quite often included in its answers units of material written in various literary genres. This composite literary character is highlighted in the title of the work by the words: "Gathered and Assembled from Written Sources" (see fol. 7r.1 and a more detailed discussion in annotation 1).

---

17. On the Armenian Embroidered Bible, see Stone 2019, 3–11.

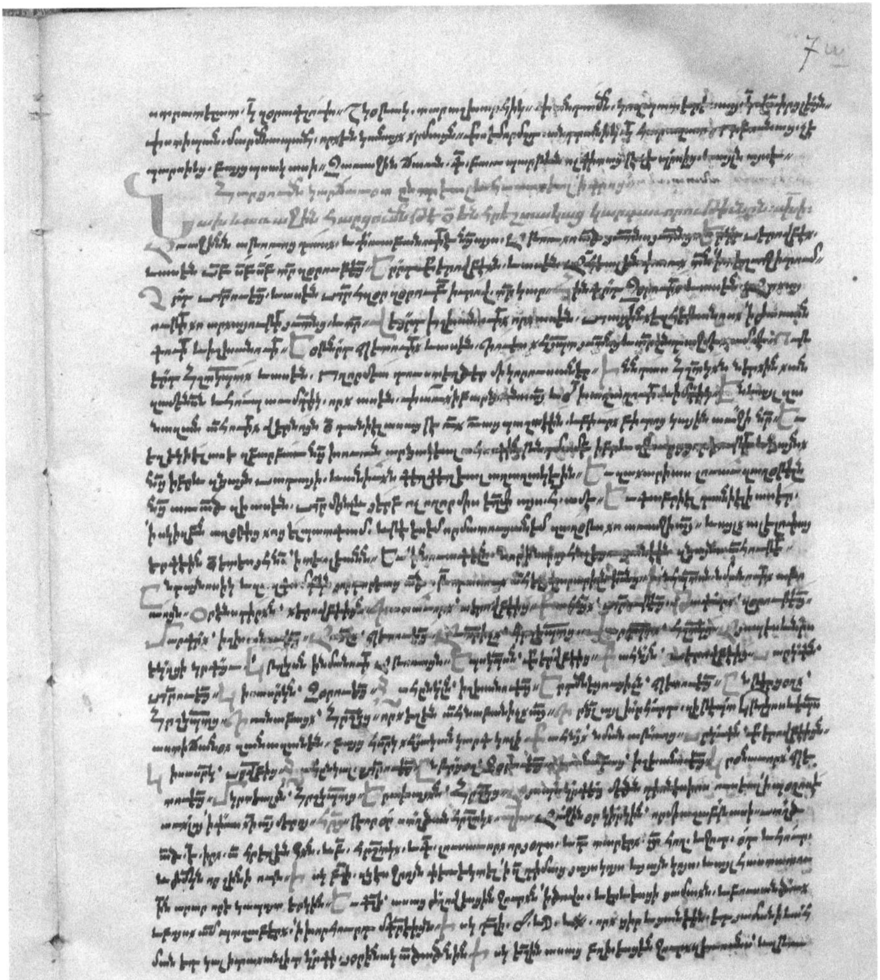

M682, fol. 7v

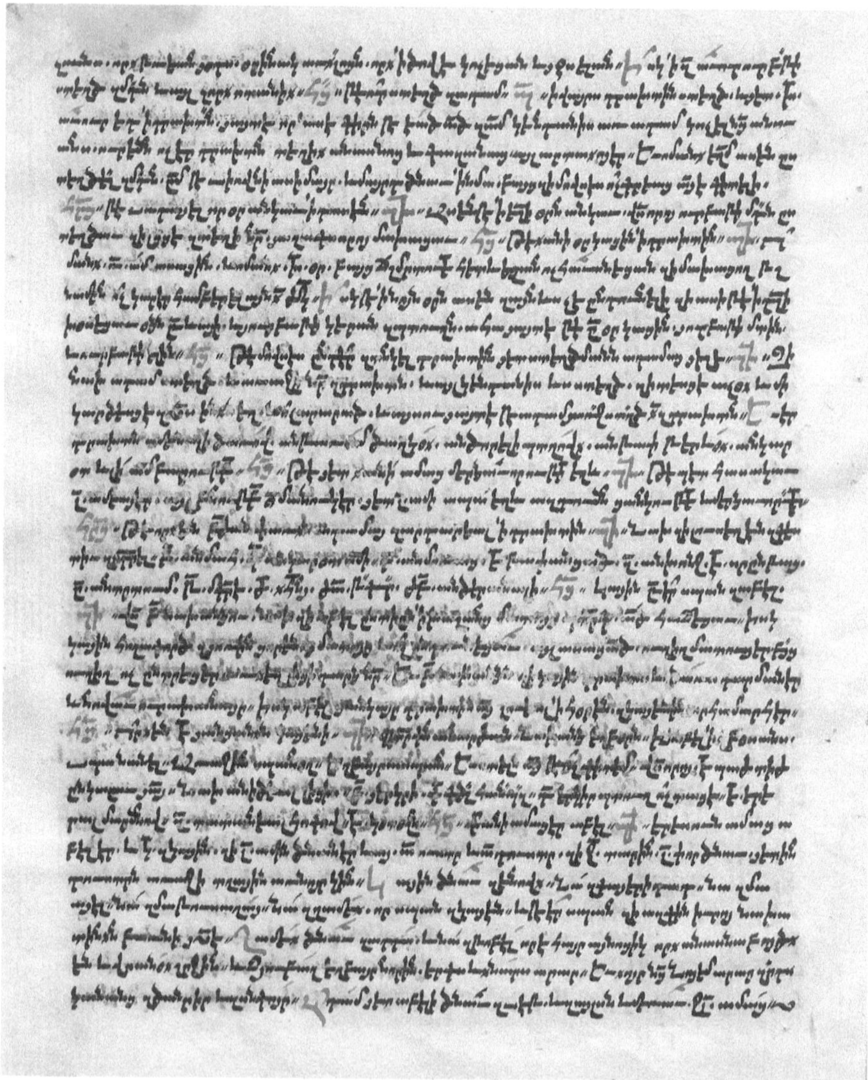

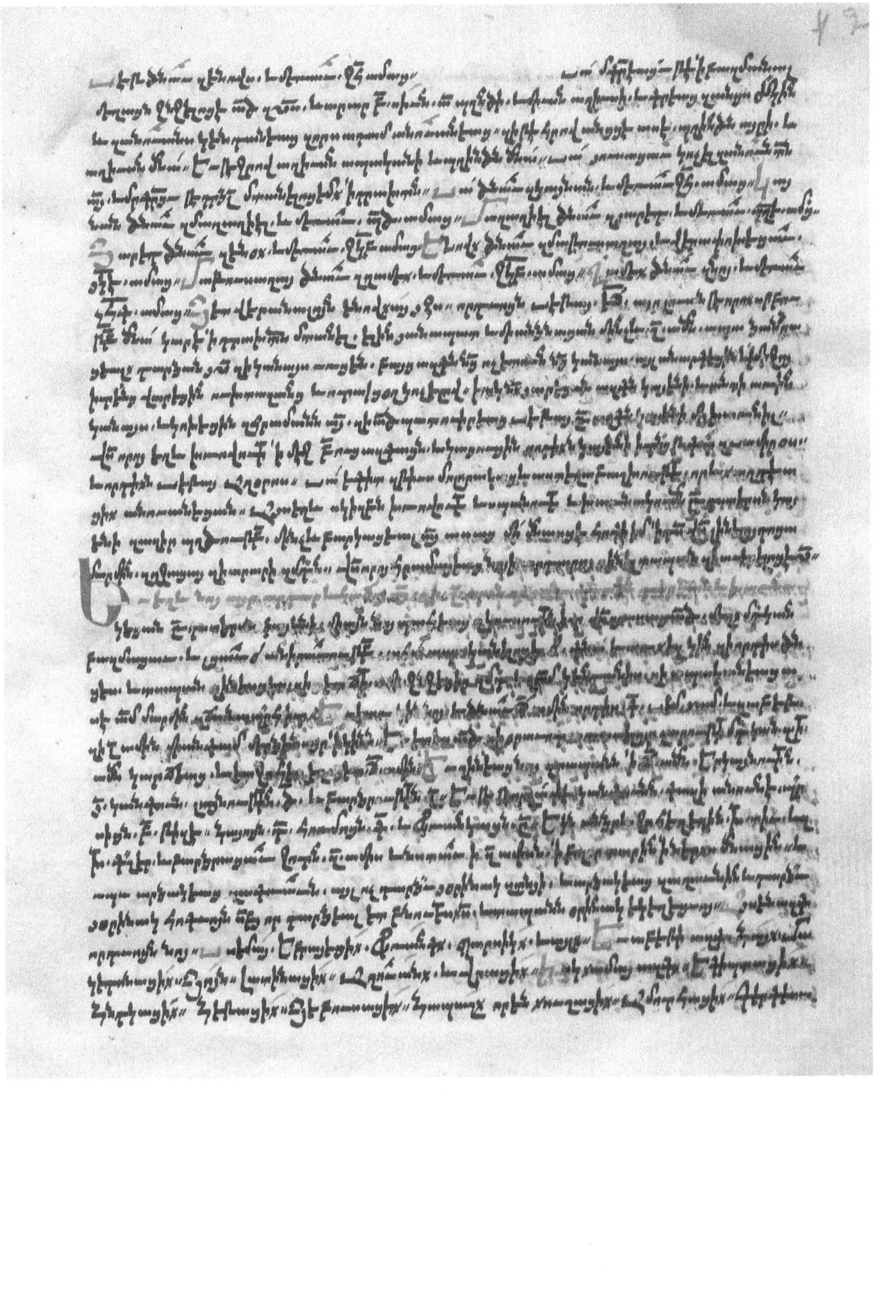

M682, fol. 7d

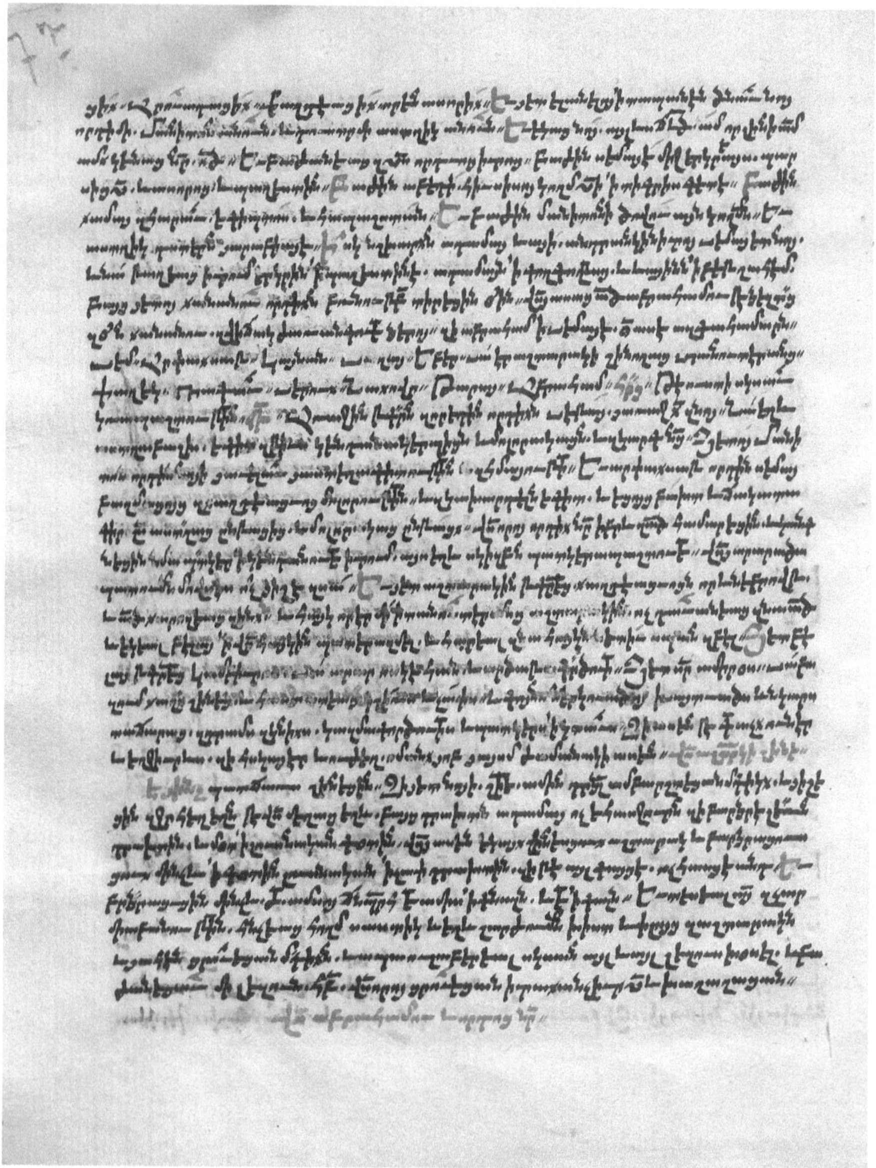

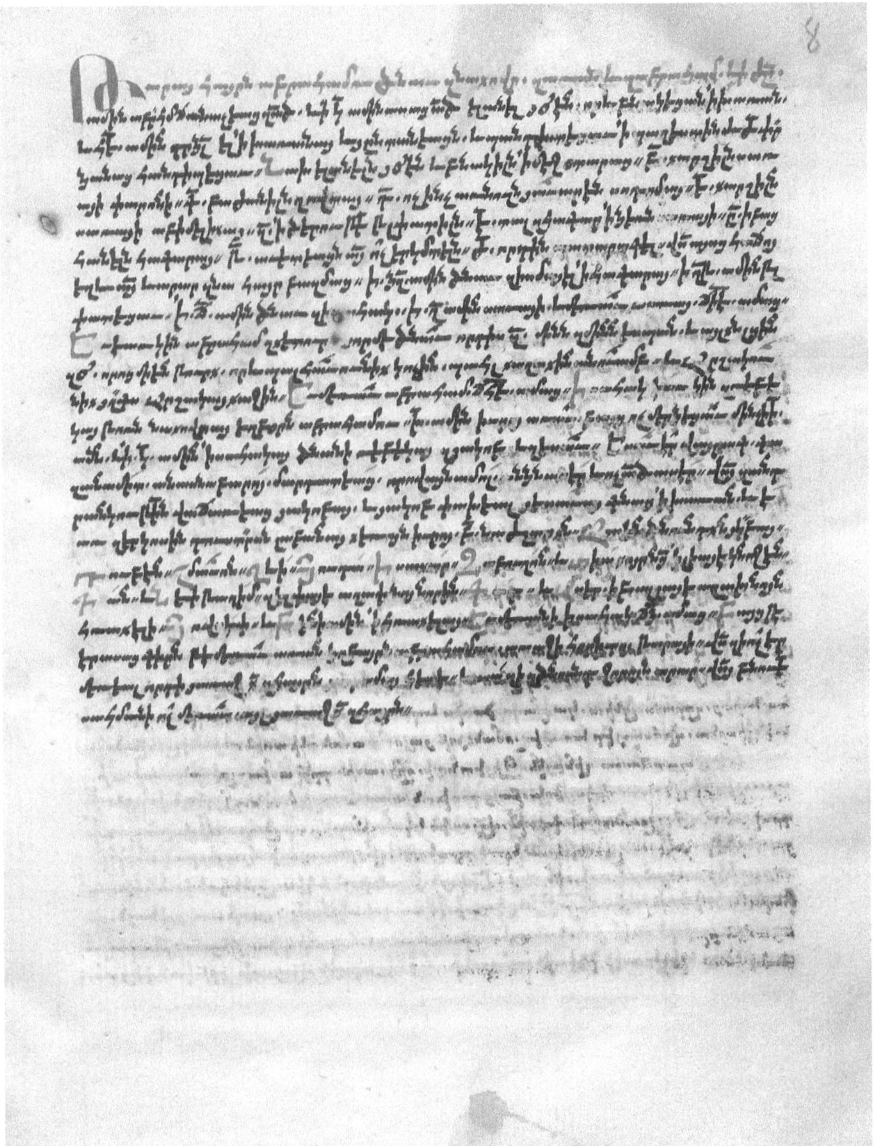

M682, fol. 8v

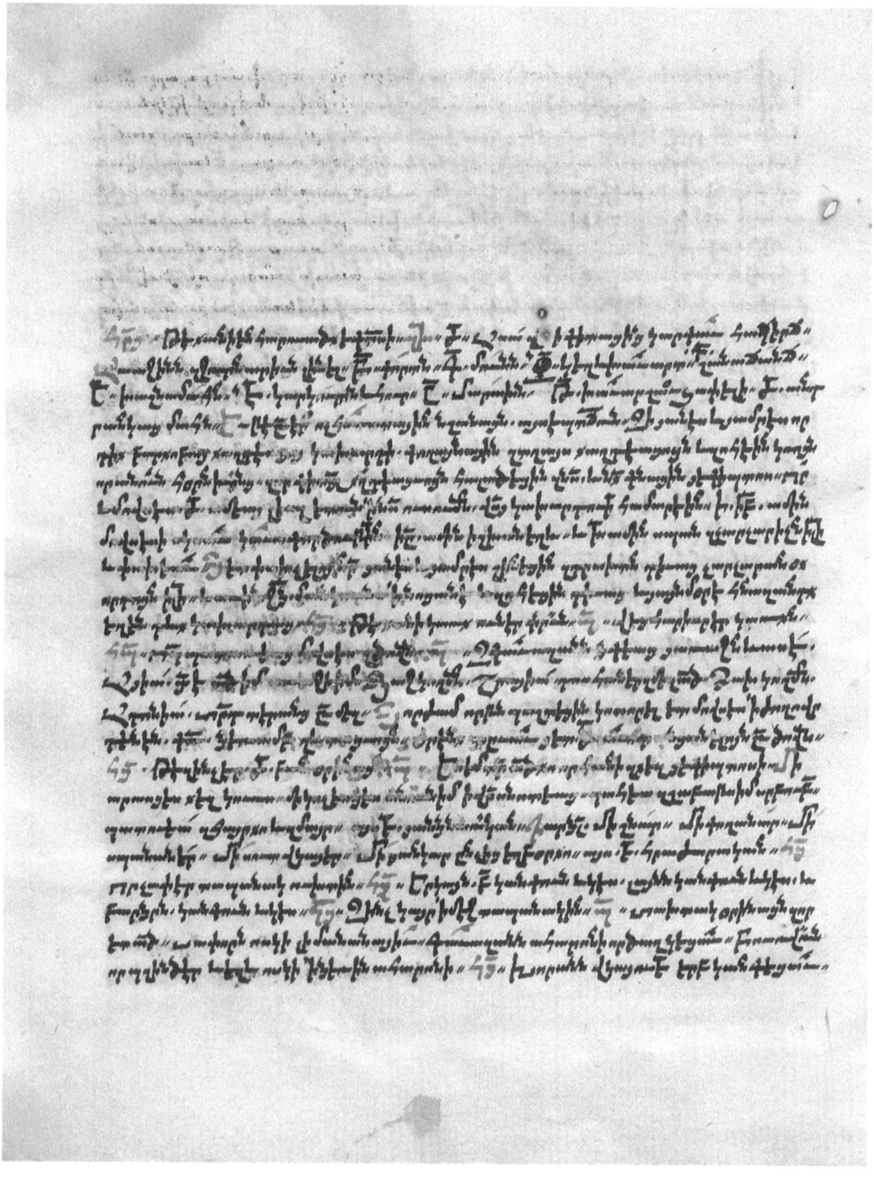

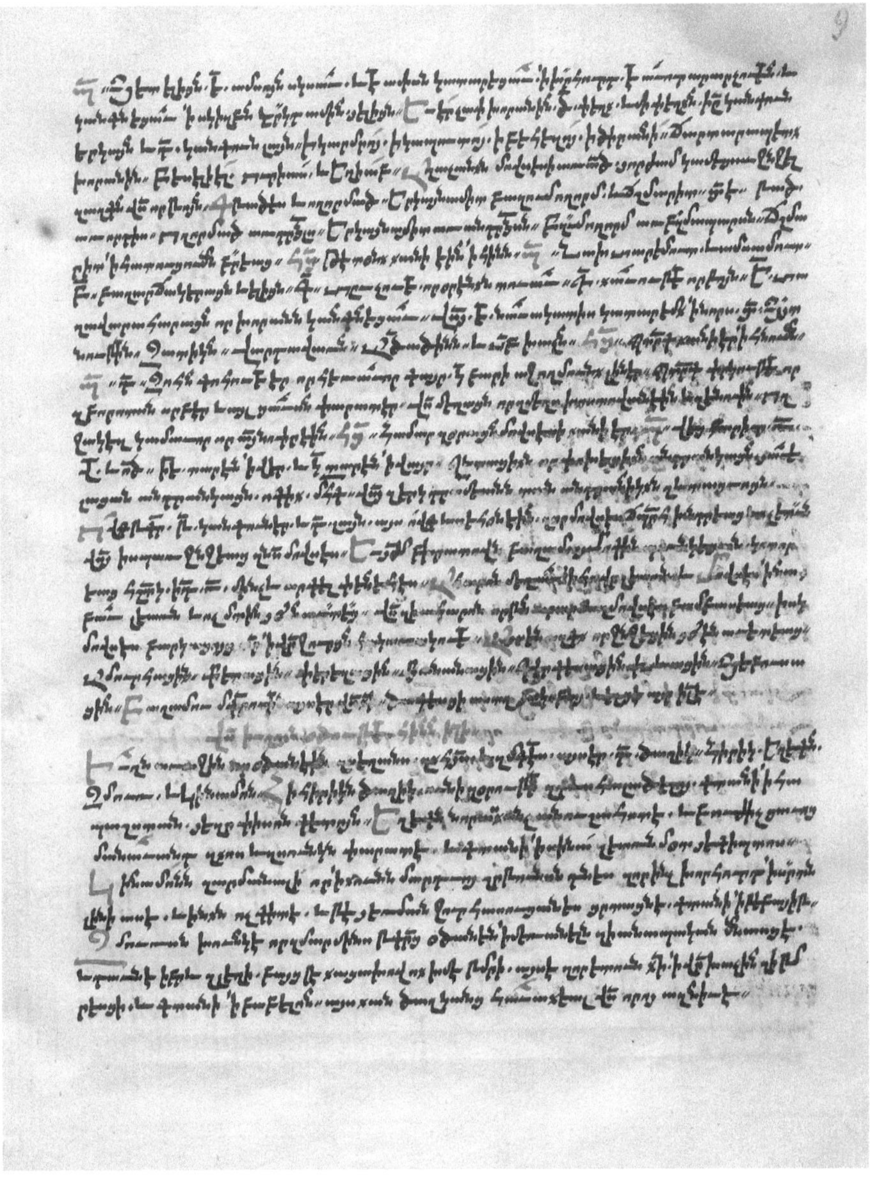

M682, fol. 9v

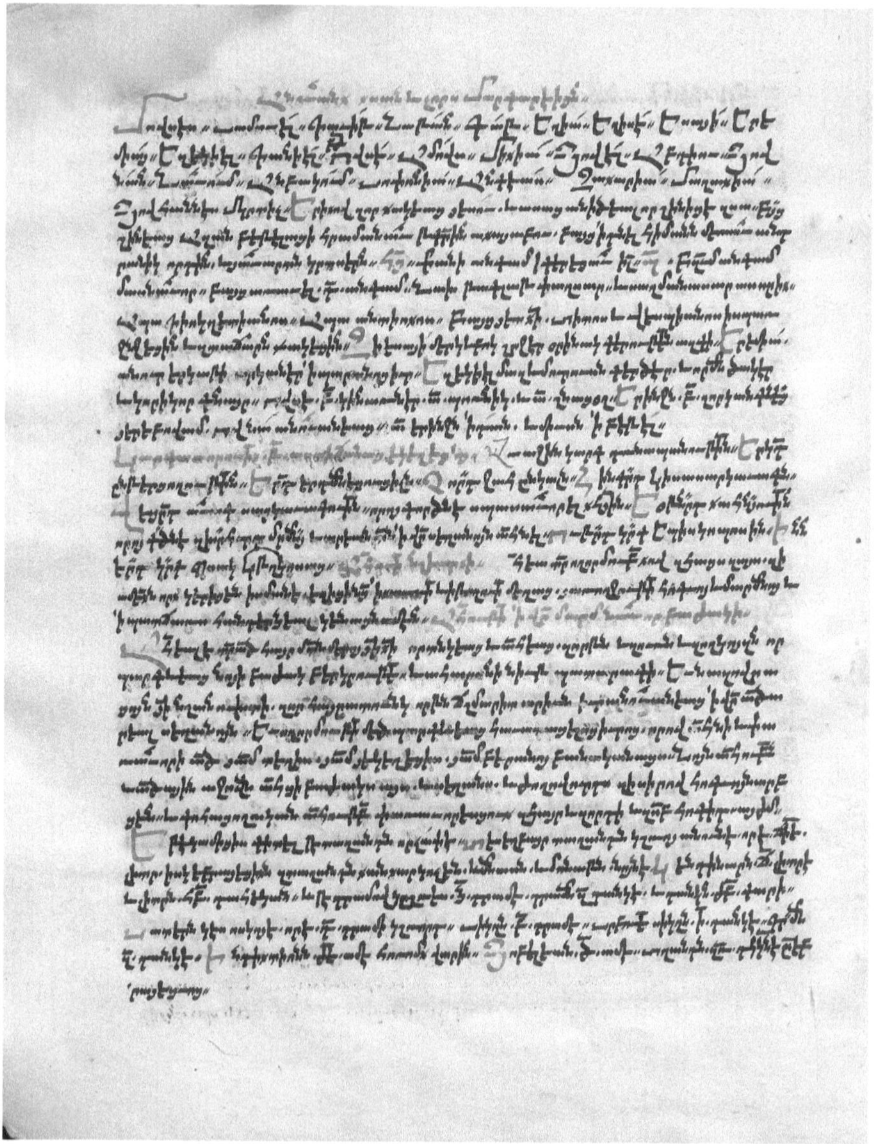

Texts, Translations, and Annotations

Parts 1–9
Questions Concerning Angels and the Garden of Eden

Parts 1–9 deal with several questions concerning angels, and my treatment of these parts here incorporates a reedition of some passages from M682 already published, as remarked above.[1] These parts concerning the angels are intriguingly enough, not included in the abbreviated copy of this document in Galata MS 154. That, of course, might just be due to the process of abbreviation, but it might indicate that the authors of the two documents held differing ideas about the heavenly world that existed before the creation of this one. This whole passage dealing with angels may have been incorporated holus-bolus into Questionnaire in M682 from an already-existing document.

---

1. See p. xxxi. This material is published in *Arm Apoc* 4:83–91.

1
The Ranking of the Angels

The first part of Questionnaire deals with the ranks and hierarchy of the angels in heaven. The author clearly holds the view that the angels are ranged into nine classes and that notion, in turn, probably derives from a Christian work, *The Celestial Hierarchy* by Pseudo-Dionysius the Areopagite, as is discussed below. These enquiries about the classes of angels and their due order, as well as the answers given to these questions, recall the descriptions of serried hosts of angels around the divine throne that are evoked by Isa 6:2, 1 Kgs 22:19 // 2 Chr 18:18, and Dan 7. These descriptions are developed considerably in both Jewish and Christian literature.[1]

The text published here is composed of two parts. The first is an enumeration of the classes of angels and the second the praise each angelic class pronounces in heaven. In every case but one, the praise specified is a verse from the Bible. The copyist strives to conclude each cited biblical verse at the end of a line, so that the name of the next class of angels can begin a new line. As a result, he often apocopates the verses. The list of verses associated with the specific angelic classes is either drawn from or (more likely) shares a tradition with Grigor Tatʻewacʻi (1344?–1409), who lists such verses in his encyclopedic work, *The Book of Questions*.[2] The author of Questionnaire either took the order of the angelic classes itself from Tatʻewacʻi's presentation or from some other source, such as the *Commentary on Genesis* by Vardan Arewelcʻi (1200?–1271).[3] In any case,

---

1. This subject is, of course, very large. A pivotal article concerning it is Rowland 1979, 137–54. On Isa 6:3 in angelic praise and its ramifications in both Jewish and Christian liturgical literature, see Stone 2024 and bibliography there, as well as annotation 3 in the present book.

2. See Tatʻewacʻi 1993, 144.

3. Consulted in MS M1267, fol. 7r.i (fifteenth century). Vardan adumbrates the same nine classes from thrones to angels in an expository sentence about each. He

as I have remarked, this order is ultimately drawn from the Armenian version of *Celestial Hierarchy* of Pseudo-Dionysius, a work of the sixth century that was translated into Armenian in the seventh century.[4] In this work, the order of the angelic classes runs from highest to lowest.[5] Pseudo-Dionysius, unlike our list and Tatʻewacʻi's, does not specify which biblical verse is sung by each angelic class. Other lists, very similar to that in M682, occur in M537 231r–232r, and we can also observe the reversed order, that is, enumeration from lowest to highest, in yet another form of this list that is also found in M537.[6] Further copies of the list of nine angelic classes and other similar documents also exist.[7]

Text

M682/ fol. 7r.4–12/

Title: 1.0/ Հարցումս կարճառօտ ընտրեալ եւ հաւաքեալ ի գրոց:

1.1/ Նախ եւ առաջին հարցումս թէ՝ Որպէս են հրեշտակաց կարգաւորութիւնքն:

1.2/ Պատասխանի. առաջինն՝ Աթոռոց դասք, եւ փառաբանութիւն է նոցա այս. Աթոռ քո Աստուած յաւիտեանս յաւիտենից:

1.3/ Երկրորդ՝ սերովբէք, եւ ասեն. սուրբ սուրբ սուրբ Տէր զօրութեանց:

---

does not indicate his source except to say եւ յայլ գիրք, "and in other book(s)," a tag common in Armenian scholastic literature. On this tag, see the introduction above.

4. See the *Celestial Hierarchy* in Luibheid and Rorem 1987, 143–91.

5. Of course, relevant rabbinic and early Jewish and Christian material is extensive and very varied. For example, orders of angels are described by 2 En. 29.3, a writing considerably older than the *Celestial Hierarchy*. Pirqe R. El. 4 mentions four classes of angels that say praise before God. The Armenian version of Pseudo-Dionysius was translated into English by Thomson 1987. Greatrex (2009, 39) remarks that Pseudo-Dionysius himself set the classes of angels in this order.

6. See *Arm Apoc* 4:81–83, no. 3.6. The difference of order may reflect the mental orientation of the author. The ascending order is that in which the classes are revealed to a seer ascending to the heavens; the descending order is that which the angels encounter as they descend to carry divine messages downwards to or to intervene among humans. Both directions are explicit in Gen 28:12, in the vision of Jacob's ladder, where the angels' ascending precedes their descending.

7. See, as a sample, the following texts: M10561, 146r–149r; M2152, 148v; M5690, 1r–1v filler; M0268, 312–313; and M10547, 44r–v. Many further related texts survive in other manuscripts.

1.4/ Երրորդ՝ քերովբէքն, եւ ասեն. Աւրհնեալ են փառք Տեառն ի տեղւոց իւրում:

1.5/ Չորրորդ՝ տէրութեանց,[8] եւ ասեն. Տէր հզօր զօրութեամբ իւրով, Տէր կար[ող]:

1.6/ Հինգերորդ՝ զօրութիւնք, եւ ասեն. Արքայութիւն քո արքայութիւն յաւիտենից. եւ տեր:

1.7/ Վեցերորդ՝ իշխանութիւնք, որք ասեն. Տացին քեզ հեթանոսք ի ժառանգութիւն եւ իշխանութիւն:

1.8/ Եօթներորդ՝ պետութիւնք, եւ ասեն. Դու ես քահանայապետ յաւիտենից եւ Տէր ընդ աջմէ քումմէ:

1.9/ Ութերորդ՝ հրեշտակապետք, եւ ասեն. Ողորմեա՛ դու ստեղծեր, մի՛ կորուսաներ:

1.10/ Իններորդ> դաս՝ հրեշտակքն, ներքին, քան զամենեսեան եւ հույա առ մարդիկ. որք ասեն. Փառք ի բարձունս Աստուծոյ եւ <յ>երկիր[9] խաղաղութիւն եւ ի մարդիկ:

Translation

1.0/ Short Questionnaire, selected and assembled from books.[10]

1.1/ The first and foremost question: Of which sort are the rankings[11] of the angels?

1.2/ Answer: The first (are) the ranks of the Thrones, and their praise is, "Your throne God is forever and ever."[12]

1.3/ The second (are) Seraphs, and they say, "Holy, holy, holy is the Lord of Hosts."[13]

1.4/ The third (are) Cherubs, and they say, "Blessed is the glory of the Lord in his place."[14]

---

8. It is unclear why this particular class name is in the genitive-dative case, whereas the others are all in the nominative.

9. This quotation is from Luke 2:14, with parallels in Luke 19:38, and Mark 11:10. Apparently, in our manuscript, երկիր has lost its preposition, and I have emended the text in light of the reading in Luke 2.

10. See the discussion in annotation 1 below.

11. Or: orderings.

12. Ps 45(44):7.

13. Isa 6:3.

14. Ezek 3:12. On the seraphs and cherubs and their biblical antecedents, see the summary by Frey 2018, particularly 122–24.

1.5/ The fourth (is) (the rank) of the Dominions, and they say, "The Lord (is) strong through his might, the Lord (is) mighty."[15]

1.6/ The fifth (are) the Powers, and they say, "Your kingdom is an everlasting kingdom, and Lord."[16]

1.7/ The sixth (are) the Rulers, who say, "The gentiles will give you for a heritage and rule."[17]

1.8/ The seventh (are) the Principalities, and they say, "You are High Priest forever and the Lord is by your right hand."[18]

1.9/ The eighth (are) the Archangels, and they say, "Have mercy, Lord, you created, do not destroy."[19]

1.10/ The nin(th) rank, the Angels, (are) lower than all and close to humans, who say, "Glory on high to God, and peace <to> earth and upon humans."[20]

Annotation 1. The Title

The title of the work given in §1.0 is "Short [կարճառու] Questionnaire, gathered and assembled from written sources." This title admirably characterizes the nature of this work. As is the case in several other Armenian parabiblical writings, the title proclaims that it is կարճ(առու), "Brief, Short." The same idea, often also expressed by the homonym համառու, occurs in the titles of Short (համառու) History of the Holy Forefathers and Short (համառու) History of Joshua.[21] Of these three works, Short History of Joshua is quite long, relatively speaking. However, it seems that in all three cases, the brevity is in comparison with the biblical text, probably not expressing the actual length of the apocryphon but its lesser prestige. The sobriquets "large/small" are also attached to some rabbinic

---

15. Ps 24(23):8.
16. Ps 145(144):13.
17. Ps 2:8. This section concerning the sixth class, the rulers, changes the formulaic verb, as does the section for the ninth class, in neither instance for any discernible reason.
18. Ps 110(109):4–5.
19. Judging from other similar verses attributed to the archangels in such lists, this is a development of Zech 1:12.
20. Luke 2:14 and see n. 10 directly above. This is the only verse of this series drawn from the New Testament; all the others are from the Hebrew Bible (Old Testament).
21. *Arm Apoc* 4:163–74 and *Arm Apoc* 5:57–108, respectively.

1. The Ranking of the Angels

compositions, presumably to distinguish them from the biblical books to which they pertain (e.g., Bereshit Rabbah, "Great Genesis"—a large fifth-century CE midrashic collection) or from one another (e.g., the mystical treatises Hekhalot Rabbati and Hekhalot Zuṭarti, "the greater" and "lesser Hekhalot," respectively). This sort of title also recalls George Syncellus's quoting of Jubilees as "lesser [ἡ λεπτῇ] Genesis."[22]

The word Հարցումն, here translated Questionnaire, is one of the terms used for "question" in the titles of erotapokritic texts. When one examines the Armenian terms for "question" in the titles of parabiblical Q&A texts, the following emerges: In the title of Questions of Ezra, we find a different, cognate but rarer word, Հարցափնունթիւնք, while in Questions of the Queen and Answers of King Solomon we find Հարցմունք, the plural of the term used here; and the same recurs in Questions and Answers from the Holy Books.[23] Indeed, the last phrase of the title of that work also rather resembles the corresponding phrase in the title of the writing being published here. Here, however, in Questionnaire, it is more specific and adds the attributive phrase: "Selected and Assembled from Books."

The Armenian word for "book," գիրք, is *plurale tantum*, so, based on the Armenian text itself, we cannot distinguish between "the Book = Scripture" and "book/books" in general. Such a determination must be made from context, and the translation chosen here calls for justification. I have already observed that several answers given in our document are units of text taken from preexisting writings.[24] I construe "selected and assembled" as relating to such answers, so that this work is clearly a quite specific type of erotapokritic writing. It is unlike Questions and Answers from the Holy Books, in which the author offers short and generally textually or tradition-based answers to the questions, for here the author has taken several of the answers completely from preexisting writings, and many of these are of considerable length. In this case then, "from books" refers to the sources he utilized. If this is so, the phrase may not refer to the Bible, as one might think initially, but to other biblically associated writings or parabiblica. The author's practice of incorporating existing literary units into the answers has also led to some rather long answers

---

22. Adler and Tuffin 2002, index, s.v. "Little Genesis." This title occurs several times in that work.

23. See Stone 1995, 293–316, especially p. 297; Yovsēpʿeancʿ 1896, 229–32; *Arm Apoc* 4:92–101. The word հարցափնունթիւն means "enquiry, questioning."

24. See above, pp. xxix–xxx and notes there.

here, while in Questions and Answers from the Holy Books the responses are brief and very focused.25 One could envisage further research on the Armenian erotapokritic texts distinguishing subgenres of questions and answers, perhaps originating in the need to serve different functions.

Since the singular in the title of the work being published here refers to a whole list of questions, I have chosen Questionnaire as its translation.

Annotation 2. Nine Classes of Angels

Part 1 names the nine classes of angels in descending order and specifies the various biblical verses of praise of God to be pronounced by each of the classes on high.26 The Hebrew Bible mentions angels, of course, but says not a word about their organization into classes or the establishment of fixed words of praise of God said by each of those classes.27

The heavenly visions seen by the prophets Isaiah (ch. 6), Micaiah b. Imlah (1 Kgs 22:19 // 2 Chr 18:18), and Daniel (ch. 7) provided the inspiration for this scene of the angels in heaven ranked in their due order around the divine throne of glory and singing the praises of God. See also Pss 89(88):6–8, 148(147):3, and 1 En. 69.22–24, which present the heavenly host singing God's praises; the celestial lauding of God features in Job 38:7 as well. That verse reads: "when the morning stars sang together, and all the Sons of God shouted for joy." In Job, in the context of creation, the stars praise God as do the "Sons of God," an expression meaning "heav-

---

25. Of course, some relationship must also exist between the point of the questions and the length of the answers they demand. In both works being discussed, it is likely that the questions, too, were drawn from existing scholastic written or oral lists or other, similar, traditional sources.

26. There exist texts where the angels are listed in ascending order, as I observe above. See further pp. 6 and 67 and nn. 42 and 43 below. On the praise of the luminaries (not angels as such), see also Bakker 2017.

27. For a fine general presentation of the angels in the Hebrew Bible, Gaster 1962a, 128–34. Morton Smith (1992) considers that these were classes of angels (*mal'akim*) from the fourth century BCE on, suggesting that different classes of divine emissaries designated by this name may be distinguished, particularly in certain Psalms: Pss 103(102):20, 104(103):4, 148:2. Angelic praise of God is also discussed in Rickles 2002, 94–98, 194. See also Martinez 1999, 8 n. 20 on the praise of the angelic ranks. Such angelic praise is described in various late antique parabiblical sources. See 1 En. 61.10, T. Levi 3, 2 En. 20.1, Ascen. Isa. 7.21.

enly beings, powers" and so, angels.²⁸ Observe the parallelism of "stars" and "Sons of God" or heavens or angels.

With the preceding descriptions, we should compare also the scenes of the heavenly court implied by Zech 3 and Job 1:6. These descriptions of a heavenly throne surrounded by the angelic hosts provide the background against which the activity of the heavenly court takes place.²⁹ In Armenian literature, this picture was adopted in toto: see, for example, Agathangelos, *Hist.* §276 (Thomson 1976). In the vision related in Rev 4, the throne is described as flanked by the four living creatures (cf. Ezek 1:5, 24–25), each with six wings (typical of the seraphs; see Isa 6:2) who sing, "Holy, Holy, Holy" (cf. Isa 6:2–3).³⁰ This scene, too, had its influence on Armenian medieval literature.

The scene of the divine throne with its surrounding angelic ranks is taken over and developed in postbiblical Jewish and Christian apocalyptic literature and is in liturgical use from the first millennium. In the apocryphal work, the Testament of Adam, the section named "The Horarium" speaks of the specific hours at which the praise of various created beings, including angels, was pronounced. Indeed, The Horarium records that the ninth hour of the night is the hour of "the praise of all

---

28. On the relation of stars and angels, see n. 32 below. The summons to praise is clear in Pss 29(28):1 and 47(46):7; see Ben-Dov 2016, 13–14 for references in the Hebrew Bible. Ben-Dov suggests that Ps 89(88):6–8 is a fragment of an older hymn that the psalmist incorporated that part here. The word "glory" often serves as a term for "God." In Samaritan usage, for example, in *TM* 1.66, God, when prophesying the death of the Egyptian firstborn, says, "My Glory will descend"; compare with Exod 11:4 and see also *TM* 1.78, 3.56 and further references in this document. Similar instances may be found in rabbinic literature.

29. See Himmelfarb 1993, 13–14. She points out the ancient Near Eastern traditions that fed into these descriptions. Visions resembling Dan 7 are found in 1 En. 14, and The Book of Giants (4Q530); see Stokes 2008. Somewhat earlier than Stokes's article, Loren T. Stuckenbruck (1997b) discussed the relationship between these two texts, Dan 7 and 1 En. 14, both of which describe the myriads of angels around the divine throne. Observe the similar description in 1 En. 71.7–9; see also the remarks of Bietenhard 1951, 54–56; Wright 2000, 120–21. Also observe Sumner 1991, 113–33. Ben-Dov (2016) argues that the divine council is an ancient, shared feature of early West Semitic religion that received a new lease of life in the Second Temple Period and was also alive among the authors of the Qumran Scrolls.

30. For an analysis of Rev 4 and its relation to the throne visions in the Hebrew Bible, Enochic literature, and later Jewish throne visions, see Frey 2018.

the angels and archangels."³¹ This is comparable with passages such as 1 En. 14.22, 2 En. 20.3–4, 22.3–4, 4Q530 (Giants^b) ii, and the Ascension of Isaiah. The liturgy or praise offered by angels is evoked likewise in Testament of Adam's specification of angelic prayer in the second hour of the day, while of the ninth hour of the night, that work says that "the angels praise God and the stars of heaven praise God."³² Angels are identified as stars in 1 En. 86.1–3 and, as noted, several other texts associate angels and stars. In T. Abr. B4, we read that "at the setting of the sun all the angels bow down before God." According to 2 En. 21.1, the angels sing the thrice-holy prayer, as they do in T. Isaac 6.5, 24, and this accords with Isa 6:3.³³ In any case, other sources witness the idea that fixed angelic prayer, a notion not encountered in the Hebrew Bible, took place at daybreak.³⁴ Lastly, it is intriguing to observe that the idea that praise was the angels' basic function is complemented by a remark of Grigoris Aršaruni (650?–729?) that humans, too, were created to praise God.³⁵

---

31. *Arm Apoc* 2:171. On angelic praise of God, see Rebiger 2007, 635; Bakker 2017. See n. 35 above.

32. See *Arm Apoc* 1:58–61, 74–75. Compare Job 38:7: "when the morning stars sang together, and all the Sons of God shouted for joy." The same parallelism occurs in 1 En. 86.1. As early as Isa 40:26, stars are spoken of as if alive. The classic study of astral religion in late antiquity is Cumont 1960; on angels and stars, see pp. 90–92. The relationship between angels and stars is also discussed by Fröhlich 2015, especially 117–18 and 121–22. Does the ninth hour feature because of the nine classes of angels? Bearing in mind that, in some texts, humans constitute a tenth class (see below), it is striking that in the Armenian text of the Horarium, part of the Testament of Adam, we read: "the 10th hour. The gates of heaven stand open, and the prayers of human beings will enter to God" (*Arm Apoc* 2:172).

33. See Stone 2024.

34. Perhaps verses like Ps 19:2 (18:3) might be seen as referring to a regular praise to God by the day and the night, but not to prayer performed by angels. However, even that would be to stretch the meaning of the verse of Psalms, which is likely a hyperbolic rhetorical figure. Gen. Rab. 78.2 explains that the angel that wrestled with Jacob according to Gen 32:27, had to return to heaven in time for the morning hymn of praise, which is comparable to T. Abr. B.4 quoted above (only there it is for evening praise). See also Budge 1933, 132–33, 148, and Gruenwald 2014, 208–9. Observe the remarks in *Arm Apoc* 1:56–57, quoting Apoc. Paul 7.

35. See Stone 2013, 44, Grigoris Aršaruni no. 1. Indeed, the human function of praise is also the point of Ben Sira 17:9–10, a much older text (early second century BCE). See also 1QH^a IX, 29–32, where the faculty of speech (רוח בלשון) is said to have been created to "make known Your glory and relate Your wonders"; 1QH^a V, 27–28 declares that God "established them from ages of old … in order that they (the

1. The Ranking of the Angels

Saul M. Olyan (1993, 31–69) argues that in ancient Judaism the names of the angelic groups or classes (he calls them "brigades") are mostly derived from the Hebrew Bible by ancient exegesis and emerged in Second Temple and rabbinic times.[36] This list of nine classes in M682, however, was not drawn directly from such Jewish sources but, as I have noted, in all likelihood goes back in the Armenian tradition to Pseudo-Dionysius the Areopagite's work *Celestial Hierarchy*, an influential writing of the sixth century CE that was translated into Armenian in the seventh century.[37] Significantly, at the conclusion of part 5, our text attributes a certain ordering of angels and ecclesiastics to "Dionysius," who is undoubtedly the same Pseudo-Dionysius the Areopagite.

A similar list of nine classes forms the basis of fragment 3 of Testament of Adam, called "The Angelology" or "The Angelic Hierarchy."[38] Steven E. Robinson argues that the main part of the Testament of Adam was composed in Syriac in the third or fourth century and that The Angelic Hierarchy is likely not much later.[39] Robinson doubts the direct derivation

---

angels or the whole of creation) might make known" his glory. This is comparable with Gen. Rab. 5.1, where God declares: "If these (the primordial waters) which have neither mouth nor speech praise me, how much more (will I be praised) when man is created!" (Theodor-Albeck 1965, 1:32). This source explicitly compares the creation's praise of God and the praise (expected) to be given by humans to God. It is intriguing to compare this material with the query in the rather later Armenian source, Questions and Answers from the Holy Books §1: "While angels and humans had not yet been created, who glorified the Divinity?" (*Arm Apoc* 6:272).

36. Olyan notes the use of the Hebrew word *mal'akim* ("angels") from the fourth century BCE on, suggesting that different classes of divine emissaries designated by this name may be distinguished, particularly in certain psalms, such as Pss 103(102):20, 104(103):4, and 148:2. Also compare Smith 1992, 285–94 and Gaster 1962a on biblical angels.

37. See *Celestial Hierarchy* 200C–261D in Luibheid and Rorem 1987, 160–72. There, Pseudo-Dionysius expounds the nine classes, their names and characters, and their descending order from thrones to angels. The Armenian texts were published most recently in Łazaryan 2013. An English translation of a previous edition was made by Thomson 1987. This ninefold list is also quoted in the thirteenth-century Syriac work called *The Book of the Bee* (Budge 1886, 9), and in many other works.

38. See Kmosko 1907, particularly 1393.

39. Robinson 1982, 142–44; 1989. On Pseudo-Dionysius's writing in Syriac, which is generally dated to the sixth century, and its attestation, see Baumstark 1922, 168; Brock 1997, 122–23. He notes that there are two Syriac translations, one of the sixth century and the other of the seventh century.

of The Angelic Hierarchy in Testament of Adam from Pseudo-Dionysius and also points out that it occurs in The Book of the Bee, a Syriac work composed in 1222 CE.[40] If he is right, then The Angelic Hierarchy in Testament of Adam might be a quite old attestation of the list of nine classes, preceding the sixth-century composition of Dionysius's *Celestial Hierarchy*. Nonetheless, The Angelic Hierarchy seems irrelevant to our search for the direct origins of the list in M682, the more so because, as far as we know today, no Armenian text of that part of Testament of Adam exists.

Pseudo-Dionysius, like The Angelic Hierarchy in Testament of Adam, enumerates nine classes of angels divided into three groups of three classes, and each group is correlated with an ecclesiastical order or rank. The division into three groups of three is an arithmetically fairly obvious, but nonetheless significant way of presenting a list of nine.[41] It should be observed that the number "nine" was considered a perfect number, not least because the digits of multiples of nine always add up to nine.[42] The view that there were nine orders of angels occurs in several other medieval Armenian sources (and, of course, can be documented further

---

40. See n. 38. One wonders whether this is the first attestation of the list of nine that Robinson found in Syriac, after Testament of Adam, or just an example of the use of it.

41. Luibheid and Rorem (1987, 5) state that "Dionysius illustrated in his own way the Platonic and Neoplatonic pattern of the three classes, three functions, and three levels. In his eyes, indeed, all reality is hierarchic and triadic.... Thus, the angelic universe includes three triads, each subdivided into three orders." Schimmel (1993, 164) remarks that "this [the idea of 9] is found in medieval Christian exegesis.... The 9 orders of angels found in such exegesis (and in Dante) are interpreted as reflections of the perfect 3, which can be completed by the all-embracing divine Unity to form the perfect 10." On the three triads in the Armenian text of Rev 4:8, see Stone 2024.

42. Schimmel (1993, 164), giving some Homeric examples, notes that the ancient view in the Graeco-Roman world was that of the "near-perfection of the 9." Compare also the nine Muses, daughters of Zeus and Mnemosyne in Hesiod, *Theog.* 52–62. For a rather later view, see "On the Ennead" in Waterfield 1988, 105–7. However, the nine is often completed by one more, to ten. Note, for example, Aristotle, *Metaph.* 1.986a in his discussion of the Pythagoreans: "Since the decad is considered to be a complete thing and to comprise the whole essential nature of the numerical system, they assert that the bodies which revolve in the heavens are ten; and there being only nine that are visible, they make the 'antichthon' the tenth." There is an interesting discussion of the numbers nine and ten in Aṙakʿel Siwnecʿi, *Adamgirkʿ* 1.10.12–1.10.20; see Stone 2007a, 141–42. That is an even later source, Aṙakʿel Siwnecʿi having written his epic on Adam and Eve in 1401–1403. Concerning the nine classes, see further in the next note.

throughout the Christian world).⁴³ The number nine was so influential that in manuscript M537 the traditional seven chief angels on occasion become nine in number!⁴⁴ Several sources, moreover, incorporate the ninefold ranking in a tenfold scheme, perhaps in an attempt to reconcile different ideas concerning the structure of the celestial world.⁴⁵

As I have remarked, ten was also regarded as a significant number, and the notion of ten as a completion of a list of nine is doubtless behind some medieval Armenian texts that count humans as a tenth class, thus complementing the usual nine angelic classes with a final category of humans. This idea is to be seen in the writings of Ignatius *vardapet* (twelfth century), who speaks of nine ranks of angels and one of humans (Stone 2013, 94). In the thirteenth century, Vardan Arewelcʻi says, զի թուեցաւ մարդն յիններորդ դասս հրեշտակացն տասներորդ, "For humans are reckoned a tenth class (added) to the nine classes of angels" (MS M1267, fol 5r), and Mxitʻar Ayrivanecʻi (thirteenth century) speaks of ten classes of angels (Stone 2013, 137, 160).

In a prayer, apparently of Jewish origin, embedded in the fourth-century Christian work, Apos. Cons. 7.35.3, nine celestial classes are mentioned: first seraphs and cherubs separately and then angels, archangels, thrones, dominions, rulers, authorities, and powers (Fiensy 1985, 66–69).

---

43. Regarding Armenian sources, it is to be found in Yovhannēs Tʻlkurancʻi's (1320?–1400?) poem, "Concerning the Creation of the World" §§19–21 and in Aṙakʻel of Siwnikʻs *Adamgirkʻ* 1.10.12, 10, 16, which was composed between 1401–1403 CE. The poem by Tʻlkurancʻi is translated in Stone 2000c. *Adamgirkʻ* is quoted from the translation by Stone 2007a. See, also, for another source, the *Commentary on Genesis* by Vardan Arewelcʻi in Matenadaran MS M1267, fol. 5r. Vardan lived between 1200?–1271. For examples of Christian sources, see the Irish text published by Herbert and McNamara 1990, text 2. In Creation and Fall §1, we read, "There were nine orders and nine grades of angels." Note further the same in the tenth-century Irish work, Saltair na Rann 4.837–840, 11.1605–1608. This important composition draws on an early form of Life of Adam and Eve; see Seymour 1922. The three triads of lauding angels, each with its praise, are likewise discussed in Golitzin 2001, 136.

44. See *Arm Apoc* 4:66. See also the discussion of the numbers 9 and 10 in n. 41 above.

45. In other traditions, observe that ten classes of angels are recorded both in 2 En. 29.2–3 and by Maimonides, *Mishneh Torah, Sefer Hamada, Yesodei haTorah* 2.7. However, no connection with nine is evident in 2 Enoch; 2 En. 20.3 [J] also lists ten ranks of angels surrounding the divine throne. Observe, however, that there are textual complications in 2 Enoch at this point. See Andersen 1983, 134–35. On lists of ten angelic classes in Jewish sources, see Charles 1913, 2:441.

The context is, significantly, the angelic liturgy of praise to God. Four of these classes, to be sure, are already mentioned in Col 1:16, in a passage long taken to be a list of heavenly beings: "thrones or dominions or principalities or authorities."[46] The list of nine was clearly developed from this list in Col 1:16, though exactly how that happened is unclear.[47] A Jewish origin for the list of nine classes is unlikely, and, all considered, this is probably a Christian touch. A similar list, but of eight classes of angels, is found in the Syriac work, Cave of Treasures (CT) 1.3, which should probably be dated between the middle of the sixth century and the first decades of the seventh century CE.[48] However, the passage in Cave of Treasures concerns the creation of the eight classes, not their praise of God.

Seven classes, likewise not in a list form, are mentioned in the Coptic *Discourse on Abbaton* by Timothy I of Alexandria (d. 385).[49] A similar list is also to be found in the Similitudes (Parables) of Enoch (61.10).[50] A prior mention of seven groups of angels is in the first century BCE document from Qumran called Songs of the Sabbath Sacrifice (4QSabbath Shirot). There, seven groups of angels are addressed in the seventh Sabbath song.[51] This work was composed not much later than 100 BCE (Newsom 2000,

---

46. In Eph 6:10–12, a somewhat analogous list of titles is related to the rulers of this world. Certain of the classes, specifically the thrones and the powers, are mentioned in T. Levi 3.8. That work, which incorporates early sources, has been dated by some to the second century CE in its present form, and others would date it earlier. A similar list of nine classes also occurs in 2 En. 20.1, though its members vary between the different recensions of that text. See Andersen 1983, 134–35 and the remarks in n. 27 above.

47. Compare Eph 1:21. Similar groups of angels are to be observed in Origen, *Princ.* 1.6.2. The addition of the four groups mentioned in the Old Testament (Hebrew Bible): angels, archangels, cherubs, and seraphs would have yielded eight classes, to which one more might have been added by virtue of the significance inhering in nine.

48. See Toepel 2013, 540; Minov 2016a, 131–49. On the Georgian version of this work, see Zurab Avalachvili 1928.

49. See Budge 1914, 480. In Budge 1933, 133 and 148, a like group of five classes may be observed. Another prose listing occurs in Ignatius, *Trall.* 5 (*ANF* 1:68). This work is usually considered to be of a second century CE date. See also the discussion in Stone 1990a, 83–84.

50. See the discussion in Nickelsburg and VanderKam 2012, 251–52, where they discuss the origin of the various terms and view this passage of 1 Enoch as a background text to Col. 1:16. In Boccaccini 2007, 415–96, there are several articles treating the date of Similitudes (Parables) of Enoch. The generally accepted opinion would set this work at around the turn of the era or a little before that.

51. See Newsom 1987, especially 14.

887–89), and the notions that there was a hierarchy of classes of angels and that different praises were sung by the different angelic classes are clearly present in that composition, which was found both among the Qumran Dead Sea Scrolls and on Masada. Except for cherubs and ophannim (4Q403 20 II, 3, 7, 9), however, the angelic terminology differs from that used by the present document and, for that matter, by other documents consulted here as well, being both idiosyncratic and obscure (see Mach 2000). Of course, those two names, "cherubs" and "ophannim," are taken or adapted from the Hebrew Bible (see below). Nevertheless, The Songs of the Sabbath Sacrifice is a striking witness to Second Temple Period Jewish views that heavenly beings offer regular prayer and praise to God according to their different ranks.[52]

At the present juncture, the name "Ophannim," which I just mentioned, deserves further comment. The Hebrew word, literally meaning "wheels," is derived from the description of God's chariot in Ezek 1. At some point, these wheels became regarded as a distinct group of angels (see 1 En. 61.10 and 71.7, Apoc. Abr. 18.3). They are a well-known angelic class in Jewish liturgy as well as in Jewish mystical texts and traditions: see, for example, 3 En. 7.25 ("Hebrew Enoch" in *OTP* 1:262, 279–80). The development of this angelic class is set forth by Christopher Rowland (1979, 143–44). They had eyes in their wheels (Ezek 1:18),[53] and they are remarkably illustrated by the image in the Armenian manuscript Bible J1925, fol. 414v (1261 CE). This presents God's chariot throne, with eyes shown around the rim of the wheel.[54] An excellent analysis of some Armenian interpretations of Ezek 1 has been presented by Theo Maarten van Lint (1999; 2014).[55]

---

52. See the edition by Newsom (1985). Readily accessible texts and translations of Songs of the Sabbath Sacrifice are also to be found in *DSSE* 2:806–41. Robinson (1985) discussed some features shared by Songs of the Sabbath Sacrifice and Testament of Adam. Both these writings include hierarchy, angelic praise, and prayer, but these commonalities do not indicate, nor does Robinson claim that they do indicate, a literary relationship between the two works.

53. This is discussed by Rowland 1979. Concerning these eyes, see also Apoc. Abr. 18.3, 12–13

54. Narkiss and Stone 1976, 73, fig. 85. See fig. 9 below.

55. A diplomatic edition of an Armenian descriptive text called Armenian Vision of Ezekiel, with translation, notes, and introduction by Michael E. Stone and an appendix by Theo M. van Lint, was published on pages 145–58 of Stone, Wright, and Satran 2000.

For the sake of completeness, we should note that various early sources quite often mention a group of four preeminent angels designated "the angels of the Presence" (מלאכי הפנים). According to 1 Enoch, they are Michael, Gabriel, Raphael, and Uriel (see Stone 1990a, 82–83) or Phanuel (see 1 En. 9.1, 10, 40.9, 54.6, and 71.8). In 1 En. 20.1, seven archangels are listed, four as above, with the addition of Reuel, Sariel, and Remiel. The four (with Sariel replacing Uriel) also appear in the War of the Sons of Light against the Sons of Darkness, a work found among the Dead Sea Scrolls (1QM IX, 14–16).[56] These groups of four or seven should not be confused with the ranks or classes of angels that were discussed above.

Eight angelic classes are mentioned in the Syriac work, Cave of Treasures 1.3 (*MOTP* 1:540), which should probably be dated between the middle of the sixth century and the first decades of the seventh century CE (Minov 2016a, 131–49).[57] In Cave of Treasures, the names of the angelic classes are not presented in a formal list or an enumeration but in a declarative prose sentence describing their creation.

In any case, the whole issue of the ultimate origins of the nine-class list is not directly relevant to our subject, for the *Celestial Hierarchy* of Pseudo-Dionysius the Areopagite was translated into Armenian in the seventh century and is well-known subsequently in that language (Thomson 1987; Łazaryan 2013). We may conclude that Armenian translation of *Celestial Hierarchy* was likely the ultimate source of our Armenian list.

Annotation 3. The Seraphic Thrice Holy

In Part 1, section 1.3, we read:

> 1.3/ Երկրորդ՝ սերովբէք, եւ ասեն. Սուրբ սուրբ սուրբ Տէր զօրութեանց:
> The second [that is, class], Seraphs,[58] and they say, "Holy, Holy, Holy is the Lord of Hosts."

---

56. The four angels there are well discussed by Yadin 1962, 237–40.
57. On the Georgian version of this work see Avalachvili 1928. The work does not exist in Armenian, as far as is known today.
58. On the seraphs, see Wagner 2006, 87–95. See also Hartenstein 2007 for the religio-historical background of cherubim and seraphim.

1. The Ranking of the Angels

The doxology[59] cited is a quotation of Isa 6:3, shortened by the scribe to fit into one line, according to the practice noted above. However, in M268, the verse of praise pronounced by the seraphs is given in full as:

Սուրբ, սուրբ, սուրբ Տէր զօրութեանց. լի են երկինք եւ երկիր փառօք քո.
Holy, Holy, Holy, is[60] the Lord of Hosts, the heaven and the earth are full of your Glory.

Many sources describe the angelic, heavenly praise as being the angels' singing of that particular doxology. After all, the prophet Isaiah says that the seraphic choirs sang these words to one another, perhaps antiphonally, in the Divine Court (Isa 6:3), so what better source of information could be adduced as to the content of angelic praise than Isaiah's prophetic citation of it? The threefold repetition of the word "holy" gained this verse the name Trishagion or "Thrice Holy."[61] Whence Isaiah took the concept, and the specific text of the praise is unknown, but the idea of prayer and praise of God by the heavenly beings is older than Isaiah, though the exact words of such praise are not explicitly cited in this fashion anywhere else in the Hebrew Bible.[62]

Examples of praise by the creations are, of course, already to be found in the Hebrew Bible in texts like Ps 89(88):6–8 and Ps 29(28):1–2 and other

---

59. Thomson (1987, 78–79) perceptively remarks concerning reapplications of this verse that "the biblical opening phrases are, as it were, the doxological constant, while the main body of the doxology is more or less in the form of a free variation on the biblical *Vorlage*." The accuracy of this statement will become evident during our discussion.

60. Or: are you. In fact, this sentence is a predicative without any explicit verb.

61. The name "Trishagion" is derived from the Greek τρίς "threefold" and ἅγιος "holy." However, the title Trishagion usually designates a specific hymn in the Orthodox Synaxis. To avoid confusion, I refer to the proclamation as it is in Isa 6:3 by the name "Thrice Holy." This verse of Isaiah also constitutes the angelic praise according to §2 of the Armenian text called History of the Discourse (*Arm Apoc* 4:104). It was early taken into Christian liturgical use and adapted and embellished. A rich study of an instance of this Christian reuse may be found in Martinez 1999. Moreover, Beck 2011, deals with the "Trishagion Hymn" as it developed in the usage of the Greek Orthodox Church. See also Golitzin 2001, 136. The Trishagion, its versions, their diverse interpretations and liturgical usages (Trinitarian and christological), and the polemics over them in ecclesiastical traditions have been much discussed by scholars. A somewhat expanded version of the present section is Stone 2024.

62. Compare, however, the cherubs' proclamation in Ezek 3:12.

similar instances, while praise as the ceaseless activity of the angels is well known in Armenian texts.[63]

This threefold glorification as a celestial song of praise was taken up and reformulated in Rev 4:8, and there it became: ἅγιος ἅγιος ἅγιος κύριος ὁ θεὸς ὁ παντοκράτωρ, ὁ ἦν καὶ ὁ ὢν καὶ ὁ ἐρχόμενος, "Holy, holy, holy, is the Lord God Almighty,[64] who was and is and is to come!"

The standard Armenian text of the same verse of Revelation reads: Սուրբ Սուրբ Սուրբ, Սուրբ Սուրբ Սուրբ, Սուրբ Սուրբ Սուրբ, Տէր Աստուած Ամենակալ որ էն եւ ես, եւ որ գալոց ես, "Holy Holy Holy, Holy Holy Holy, Holy Holy Holy Lord God Almighty, who is and are and who are coming."[65] This, the text in Zohrab's Bible (Zohrabean 1805), has the Thrice Holy praise thrice, thus reading the word սուրբ "holy" nine times in all. The other known, ancient Armenian translation of Revelation, edited by Frédéric Murad (1905), reads: Սուրբ, սուրբ, սուրբ Տէր Աստուած ամենակալ, որ էն եւ էն, եւ գալոց է, "Holy, holy, holy is the Lord God Almighty, who is and is and is coming." Here սուրբ occurs three times, as in the Greek text.[66]

The striking, ninefold repetition of սուրբ "holy" in the Zohrab Bible, where Murad's text has it three times, as does the Greek of Revelation, is to be explained as three times Thrice Holy, making nine in all. The number nine of the angelic classes, descending from thrones to angels, is already found in the *Celestial Hierarchy* 200c–261d (see Luibheid and Rorem 1987). There, Pseudo-Dionysius expounds on the nine classes, their names and characters, and their descending order.[67]

---

63. See *Arm Apoc* 4:97, 104; Martinez 1999, 8 refers to the praise of the angelic ranks. See above, annotation 2, pp. 11–12.

64. In the Greek Bible, the Hebrew divine epithet צבאות ("of hosts") is often translated as τῶν δυνάμεων "of the powers, armies" or παντοκράτωρ "ruler of all, Almighty." This latter is, in turn, translated ամենակալ "Almighty" in Armenian. In the instance in Isa 6:3, however, Greek has, not unusually, a third rendering of צבאות, the transliteration σαβαωθ, while in Rev 4:8 we find ὁ παντοκράτωρ. This implies that the Greek text of Isa 6:3 that stood before Revelation contained a reading varying from that of the Septuagint as we now have it.

65. The relevant verse is to be found on p. 515. The second էն, which is found in Murad's text where Zohrabean reads ես ("you are"), may be taken as "He who is," that is, է with the substantivizing article. Note the shift from 2nd person to 3rd person.

66. էն2° is odd, and Murad records a variant: էին. That is not any clearer.

67. This is discussed in detail in annotation 2.

1. The Ranking of the Angels

The Thrice Holy proclamation occurring in Rev 4:8 is in a passage, features of which are adapted from Ezek 1. In the said passage, the four living creatures that sing the Thrice Holy as praise in heaven are drawn from Ezek 1:5–21 and 24, and they play the role of the seraphs of Isa 6.[68]

According to 1 En. 39.12, "those who sleep not" (that is, the Watchers, a very elevated angelic class) praise God, saying: "Holy, holy, holy is the Lord of Spirits, he fills the earth with spirits." Johann Maier (1990) argued that the use of the Thrice Holy formula in this early Enoch writing outside the Bible, as well its rareness in the Dead Sea Scrolls from Qumran but its wider use in later texts, reflects a change, in which an originally arcane tradition came into broader use after 70 CE.[69] In the form with "heaven and earth," the same verse is the praise of the seraphs and cherubs that surround God's throne according to 2 En. 21.1.[70] The invocation "Holy, holy, holy," is also to be found in 4 Bar. 9.3.[71]

Analogously, the Hebrew tradition integrated the seraphic Thrice Holy praise of Isa 6:3 into the heavenly liturgy, itself paralleled in human prayer. This process resembled *mutatis mutandis* the development in early Christian texts that ultimately led to the Thrice Holy being the typical praise of the class of seraphs in the list in Questionnaire. Its significance for the present investigation lies in this similarity, which I shall trace briefly.

In Hebrew, the Thrice Holy praise is called the Qedushah ("holiness"), and it occurs regularly in the Jewish liturgy. At its heart stands the seraphs' praise in Isa 6:3, together with a text based upon Ezek 3:12, which

---

68. These living creatures produced sounds; see Ezek 1:2, 24, 10:5. There are several similar adaptations of the Thrice Holy in the early Christian centuries, of which the Sanctus prayer is one. Martinez (1999, 8) discusses the praise of the angelic ranks. On the praises in Rev 4–5, see Frey 2018, particularly 124–26. Lucetta Mowry (1952) has suggested that a Jewish liturgical background combined with Eastern court practice served to provide the context for Rev 4–5.

69. Maier's article is further discussed in Warren 1994. The main point of Warren's article is to identify an embedded use of the Thrice Holy formula in 4QSam^a II, 11–10. This had first been discerned in the Septuagint of that passage by Thackeray 1914. Warren (1994, 284) argues that Maier's dating of the introduction of the Thrice Holy formula into general usage is too late, and the change in usage happened rather earlier than 70 CE. This formula may serve to conclude the first part of 1 Enoch as is suggested by Gruenwald 2014, 78–79.

70. This is the form of the text translated by Andersen (*OTP* 1:134).

71. This is discussed in *Arm Apoc* 6:20, 32, 47.

latter verse reports the song of the cherubs before God: "Blessed be the glory of God from his place." The Qedushah was established in the Jewish fixed liturgy from early times, and it came to highlight the complementarity of the human recital of these two verses with these angelic prayers (Hartenstein 2007).[72]

So, in the usual Ashkenazi rite, the Qedushah opens with the invocation, "Let us extol you and sanctify you, according to the counsel of discourse of the holy seraphs, who sanctify your name in holiness, as was written by your prophets: 'and they called to one another and said, "Holy, holy, holy."'"[73] The earthly worship here deliberately resembles and explicitly evokes the angelic.

First Clement 34, dating from the early second century CE, refers to the angelic praise and quotes the Isaianic verse, with the substitution of "creation" for "earth."[74] The Apotelesmata of Apollonius of Tyana, which is another recension of the Horarium included in the Testament of Adam, mentions the "Trishagion of the angels," that is, the Thrice Holy that it says the angels sang in the second hour of the day.[75] The details of the angelic Thrice Holy prayer are also given in 3 En. 40 (also known as Hekhalot Rabbati).[76]

---

72. See Heinemann 1977, 24, 36. Note also Gruenwald 2014, 208–9, which deals with the connection of the liturgical Qedushah and the early Jewish mystical *hekhalot* hymns, on which, see the next note. See further the description of the heavenly Qedushah in Gruenwald 2014, 293.

73. See also Martinez 1999, 6. The Qedushah is also referred to in t. Ber. 1:11. Scholem (1954, 60) remarks that the angelic hymns in the *merkabah* mystical text Hekhalot Rabbati all end in the Isaianic *Trishagion*. Scholem discusses the mystical effect of the repeated Thrice Holy from the point of view of ecstatic religious experience. These hymns are claimed to be the oldest part of the *hekhalot* literature and can be dated at the earliest to the early Byzantine period.

74. And not "heaven and earth," as is discussed in the next paragraph.

75. This is discussed on p. 19 and in n. 61 above. The Testament of Adam is probably from the fourth century CE. See the discussion on pp. 13–14 and in n. 39, above. See Robinson 1982, 142–44; 1985; and 1989. The phrase "Trishagion of the angels" is cited from *Arm Apoc* 1:72. The Christian text conventionally called "Pseudo-Epiphanius" has also been read as reflecting a heavenly liturgy. It is discussed in Dorfmann-Lazarev 2020a, 319–21.

76. Odeberg 1928 lists several instances, such as on pp. 56 ("time … for the saying of the 'Thrice Holy'"), 71, and 116 ("those who utter 'Holy' and those who utter 'Blessed'"). This last reference is to the Qedushah, citing both of its verses. Other cases are listed in his index, s.v. "קדוש." See also *OTP* 1:291–92 and 305.

1. The Ranking of the Angels

The Thrice Holy occurs in the list like the present one that Grigor of Tatʻew (1346–1409/10) included in *The Book of Questions*. Relating to the Thrice Holy pronouncement, that list says: "The seventh (class) is of the Cherubs:[77] and they say, 'Holy, Holy, Holy is the Lord of Hosts,' just as Isaiah heard. The eighth class is of the seraphs: and they say: 'Blessed is the Glory of the Lord from his place.'"[78] The cherubs are the seventh of the nine angelic classes ascending from the lowest; above them are seraphs and then the thrones, which are the closest to the Divinity. Grigor Tatʻewacʻi's list of the angelic ranks in his *Book of Questions* is very like those being published here but is in ascending order from angels (lowest) to thrones (highest).

In documents both earlier and later than Questionnaire, seven steps of ascent of souls to the heavens are described.[79] This idea connects with the notion that the earth is surrounded by seven spheres counting from the moon up and in each of which there is a luminary,[80] that is, the moon, the sun, or one of the five planets. Beyond or as the seventh sphere is that of the fixed stars. This is, of course, the background to the seven steps of ascent, which are mirrored subsequently in the seven descending steps to Tartarus.

In most Armenian texts dealing with angelic praise and deriving from Isa 6:3,[81] the laudation reads as follows: "Holy, Holy, Holy is the Lord of

---

77. One would expect seraphs, since in Isa 6, the seraphs are explicitly said to be those who sing this laudation.

78. See Tatʻewacʻi 1993, 144. Observe that the praise that Grigor attributes to the seraphs is taken from Ezek 3:12, where it is associated with the living creatures, identified generally as the cherubs.

79. On the seven steps of ascent of the righteous souls and the seven steps of the descent of the wicked, see 4 Ezra 7.80–98 and the discussion in Stone 1990a, 243. This work is of the late first century CE. Also compare Questions of Ezra A 19–21 and Questions of St. Gregory Recension I. In the latter work, there is a partial list of seven steps in §§24–29 and another complete one in §§42–48. See Stone 1995, 293–316; Stone 2018, 141–72. See also *Arm Apoc* 1; Stone 2022.

80. Lewy (1956, 412–20) discusses the idea of the ascent and descent of the soul through the seven heavenly spheres. The number seven of the spheres is constituted of six for the planets, sun and moon, and one for the fixed stars. On the development of this cosmology, see Bietenhard 1951, index, s.v. "Himmel."

81. An early Armenian reference to angelic praise of God is in Agathangelos §272, and see Thomson 2001, 79. Agathangelos says that the angels were created with the purpose of offering unceasing praise to the Creator.

Hosts. The heavens *and earth* are full of your glory."[82] This variant form of the Thrice Holy, with addition of the words "and earth," is also found in the Sanctus Prayer in the Divine Liturgy of the Armenian Apostolic Church.[83] It is also attributed to angelic choirs in 2 En. [J] 21.2.[84] It may be assumed plausibly that this form of the Thrice Holy also occurred in the *Vorlage* of M682 here, and it was apocopated, though, of course, the fragment of the formula preserved does not permit a decisive conclusion.

---

82. See M268, fol. 312r, published in *Arm Apoc* 4:78–81, and M266, fols. 90v–91r, published in *Arm Apoc* 4:81–82. A quite different composition, also preserved in M682 (*Arm Apoc* 4:102–4), mentions the Thrice Holy as sung by the highest class of angels but does not quote the second half of the verse. The formula is also found in this form in the Greek Trishagion text published by Martinez 1999, 7.

83. See Nersoyan 1984, 66–67. For a study of the Sanctus and its manifold reverberations, see Winkler 2002.

84. Although 2 Enoch is accepted as a Jewish work, it would be difficult to infer from this fact that the form of the Thrice Holy found in the surviving Slavonic text of the book is, therefore, Jewish. The addition to a biblical quotation of two words from a formula found in the church liturgy is quite possible during two translation procedures, from Semitic to Greek or from Greek into Slavonic, or while copying in Greek or Slavonic, or during the process of transmission and editing of the Slavonic that resulted in the two Old Church Slavonic recensions of 2 Enoch preserved in the surviving manuscripts. On the transmission of this work, see *OTP* 1:92–94.

2
Angels and Prophets' Praise

The preceding part 1 of Questionnaire discussed the celestial ranking of the angelic classes and the angels' praise of the Almighty. This second part deals with the praise of God pronounced by prophets. It gives five prophetic names (more exactly, the names of four different prophets, since Daniel is mentioned twice) and records a biblical verse in which each of these particular prophets spoke about the angelic praise of God or else uttered a prophetic dictum relating to that celestial praise, as well as to the prophet's own reverence of God.[1] This may be taken as a descent of one level from the preceding section, that is, the descent from angels' praise of God to the prophets' celebration of angelic praise. This type of list is new to my experience, and I have not encountered its like previously in Armenian, neither in manuscripts nor among published texts. However, the Armenian tradition does know praise of, invocation of, and prayer to angels and not only in apotropaic texts and amulets. In the past, I have published some such prayers to angels, as have some of my scholarly predecessors, as is set forth below in annotation 4, "Prayer and Angels."

Text

M682/ fol. 7r.12–18/

2.1/ Են եւ այլ զանազան աւրհնութիւնք վերնոցն, որպէս Դանիէլ ասաց թէ՝ Ո.ք (հազարք) Ո.աց (հազարաց) պաշտէին եւ բիւրք բիւրոց կային առաջի նորա։

---

1. Compare John's vision in Rev 14:2–3.

2.2/ Եւ Եզեկիէլ ասէ. Ջրարբատ նոցա խուռն արձակեալ ահագին թնդմամբ իբրեւ գշուրց ցոր[...]ութիւն² եւ ձայնք նոցա իբրեւ զձայն Սադայի. եւ անիւքն գեղգեղեալ աղաղակէին։

2.3/ Եւ Զաքարիաս³ լուաւ զաղօթելն նոցա առ Աստուած զի ասեն. Տէր մինչեւ յերբ ոչ ողորմիս Երուսաղէմի, այս Հ.(70) ամ է:

2.4/ Եւ Գաբրիէլ Դանիէլի ասէր. Ի սկիզբն աղօթից քոց ելի պատգամ. եւ թէ՛ Ես եմ որ մատուցանեմ զաղօթս քո առաջի Աստուծոյ.

2.5/ եւ այլք՝ Ալելուիա երգէին, որպէս եւտես Յովհաննէս ի տեսլեանն. Եւ ի նուազելն նոր ի նորոյ հնչեցուցանէին զձայն ալրհնութեան:

Translation

2.1/ There are also various blessings of the celestial ones,[4] such as Daniel said, "A thousand thousands were serving and a myriad myriads were standing before him."[5]

2.2/ And Ezekiel said, "Their speech was (like?) a tumult/multitude resounding with a mighty clamor like [*illegible*] waters and their voices like the voice[6] of Shaddai and the wheels[7] singing pleasantly, were calling out."[8]

---

2. This word is partly illegible, and no obvious restoration comes to mind.

3. Observe the Greek or Latin ending on this proper noun. This is the prophet Zechariah. The same phenomenon may also be observed in one instance in part 18.1 in "List of 24 Prophets" at n. 7. This ending often occurs in works translated from Latin or Greek, but also occasionally in works composed in Armenian: see *Arm Apoc* 1:159.

4. That is: pronounced by the celestial ones.

5. Dan 7:10. This verse, and in particular the word "serving," is apparently interpreted as the singing of praise by the angels. The passage in Daniel has influenced Rev 5:11: "many angels, numbering myriads of myriads and thousands of thousands." In 2 Bar. 48.10, we read, "Armies without number stand before you (that is, God)"; compare 4 Ezra 8.21, which says: "before whom hosts of angels stand trembling." See also 1 En. 40.1, 71.8, which conflate the angels' numerousness with their innumerability (cf. Job 25:3). [Similar sensitivity, and even similar formulations, appear in rabbinic sources. See Sifre Num. 42; Pesiqta of Ten Commandments 1, (Pesiq. Rab. 21, fol. 103a–b); Efrati 2019, 2:11–13. The rabbinic sources are discussed in relation to 1 En. 40 in Efrati 2019, 1:179, §9 –S.E.].

6. Or: sound.

7. The word "wheels" presumably refers to the wheels of the divine chariot, described in Ezek 1:15–21 and 3:13. They become the angelic class of ophannim (literally: "wheels").

8. The preceding text is difficult to read in places due to the physical damage that the manuscript has sustained. The biblical reference is to Ezek 1:24. Interestingly, the

2. Angels and Prophets' Praise 27

2.3/ And Zecharias[9] heard their praying to God, that they were saying, "Lord, how long will you not have mercy on Jerusalem, it is (already) seventy years."[10]

---

text given here is different from that of the Armenian Bible in its wording, though agreeing with it in sense. Was this part of the text translated from Greek or Latin, as is perhaps suggested by the name-form Zecharias that was considered in n. 3 to the present section? No determination can be made.

Efrati adds: [The main verse used is certainly Ezek 1:24, but apparently it is paraphrased and conflated with other verses, as follows:

(1) Dan 10:6 describes the voice of a mighty angel, saying: קול דבריו כקול המון, "the voice of his words is like the voice of a multitude." This phrase corresponds with the clause in the present text qբաṛբառ ձնգս խուռն, "his speech was (like?) a multitude/tumult." However, it should be noted that the Armenian version of Dan 10:6 reads բարբառ բանից նորա իբրեւ զբարբառ զօրու, "the speech of his words is like the speech of the army/ power (?)." The different reading of Dan 10:6 implied by Questionnaire here is not to be found in either the text or the apparatus of Daniel edited by Cowe 1992, 210, and perhaps should be seen as a free paraphrase (or, perhaps, a quotation from memory) rather than an actual variant text. The conflation of Dan 10:6 with Ezek 1:24 could have arisen both from the similar subject matter and, more specifically, from the fact that the Armenian version of Ezek 1:24 has an explicit ձայն պատգամաց, "sound of pronouncement (words)," as a translation of MT קול המלה (that is reading הַמִּלָּה, "the word," instead of הֲמֻלָּה, "tumult, noise").

(2) The phrase of Ezek 3:12–13, קול רעש גדול, "a mighty sound of noise/tumult/earthquake," corresponds here to արձակեալ ահագին թնդմամբ, which may be translated as, "resounding with/by means of a mighty clamor" or the like. Under the lemma արձակեմ, Bedrossian (1973) records the collocation թնդումն արձակել in the sense "to resound, to make a noise," which seems appropriate here.

(3) Ezek 1:24 כקול מים רבים כקול שדי, "like the sound of great waters, like the sound of Shaddai (the Almighty)," which resembles the section here.

(4) Ezek 3:13 וקול האופנים, "the voice/sound of the wheels." This is probably the basis of the final part of the verse here.

Perhaps also (5) Isa 6:3 וקרא זה אל זה, "and one **cried** unto the other," Armenian աղաղակէին, which is the same verb as "calling out" here. Note that according to Ezek 3:13 MT the voice of the wheels is "over against them" (לעמתם), like the "one unto the other" in Isaiah. –S.E.].

9. See n. 3, above.

10. Zech 1:12. The seventy years are those foretold as the length of the exile by Jer 29:10 and taken up by Zech 7:5, 2 Chr 36:21, and Dan 9:2, 24. Later, the topos of seventy years or periods was used in apocalyptic eschatological predictions: see T. Levi 16.1, 1 En. 89.59, etc. The same is repeated in Armenian apocrypha; see Jeremiah, Susanna and the Two Elders §2 (*Arm Apoc* 4:200), Story of Daniel §3 (*Arm Apoc* 4:212). See also Adler 1996.

2.4/ And Gabriel was saying to Daniel, "At the beginning of your prayer a pronouncement went forth" and "I am he who brings your prayers before God."[11]

2.5/ And the others were singing "Hallelujah," as John saw in his vision. "And in the singing of new, anew they were uttering the voice of blessing."[12]

Annotation 4. Prayer and Angels

As noted in the introductory remarks to part 2 above, this part is a collection of testimonies to the angels' praise of God as they occur in the writings of the biblical prophets and the Revelation of Saint John. It is quite an unusual document, and it is a clear indication of the important role angels play in Armenian beliefs. Since some angels, notably Michael and Gabriel,[13] are celebrated in the ecclesiastical calendar, prayers to angels extend beyond popular milieux and into various formal ecclesiastical contexts. This attitude toward angels is also expressed in the many prayers addressed to angels and in the angel-related invocations and charms to be found in Armenian amulets.[14] These amulets are typically scrolls, narrow

---

11. An approximate quotation of Dan 9:21–23. To bring the prayers before God is the task of the archangels according to Tob. 12:12, 15; 1 En. 9.2. See also 3 Bar. 12.1–8 and Philo, *Somn.* 1.141. On angels as intercessors, see the remarks of Kulik 2010, *ad* 3 Bar. 12.1–8. In Exod. Rab. 21.4, the angel responsible for prayers is said to weave a crown from the prayers of humans and present it to God. See further discussion on pp. 16–17 and Rebiger 2007.

12. This is based on Rev 14:2–3, which uses a common phrase from the Hebrew Bible, "to sing a new song"; see Ps 33 (32):3, Isa 42:10, and more.

13. The intercessory role of these two angels in some Jewish circles is implied by the talmudic statement in y. Ber. 9:1, 13a, placed in God's mouth: "When troubles beset a man, let him not cry out to Michael nor to Gabriel—but let him cry out to Me, and I will answer him immediately." Had such invocations of angels not been current, this dictum would have been irrelevant. [It is perhaps worth noting that this statement denigrates crying out or praying to angels but does not forbid it—it is not a sinful act but simply an unnecessary one and apparently not a matter of great concern for the rabbis. See concerning worship of and prayer to angels, Stuckenbruck 1995, 63–67. –S.E.]

14. In the New Testament, in Col 2:18, excessive prayer to angels is condemned; compare also Heb 1:4–8. Examples of such Armenian prayers to angels are published and translated in *Arm Apoc* 6:29–37. Many similar prayers are to be found in the various printed collections of Armenian apotropaic prayers cited in the next footnote.

2. Angels and Prophets' Praise

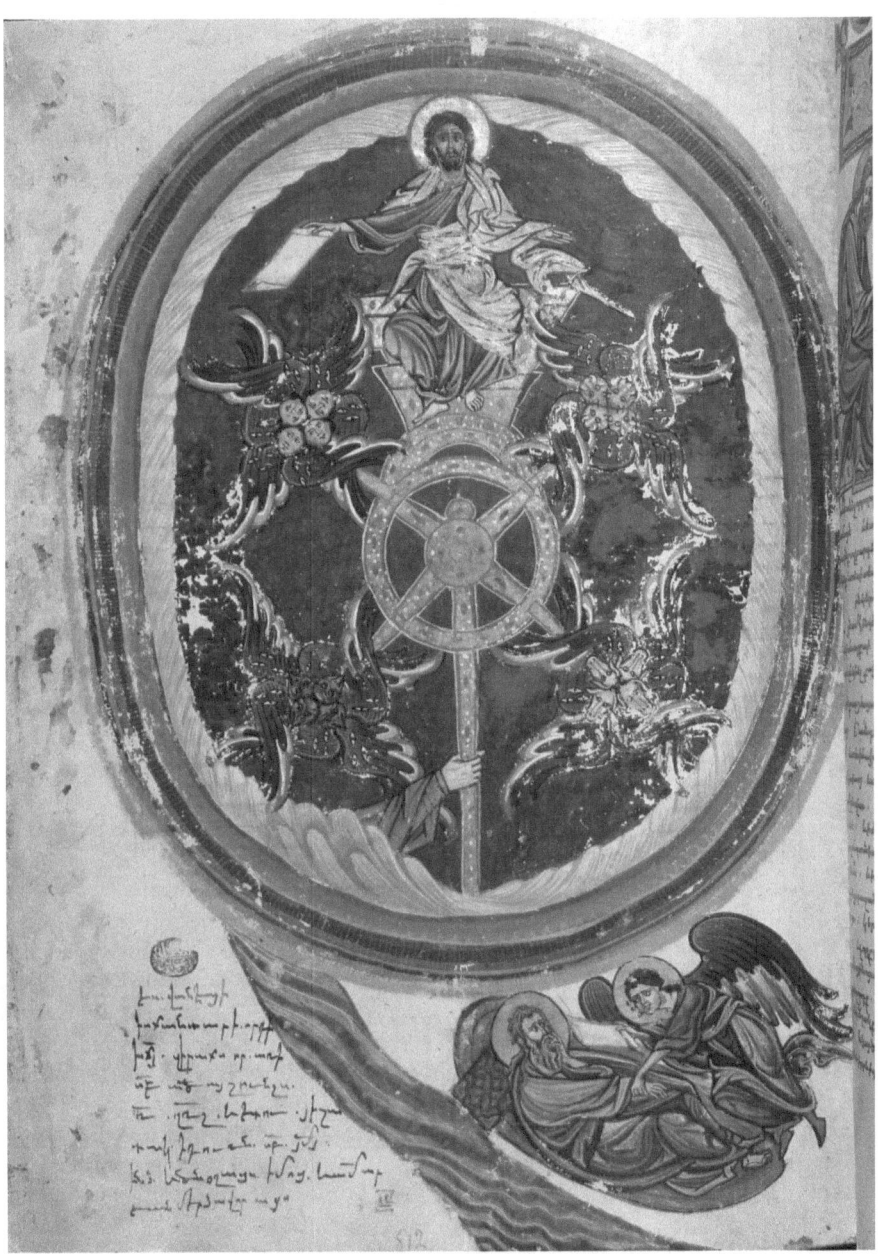

Figure 9. J1925, fol. 414v (Ezekiel's Vision of the Divine Chariot)

and quite long, on paper or parchment. Many have been copied by hand, but several printed scrolls have also been noted to exist, and doubtless many more, both handwritten and printed, survive unstudied in libraries, in museums, and in private hands.[15]

A few studies concerning the amulets and a substantial number of their invocations of angelic intercession have been published. Sargis Harutʻyunyan collected quite numerous, similar prayers for angelic help among the many charms and prayer texts assembled in his work on Armenian popular prayers.[16] In addition to various lesser publications, Frédéric Feydit published a collection of such texts drawn from the amulet scrolls (*hmayils*) in the Library of the Mekhitarist Fathers in Venice. He presented them with translations into French and reproduced the images that are also part of this apotropaic tradition, often of angels or saints. As part of that collection, Feydit edited, translated, and published a group of twelve different prayers taken from such *hmayil* amulets and directed to angels or calling on angels to intercede.[17] This work is a rich and extremely interesting corpus of Armenian prayers mainly of antidemonic and apotropaic character. Where possible, Feydit also notes

---

Later Jewish tradition also disapproves of such prayers, which condemnation most likely shows they must have been practiced, as I observed immediately above. See, for example, Weiss 2020. In the Jewish magical Book of Mysteries (Sefer Harazim) the invocation of angels for diverse purposes is rife. It is sufficient to consult the index in Morgan 1983, 94–95 to be convinced of this. See also the clear discussion in Bohak 2008, 46 and 171–72 (on angels in Sefer Harazim). On the four archangels in a magical context, see Bohak 2008, 197; on the adjuration of them, see p. 382 there.

15. They also appear in the form of small codices. On Armenian amulets, see Feydit 1986. Feydit published the scrolls in the Library of the Mekhitarist Fathers in Venice. Further note Vardanyan 2012. See also the publication of texts from the oldest surviving dated amulet scroll in Loeff 2002. Feydit (1973) discusses Armenian demonic or legendary animals against which such amulet prayers were pronounced. There is much interest concerning this subject in James Russell 2011. He deals with the same childbirth demon concerning which Feydit writes, and I may add that that class of demons was often the object of charms such as a number of those published by Harutʻyunyan. Russell presents interesting ideas and insights about the illustrative tradition of the amulets, as well as describing one specific scroll belonging to the Armenian Library and Museum of America. See also Ghazaryan 2018. Another amulet scroll has been studied in some detail by Uluhogian 1984.

16. In his work, he assembled a substantial corpus of Armenian folk prayer texts: see Harutʻyunyan 2006, nos. 1, 3, 4, 6, 19, etc.

17. Feydit 1986, 213–27; see n. 15 above for bibliography on this subject.

2. Angels and Prophets' Praise

the provenance of each prayer. The connections between Armenian magical texts and nonmagical traditions need investigation, and this field of learning and research still has great potential.

Manuscript Oxford Bodleian Arm f27 preserves three such prayers that have been edited and translated; one prayer is directed to angels, archangels, cherubs, and seraphs; one to the archangel Michael; and one invokes twelve guardian angels.[18] These prayers are actually in a manuscript codex of prayers, which also contains other prayers directed to angels and compositions by such luminaries as Saint Grigor Narekacʻi and Saint Nersēs Šnorhali, among many others (Baronian and Conybeare 1918, 149–153, especially 151).[19] Another prayer to the archangels is to be observed in the amulet roll Oxford Bodleian g4 (dated 1706/7) (Baronian and Conybeare 1918, 73–74). It is directed to the archangels Gabriel and Michael and all the heavenly host.[20] A similar prayer title, "to all the archangels, to Gabriel," may be seen in manuscript Chester Beatty Library 636, which is also an amulet fragment. It opens with a list of angelic names.[21] These are a few examples of a very rich and understudied corpus.

The idea of angelic helpers for human prayer is most graphically presented in 3 Bar. 12.[22] The notion is quite widespread, and the angels are often characterized by the tag "guardian." Examples may be seen in LAE 31 and the Armenian list of twelve guardian angels published in *Arm Apoc* 4:110–11, no. 3.12.[23] It is clear, then, that the role of angels in Armenian religious life was significant.

In conclusion, I may remark that quite numerous adjurations by angels are to be observed in Near Eastern Aramaic incantations and spells from late antiquity.[24] It would be interesting to see how far the tradition

---

18. These are published in *Arm Apoc* 4:107–11.
19. The manuscript is dated to 1611 CE, and the location of its copying remains unknown.
20. This is published with commentary in *Arm Apoc* 6:29–37.
21. Stone and Stone 2012, 190–97, especially p. 193. Further amulet fragments are catalogued there on pp. 197–214, but none contains prayers to angels.
22. I have discussed it elsewhere: see *Arm Apoc* 5:44 n. 42. See for a most insightful and exhaustive discussion: Kulik 2010, 343–54 and see n. 11 to this part.
23. For further discussion see in *Arm Apoc* 4:43–44 nn. 45–46; 165 n. 94; and *Arm Apoc* 3:98. Consult also Kulik 2010, 349–51 and Hannah 2007.
24. See, for example, Naveh and Shaked 1993, amulet 10.3–4 (pp. 86–87) from Ḥorvath Rimmon, ca. 30 km north of Beersheba, Israel; bowl 10.12–13 (p. 181); and Cairo Genizah 4.13–14 (pp. 224–25). Guardian angels play a considerable role in

embedded in Armenian amulets resonates with the Jewish, Syriac Christian, and Mandaean magical bowls and with other magical texts, such as those that are preserved in the Cairo Genizah.[25] The Greek and the Coptic magical papyri are yet another branch of this tradition and a good number of texts can be consulted in their translation by Hans Dieter Betz (1992).[26] This bibliography could be considerably expanded.

Apoc. Paul 12, 16, etc.; see also Supplication about Sodomites and Gomorreans §5 in *Arm Apoc* 5:43–44 and n. 42. Other similar texts are numerous.

25. More material is presented in Naveh and Shaked 1998; Bohak 2008, 197.

26. See for bibliography: Bohak 2019, 388–415. There is a very considerable literature on the magical bowls due to particularly intensive study of them in recent decades. The Matenadaran in Erevan holds one unpublished bowl.

3
Nine Ranks of Angels and Human Leaders

The third part of Questionnaire is a list of nine classes of biblical holy leaders, which specifies that each of these nine types of leaders is typologically correlated with one of the nine angelic classes. This correlated material does not appear in the sections associated with angelic praise in the fourteenth-century encyclopedic *Book of Questions* by Grigor of Tat'ew (1346–1409/10) nor, indeed, in the much older *Celestial Hierarchy* by Pseudo-Dionysius the Areopagite (sixth century CE).[1] However, presumably, it reflects an Armenian ideal of society informed and structured by the Christian church, headed by patriarchs (in the biblical sense) and concluding with the վարդապետք "the Doctors, teachers."[2]

TEXT

M682, fol. 7r.19–21/

3.1/ Ընդ այնոսիկ եւ զազգս մարդկան յորդորեաց Աստուած Թ.(9) դասուք, աւրինել զԱրարիչն իւրեանց.
3.2/ ի նահապետսն նմանութիւնք աթոռցն,
օրէնսդիրքն՝ քերովբէիցն,
դատաւորք՝ Սերովբէից,
քահանայք՝ տէրութեանց,
թագաւորք՝ զորութեանց,
3.3/ մարգարէք՝ իշխանութեանց,

---

1. See *Arm Apoc* 4:77 and the discussion there of Pseudo-Dionysius's *Celestial Hierarchy* as a source used by Grigor Tat'ewac'i.

2. It should be noted that the word վարդապետ, rendered "teacher" and, more specifically, "one authorized to teach religious doctrine in the church," does not occur in the Armenian translation of the Bible.

առաքեալք՝ պետութեանց,
աւետարանիչք ՝ հրեշտակապետաց
վարդապետք՝ հրեշտակաց:

TRANSLATION

3.1/ In place of this,[3] God exhorted the race of humans to bless their Creator in nine ranks:

3.2/ Among the patriarchs, the likenesses of the Thrones.
The lawgivers, of the Cherubs.
The judges, of Seraphs.
Priests, of Dominions.
Kings, of Powers.
3.3/ Prophets, of Rulers.
Apostles, of Principalities
Evangelists, of Archangels.
Teachers,[4] of Angels.

---

3. That is, the praise of the angelic ranks, described in part 2, above. Here the text gives the equivalations of angelic and human ranks.

4. Or: doctors, that is, of the church.

4
Nine Ranks of Angels and Ecclesiastics

Below, part 5.1 refers to the list presented in part 4 as a խորհուրդ, which means "mystery, counsel," perhaps borrowing the term from Pseudo-Dionysius, who views the understanding of the correspondence of the celestial orders or ranks and the terrestrial church orders to be special knowledge that issued from meditation.[1] This correlation of heavenly and earthly order is to be observed in other texts as well.[2] Here, it is interesting to see the extent to which the pseudo-Dionysian list of nine has served as a pattern for the various categorizations of angels and of society, clerical and lay.[3] That correlation was taken as demonstrating the divine intent and order that penetrate all of creation, with the heavenly correspondence of the church's ranks making its divine character evident. Part 4 concludes the response to the question asked at the beginning of the whole document (see §1.2), "The first and foremost question: Of which sort are the rankings[4] of the angels?" Together with the preceding parts, it has thus presented the rank and order of the angels.

Text

M682, fol. 7r.21–24

4.1/ Այսպէս եւ նորս եկեղեցի կարգեցաւ.

---

1. La Porta 2008, 124. The correlation of cosmic order and that of the church in early Syriac sources is discussed in Murray 1990, 151. Praise, suitable for the heavenly realm, is also afforded to the Christian ascetics, see Murray 1990, 151.

2. See *Arm Apoc* 4:77–81, no. 3.5.

3. See part 3, introductory remarks, and *Arm Apoc* 4:77–81. Above, in part 1, n. 42 the various numbers of the groups of highest angels are discussed.

4. Or: orderings.

կաթողիկոսն՝ ի նմանութիւն աթոռոցն,
եպիսկոպոսն՝ քերովբէից,
քահանայն՝ սերովբէից,
սարկաւագն՝ տէրութեանց,
կիսասարկաւագն՝ զօրութեանց,
4.2/ ջահընկալն՝ իշխանութեանց,
երդմնեցուցիչն՝ պետութեանց,
ընթերցողք՝ հրեշտակապետաց,
դռնապացք՝ հրեշտակաց, որք եդեն աւրհնաբանիչք Աստուծոյ։

Translation

4.1/ Thus, also this new church was ordered:
The Catholicos, in likeness of the Thrones,
The bishop, of Cherubs,
The priests, of Seraphs,
The deacon, of Dominions,
The subdeacon, of Powers,
4.2/ The acolytes, of Rulers,
The exorcist,[5] of Principalities,
The lectors, of Archangels,
The doorkeepers, of Angels, who[6] were glorifiers of God.

---

5. No reason may be discerned for the exorcist being in the singular and the other eight classes, except, of course, the Catholicos, being in the plural.

6. Presumably, all the above.

5
Another Ordering of Angels and Ecclesiastics

In this list, the sequential order in the individual lines of the preceding list is reversed so that the human element is presented first and then the angelic. This list, however, also differs from the preceding part 4 in matters of content. The catholicos and bishop are mentioned in the preliminary sentence. That sentence makes the point that, though they differ in rank, they are equals as priests. Then ensues a list of nine ecclesiastical ranks, six of which appear in part 4 and three are additional to that list. The exorcist of part 4 is omitted and, because catholicos and bishop have been mentioned in the opening sentence, they, too, are excluded from the list. Three categories are added to it: the monk, the baptised, and the catechumens. All Christians are included here in the list of the church and not just its office holders or clergy.

Text

M682, fol. 7r.21–24

5.1/ Դարձեալ այլ խորհուրդ. զի թէպէտ կաթողիկոս եւ եպիսկոպոս աստիճանօք զանազանեն. բայց հասարակ քահանայական կարգ կոչի.
    քահանայք նման աթոռոց,
    սարկաւագն՝ քերովբէիցն,
    կիսասարկաւագ՝ սերովբէից,
    ջահընկալ՝ տէրութեանց,
    ընթերցող՝ զօրութեանց,
    5.2/ Դռնպաց՝ իշխանութեանց,
    Կրօնաւոր՝ պետութեանց,
    Մկրտեալքն՝ հրեշտակապետաց,

Երախայքն՝ ընրեշտակաց,
Այսպէս կարգեաց մեծ Դիոնեսիոս՝ ուսեալ ի Պօղոսէ առաքելոյ.
ի փառս Քրիստոսի Աստուծոյ մերոյ։

Translation

5.1/ Again, another mystery:[1] although a Catholicos and a bishop are distinguished by rank, yet they are called equal in priestly rank.

Priests (are) like to Thrones,
The deacon, to the Cherubs,
Subdeacon, to Seraphs,
5.2/ Acolyte, to Dominions,
Reader, to Powers,
The doorkeeper,[2] to Rulers,
Monk, to Principalities,
The baptized, to Archangels,
The catechumens, to Angels.

Thus, the great Dionysius ranked (them), having learned from the apostle Paul.[3]

For the glory of Christ, our God.[4]

---

1. The mystery or the symbolic value is the hierarchic order within the church, which thus partakes of the divine. See part 4, n. 1.

2. Literally: the door-opener. The use of the article/demonstrative -ն is inconsistent in this text, and that inconsistency is reflected in my consequently inconsistent use of the English article "the."

3. Acts 17:34 relates that, when Paul preached in Athens, Dionysius the Areopagite joined him. This is the Dionysius to whom the *Celestial Hierarchy* was attributed. Several verses in the New Testament epistles mention the names of groups of super-terrestrial beings: see Col 1:16, Eph 3:10, 6:10–12, and 1 Pet 3:22.

4. Such short doxologies often mark the end of a writing or of one of its major parts.

6
On Which Day Were the Angels Created?

Following the presentation of the heavenly order, a new question is posed about the day of the angels' creation. This question as to which day was that of the angels' creation is one concerning which there were differing opinions in antiquity and medieval times, which will be discussed below. It marks the movement of our document's center of interest from the angels' ranking to their origins and actions. These subjects will occupy the immediately following part as well. The present part is one of many texts surviving in various languages that enumerate the six days of creation and list the creations made on each day. Such texts are called "Hexaemera," that is, "Six Days."[1] Such lists are quite old in Judeo-Christian tradition; compare, for example, 4 Ezra 6.35–59 (last decade of the first century CE), and there are many other sources, both longer or shorter.[2] An ancient and very important patristic work in this genre is the *Hexaemeron* of Basil of Caesarea (fourth century), which was early translated into Armenian.[3]

Text

M682, fols. 7r.28–7v.2

6.1/ Հարց. թէ որ օր ստեղծան հրեշտակք։
Պատասխանի. Առաջին օր կիրակէ՝ որ միաշաբաթ ասի. ստեղծ Աստուած է.(7) իրք՝ Ա.(1) հրեղէն երկինք. եւ Բ.(2) հրեշտակք, եւ Գ.(3)

---

1. See also Armenian manuscript illustrations such as M187, fol. 4v and M203, fol. 12v. Plentiful examples could be assembled from the art of other Christian cultures as well.
2. For a general survey, see Robbins 1912.
3. Thomson 1995. The most recent edition of the Armenian text is K. Muradyan 1984.

լուսաւորք որ յօդս, եւ Դ.(4) տարերք, այսինքն հող, եւ ջուր, օդ եւ հուր, եւ ժամանակն որ լինի ութ։

6.2/ Իսկ Բ.(2)շաբթի՝ զկէս ջրոյն վերեկոտել ի Զ.(6) դիմաց յայսկոյս եւ յայնկոյս, եւ այլ հաստատութիւնն արար որ է կապոյտ երկին։

6.3/ Գ.(3)շաբթի՝ ասաց ժողովեցին ջուրքն ի ծովս․ եւ երեւեցի ցամաքն։ Եւ բուսան ծառք եւ բոյսք ամենայն պտղաբերք․ ի խորհուրդ մարգարէիցն։

6.4/ Իսկ Դ.(4)շաբթի՝ արեգական եւ լուսին եւ աստեղք, որք ցիր եւ ցան էին, եղ յամանի եւ սահման եղ կալ իւրաքանչիւր կարգի, յօրինակ Աստուածածնին։

6.5/ Իսկ Ե.(5)շաբթին ասաց. Բղխեսցեն ջուրք զեռունս եւ qթn/ fol. 7v /չունս, որք թռեան յօդս՝ օրինակ առաքելոցն, որք ի ծովէ կոչեցան եւ յերկինս ելան։

6.6/ Իսկ ի Զ.(6) աւուր ուրբաթի, ստեղծ զմարդն եւ այլ չորքոտանիք։

Translation

6.1/ Question: (On) which day were the angels created?

Answer: On the first day, Sunday,[4] which is called the first of the week, God created seven things: (1) fiery heavens,[5] and (2) angels, and (3) the luminaries which are in the atmosphere,[6] and (4) the elements, that is earth and water, air and fire; and time, which makes eight.

6.2/ Then on Monday, having divided half of the water into six aspects, hither and thither,[7] and also, he made the firmament, which is the blue heaven.[8]

---

4. The Armenian Կիրակին derives from Greek κυριακή and may be translated also "Lord's day." See Malxaseancʽ 1944, s.v.

5. The upper heavens were of fire, according to many sources: see, for example, *Arm Apoc* 4:8; CT 1.8.

6. In Gen 1:3, the creation of light is recounted. These luminaries seem to be distinct from the sun, moon, and stars, the creation of which is attributed to Wednesday; see §6.4 below. Just what is intended here is unclear, perhaps the planets in contrast to the fixed stars.

7. The reference seems to be to the waters above the earth and those under the earth, see Gen 1:6–7. Observe Pseudo-Zeno 1.0.1 which passage talks of six positions (դիրք), an idea developed in 1.1.0–1.6.18: see Stone and Shirinian 2000, 51–66, 127–39. The number six plays a major role in that work.

8. Gen 1:6–8.

6. On Which Day Were the Angels Created?

6.3/ On Tuesday he said, "Let the waters be gathered into the seas, and let the dry land be seen." And all fruit-bearing trees and plants sprang up as a pattern of the prophets.[9]

6.4/ Then on Wednesday, (he created) the sun and the moon and the stars,[10] which were scattered. He set (them) in a vessel,[11] and he set a limit for each order to remain within (that is its vessel), as a type of the Mother of God.[12]

6.5/ Then, on Thursday he said, "Let the waters bring forth crawling things and birds that flew in the air," as a type of the apostles, who were summoned from the sea and ascended to the heavens.[13]

6.6/ Then on the sixth day, Friday, he created humans and also the quadrupeds.

ANNOTATION 5. THE DAY ON WHICH THE ANGELS WERE CREATED

There are differing traditions about the day on which the angels were created, for the angels are mentioned neither in the creation story in Gen 1 nor in Gen 2. The present text says that their creation took place on the first day of creation. This view is already reflected in ancient Judaism in the extraordinary list of angels in Jub. 2.2 and perhaps is implied by 4 Ezra 8.22. Second Baruch 21.6, which speaks of "hosts which you made from

---

9. In other words, the fruit-bearing plants symbolize the prophets, who produce the word of God, which is their fruit and through it they (spiritually) sustain humanity.

10. The sun, moon, and stars are represented by ideographs, not uncommon in Armenian manuscripts; see Abrahamyan 1973, 223–43 with tables.

11. Rabbinic sources mention the נרתיק / נושתק, "vessel," of the sun: see b. Ned. 8b, Gen. Rab. 6.6. This is a loanword from Greek νάρθηξ; see Krauss 1899, 2:367–68; Perles 1917, particularly 302.

12. Gen 1:14–18. The author reads this passage as saying that the vessel in which he set the luminaries was like the Virgin Mary, within whom Christ was put. Additionally, perhaps the simile is influenced by the iconography of the Virgin standing on the crescent moon among the stars, see, Bergamini 1985, especially 1–32; Reau 1957, 80. This iconography connects the Virgin specifically with luminaries.

13. Gen 1:20–22. In this section, the verb "flew" is in the aorist indicative tense, which is odd. A present indicative or a subjunctive would be expected. Here is a generalization, extended to the body of the apostles, of features that the gospels record relating to certain specific apostles. Thus, Simon Peter and Andrew were fishermen (Matt 4:18, Mark 1:16), as were James and John, sons of Zebedee (Matt 4:21). According to 2 Cor 12:2–4, Paul claims that someone ascended to the third heaven.

the beginning," may also point specifically to the first day.[14] The view promoted by Questionnaire is clearly based on a particular understanding of Gen 1:3–4 that included various other items in addition to light and darkness in the list of the first day's creations.[15]

Oddly, at the start of this paragraph, God is said to have created seven things on the first day, and at the paragraph's end, there are said to be eight, including time. Time seems to have been added to a preexisting list and causes a contradiction between the last and the first sentences. One may assume that the author's source spoke of seven things, and the eighth was added by the author himself as an afterthought, from a different tradition, or by some analogous process.[16] About a millennium later than Jubilees and 4 Ezra, which I have just cited, is CT 1.3, which reads, "on the first day, the Lord made … the angels, archangels, thrones, authorities, powers, rulers, cherubs and seraphs" (*MOTP* 1:540). Notably, considering the preceding discussion of the classes of angels, here the document mentions eight angelic ranks, not nine, nor does the order of the ranks accord with the usual Armenian list, as is evident from comparing it with the preceding parts of Questionnaire.

Implying that the angels are created on Day 1, Herm. Sim. 3.4.1 characterizes them as "first-created."[17] That their creation was on the first day is also maintained by an unpublished text in Armenian manuscript M10725, fol. 216v. Second Enoch 29.3, however, mentions the second day as that on which God created the angels. In b. Hag. 12a, R. Judah reports in the name of Rab that ten things were created on the first day. According

---

14. This was also a Western view, see Auffarth 2004, especially 199–203, see also on pp. 268, 277. This was also the view of Augustine, see Teske 1990, 158. See also Cowley 1988, 240–41, who reports than the Ethiopian tradition holds that the angels were created on the first day, though a few texts talk of the second or the fifth days.

15. On the four elements' creation on that day, which is a common idea in the Armenian tradition, see Stone 2013, index, s.v. "elements."

16. The dissonance of seven and eight is also found in Jub. 2.2–3, which enumerates eight things and concludes by saying "seven great actions." Philo, *Opif.* 29, however, enumerates seven things created on the first day. See also Kister 2006, especially 241–45. In Jansma 1958, 96, there is a discussion of time in connection with creation according to Syriac sources.

17. A quite different narrative about the creation of angels, according to which, nevertheless, they are the first of created things, is found in the Slavonic work, Sea of Tiberias; see Badalanova Geller 2011, 68–69. In some Syriac sources, angels are considered to have existed before creation; see Jansma 1958, particularly 98.

6. On Which Day Were the Angels Created?

to Pirqe R. El. 3, seven things existed before the creation and eight other things were created on the first day. However, none of these rabbinic or Hebrew sources mentions the creation of the angels.[18]

Indeed, in rabbinic literature, there are two views concerning the day the angels were created, which are usually set forth in debate with one another. The competing opinions are (1) that the angels were created on the second day and (2) that they were created on the fifth day. The dominant view is that it was on the second day.[19] The idea that they were created on the first day is strongly opposed in some sources, see, for example, Gen. Rab. 1.3, Midr. Tanh. Bereshit 1.1, Midr. Teh. 24.4, 86.4. The creation of angels on the first day is rejected because that might raise the possibility that the angels had a part in creation. In turn, that view would threaten the idea that God created on his own. The rabbis read the creation passage in Job 38:7 ("when the morning stars sang together, and all the Sons of God shouted for joy") to refer to the creation of angels, but no specific day or temporal sequence can be inferred from that passage. The matter of creation of the angels is clinched for rabbinic interpreters by Ps 104(103):1–4, and particularly verse 4: "who makest the winds thy messengers, fire and flame thy ministers." In this verse, the Hebrew word translated as "messengers" is *mal'akîm*, which became the usual Hebrew word for "angel(s)."

The earliest Armenian theological discourse, the *Teaching of Saint Gregory*, which is preserved in the writing of the fifth-century author called Agathangelos, speaks in §265 of the creation of humankind and of angels, but does not say on which day angels were created (Thomson 2001, 66–67). Vardan Arewelcʻi (1200?–1271) suggests that the angels were created on the first day because in the term "heaven" (Gen 1:1), Scripture includes all the inhabitants of heaven and thus also the angelic ranks, all of which were created on that day.[20] Grigor Tatʻewacʻi (1344?–1409) in his

---

18. See Jansma 1958, 99–101 on comparable Syriac traditions and their context.

19. See Gen. Rab. 1.3; Midr. Tanh. Bereshit 1.1. See also Pirqe R. El. 4 and Midr. Konen 1.25. See for this last text: Jellineck 1938, 2:25. For the second day alone, not in an argumentative context, see Gen. Rab. 11.9; Song Rab. 15.22; Midr. Tanh. Hayye Sarah 3; Midr. Teh. 104.7; Targum Pseudo-Jonathan to Gen 1:26. More rabbinic sources could be adduced. See also Bamberger et al. 2007, 156 and further references there. In Exod. Rab. 15.22, the sequence "firmament—angels" is derived from Ps 104(103):4; see the discussion in Reiterer, Nicklas, and Schopflin 2007, 631.

20. See his *Commentary on Genesis* in manuscript M1267, fol. 7r.i. The manuscript copy is of the fifteenth century. On the different classes of angels, see above, parts 1–5.

Book of Questions enumerates seven creations of the first day: heavens, earth, angels, and the four elements and light as well.[1]

---

1. On creation of the four elements, see *Arm Apoc* 4:89 and compare Stone 2013, index, s.v. "elements." The Samaritan work TM 2.4, 4.16–17 also speaks of the four physical elements. See further in part 6, n. 1. On light, see Tatʻewacʻi 1993, 193. On light as an eighth, see above, n. 15.

7
Where Did He Create Adam?

Genesis does not specify the site of Adam's creation. Was it in the garden of Eden, outside the garden of Eden, or on the future site of Jerusalem? These are the main options that ancient sources offer as possible locales for the creation of Adam. Our author does not make a clear exegetical choice and leaves the determination to "God alone." Apparently, despite his exegetical ingenuity, he is stumped, or perhaps he knows no clear tradition. In annotation 6 below, I present some of the answers that were suggested by other ancient exegetes. In fact, many sources connected the locale of Adam's creation with christological ideas, which makes our author's professed agnosticism in this matter the more striking.

TEXT

M682, fol. 7b.2–5

7.1/ Հարց, թէ՛ Ուր ստեղծ զԱդամ:
7.2/ Պատասխանի. ի վայրս դրախտին ստեղծ. եւ յետ աւուր, եդ ի դրախտին. Յայտ է որ ասէ գիրն, թէ՛ Էած Աստուած զամենայն կենդանիս առ Ադամ կոչել նոցա անուանս, ուրեմն ոչ էր դրախտն տեղիք անասնոց եւ զազանաց, այլ արտաքոյ էր:
7.3/ Եւ ոմանք Երուսաղէմ ասեն ստեղծեալ զմարդն. ըստ այնմ թէ Սիովնի ասի մայր, եւ մայրդ ծնաւ ի նմա: Բայց զի Մովսէս ոչ գրեաց, Աստուծոյ է գիտելի:

TRANSLATION

7.1/ Question: Where did he create Adam?

-45-

7.2/ Answer: He created (him) in the environs of the garden. And after a day, he put (him) in the garden.[1] That which Scripture says is clear, that God brought all the animals to Adam to call them names.[2] Therefore, the place of the animals and beasts was not the garden, but outside (it).

7.3/ And some say that he created man in Jerusalem, according to that Zion was called mother,[3] and this mother gave birth in it. But because Moses did not write (about this), it is knowable to God (alone).

ANNOTATION 6. THE PLACE OF THE PROTOPLASTS' CREATION AND BURIAL

In Jub. 3.8–9, the angelic informant says to Moses:

> In the first week Adam was created and also the rib, his wife. And in the second week he showed her to him. And therefore, the commandment was given to observe seven days for a male, but for a female twice seven days in their impurity.[4] And after Adam had completed forty days in

---

1. Gen 2:8.
2. Gen 2:19.
3. Cf. Isa 66:13, Jer 4:31, 31:15, Matt 2:18.
4. The reference is to Lev 12:2–5, which reads: "2 Say to the people of Israel, If a woman conceives, and bears a male child, then she shall be unclean seven days; as at the time of her menstruation, she shall be unclean. 3 And on the eighth day the flesh of his foreskin shall be circumcised. 4 Then she shall continue for thirty-three days in the blood of her purifying; she shall not touch any hallowed thing, nor come into the sanctuary, until the days of her purifying are completed. 5 But if she bears a female child, then she shall be unclean two weeks, as in her menstruation; and she shall continue in the blood of her purifying for sixty-six days." This text mandates a forty days' exclusion of the mother of a new-born son from the tabernacle and eighty days of exclusion in the case of a daughter. The week plus forty days and two weeks plus eighty days periods in Jubilees correspond to the same periods of time in Lev 12:2 and 5. This implies that, for Jubilees, the garden of Eden was at the level of purity of the tabernacle and the temple. On this matter, see Baumgarten 1994, 3–10. This idea is also found in a quotation from a lost Adam apocryphon in the *Chronography* of George Syncellus (early ninth century). See Adler and Tuffin 2002, 6–7, quoting Little Genesis, also called Life of Adam. See their n. 4 on p. 6 for further sources and ramifications of this idea in Byzantine literature. The connection of the garden of Eden with the sanctuary is greatly stressed in Elior 2014. However, her hypothesis of the existence of alternative, priestly narratives of the incidents related in Genesis and in the first twenty chapters of Exodus raises considerable difficulties. The intimate connection of the garden of Eden and the temple is discussed further in nn. 12, 26, and 130 to annotation 13.

the land where he had been created, we brought him into the garden of Eden to till and keep it, but his wife they brought in on the eightieth day, and after this she entered the garden of Eden.

Robert H. Charles (1902, 22–24), in a long note to this passage, points to its use by the chronographer George Syncellus (d. after 810 CE) and other first-millennium CE authors.[5]

The passage of Jubilees clearly professes that Adam and Eve were created outside the garden, and, indeed, such a view is also the plain sense of Gen 2:7–8.[6] That passage relates God's creation of Adam, after which God put Adam in the garden.[7] In annotation 7, which follows below, I consider the associated question of how many days passed between Adam's creation and his establishment in the garden. At the present point, however, our concern is solely with the locale of Adam's creation.

One tradition holds that Adam was created at the center of the earth. Victor Aptowitzer (1924, 148, 152–54) discusses this view as it occurs in rabbinic sources and the linked notion that Adam was created in Jerusalem, the world's center (Ezek 38:12). Aptowitzer traces rabbinic traditions that Adam was created not only at the mid-point of the earth but with dust taken from the whole earth or from its four corners.[8] This, of course, became bound together with the idea that Adam was created in Jerusalem.

---

5. See Adler and Tuffin 2002, 6. The matter had been discussed at some length by James 1920, 5–8.

6. So also, the Latin LAE 29 and Aptowitzer 1924, 150–51.

7. John Chrysostom, *Hom. Gen.* 14, says that Adam was created outside the garden and immediately brought into it.

8. Aptowitzer also refers to the Latin LAE 29, which shows that Adam was created outside the garden. [A Talmudic tradition in b. Sanh. 38a–b speaks of Adam's head being created from the land of Israel, his body from Babylon, and his limbs from "other countries," thus giving a characteristic rabbinic turn to the motif of his being created from dust from the four corners of the earth. –S.E.] According to Pirqe R. El. 11, he was created in "a clean place," that is in the temple (Friedlander 1981, 78). In addition, in the Beta Israel (Falasha) writing, *Teʾezaza Sanbat*, Adam is said to have been created from clay from the land of Dudālēm, a legendary country; see Leslau 1951, 25 and 144 n. 23 concerning the "land of Dudālēm." According to the Armenian Homilies of Pseudo-Epiphanius, after his creation, Adam was led to Golgotha, and there, God and he sat on thrones; Dorfmann-Lazarev 2014, 285–333. Christ, in the New Testament, is said to sit at God's right hand in the future; see Matt 26:64; Mark 14:62, 16:19; Luke 22:69; etc. He is the new Adam, replacing the old Adam in his position, which coincides with the site of the old Adam's creation.

According to Jewish texts, he was created on the spot of the temple and, according to some Christian texts, on Golgotha. From a Christian perspective, Golgotha took over the site of the center of the earth from Jerusalem or the temple or its altar.[9] It also explains the idea that the dust of which God molded Adam was taken from the four corners of the earth.[10] The earth's four corners, some Jewish Greek texts maintain, are indicated by the name Adam, which is an acrostic of the initial letters of the Greek words for the four directions or the four winds (2 En. 30.13 J; Sib. Or. 3.26).[11] The idea expressed by this acrostic is anchored once again in the view attested in various sources that Adam was created in the center of the earth, which is sometimes specified as Jerusalem or Golgotha.[12] Moreover, Aptowitzer remarks that Abraham's ram was offered on the same spot, on Mount Moriah. He also notes that a tree was said to grow there in which the ram, Isaac's substitute, was entangled and that Melchizedek made an offering there (Aptowitzer 1924, 150). These traditions recur in a Christianized form in the interesting Armenian apocryphon, The Tree of Sabek.[13]

Another, rarer formulation of this idea located Adam's creation on Mount Zion, but in that context "Mount Zion," too, may well be another name for the Temple Mount.[14] Yet a further formulation of the idea of Adam's creation, which event both indicated and somehow contained the rest of creation, is the view that he was created from all the four elements. Apparently, it first occurs in Armenian literature in Yačaxapatum čaṙk'

---

9. See CT 2.15–17 (*MOTP* 1:541), which says that Adam first stood erect "on that place where the cross of our Savior would be erected," a typological interpretation indeed, and pointing to Golgotha. See Grypeou and Spurling 2009, 237–38 and further on p. 93 below.

10. See n. 9.

11. See also Gos. Barth. 4.53 and further Adler 2020, 64–94 and especially 76 n. 24. The same idea is to be observed in the Old Irish biblical poem Saltair na Rann 4.1053–1056.

12. According to CT 2.16 (*MOTP* 1:541), Adam was created in Jerusalem. See also Stroumsa 1983.

13. See *Arm Apoc* 3:94–100. See annotation 15 in this book concerning Abel's sheep and Isaac's ram.

14. See Dorfmann-Lazarev 2020a, especially 314 n. 37. Adam, his source says, was created from the dust of Mount Zion and the water of the source of the brook of Kedron. On the location of Mount Zion, see Wilkinson 1977, 171–72 and Barrois 1962.

7. Where Did He Create Adam?

3 (sixth century), and it is common in subsequent Armenian compositions.[15] Earlier, Philo also says that humans are created of the four elements, and thus they are at home in all of them (Philo, *Opif.* §146).[16] So also says CT 2.6–7 (*MOTP* 1:541), though that work is rather later.[17] This idea highlights another aspect of Adam's special role in creation.[18]

The view that Adam was created in Jerusalem is clearly one of the ideas underlying the notion that he was buried on Golgotha. That idea is analyzed by Alexander Toepel (2012, 315), who places its origin late in the fourth-century CE.[19] "Golgotha" is the Aramaic word for "skull," and it is, of course, mentioned in the gospels, together with the gloss "skull" as the site of the crucifixion.[20] Golgotha as Adam's burial place is first testified in surviving witnesses by Origen in *Comm. Matt.* 27.33 and is to be found in a number of other Greek and Latin patristic works. Nikolai Lipatov-Chicherin discusses the shift from Jerusalem to Golgotha and further argues that Golgotha became central to the tradition of Adam's burial in the last decades of the fourth century.[21] A Greek tradition attributed to Epiphanius of Salamis quotes the burial of Adam on Golgotha and says

---

15. See Stone 2013, index, s.v. "elements."

16. Observe that the Falasha *Te'ezaza Sanbat* (Leslau 1951, 25) says that Adam was created from fire, wind, water, and crushed stones, which might be a variant on this theme. It is odd, considering that Gen 2:7 explicitly says that God molded Adam from the dust of the earth.

17. On this question, see also Toepel 2012, especially 317. On the creation of Adam according to Cave of Treasures, see Minov 2016a, 245. According to that work, Adam is created from the four elements, is given authority over all creatures, including the angels, and is endowed with prophecy, kingship, and priesthood.

18. Before his sin, Adam was of supernatural size; see Ginzberg 1909, 1:76, 5:79 n. 22: see also b. Hag. 12a. Rabbinic views of Adam's size and nature are well set forth by Schäfer 1986, 69–93. Concerning superhuman or heavenly beings of enormous size, see Stroumsa 1981, 42–61. The subject is very extensive, and these references should be taken as indicative.

19. See Heither and Reemts 2007, 278–80 for the Western traditions. See further, Lipatov-Chicherin 2019b, particularly 158–59. On the iconographic evidence, see Frazer 1974, particularly 153–55.

20. See Matt 27:33, Mark 15:22, and John 19:17. In general, on the site, see Wilkinson 1977, 177. Aptowitzer (1924, 145) suggests that the old form of the Christian Golgotha tradition spoke only of Adam's skull being buried on Golgotha.

21. See Lipatov-Chicherin 2019a, 31–50; concerning Golgotha as Adam's tomb see also 33–37. The same tradition also occurs in *The Conflict of Adam and Eve with Satan* 3.20 (see Malan 1882); CT 22.6, 23.16–17 (*MOTP* 1:556–557).

that the Golgotha tradition derived from Ἑβραῖοι.²² A certain Epiphanius, styled the Monk, in *Holy Places* 1.10 speaks of "a church, the Tomb of Adam." A similar description is to be found in the Armenian list of Anastas *vardapet*.²³

Aptowitzer (1924, 140–50) and Louis Ginzberg (1909, 5:126) suggest that Golgotha as Adam's burial place was a development of the Jewish tradition of Jerusalem transmitted to Christian thinkers through Syriac intermediaries. Ginzberg points out that the Syriac *Cave of Treasures*, which uses the formulation "center of the earth" as well as "Golgotha,"²⁴ retains the Jerusalem identification. Its tradition, I may add, apparently influenced *The Conflict of Adam and Eve with Satan* in Ethiopic.²⁵ Similarly, in Armenian, David the Invincible Philosopher (sixth–seventh century) speaks of Adam's burial on Golgotha as being a Jewish tradition, saying "For the summit of Golgotha, the place of the execution, the Jews say is also the tomb of the first man."²⁶ Pilgrim itineraries also evidence this view, as John Wilkinson points out.²⁷

Quite different is the Syriac *Testament of Seth*, which says Adam was buried "east of Eden," over against the "city of Henoch" (see Gen 4:17), where the founding of this city is mentioned.²⁸ This testimony is not attributed to Jews. Theophilus, *ad Auctolycum* 2.19 sets Adam's burial on a mountain in Arabia. Nonetheless, it is Jerusalem and Golgotha that have pride of place as claimants to Adam's tomb.

The highlighting of Golgotha, of course, taps into the correlations between Old Adam and New Adam, of the Old Adam's mortal sin and the related expiatory death of Christ, who was viewed as the New Adam. Indeed, in Christian iconography, Adam's skull is often shown underneath Christ's cross, and Christ's blood flows from the wound in his side

---

22. See Hultsch 1864, 1:275 §86, 10.2–4, and also in Epiphanius, *Pan.* 46.5. On the latter, see Govett 1880.

23. Wilkinson 1977, 158, 177, 200; On Anastas *vardapet*'s list, see Sanjian 1969. This list has been presented most recently by Tchekhanovets 2018, 20–21. See also recently Terian 2016.

24. See Malan 1882, 3.18 n. 29, and 3.20; CT 22.6, 23.16–17 (*MOTP* 1:556, 557).

25. The Conflict of Adam and Eve survives in Ethiopic and Arabic. See Stone 1992, 98–101 and bibliography there.

26. Cited in Stone 2013, 301.

27. See the "Gazeteer" in Wilkinson 1977, 174–78. The earliest pilgrim reference is Egeria, *Travels*, 25.8–12. On this work's testimony, see also Wilkinson 1981, 127–28.

28. See James 1920, 4. See p. 52 below.

7. Where Did He Create Adam?

and washes Adam clean of sin and guilt. In certain medieval representations, not only is Adam's skull visible underneath the foot of the cross, but some of his bones are shown below it.[29] That iconography expresses the same correlation between Adam's sin and Christ's redemption that inheres in the idea of Adam's burial on Golgotha.

The earliest known image of the cross standing over Adam's skull is, apparently, on a seventh- to eighth-century icon in Saint Catherine's Monastery in the Sinai.[30] Kurt Weitzmann (1976, 57) says about it: "Blood flows quite freely from the wounds in both hands and also down the suppedaneum into the cave in the red-coloured hill of Golgotha and then into what seems to be the top of Adam's cranium." The same scene, without the cave, is to be observed on an eighth- to ninth-century bronze crucifix now in Providence, Rhode Island.[31] Other examples can be traced back to the tenth century, and they become more frequent around 1000 CE.[32] This is rather later than the literary evidence discussed here, but is an interesting corroboration of it.

A variation on this theme occurs in a Greek folktale recorded by George A. Megas. Belonging to the Cheirograph cycle, it relates that on Golgotha, it was not Adam's skull that Christ's blood did wash clean, but his hand, upon which the Cheirograph had been incised. This, of course, exhibits the same dynamic as the skull story but is focused on the hand because of the Cheirograph legend.[33]

In turn, this narrative integration of Adam's creation into salvation history begets yet a third tradition complex, the story of the remains of Adam and Eve. The basic element of this complex tale concerning the protoplasts' burial relates that their remains were borne through the flood in Noah's ark and were finally buried in Jerusalem on Golgotha (Adam) and in Bethlehem in the Grotto of the Nativity (Eve).[34] Eve rises from the dead

---

29. See Matt 27:33, Mark 15:22, and John 19:17 for the skull etymology. On the iconography of this idea, see Frazer 1974, 153–61.

30. See Weitzmann 1976, 1:57–58, no. B.32, 57–58. See also the discussion of this iconography in King 2017, 130–37 and Harley McGowan 1970.

31. See Montesano 2013, especially 21–22.

32. Personal communication from Christina Maranci on 13 May 2021. One source is Montesano 2013.

33. Stone 2002, 102; Megas 1928. See also Stone and Timotin 2023.

34. Stone 2021c, 344–57. See also similar material since discovered in Armenian manuscript M10725, fol. 199b, which also says that the relics of Adam and Eve illuminated Noah's ark. The same is to be found in manuscript M4618, fol.53r, bottom.

in Bethlehem at time of the nativity to care for the Christ child.³⁵ Another variant of the tradition would put Adam and Eve's burial in Hebron in the Double Cave, that is, the Cave of Machpelah, where the patriarchs of Israel were buried with their wives.³⁶

There seem to be three individuals whom tradition associated with the burial of the remains of Adam and Eve after the flood: Noah, Shem, and Melchizedek. There are separate traditions that each of the three buried Adam's (and often Eve's) remains. There is also a tradition, also found in Armenian sources, that relates that Shem and Melchizedek (or Zēdēk) together buried him.

This is another variant of the tradition preserved in Cave of Treasures, which has Seth and Melchizedek burying Adam in a cruciform tomb on Golgotha (CT 5.10–12, cf. 23.18 [*MOTP* 1:544, 557]). After his death, Adam was buried, Cave of Treasures relates, in the wondrous cave on the mountain on which Eden was located (CT 6.12 [*MOTP* 1:545]).³⁷ There, Adam's remains were revered by the descendants of Seth and thence his body was taken by Noah and carried through the flood in the middle of the ark (CT 17.20 [*MOTP* 1:553]). On his death-bed, Noah commanded Shem to take Adam's body secretly from the ark. Shem took Melchizedek as an assistant, and they travelled to Golgotha, where the earth opened a

---

35. Dorfmann-Lazarev 2014, especially 289–90, 293–98; Stone 2000b. Eve is sometimes represented in medieval miniature paintings of the nativity as a woman without a halo, washing the infant.

36. See Aptowitzer 1924, 152–54; Spurling and Grypeou 2007, especially 234. Note that according to Testament of Adam, their remains were buried over against the first city founded on earth (Kmosko 1907, 1309–60, 1393, 1396). A similar tradition occurs in the Syriac Testament of Seth, discussed at p. 48 above. Jerome, however, says that Adam was buried in Hebron (*Ep.* 108 [to Eustochium] 11.3; *Qu. hebr. Gen.* 23.2; see Wilkinson 1977, 50). Likewise, the late seventh-century traveler Adomnan, in his travel journal called *The Holy Places* 2.9.5, gives details of Adam's tomb in the Cave of Machpelah (Wilkinson 1977, 105); see also Heither and Reemts 2007, 278–80. This tradition is also discussed by Lipatov-Chicherin 2019b, 155–59. Ginzberg (1909, 5:126) characterizes burial in the Double Cave in Hebron as the prevalent rabbinic view. See also Spurling and Grypeou 2007, 234–36. The Samaritan work TM 5.31 has a tradition of four significant caves, one of which is Machpelah. That is discussed by TM 503. For the burial of the prophet Jonah in a cave see Stone, *Arm Apoc* 6:192.

37. The mountain of Eden is discussed by Brock 1979a, especially 216–17, and I discuss this tradition as it occurs in Questionnaire in part 11, n. 46 in annotation 16 below.

cruciform tomb, and they buried Adam there (CT 6.20–21, 22:4 [*MOTP* 1:545, 556]).

The Death of Adam §40 reads: "And Adam was placed in a grave until Noah received an order from the angel who instructed (him) to open the place and to take the bones of Adam and Eve into the Ark."[38] This text does not contain any information on the postdiluvian fate of the remains of Adam and Eve.[39]

The Armenian text, The Tree of Sabek §§2–3, preserved in a seventeenth-century manuscript, has a somewhat variant tradition combining Shem's deposition of Adam's body on Mount Zion with traditions drawn from the Melchizedek narratives.[40] It adds that Abraham's ram was offered on the same spot and that it symbolized Christ. Melchizedek also made his offering of bread and wine to Abraham there, which event was later interpreted eucharistically. A similar narrative about the location of the eventual burial of Adam and Eve occurs in Repentance of Adam and Eve (Lipscomb 1990, 233). In §97 of that writing, the story runs as follows: Noah took their bodies into the ark, and, after the flood, he gave the bodies to Shem. Shem took them and buried Adam in Hebron in the Double Cave, that is, the Cave of Machpelah, where the patriarchs of Israel were buried with their wives, in his own territory, called Šamatun.[41] He buried Eve in the cave or grotto in Bethlehem. There, Christ was born over Eve's tomb.[42] Shem buried Adam on Golgotha, and there Christ was

---

38. *Arm Apoc* 2:286. See the same tradition in CT 16.19 (*MOTP* 1:552). His remains lighted the ark according to Armenian manuscript M4618, fol. 53r (bottom).

39. According to CT 16.19, 22.6 (*MOTP* 1:552, 556), Seth is instructed to put Adam's body in the center of the earth.

40. See *Arm Apoc* 3:94–100. Cave of Treasures has a similar tradition: see CT 6.20 (*MOTP* 1.552). The connection of Melchizedek with Golgotha and Adam's tomb is clear in the various Melchizedek narratives: see CT 22.6 (*MOTP* 1:556) and Stone 2013, 239; for a discussion see Dorfmann-Lazarev 2020c, 296. A different tradition about burial in a cave may be observed in the Armenian apocrypha Jonah 1 and Jonah 2, in *Arm Apoc* 6:170–92. On Melchizedek and Adam's burial, see Dorfmann-Lazarev 2020c, 297–99.

41. See Lipscomb 1990, 233. More generally, on the foundation of cities, see Gen 4:17, referring to the Cainite line as the founders of cities. The name Šamatun is only known to me so far from this occurrence. Perhaps it means "house of Shem." It does not occur in Hakobyan, Melikʻ-Baxšyan, and Barsełyan 1998.

42. This specific detail is not usually noted. See Repentance §102. The general location of Eve's tomb in the grotto in Bethlehem is well known see also Dorfmann-Lazarev 2020c, especially 298–99.

crucified over his head (Repentance §§99–103).[43] The tradition of Adam's sepulcher on Golgotha and Eve's in Bethlehem is found in other Armenian sources and has been discussed above.[44]

A different form of the tradition about Adam's bones also occurs in a work called The Bones of Adam and Eve §1, which relates that after the flood the Hebrews preserved the protoplasts' bones, and when they moved around, they took them along just as the Israelites later did with the bones of Joseph (Exod 13:19).[45] The bones were brought by Melchizedek to the entrance of the cave in Bethlehem. There, the heifers drawing the wagon sat down and did not move. There, they buried the bones of Eve "by the entrance of the cave where the Holy Virgin bore Christ and the curse of Eve was undone." Adam's bones were then brought to Golgotha, where he was buried and remained until the time of the crucifixion.[46]

Michael, patriarch of the Syrians, lived between 1126–1199 CE and wrote a major chronography, which was twice translated into Armenian soon after its composition. The Armenian translation of Michael's *Chronography* says that Maniton, the apocryphal fourth son of Noah, asked for some of Adam's bones from Noah after the flood. Noah gave him Adam's knee bones.[47] This confirms the tradition that Noah carried Adam's remains in the ark during the flood to which I referred above.[48] The connection between Noah and Adam's remains, however, is much older than the thirteenth-century *Chronography* of Michael the Syrian. Lipatov-Chicherin (2019a, 36) observes that in the *Commentary on the Prophet Isaiah* (5.141) by Basil of Caesarea (330–379 CE), Noah is introduced as the

---

43. This, of course, is parallel to Christ's birth above Eve's tomb.

44. See further also Zak'aria Catholicos (ninth century), "Homily on the Life-giving Passion," in MH 9:195, §185. There, Zak'aria says that, after the flood and under the influence of the Holy Spirit, Noah buried Adam on Golgotha and Eve in Bethlehem. Another source is in the document The Bones of Adam and Eve, discussed immediately below; see Stone 2000b. It is undated, but the manuscript containing it was copied in 1618 CE.

45. The work is discussed in Stone 2000b.

46. Bones of Adam and Eve §1. For a comparison of this work with the Pseudo-Epiphanian *Homilies*, see Dorfmann-Lazarev 2020b, 271–72, 292.

47. See *Arm Apoc* 2:116. The second Armenian translation, although, in fact, a different recension of Michael's *Chronography*, does not differ at this point: see *Arm Apoc* 2:117. The tradition about Maniton, Noah's fourth son, is discussed below in annotation 21 to part 13.

48. See pp. 52–53.

7. Where Did He Create Adam?

one who preserved the memory of Adam's tomb being on Golgotha. The figure of Maniton and the connection between the protoplasts' remains and Noah are discussed in detail in annotation 6.

I have pointed out that the fifth-century Armenian author Ełišē's tradition that Adam was in the garden for forty days is apparently a misunderstanding of the teaching of the passage on ritual impurity of the newly created beings discussed at the beginning of the present annotation (see Stone 2013, 36, 74). Our text, Questionnaire, agrees with the view of Grigoris Aršaruni (seventh–eighth century) that Adam was created on the sixth day and entered the garden on the fortieth day, which is a parallel outgrowth of the tradition already to be found in Jubilees (second century BCE).[49] Questionnaire, however, does not call upon the tradition of forty days, though that does occur in other Armenian apocrypha, such as Adam Story 2 §3 (*Arm Apoc* 2:111).

---

49. This means the fortieth day of his life and not the fortieth day since the beginning of creation, for Grigoris Aršaruni says he was in the garden for the same number of days as his age when he first entered it (Stone 2013, 312). For further Armenian sources for Adam's creation on the sixth day, see Stone 2013, 87. This is, of course, the biblical view, see Gen 1:24–2:1.

8
On Which Day Did Sadayēl Fall from the Garden?

The subject of this very brief part is the angel Satan or Satanel, who is also familiar in some Armenian texts designated with the by-form Sadayēl, his fall from the garden, and his transformation into an envious, evil, supernatural power on earth.[1] Thus, it continues the process of clarification of the details of the events preceding creation and progressing down to Adam's entering the garden of Eden. In fact, some forms of this tradition viewed the fall of the angel Sadayēl as having transpired before the creation of Adam.[2] I have discussed elsewhere the hubris and fall of Helel ben Shaḥar (Day Star son of Dawn) in Isa 14:12–13, which was exegeted as also referring to the fall of Satan.[3] The story is told in brief compass in History of the Discourse §§1–2.[4]

---

1. The fall of Satan, also called Satanael or Sadayēl, is discussed in further detail in Stone 2021d. The tradition is also well known in the West already from early times and is traced by Jeffrey Russell 1981; a striking retelling of it is incorporated in the tenth-century Old Irish work, *Saltair na Rann* 4 (see Greene and Kelley 1976, 10–13). This part is included in the extract from M682, fols. 7a–7b that was published in *Arm Apoc* 4:83–91. This is the last section printed there, and I gave it the title, Question about Sadayēl. Here I have changed its title and brought it into accordance with the titles of the other parts, which are taken directly from the manuscript. For the name Sadayēl, see annotation 7 below. Satan is also known by the name Satanayel, constructed upon the Armenian սատանայ (*satana*), itself going back to Syriac, with the theophoric element "el" added (see *Arm Apoc* 4:104). This element is common in angelic names, such as Micha-el, Rapha-el, etc.

2. See Rose 1958, 22–23 on such primordial conflicts. Compare also the Ancient of Days and the One Like a Human in Dan 7 (see Cross 1973, 17), which draws on Canaanite patterns of strife between an old god and a young god, which may lie in the background of the idea of Satan's rebellion against God. The Byzantine Greek Palaea Historica sets the rebellion of Satan on day 4 (see PH 3.6 [*MOTP* 1:600]). See further in n. 3, immediately below.

3. See Stone 2021d, 478–88. The name Helel appears in the Hebrew Bible only

Down to this point, Questionnaire may thus be said to constitute an erotapocritic text dealing with angels and Adam and Eve. The question about Sadayēl fits seamlessly into this genre and context.

Text

M682/ fol. 7v.6–7

8.1/ Հարց, թէ՝ Սադայէլ ո՞ր օր անկաւ ի դրախտէն:
Պատասխանի. Ասեն թէ ի Ե.(5)շաբթի օրն անկաւ, վասն որոյ ուրբաթի մարդն ստեղծաւ, զի լցցէ զտեղի նորա, յաղագս որոյ մախացաւ:

Translation

8.1/ Question: On which day did Sadayēl[5] fall from the garden? Answer: They say that he fell on Thursday, because of which man was created on Friday, so that he might fill his place.[6] On account of this he was envious of humans.[7]

---

at this point; concerning it, one may profitably consult Watson 1995. In Canaanite mythology, Šaḥar "dawn" was a deity, a son of 'El, the high god: see see Cross 1973, 22. There is a substantial body of exegesis that arose around the identification of Helel, son of Dawn with Satan. Moreover, in its Latin form, Lucifer, this name had a ramified history in Western European thought. I discussed it as it occurs in Armenian sources in Stone 2021d, 478–88 and above in n. 1 to this section. See also PH 3.1–9 (*MOTP* 1:600). Satan's revolt and his name Satane/il, and the connection of these with Isa 14:12–13 in some Slavonic sources are discussed by Gaylord 1982. See on the possible Christian origin of this motif as found in the Latin LAE 15.3; see Minov 2015, particularly 243.

4. *Arm Apoc* 4:104.

5. In his study of names of the Enemy—that word being itself another name for the Devil—Turdeanu (1981, 15–74) attempts to separate different streams of ideas and different periods by analyzing the use of the various Satanic names. His results are not uniformly convincing.

6. For the idea that humans fill the place of the fallen angels, see *Arm Apoc* 4:91. The particular text cited there may have been of Catholic origin but, nonetheless, this concept is to be found in Armenian sources; see pp. 64–65. See also Orlov 2011, especially 14–15.

7. See Stone 2013, 358. There this is said to be the view of Zak'aria Kat'ołikos (ninth century). In the Life of Adam and Eve referred to below, a different but equally

8. On Which Day Did Sadayēl Fall from the Garden?

Annotation 7. The Name Sadayēl

The name of the fallen angel is said to be Sadayēl (and variants), and an alternative spelling found in manuscripts—Sadaēl.[8] I have proposed that Sadayēl is formed from "Satan" or, perhaps better, from Armenian *satana* > satanael > sat/dayel. This is a name for Satan, whom some traditions also name Satanael. After the word *satan* changed from denoting a particular sort of demon and became the personal name of the Devil, due to the idea that Satan was a fallen angel, in some circles, the name was refashioned on the pattern of the many theophoric names of angels that are structured with the addition of the divine formative -el, which godly element Satan was then said to have lost on the occasion of his fall.[9] The addition of the theophoric ending -el to Satan's name takes place in other language traditions as well. For example, the name Satanael is to be found in Slavonic 3 Bar. 4.8 at a point at which the Greek of the same work has Sammael.[10] The form Sadayēl (Sadaēl) is not biblical,[11] yet it occurs regularly in the

---

pointed reason is offered for Satan's particular animus against humans; see also Minov (2015, 230, 235–37). The apocryphal Life of Adam and Eve was translated twice into Armenian, once from a manuscript close to the extant Greek version called Apocalypse of Moses and once from a quite different Greek recension, allied with the ancestor of the Georgian Life of Adam and Eve. The first translation is known as Գիրք Ադամայ (Book of Adam), and the second is called Ապաշխարութիւն Ադամայ (Penitence of Adam). Concerning these two recensions, see Stone 1992, 12–13, 36–37. Bibliography of the editions and translations is provided there. The Georgian translation is also discussed in that book, on pp. 37–39.

8. On the story of the fall of Satan (Sadayel), see also nn. 1 and 3 above.

9. See Theodore H. Gaster 1962b. On this change in the denomination of "satan," see p. 225 in particular. See Badalanova-Geller 2021c, 18–19. Gaylord 1982, 303–9 discusses this loss of "el." The name is also considered by Turdeanu 1981, 17–21, 23–24.

10. See Kulik 2010, 187 and commentary on p. 190–91. He adduces several other occurrences of this name in Eastern Christian sources. See also Gaylord 1982 and see further on Satan and Sammael, Rebiger 2007, 639. Moreover, the attribution of multiple names to Satan in the Ethiopic tradition is discussed by Witakowski 2019, particularly 458–62. Witakowsky dates this to the mid-sixteenth to mid-seventieth centuries (462).

11. Contrast, in addition to Satan, the names Beliar and Beelzebub which are biblical (2 Cor 6:15; Matt 10:25; 12:24, 27). See Grigor Narekacʻi, *Book of Lamentation* 4.2.35 and 64.4.3 (tenth century). Grigor was one of the first Armenian authors noted to use the devilish name Beliar (see *NBHL*, s.v.). Both names may well occur in earlier Armenian texts that have not been plumbed for this usage, and the uses cited here are the first to be found under the respective entries in *NBHL* and in the index in Stone

apocryphal Armenian Adam writings. There it is nearly always connected with the myth of the primordial angelic revolt against God.[12]

In Creation and Transgression of Adam, Satan is described as "adorned gloriously, and ... higher than all the angels and all the divisions of angels" (Lipscomb 1990, 108, 118). In this work, he stands at the peak of the angelic hierarchy, which of course makes his fall into darkness with his "division"[13] the more striking.

Yovhannēs Erznkacʻi Pluz, an Armenian poet of the thirteenth century, describes the fall of Satan (Sadayēl, Sadaēl) as follows:

> From the heavenly orders,
>   Sadaēl had turned his face;
> From heaven,
>   he descended into the abyss,
> And from light,
>   he lived in darkness.[14]

The figure of Sadayēl regularly features in the apocryphal Armenian Adam books in connection with the myth of the primordial angelic revolt against God. For example, manuscript Y of History of the Creation and Transgression of Adam and Eve §2 reads, "now the wicked Sadaēl and Beliar were heads of the divisions of Satan" (Lipscomb 1990, 118). This section of Creation and Transgression mentions three names, all of which are used in various sources for the Devil, namely, Sadaēl, Beliar, and Satan. Creation and Transgression accounts for the existence of these three different devilish names by turning them into three different figures, two of whom, Sadaēl and Beliar, are subject to the third, superior figure, Satan. Manuscript D's text of the same passage mentions Beliar alone, and from §3 on, both manuscripts only use the name Satan.

2013. "Beliar" occurs in the Armenian translation of the Testaments of the Twelve Patriarchs, which is probably early; see Stone and Hillel 2012. The name recurs in the tenth-century epitome of that work; see Stone 1986–1987. The use of these various names calls for further investigation.

12. Turdeanu (1981, 15–74) attempts to distinguish separate streams of ideas and various periods, by analyzing the use of the different names. See n. 5 above.

13. The group or host of angels, of which Satan was the chief.

14. This work is translated in Stone 2013, no. 10. A similar description by Jacob of Edessa is quoted by Greatrex 2009, 39. Note also PH 3.7 (*MOTP* 1:600).

8. On Which Day Did Sadayēl Fall from the Garden? 61

Annotation 8. Why Did Satan Fall?

Satan's fall is already known to the New Testament (Luke 10:18, Rev 12:2–4), and certain passages in the Hebrew Bible also were widely interpreted in light of this incident, particularly Isa 14:12–14, which passage I have already discussed in the introductory remarks to this part. Among other later sources, it is also found in 3 Cor 2.16–17, which was included in the Armenian Bible and was cited in Agathangelos §26 (fifth century), which is one of the oldest writings in Armenian.[15] Further Armenian attestations to Satan's fall are discussed in the context of annotations 8 and 9 here.

The angelic fall is intimately related to the name Sadayēl in an Armenian amulet scroll (*hmayil*), apparently one of the oldest such, Matenadaran no. 115, dated 1428 CE (Loeff 2002, 35–36). In it, Sat/dayēl is commander of the fallen angels and builder of hell.[16] In this document, the demons describe themselves as angels who fell due to their unwillingness to give glory to God.[17] They were responsible for Adam's expulsion from the garden. This angelic refusal and rebellion, of course, is a well-known theme in the Armenian tradition, and this incident is recounted much earlier in the widely diffused Adam apocryphon, Life of Adam and Eve (12.1–15.1).[18] The amulet, therefore, knows the story of the prideful rebellion and the fall of Satan–Sadayēl before creation[19] and the subsequent construction of hell. In time, moreover, some of these actions

---

15. On this epistle, included in the Armenian Bible, see Hovhanissian 2000. See also Stepʻanos Siwnecʻi no. 2 in Stone 2013, 320; Zakʻaria Catholicos no. 5 in Stone 2013, 358–59.

16. The idea of hell as a sort of prison in which the human dead are incarcerated until Christ's descensus ad infernos is common in medieval Armenian thought and is, in one of its aspects, encapsulated in the term ազատել ("to free, set free") used of delivering souls from their captivity in the prison of hell. See, for example, Questions of Ezra A7 and B6, and numerous other texts.

17. See Aṙakʻel of Siwnikʻ, *Adamgirkʻ* 1.21.8 (Stone 2007a, 206).

18. Further discussion of the fall of Satan and the allied traditions may be found in Minov 2015.

19. See also Gos. Barth. 4.53–55. In a gnostic myth, referred to in Irenaeus, *Haer.* 1.30.6 (*ANF*), we read, "On this account, Ialdabaoth, becoming uplifted in spirit, boasted himself over all those things that were below him, and exclaimed, I am father, and *god*, and above me there is no one." See further on the text of Irenaeus and a discussion in Rudolph 1957.

are transferred from Sadayēl/Satan to the demons in general, as happens in the said amulet.

Proverbs 18:12 says: "Before its breaking, the heart of man is haughty; and before thought it is destroyed." Well before the composition of the amulet just cited, the learned Armenian scholar Hamam Arewelcʻi (825?–890? CE) says the following in his commentary to Prov 18:12:

> Before the breaking, the heart of Satan became haughty, who by rebelling, wanted to become more elevated than his fellows. And, therefore, he was abased to this great rupture before mighty God. And … he was cast down and abased before everyone. He who was a brilliant light bringer/Lucifer, on account of his haughtiness was named and became, darkness.[20]

The passage quoted plays upon the meaning of the name and thus speaks of "light-bringer" (Lucifer, Armenian լուսաբեր) becoming "darkness." Here, pride is the chief motive noted.

This is not surprising, since Lucifer's hubristic rebellion against God and his fall had already been familiar to Armenian authors from the beginning of Armenian literacy in the fifth century.[21] Lucifer was identified as Satan as far back as 1 En. 54.5–6 and Latin LAE 15.3[22] as well as in the *Teaching of St. Gregory*. My previous analysis of the interpretation of Isa 14:12–16 renders the presentation of a detailed discussion otiose here, so I forebear to weary the reader with it.[23] However, observe that, according to the text here, the great angel Satan rebelled against God's command because of his jealousy of Adam. That idea occurs already in the Armenian Penitence of Adam 12–16, where it serves as Satan's explanation of his enmity toward Adam and Eve.[24]

---

20. Thomson 2005, 133, 183. The biblical passage dealing with Lucifer is, as I have said, Isa 14:11–14. The translations given here, however, are my own. See the comments on this matter by Greatrex 2009, 39. Compare also Frikʻs *Poem on Adam*, l. 49 in Tirayr 1952, 532.

21. Stone 2013, 193–99, 229 quoting Agathangelos, *Teaching of St. Gregory* §278.

22. On the Lucifer figure in the West, see Jeffrey Russell 1984. Similar Muslim sources relating to Iblis are discussed by Kuehn 2019, especially 176–79.

23. Compare also Ezek 28:2. See my most recent consideration of these issues in Stone 2021d, 486–96. Isa 14:12–14 is analyzed in that paper as well as in the present part.

24. The Armenian translation of the Life of Adam and Eve, which is called Penitence of Adam, is quite old, though we cannot fix its date with precision: see above n.

8. On Which Day Did Sadayēl Fall from the Garden?   63

ANNOTATION 9. SATAN'S ENVY OF AND ENMITY TOWARD HUMANS

In Life of Adam and Eve, Satan's enmity toward humans is attributed to his rebellious refusal to obey a divine command to worship Adam, who, as is specified in Gen 1:26, was created in God's image.[25] Because of this refusal, Satan and his band of angels were expelled from heaven (LAE 13–16). The connection between Satan and envy, which is made in our text here, is rather old, and it already occurs in Wis 2:23–24, which reads: "for God created man for incorruption and made him in the image of his own eternity, but through the devil's envy death entered the world, and those who belong to his party experience it." Pseudo-Solomon's well-known phrase "but through the devil's envy" means, at the very least, that the διάβολος was jealous of humans because they were made "in the image of God's eternity." Some story such as that in Life of Adam and Eve must have been known, therefore, in the last century BCE or early first century CE to the author of Wis 2:23–24, otherwise his statement is inexplicable.[26] Wisdom of Solomon is included among the wisdom books in the Armenian Old Testament, as is the case in the Greek and Syriac Bibles as well.

In Agathangelos's *Teaching of St. Gregory* §278, the oldest theological treatise in Armenian, Satan is described as jealous of the "good things"[27] that God bestowed on Adam and of Adam's obedience to God's com-

---

7 to the translation of the present part. See also PH 4.2 (*MOTP* 1:601) on Satan's rebelliousness and for further discussion of Satan's envy of humans in Stone 2013, 26–28.

25. The angels were commanded to worship Adam upon his creation: see LAE (Lat., Arm., Georg.) 14.1; CT 2.25 (*MOTP* 1:542). According to TM 6.19 (Tal 2019, 535) the angels assembled to honor Adam, apparently on his creation. Toepel (2012, 322–24) discusses angelic worship of Adam, and this theme can be documented further. See also Minov 2015, and Schäfer 1986, 71.

26. See Winston 1979, 20–25. In Stone 2013, 64–66, for example, three reasons for Satan's envy, occurring in fifth- and sixth-century Armenian sources, are discussed: first, Satan's envy of Adam's priority of rank; second, his envy of the good things Adam was destined to receive; and third, his envy of the goods that Adam had already received. Satan's grudge against Adam is also mentioned in *Adamgirkʿ* 2.1.54 (Stone 2007a, 274). On Satan's jealousy of Adam in medieval Jewish sources, see Ginzberg 1909, 84–85 nn. 34–35. This motif is hardly attested in classical rabbinic literature. For Muslim sources reflecting this idea, see Kuehn 2019, 174.

27. Concerning the term *goods* or *good things* that in Armenian texts often denotes eschatological reward, but here refers to protological benefits, see Stone 1990b, xx and 159. The pattern of *Urzeit-Endzeit* is clearly at work in the present context.

mand. Therefore, he became envious and caused Adam to fall (Thomson 2001, 72–73).[28] Among other Armenian sources, Yovhannēs Mandakuni (fifth century) says that "the fall of Satan was because of pride" (Stone 2013, 25).[29] In the Armenian version of the Life of Adam and Eve that is called Penitence of Adam, Satan responds pridefully to Michael's call to bow down to Adam, the image of God: "Go away, Michael! I shall not bow [down] to him who is posterior to me, for I am former. Why is it proper [for me] to bow down to him?" (14.3).[30] Questionnaire, however, discloses no cause for Satan's enmity, and the author's chief interest is focused on showing that God did not create evil but gave both humans and angels, including Satan, free-will, so that disobedience to the divine command was possible but not necessary.

Another aspect of Satan's enmity is also presented in Questionnaire. The work argues that Sadayēl, as Questionnaire calls Satan,[31] had to have fallen on the fifth day, that is, Thursday, because he was replaced in the heavenly array by Adam, who was created on the sixth day (§8.1). The idea that Adam or humans replaced Satan or his cohort of angels in their heavenly dwelling is found in other Armenian texts. Yačaxapatum Čaṙk' (sixth century) entertains this concept, as does Zak'aria Kat'ołikos

---

28. As for the benefits given him by God, see the Armenian lists of blessings or benefits that Adam lost when he sinned, which are presented in the present volume, on pp. 82–87. Satan's own fall is not mentioned here, but it is implied. A similar view is forwarded by Eznik §§32–33 and see also the remarks of Stone 2013, 253; similar is CT 3.1 (MOTP 1:542) and see further in n. 30 below. Indeed, the two chief reasons offered for Satan's refusal to bow down to Adam are envy, as here, and pride, as in Life of Adam and Eve. Chronologically, in the present section Questionnaire puts Satan's fall directly preceding Adam's creation on the sixth day. Cave of Treasures combines pride with envy and puts Satan's fall after the creation of Adam

29. See also the pseudo-Epiphanian *Homilies* cited by Dorfmann-Lazarev 2020c, 264–95, 315–16.

30. For the fifth-century evidence about Satan's envy, see Stone 2013, 26–28. A summary statement of the various causes that Armenian sources attribute to Satan's envy is set forth in Stone 2013, 203–4 and in n. 26 above. Eznik (fifth century) §§51–52 discusses Satan, whom the author identifies explicitly as the serpent, and his deception of Adam. Free will is attributed to humans and angels which makes their disobedience possible. This was of considerable interest to our author, see also p. xxx above and p. 66 below. Here, as is also the case in *Teaching of St. Gregory*, Satan's actual fall is not mentioned; cf. n. 28 above. In Pseudo-Epiphanius, *Homilies* the angels are said to bow down to Adam; see Dorfmann-Lazarev 2020a, 315.

31. See annotation 7 above on the name Sadayēl.

(ninth century) when he says, "to obey the command of the Creator, and go forth, fill the encampment of the fallen angels" (Stone 2013, 358–59).[32] Zak'aria is of the view that the garden of Eden was originally Satan's camp and was taken over by humans. Thus, humans not only replaced Satan in his heavenly dwelling, but when Satan had fallen, Adam was to take his place in Eden. This also seems to be Questionnaire's opinion, as it states that Sadayēl fell from the garden rather than from heaven.

According to the Syriac Cave of Treasures, the Sethites, when they ascended the mountain (that is, of paradise), filled the place of the rank of the Demon (Satanel) and his host, who had fallen (CT 7.4 [*MOTP* 1:545]). This is an extension of the idea of replacement just discussed. Such traditions provided a solid basis for Satan's envy.[33]

This tradition about Satan's envy and fall functions in significant ways in religious thought.[34] Greatrex (2009, 39), citing Gregory Nazianzus (329–390 CE) and Jacob of Edessa (640–708 CE), remarks that Satan fell from highest to lowest and he was transformed from light to dark.[35] This is a response, she concludes, to the question of the origin of evil in a God-created world.[36] Evil is caused by Satan, a fallen great angel, usually described as falling together with his heavenly host who followed him and became his demonic army. Satan, with whom the Edenic serpent was identified or closely connected, gave evil its entrée into this world by possessing the serpent and through it is tempting Eve and Adam so that they sinned.[37]

---

32. See Yačaxapatum Čaṙk' 16 and 23 and further, Terian 2020, 238 for other references. (Dr. Terian graciously communicated this information and a copy of his fine article.) For the idea that humans fill the place of the fallen angels, see Stone 2013, 46–47, and see also *Arm Apoc* 4:72–75 where it is found in the writing called Question about Archangels, which discusses the nature of the angelic rebellion. It also occurs in Creation and Transgression §5; see Lipscomb 1990, 109, 199.

33. The Sethites are discussed in part 11 below. See n. 46 to annotation 16 concerning the mountain of paradise.

34. Ginzberg (1909, 5:84–85) argues that some such legend of angelic fall must have been current early in various rabbinic sources and later displaced. See also CT 4.4 (*MOTP* 1:543) concerning Satan's envy.

35. The use of dark and light as indicators of good and evil is very ancient and widespread. The darkening of bright faces is a mode of expression applied to sinners, and its reverse, to the successful penitent: see Stone 1990a, 244–45 and 259 and see further Stone 2013, 152–53, as well as the Samaritan text TM 4.96–97.

36. So, Jacob of Edessa, as presented by Greatrex 2009, 38. Note the use of Isa 14:13 to this end. See the discussion above on pp. 62–63.

37. On the relation of Satan and the serpent, and the various ways it was expressed,

In earliest Armenian written texts, Satan and the serpent are sometimes identified, especially in the context of the garden (see Eznik §35; Stone 2013, 256). The serpent's possession by Satan is described in CT 4.5–11, while CT 5.27 and 21.11 say that Cain was possessed by Satan when he killed Abel and another instance of demonic possession is related in CT 11.2.³⁸ According to David bar Pawlos, a West Syrian writer (eighth or ninth century) Satan was identified as a dragon.³⁹

This formulation of the relationship of Satan with the serpent resolves the theological conundrum of the origin of evil in terms of the myth of the primordial fall of Satan and his host. Questionnaire here asserts two allied ideas: first, that both angels and humans have free will (անձնիշխանութիւն, "autonomy"), and in exercising that autonomy, they sometimes make the wrong choice. Second, this myth is an implicit denial that God created evil or, alternatively, a denial that evil was preexistent.⁴⁰

---

see Stone 2013, 177–210. Schäfer (1986, 77–78) gives an overview of rabbinic views of this matter. For a similar Muslim view, see Kuehn 2019, 186. Demonic possession, specifically by Satan, is mentioned in Luke 22:3. The idea was certainly current, but to present it, even briefly, would take us too far from our topic.

38. See *MOTP* 1:543, 544, 555, and 548. So also, in the Ethiopic work called *Qälamenṭos*; see Witakowski 2017, 531 and compare 536. Witztum (2011, 89–92) discusses the relationship between Satan and the serpent in the Qur'an.

39. See Sergey Minov 2020, 74–75. On a dragon-serpent as a form of Satan, see Stone and Timotin 2023, 22–34; and Stone 2023. See Orlov 2023 for the history of this complex of ideas. Witakowski (2017, 525–35) discusses the Cain and Abel story in Ethiopian texts. In the Vienna Protology, a late Ethiopic retelling of the *Urgeschichte*, dated to sometime between the mid-sixteenth to the mid-seventeenth centuries (see Witakowski 2019, 462), Satan accosts Cain, puts the idea of killing Abel into his mind, and shows him how to kill Abel with a stone (526). Other Ethiopian variants of this incident may be found on p. 530 of Witakowsky (2017). By implication, these stories too, address the question of the origin of evil.

40. This is discussed, in different context, by Greatrex 2009, 37–38. See above p. 63 and further references there. Schäfer's (1986, 80–81) presentation of the rabbis' view indicates that, for them, evil is part of creation, but there he also notes that to present the ideas in these terms in fact involves an over-simplification and that more complex ideas are present. [Indeed, there are rabbinic sources that emphatically deny that God created (moral) evil and stress that it is human-made: Sifra Beḥukotai 4:1 [111c]; Pesiqta of Ten Commandments 4 (Pesiq. Rab. 24, fol. 125b; Efrati 2019, 2:60–61); Tana deBei Eliyahu Zuta 3: compare a similar formulation in 1 En. 98.4. For a related idea in Philo, see *Opif.* 75; *Conf.* 178–179; *Fug.* 70; and the discussion in Runia 1986, 243–47.–S.E.]

8. On Which Day Did Sadayēl Fall from the Garden?

The question of whether God created evil considerably exercised ancient theologians and exegetes and, of course, had polemical as well as theological implications. Aṙakʻel Siwnecʻi's epic poem *Adamgirkʻ*,[41] for example, struggles to explain the origin of Satan or of evil, which, this theologically active poet asserts, was not created by God. Notably, Aṙakʻel asks the question in terms of philosophical theology rather than those of mythology.

---

41. Version 1.8 in Stone 2007a, 127–36.

9
Adam and Eve in the Garden

This section, following §8 about the fall of the angels, continues with questions concerning Adam and Eve and relates the primordial history down to the expulsion from Eden. Questionnaire raises several extremely interesting issues in this section. Each of these queries concerns a detail of events not mentioned explicitly in Genesis, an approach that is typical of the parabiblical works and traditions that constitute the Armenian Embroidered Bible.

Text

M682, fols. 7b.7–7c.19

9.0/ Հարց. թէ՝ Քանի̊ օր կացին ի դրախտին։

9.1/ Պատասխանի. Ոմանք Ռ. (1,000) ամ ասացին, եւ ոմանք՝ Խ(40) օր. բայց ճշմարտութեան հետեւել[1] ոչ հաւանեցան, զի մախացող թշնամին ոչ կարէր համբերել այնքան ժամանակ։

9.2/ Իսկ թէ ի նոյն օրն ասեն, զայն եւս չէ ընդունելի, զի ասի թէ ի Դ.(4)շաբաթի խոսեցաւ օձն ընդ Եւայի եւ յուրբաթի կերան զպտուղն։ Ահա յայտ է թէ Ը. (8) օր կացին. յուրբաթի մտին եւ ուրբաթի ելին։

9.3/ Հարց. թէ՝ Մովսէս ընդէր զտնկել դրախտին յետ ստեղծմանն Ադամայ յիշէ։

Պատասխանի. Զի նախ Ադամ ստեղծ, եւ առաջի նորա զդրախտն. եւ այլ կենդանիս եւս ստեղծ, զի տեսցէ աչօք եւ մի կարծեցէ զաշխարհս

---

1. The scribe seems to have first written հետեւեցան, of which word the ending -ցան is an erroneous dittography of the ending of the next word, and then to have corrected it to հետեւեալ, which is correct, but he did not erase the erroneous -ան.

ինքնեդ եւ ոչ արարած։ Եւ այսու յայտ է թէ Ադամ յառաջ ստեղծ քան զդրախտն:

9.4/ Եւ էր դրախտն ամենայի ծառով անթառամ ծաղկօք, անձրելի պտղովք, անթափ տերեւօք, անկարօտ եւ լի ամենայն բարութեամբ:

9.5/ Հարց, թէ՝ Յետ քանի՞ ամաց մերձաւորութիւն եղեւ:

Պատասխանի. Թէպէտ հասակաւ Լ. (30) ամեայ էր, այլ բնութեամբ որպէս մանուկ էր. յետ Լ. (30) ամի ապա եղեւ ազդումն ցանկութեան եւ մերձաւորութեան:

9.6/ Հարց, թէ՝ ո՞րք են ԲԺ.(12)ան.(երկոտասան) փարք Ադամայ զարդարեալ ի դրախտին:

Պատասխանի. Նախ՝ զի լուսեղէն զգեստիւ զարդարեալ, Բ, (2)՝ անմահ, Գ, (3)՝ անկարօտ ամենայնի, Դ, (4)՝ անմռաց, Ե, (5)՝ թափանցած, Զ, (6)՝ անխոնչ, Է, (7)՝ սրբնչաց, Ը, (8)՝ անտրտում, Թ, (9)՝ մարգարէ, Ժ, (10)՝ քահանայ, ԺԱ, (11)՝ թագաւոր, ԺԲ, (12)՝ անծերանալի:

Translation

9.0/ Question: How many days did they stay in the garden?

9.1/ Answer: Some said one thousand years,[2] and some, forty days, but to tell[3] the truth, they were not persuasive,[4] for the envious Enemy could not be patient[5] for so long.

9.2/ But, if they say, "on the same day,"[6] that also is not acceptable, for it is said that the serpent spoke with Eve on Wednesday, and they ate the fruit on a Friday. Behold, it is clear that they remained in the garden for eight days. They entered on a Friday and went out on a Friday."[7]

---

2. So Ełišē, *Commentary on Genesis* cited in Stone 2013, 35.

3. Literally: following.

4. That is, those who proposed the periods of a thousand years and of forty days were not persuasive.

5. That is, wait. The sense is that the Enemy could not have waited for so long, and so the sin must have followed shortly after the entry into the garden. "Enemy" is another name for Satan. On Satan's envy, see annotation 10. I have not seen a similar reference to Satan's impatience in other sources.

6. They were expelled on the same day on which they entered the garden. So Pseudo-Basil (sixth century; see Stone 2013, 294 and 300, no. 2) and Yovhannēs Ojnec'i (eighth century: Stone 2013, 335–38, nos. 7–9) and CT 5.1 (*MOTP* 1:543).

7. The argument appears to be that, if the serpent spoke with Eve in the garden, this must have been on the first Friday after their creation, which itself was on Friday (see Gen 1:26, 31), and so they ate the fruit on the second Friday. While Genesis does

9. Adam and Eve in the Garden

9.3/ Question: Why does Moses mention the planting of the garden after the creation of Adam?

Answer: For he created Adam first, and (he created) the garden in front of him.[8] And he also created the other living beings[9] so that he (Adam) might see (them) with his eyes, and so that he should not think that the world was self-existent and not created.[10] And from this it is evident that he created Adam before the garden.[11]

9.4/ And the garden was completely full of trees with unfading flowers, nondropping fruit,[12] leaves fresh, plentiful and full of all goodness.[13]

---

put their creation on the first Friday, it says nothing explicitly about the day upon which they sinned. In Stone 2013, 312, 394, I discuss, among others, the views of Grigoris Aršaruni (seventh–eighth centuries) and of Tiranun *vardapet* (tenth century). Grigoris says that Adam was expelled on the same day on which he was created. Tiranun states that it all happened between the first and the second Fridays, thus agreeing with our text here. Both these views are mentioned by Questionnaire. However, the writer of Questionnaire does not make explicit why he opined that it was on a Friday that the serpent spoke to Eve and on a Friday that they sinned. Perhaps he inferred this from the typological matching of the sin in the garden and Adam and Eve's expulsion with the crucifixion of Christ who died on a Friday (Good Friday). Thus, Christ's expiatory death took place on the same day of the week upon which Adam sinned. This type of patterning is discussed in Stone 2013, 76–77, 110–11. Friday, of course, became a special day in Christian tradition because it was the day of the Crucifixion. A parade example of this type of patterning is the Slavonic work The Twelve Fridays, (see Badalanova Geller 2017a, 183–279; the text and translation of this Slavonic work are on pp. 246–54). There, not only are events listed that took place on Fridays, but also the calendar dates of those Fridays. In Questionnaire, too, several special and ominous Fridays are mentioned; humans were created on a Friday (6.6); Adam and Eve ate the fruit on a Friday (9.2); the serpent deceived Eve on Friday (9.2).

8. In front of, that is, before his eyes. The idea that the world was made of preexistent matter is one that Armenian thinkers energetically combatted, see pp. xxx–xxxi and 78–79. That is the point made by stressing that the creation of the garden was "before Adam's eyes."

9. That is, after Adam's creation. That, of course, runs against the sequence of the creative events according to Gen 1.

10. See Ełišē, §10 cited in Stone 2013, 23. The present passage seems to draw upon this section of Ełišē, *Commentary on Genesis*. See also Vardan Arewelc'i (1200?–1271) *Commentary on Genesis*, M1267, fol. 5v (viewed in manuscript).

11. See n. 8 above, where this subject is discussed.

12. These attributes of the garden are often encountered in Armenian parabiblica and not just there. On the green fructifers in the garden and in the temple, see Mazor 2012, 9–16. According to Repentance of Adam and Eve §87, there was an oil-producing tree in the garden that Eve and Seth sought when Adam fell mortally ill. Rabbi L.

9.5/ Question: After how many years did intercourse take place?

Answer: Although in stature (age) he was thirty years old (when he was created), in nature he was like a child. After thirty years, then the instinct of desire and intercourse came into being.[14]

9.6/ Question: Which are the twelve glories of Adam with which he was adorned in the garden?[15]

Answer: First, that (he was) ornamented in a luminous garment.[16]

Rabinowitz remarked to me several decades ago, that this implies that the tree of life was an olive tree (see also Stone 1972). Though this is *prima facie* obvious, perhaps one should remember that other plant oils were current, of which a prominent example is cedar oil. On that, see Stone 2015. The oil of Eden is mentioned in the context of the story of Adam's illness and the quest of Seth and Eve for Edenic fruit is found already in the Greek LAE 9.1–13.5) and in the Latin version. For the second Armenian version, The Penitence of Adam, see Stone 1981b and see the Georgian and Slavonic versions 35.1–42.4. The same story is found, with variants, in the Armenian parabiblical texts, Adam Fragments 1 and 2 and in The Words of Adam to Seth (see *Arm Apoc* 1:2–13; Stone 2000a). The study by Quinn (1962) deals with the quest story in the broader context of medieval Christian traditions. Similar in scope is Baert 2005, 310–33. This story is focused on the idea that at the end of days the righteous will be anointed with the oil of the tree of life; with these ideas compare the heavenly oil mentioned in 2 En. 22.8–9, as well as "the oil of the tree (wood) of life" in 3 Ezra (2 Esdras) 2.12.

13. Such stereotypical descriptions of paradise are often encountered in Armenian sources. See annotation 10 below.

14. Thirty years of age was considered the age of physical acme; see the discussion of many sources in Stone 2013, 91 and 44–45 n. 35. The tradition in Adam and His Grandsons §1 also says that thirty years passed before Adam and Eve had intercourse (see *Arm Apoc* 2:183). The view that Questionnaire forwards here is shared by Vardan Arewelc'i (thirteenth century) (see Stone 2013, 102). Intriguingly, in the substantial body of sources assembled in Stone 2013, though a period of thirty years is posited for Adam and Eve's first intercourse, the issues raised in our text which are the protoplasts' maturity and inception of sexual activity, are not discussed. Moreover, Questionnaire here does not make explicit where this happened, in the garden or outside the garden after the expulsion. On ancient Jewish and Christian views as to where Adam and Eve's first sexual intercourse took place, see the insightful analysis by Anderson 1989. The role of this concept in early Christian thinkers is discussed by Toepel 2012, 315. See further CT 5.18 (*MOTP* 1:544).

15. This is one of several lists of twelve boons that Adam had in the garden and which he lost (see *Arm Apoc* 4:10–16, where three allied but different lists are published). The present list differs again to a considerable extent from them. Below, in an annotation to this part, a table of these four lists is presented. See for comparative rabbinic lists Ginzberg 1909, 1:79, 5.102 n. 87 and Pirqe R. El. 14.

16. This is most likely supported by or, less likely, inferred from Ps 8:5. Adam's

9. Adam and Eve in the Garden

Second, undying.[17] Third, not needy of anything.[18] Fourth, not forgetting. Fifth, penetrating. Sixth, untiring.[19] Seventh, speedy. Eighth, not gloomy. Nine, prophet. Tenth, priest. Eleventh, king.[20] Twelfth, unageing.

ANNOTATION 10. STORIES OF PARADISE

In §9.1, in response to the question about the length of Adam and Eve's residence in paradise, Questionnaire says, "Some said 1,000 years, and some, 40 days."[21] This statement is apparently drawn from Ełišē's *Comm. Gen.* 10, where it is found verbatim. However, the passage in M682 in which it occurs is most likely not directly dependent on Ełišē's *Commentary on Genesis* since the latter, as far as is known, did not survive down to the later medieval period as an integral work. Indeed, M682 may actually have taken this statement from a third work that cited Ełišē, for Questionnaire is most likely a medieval composition.[22] Quotations from Ełišē's *Commentary on Genesis* are known from Vardan Arewelcʻi's *Commentary on Genesis*, which is partly a *catena* and contains many excerpts from Ełišē and other patristic authors.[23] Unfortunately, Vardan Arewelcʻi's *Commentary on Genesis* is, at present, still unpublished, but I have examined it in manuscript, and I accept the attribution of Vardan's passage relevant to this matter to Ełišē, which was proposed by Levon Xačʻikyan.

A period of one thousand years is taken as one divine day, an idea based on an exegesis of Ps 90(89):4, "For a thousand years in thy sight are

---

luminous robes are mentioned in many Armenian sources; see Stone 2013, index s.v. "glory" and section 4.2.3 in each of that book's chapters of the analysis. See the further discussion in annotation 13 below.

17. This is implied by the curse in Gen 3:19.
18. All Adam's needs were supplied; that is inferred from Gen 2:16.
19. The reverse of the curse in Gen 3:17–19.
20. The three offices, prophet, priest, and king were also qualities of Christ's, who was seen as the new Adam; see Stone 2013, 57, 92–93, etc. These three qualities of Adam's are called "seals" in CT 16.8 (*MOTP* 1:552). Note the crowned figure of Adam in Eden depicted in Armenian miniatures, evoking his kingship; see, for one example, Stone 2013, 52–53. The same view may be found in Pseudo-Epiphanius; see Dorfmann-Lazarev 2020c, 297, 304–5. On Adam as priest in postbiblical literature, see Mazor 2012, 32 discussing Jub. 3.27–28.
21. So Ełišē, *Commentary on Genesis* cited in Stone 2013, 35.
22. See the section on dating in the introduction to this volume, on p. xxviii.
23. See Xačʻikyan 1992 and Xačʻikyan, Kēoseyan, and Papazian 2004.

but as yesterday when it is past." If God's day is one thousand years, so the exegetical logic runs, then the text of Gen 2:17, "for in the day that you eat of it you shall die," must mean during divine day one. Since they became mortal on the (divine) day one it is inferred that on that day they must have been expelled from Eden and on it they became mortal. It was, as I have explained, a thousand years long. This understanding of Ps 90(89):4 is found in rabbinic sources such as Gen. Rab. 19.8, as well as in Christian ones.[24]

The second view adduced by Ełišē, that Adam was in the garden for forty days, is also the opinion of Grigor Aršaruni (eighth century), who says that Adam "was created on the sixth day and entered the Garden on the fortieth day, and came out after an equal period."[25] This is based on apocryphal and probably ultimately Jewish sources concerned with the ritual purity of Eden.[26] An analogous, but different idea is the view of the Armenian apocryphon called Adam Story 2, which relates that Adam was put into Eden on the fortieth day, and on the next Friday, eight days later, he sinned and was expelled.[27]

"On the same day" means that on the very day of their introduction into the garden, they sinned and were expelled. This is the third opinion recorded by Questionnaire §9.2. It is already found in Armenian sources as early as the sixth century[28] and is, of course, based on different exegesis of Gen 2:17, "on the day you eat of it."[29] In addition to the Armenian sources, Pseudo-Basil (sixth century) and Grigoris Aršaruni (seventh–eighth century), a number of rabbinic sources support the same view.[30]

---

24. See Ginzberg 1909, 1:75–76 and 5:98–99 n. 72 and the many Jewish and Christian sources cited there.

25. Stone 2013, 312, no. 7.

26. Concerning the forty- and eighty-day periods from the creations of Adam and of Eve until their respective entries into the garden, the oldest source is Jub. 3.8–9. This period of forty days is discussed in annotation 6 above. Applying the temple purity rules prescribed in Leviticus to Eden involves investing Eden with the degree of purity which was attributed to the temple; see part 7 n. 4 above and the article by Baumgarten 1994 cited there. Thus, it relates to the idea of Adam's priestly function, which will be discussed more extensively below. This matter is also analyzed by Ginzberg 1909, 5:106 n. 97. See also the discussion in Schäfer 1986, 72, as well as Mazor 2012.

27. See the discussion in Stone 2013, 76–77.

28. See n. 6 above.

29. See the treatment of Adam's creation on Friday in Stone 2013, 41.

30. See Stone 2013, 76. Various rabbinic sources list the first twelve hours of Adam and Eve, from (before) their creation until their sin and expulsion. See the references

9. Adam and Eve in the Garden

This third view is opposed by Questionnaire §9.2 on the grounds that the serpent's talk with Eve, the eating of the fruit, as well as what ensued on these actions were too much activity to take place on the same Friday as Adam's creation.

A variant of this opinion is that of Tiranun *vardapet* (tenth century),[31] who maintains that "on the day, etc." means on the same day of the week. Genesis 1:26, of course, puts Adam and Eve's creation on the sixth day, that is, on the first Friday. So Tiranun *vardapet* says that all these events in the garden happened between the first and the second Friday, which makes eight days (counting both Fridays). Thus, Tiranun *vardapet* agrees with our text here.

In addition to the answers to the question, "How many days did they stay in the garden?" (§9:0), which I discussed immediately above, the following associated concept should be mentioned. Grigoris Aršaruni, and not only he, makes much of the symbolism of Friday. Adam and Eve were created on Friday, and on the next Friday, they sinned and were expelled from the garden. Humans, he says, found salvation through the cross "on Friday in the six-thousandth year," for Christ was crucified on Friday.[32] A chiliastic understanding of history lies in the background of the statement: "in the six-thousandth year." The concept of a world-week developed and became related to the interpretation of Ps 90(89):4, as it was presented on pages 73–74 above. The basic idea became the following: the world is to last a week of God's one thousand-year days, which is then counted as six thousand years with a seventh eschatological Sabbath "day" of another one thousand years to come.[33] Intriguingly, Grigoris Aršaruni puts Christ's

---

in Ginzberg 1909, 5:106–7 n. 97 and Pesiq. Rab. 46, fol.187b, which expresses the same view. [Such lists are found in numerous rabbinic sources, from classical Amoraic midrashim and the Babylonian Talmud onward. See the analysis in Efrati 2019, 1:206–7. –S.E.]

31. See Stone 2013, 76 for this subject and for a further discussion of Tiranun *vardapet*'s view.

32. See Stone 2013, 312–14. On p. 77 there, Stone gives a table in which the timetable of Adam and Eve's actions in Eden is correlated with the events of the Friday of Christ's crucifixion. That table was drawn up following the indications of Pseudo-Basil. See the discussion of the Edenic timetable in Ginzberg 1909, 5:106–7. Furthermore, the sixth millennium was, as it were, the "Friday" of the world-week of seven thousand years.

33. See several such opinions in b Sanh. 98a–b. In Christian millenarianism, Christ was believed to have come during the sixth millennium-long day. Some sources,

crucifixion at 6,000 a.m. and not in the year 5,198 a.m., which is the date commonly found in Armenian sources.[34]

There are variant views according to which the Sabbatical millennium is said to be an ideal messianic period and that the end of history will coincide with its conclusion. Then, at its end, the world-to-come commences. The first act in the drama of the end is the resurrection to the otherworldly day of judgment. Some Armenian chronological lists implying a millennial calculation have been published, such as Concerning the Millennia 1, 2, and 3. These are lists of seven plus one millennia.[35]

In 4 Ezra 7.26–32 (late first century CE), the same sequence of events is set out, but there without a precise chronology:

> 26 For behold, the time will come, when the
> signs which I have foretold to you will come,
> that the city which now is not seen shall appear,
> and the land which now is hidden shall be disclosed.
> 27 And everyone who has been delivered from the evils that I have foretold shall see my wonders. 28 For my Messiah shall be revealed with those who are with him, and he shall make rejoice those who remain for four hundred years. 29 And after these years my son (or: servant) the Messiah shall die, and all who draw human breath. 30 And the world shall be turned back to primeval silence for seven days, as it was at the first beginnings; so that no one shall be left. 31 And after seven days the world, which is not yet awake, shall be roused,
> and that which is corruptible shall perish.

---

for instance, CT 44.51–55 (*MOTP* 1:574), say that he came in 5,500 a.m. Armenian chronological summaries built on the division of history into one-thousand-year periods, with the sixth marking the life of Christ and the seventh the eschatological state, have been published in *Arm Apoc* 4:34–41. In that work, I am much indebted to Eynatyan 2002, 99–101, 136–37, 154–55.

34. Armenian chiliastic chronological summaries are discussed in the preceding note. Down to the sixth millennium, this same sequence also occurs in Concerning Millennia 3 (*Arm Apoc* 4:36–37), and other chronological texts in *Arm Apoc* 4:39–41 have the same sequence, but their division is into ten periods, reckoned by event and not by millennia. On the importance of the number 10, see above n. 42 to part 1.

35. See the preceding note and the discussion in *Arm Apoc* 4:27–28, 34–38. Al-Ṭabari (ca. 839–923) attributes millennial views the "the Jews." See Rosenthal 1989, 172–74, §1.8. There, a tradition is quoted that the length of time is seven thousand years, and other traditions that maintain that it is six thousand years. In rabbinic sources too, millennial calculations are known; see Urbach 1979, 677–78 and 1000–1001 nn. 94–96.

32 And the earth shall give back those who are asleep in it,
and the dust those who rest in it.
and the treasuries shall give up the souls which have been committed to them. (Stone, 1990a, 202).

The renewal of the world and the general resurrection are followed by the judgment and eternal life or death.

In the Armenian text called Concerning Millennia 1, the same sequence occurs:

In the sixth era, the Incarnation of the Word God took place.
In the seventh era will be the completion of life.
At the inception of the eighth, the resurrection of all humans.[36]

The same question asked here in Questionnaire is also posed in Questions and Answers from the Holy Books §7, but the answer differs. The text of that question and answer are:

Question: How long did Adam remain in the garden, for some books say a lot and others, not one day?
Answer: Because in the garden there was no day and no night, but it was always light, therefore, no one knows the limits of Adam's life.[37]

The idea of continual light in paradise mentioned here is part of a complex tradition found in rabbinic thought about the special light of the seven days of creation and in Eden.[38] In Christian sources, one may also observe the idea of the light of Eden, which is a central element of the Legend of the Cheirograph of Adam.[39] The role of Edenic light is discussed extensively in paradise language highlighting trees that is used both in an encomium to Grigor Tat'ewac'i by Aṙak'el of Siwnik' and also in the long description of

---

36. *Arm Apoc* 4:34–36. See further on various chronological issues Eynatyan 2002.

37. *Arm Apoc* 4:97–98.

38. See y. Ber. 8:5, 12b; Gen. Rab. 11.2; Pesiqta of Ten Commandments 3 (Pesiq. Rab. 23, 118a–b; Efrati 2019, 2:42–43). On the special light of the first day see, e.g., Gen. Rab. 3:6 and the extensive discussion in Ginzberg 1909, 1:8–9, 5:8–9 n. 19, 5:112–13 n. 104. On the primaeval light in Jewish Hellenistic and rabbinic literature, see further Kister 2015, 163–78.

39. See Stone 2002, 102; Megas 1928, 89–90 and index, s.v. "light." See also Stone and Timotin 2023, index, s.v. "light."

Eden in *Adamgirkʻ* 1.14.1–14.⁴⁰ The same special light is portrayed in the Adam cycle in the exterior murals of the Romanian churches of Voroneț, Moldovița, and Sucevița (Stone and Timotin 2023, 112–13).

Annotation 11. The Creation of Eden

§§9.3 broaches another issue with considerable theological ramifications. The question is simple and focuses on a seeming contradiction in Genesis. The plants were created on the third day, so Gen 1:11–12 relates. Moreover, in Gen 1:29, God blesses Adam at the end of the creative process and gives him "every plant yielding seed which is upon the face of all the earth, and every tree with seed in its fruit." Later, however, Gen 2:8 speaks of God planting a garden in Eden after Adam's creation. These verses, our author thinks, are in conflict, for the garden should have been included in the enumeration of the creative events of Gen 1:11–12, which describe the creation of all vegetation. Therefore, he reasons that the later creation of Eden must have had a special purpose; that purpose was so that Adam himself could witness the creation of the flora and fauna and thus would know that it was created, that is, created from nothing. This was done to combat the idea that the world was created from preexistent matter, an idea that is energetically opposed by Armenian thinkers. Questionnaire expresses that opposition in explicit terms.

The remarks of Vardan Arewelcʻi (1200?–1271) in his *Commentary on Genesis* concerning Gen 1:1 concord with this view:

> In the beginning he made—It teaches that the existent things had a beginning, lest we think that they are without beginning. And then this, that God is the creator, and they are not self-existent things, (as they are) according to the Greek view.⁴¹

In general, the issues of *creatio ex nihilo* and its correlative, the denial of preexistent matter, seem to have been of great importance to the author. Moreover, he most emphatically makes the point that God himself cre-

---

40. This was translated into English in Stone 2007a, 83. The description of Eden is found in *Adamgirkʻ* 1:14.1–14 (Stone 2007a, 166–68).

41. Viewed in Matenadaran manuscript M1267, fol. 5v. The Greek notion was a rather common philosophical view in the late antique world (D. Runia, personal communication). It developed, in Christian usage, from Aristotle; see briefly in Cross and Livingstone 1974, 890 and there are many other sources.

ated without any other power associated with him in the creative act. The present text, then, has as one of its polemical objects to attack views that hold the Greek notion of the preexistence or self-existence of matter. It was created by God alone without any angelic or other helper; Questionnaire implies this, but does not state it outright.

Questionnaire's view that the garden was created after Adam is not the only view represented in Armenian literature. In a more exegetical mode and as early as the fifth century, in his *Refutation of the Sects* (= *de Deo*) 162–63, Eznik of Kołb argued that Adam was created on the sixth day, for "first the house and then the householder, first the possessions and then the possessor, first the servants and then the master."[42] This statement, of course, implies that the creation of the garden preceded the creation of Adam and so contradicts the view forwarded by Questionnaire §9.3 concerning the creation of the garden.

Vardan Arewelcʻi's *Commentary on Genesis* as it is preserved in manuscript M1267, fol. 21v, clearly states that the garden of Eden was created on the third day, together with the other plants and vegetation.[43] This is also the view of Samuel Anecʻi (twelfth century), who says the following concerning the third day: երրորդ օրն՝ բոյսք եւ տունկ<կ>ք եւ դրախտն, "(on) the third day, shoots and plants and the garden."[44]

That the creation of the garden of Eden was on the third day is a view already current in the second century BCE, as we may see in Jub. 2.7. The same idea of Eden's creation on the third day may also lie behind 4 Ezra 6.2 and 44, though it is not explicit there. Fourth Ezra, stressing the purposive nature of creation, asserts that God planned things in advance, before creating many heavenly and meteorological phenomena, among which were the laying of "the foundations of the garden," and the creation of "the beautiful flowers" (4 Ezra 6.2–3). Without a doubt, this

---

42. Stone 2013, 269. [A related idea is that, like one who prepares a feast and then invites the guests, God first prepared all of Adam's provisions and then created him. See Philo, *Opif.* 77–78; Gen. Rab. 8.6; Aphrahat, *Demonstration* 17.7 –S.E.]. Also compare 4 Ezra 8.52.

43. That is already the explicit view of Jub. 2.7, a work of the late second century BCE; see annotation 11. There does not seem to have been a translation of Jubilees into Armenian, though some traditions first attested in Jubilees were transmitted in that language, having entered Armenian culture via Greek and predominantly Syriac sources.

44. Abrahamyan 1952, 2:43. The fifth word is corrupt in Abrahamyan's text, reading տունք "houses" for տունկք "plants." Armenian manuscript M10725 (seventeenth century), fol. 218v, also puts Eden on the third day.

collocation refers to the garden of Eden. The Armenian version of 4 Ezra, a fifth-century translation from a longer Greek text than that behind the Latin and Syriac versions, expands on this list of created things, and in 6.2–3 reads "before the establishment of the pavements of the garden, and before the appearance of its beauty."[45] Thus, the Armenian version makes the reference to Eden quite explicit.

In rabbinic thought and literature, we find two opinions. One of them sets Eden's creation on the third day, together with all the other vegetation (e.g., Gen. Rab. 11.9). According to the other view, the garden of Eden was one of seven things that were created before the creation of the world.

The first rabbinic view follows the same line of exegesis as occurs in Questionnaire, asserting the precreation of the garden. It is found, for instance, in b. Pesah. 51a, 54a, b. Ned. 39b and Pirqe R. El. 3, Gen. Rab. 11.9 in a hexaemeral passage, and in Gen. Rab. 21.9, all put the garden's creation before that of the world, The later works, Seder Gan Eden (Jellinek 1938, 3:132) and Midrash Konen (Jellinek 1938, 2:1.6) also concord with this view. Both these works are difficult to date but are likely very late first millennium or early second. The prooftext for this opinion is Gen 2:8: "The Lord God planted a garden in Eden *from before*," understanding the Hebrew word מקדם of Gen 2:8 not as "in the east" but rather as "beforehand."[46] The same exegetical assumption is both used in and refuted by Gen. Rab. 15.3; according to this source מקדם does indeed mean "beforehand," meaning not before the creation of the world but instead, before the creation of Adam, that is, on the third day.

Among patristic authors, note that Jerome (ca. 342–347–420 CE) in *Hebrew Questions on Genesis* also interprets the crux מקדם in Gen 2:8 to mean "previously, in advance" rather than "in the East."[47] John Chrysostom (ca. 347–407 CE), *Hom. Gen.* 13.14 also seems to hold that Eden was created before Adam, and John Damascenus (ca. 675–749 CE) expresses the same idea in *Orthodox Faith* 2.11 (*NPNF* 30.61–72). This

---

45. Stone 1979, 87. Indeed, the list of created things in 4 Ezra 6.1–5 is an important catalogue of natural phenomena.

46. According to b. Pesah. 51a, the seven things that were created before the creation of the world are: the Torah, repentance, the garden of Eden, Gehenna, the throne of glory, the temple, and the name of the messiah. The same argument from Hebrew מקדם is presented by Jerome; see annotation 11 n. 47 below.

47. See Hayward 1995, 108–9; Kamesar 1993, 141–44.

9. Adam and Eve in the Garden

view, then, shared by rabbinic and patristic exegesis, sets the creation of Eden before that of Adam, just like Questionnaire.

Paradise is also described in Questionnaire §9.4 utilizing stereotypical descriptions of its trees and fruit that are often encountered in Armenian sources. The "unfading flowers" and the "non-dropping fruit" are two of the commonest phrases shared by these descriptions.[48] Many clear examples of such stereotypical language occur in the *Book of Adam* or *Adamgirkʻ* (Ադամգիրք) by Aṙakʻel Siwnecʻi (1356?–1422?) and in the *Book of Paradise* (Դրախտագիրք) by the same author, as well as in other sources.[49] Grigor Magistros (990?–1059) evokes this language in his Epistle 11 in a mention of "unfading crown," and it occurs in Vardan Anecʻi's (tenth–eleventh century) poem on Ezek 1, in the context of Eden.[50] Similar expressions are used in the thirteenth century, in Vardan Arewelcʻi's *Historical Compilation*,[51] and in one of his hymns cited there: ի դրախտին դնելով, բազմախիտ ծառով, կանաչ տերևով. / զանազան պտղով, անթառամ գունով, եւ անուշ հոտով. "Being put in the Garden, with very leafy trees, with green leaves, / With various fruit, with unfading colour, and with sweet fragrance." Similar language is also encountered in Yovhannēs Tʻlkurancʻi's (1320?–1400?) description of the garden of Eden.[52]

I add here a striking quotation from the theologian Grigor Tatʻewacʻi's (1346–1409/10 CE) writing called *That the Garden Is Incorruptible*. He says: "In that, the wood of the garden does not putrefy, and the leaves

---

48. For edenic flowers, see, e.g., Stone 2007a, 81, 90–92, 147, 166–67, 281, and 283. This is a widespread topos. Fruit of paradise is mentioned in Irenaeus, *Haer.* 5.33.3. In the hexaemeron in 4 Ezra 6, the description of the third day reads "For immediately fruit came forth in endless abundance and of varied appeal to the taste; and flowers of inimitable colour; and innumerable beautiful trees; and inexpressible fragrances. These were made on the third day." Although, in context, this is the description of all vegetation, the language is typical of that used of the garden of Eden. Similarly, in 4 Ezra 7.123, paradise is revealed, "whose fruit does not spoil." See also Odes Sol. 11.16. Thus, the terminology used commonly in Armenian literature can be already discerned in Jewish writings of the Second Temple period.

49. The *Book of Adam* or *Adamgirkʻ* has been translated into English, but the *Book of Paradise* is known to date only in Armenian. For *Adamgirkʻ*, see the edition of Madoyan 1989. The English translation of the complete *Adamgirkʻ* is in Stone 2007a. The *Book of Paradise* may be consulted in the edition of Tēr Nersēsean 1956.

50. See Lint 2014, 232.

51. See Stone 2013, 480. The full translation of the *Historical Compilation* is Thomson 1989.

52. Stone 2013, 598. See Anderson 1988, 202 on the fragrance of Eden.

do not rot, and the fruit (is) undroppable, and the flowers (are) unfading, and God had planted them with his hands."[53] This work draws upon the same literary topoi and the same vocabulary featured in the preceding paragraph. In the apocryphal text bearing the title Creation of Eve and Disobedience in §4, this same floral terminology clusters around a mention of Eden, "the beauty of the garden, with trees, fruit, unfading [անթառամ] flowers, leaves." See similarly Grigor Taranałc'i (1576–1643), *Chronicle* 84.[54] The same phrase using the word անթառամ "unfading" recurs in M2245 of the year 1689, in *Questions of St. Gregory*, fol. 237v.[55] Such citations could readily be multiplied, and these attributes were clearly formulaic topoi in medieval Armenian descriptions of the garden of Eden. In Ezek 47:12, similar ideas are already encountered, but elements of the typical Armenian paradise vocabulary of which I am speaking are not to be found there.

Annotation 12. The Twelve Gifts that Adam Lost

The list of the blessings and advantages that Adam lost through his sin recurs in several Armenian manuscripts in various contexts, and Questionnaire includes this list in its running text in §9.6. In the first table below, I present the lists of the twelve gifts that Adam lost, as they are found in four different manuscript versions. It can be remarked that, except for M2182 dating from 1647 and 1731 CE, all these lists enumerate twelve blessings that Adam lost, though the reason for them to be twelve in number is unclear.[56] One list occurs in two of the manuscripts and the other three lists are not identical with that particular list or with one another. Even

---

53. See Stone 2013, 526.
54. See Daranałc'i 1915.
55. It is published in Stone 2022.
56. In rabbinic sources, between seven and twenty-four blessings are mentioned that Adam lost when he sinned; see Ginzberg 1909, 5:112–13, 114 n.105, and the sources cited there; Gen. Rab. 12:6. In 1:86, for instance, Ginzberg lists: celestial light, resplendent countenance, (eternal) life, tall stature, fruits of the soil, fruits of the tree, and the (special shining of) luminaries. Some of these overlap with the Armenian lists, but the two traditions do not appear to depend on one another. As already noted, these seven qualities are increased to twenty-two and twenty-four by other sources. The messianic age will bring about the restoration of the lost gifts. See Gen Rab. 12.6; Tanh. Ber. 6.2; Num. Rab. 13.12; Sifra Beḥukotai 1:2–6 [110d]. [In fact, the list of seven is Ginzberg's own synthesis, which is not found in any of the sources. The Sifra passage

where they share items, the order of presentation varies. I think it is more than likely that a systematic search would turn up substantially more copies of such lists and further variations of their order and content. I may also remark that the items common to M10720 (eighteenth century) and M2182 (1674, 1731) are virtually identical in wording, while M2182 seems to have lost the last few items.

Although M682, that is Questionnaire, and M9121 have the full twelve gifts, they differ in formulation and, for the most part in content, from the list shared by M10720 and M2182.[57]

TABLE 2: THE TWELVE GIFTS THAT ADAM LOST

	M682 (seventeenth century)	M9121 (1732–1733)	M10720 (eighteenth century)	M2182 (1674, 1731)
1	that (he was) ornamented in a luminous garment	health without sickness	vision of God	vision of God
2	undying	childhood without (old) age	conversation (that is, with God)	conversation (that is, with God)
3	not needy of anything	satiety without tediousness	immortality	the immortality
4	not forgetting	freedom without slavery	a luminous garment	a luminous garment
5	penetrating	beauty without ugliness	un <blemished> life	life without blemish
6	untiring	impassibility subject to immortality	unageing status	unageing status
7	speedy	abundance without lack	enjoy<ment without toil> of the garden of delights	enjoyment of the garden's delight without labor.

asserts that if Israel does God's will, the land will be as fertile as in Adam's days; this is related to the tradition of Adam's gifts, but no actual list is given there. –S.E.]

57. Except for the list in Questionnaire, which I am publishing here, the Armenian texts and full translations of the other lists have been edited and are published in *Arm Apoc* 4:10–16.

8	not gloomy	peace without turbulence	cultivation of God <that is the agriculture and gardening> of the immortal tree	cultivation of God
9	prophet	freedom from care without fear	love and pity of God upon humankind through the obedience to the commandment that came to him	
10	priest	knowledge without ignorance	kingdom over all the things made by hand	
11	king	glory without dishonor	priesthood	
12	unaging	happiness without grief	prophecy	

The encyclopedic work, *Book of Questions* by Grigor Tatʻewacʻi (1346–1409/10), presents a list of twelve blessings that Adam lost, together with a somewhat longer explanatory exposition.[58] Grigor's list is basically identical to that in M10720 and M2182. Considering the late date of these two copies, they may well have derived from Grigor Tatʻewacʻi's composition. Because considerable interest inheres in this list and because of the central role Grigor's *Book of Questions* played in the intellectual life of subsequent generations, I have transcribed and translated the whole chapter.[59]

Վասն ԺԲ. (12) պարգեւաց Մարդոյն
Երկոտասան պարգեւք էին ի դրախտին զոր կորոյս Ադամ:
1. Նախ՝ տեսութիւնն Աստուծոյ:
2. Երկրորդ՝ խոսակցութիւնն:
3. Երրորդ՝ անմահութիւն:
4. Չորրորդ՝ լուսեղէն պատմուճան:
5. Հինգերորդ՝ անախտ կեանք:

---

58. Grigor Tatʻewacʻi 1993, 278–79; it is most likely that that further copies and forms of this list exist.

59. I have introduced a numbering of the graces or blessings to facilitate comparison.

9. Adam and Eve in the Garden

6. Վեցերորդ՝ անձերանալի հասակ:
7. Եօթներորդ՝ վայելչութիւն անաշխատ փափկութեան դրախտին:
8. Ութերորդ՝ մշակութիւն Աստուծոյ. այսինքն անմահ տնկոց երկրագործ եւ պահապան:
9. Իններորդ՝ սէր եւ զուլթ Աստուծոյ ի վերայ մարդոյն հնազանդութեամբ պատուիրանին որ զայր ադ նա:
10. Տասներորդ՝ թագաւորութիւն ի վերայ ամենայն ձեռակերտաց:
11. Մետասաներորդ՝ քահանայութիւն:
12. Երկոտասաներորդ՝ մարգարէութիւն:

Ճայս ԺԲ. (12) պարզեւս էհան ի մէնչ Եւա:
1. Նախ՝ ի տեսութենէն. զի ոչ եւս յաւել տեսանել զԵրեսս Աստուծոյ.
2. Ի խօսակցութենէն, զի մինչ ի Յորդանան այլ ոչ ասի հօր Աստուծոյ խօսիլ ընդ մարդկան:
3. Իսկ յանմահութենէն՝ զի վճիռ եհատ ասելով (հող էիր եւ ի հող դարձիս):
4. Ի լուսաւոր պատմուճանէն, յորժամ կերին ի պտղոյն եւ ծանեան զի մերկ էին եւ արարին սփածանելիս:
5. Իսկ յանախտ կենացն, (տրտմութեամբ եւ քրտամբ կերիցես զհաց:)
6. Իսկ յանձերանալի հասակէն, (փուշ եւ տատասկ բուսցին ի քեզ:)
7. Ի պահպանութենէն, (յորմէ պատուիրեցի չուտել՝ կերէր արդեօք ի նմանէ:)
8. Իսկ ի վայելչութենէն, ասէ (էհան զնոսա եւ բնակեցոյց ընդդէմ դրախտին փափկութեան:)
9. Իսկ ատելութեան ցոյց, (զուցէ ձգիցէ զձեռն իւր:)
10. Ի թագաւորութենէն, (մարդ ի պատիւ էր, եւ ոչ իմացաւ. հաւասարեաց անասնոց անբանից:)
11. Ի քահանայութենէն, զի ոչ իշխեաց պատարագ մատուցանել ի կեանս իւր:
12. Իսկ մարգարէութիւնն լռեաց, զի ոչ եւս երեւի բան մի յիշատակ շնորհաց նորա:

Concerning the Twelve Gifts to Humans
1. First, the Vision of God.
2. Second, the conversation.
3. Third, immortality.
4. Fourth, luminous garment.
5. Fifth, life without blemish.

6. Sixth, unageing status.

7. Seventh, enjoyment without toil of the garden of delight.[60]

8. Cultivation of God, that is the agriculture and (being) guardian of the undying trees.

9. Ninth, love and pity of God upon humans by the obedience of the command that came to him.

10. Tenth, kingdom over all things made by hand.[61]

11. Eleventh, priesthood.

12. Twelfth, prophecy.

Of these twelve things, Eve deprived us:

1. First of the vision, no longer to see the face of God.

2. Of conversation, for up to the Jordan,[62] God is not again said to speak with mankind.

3. Then, of immortality, for he declared a sentence, saying ("you are dust and to dust you will return").[63]

4. Of the luminous garment, when they ate of the fruit and knew that they were naked, and they made aprons.[64]

5. Then, of unblemished life, ("in the sweat of your face you shall eat bread").[65]

6. Then, of unageing status, ("thorns and thistles it shall bring forth to you").[66]

---

60. That is, of Eden.

61. That is, God's hand. Several older sources stress that God created humans with his right hand. This idea derives from Gen 2:7. Adam is frequently represented with royal attributes and characteristics. His kingdom is usually, as is the case here, associated with priesthood and prophecy; see part 7 n. 17.

62. Grigor is referring to Jesus's baptism in the Jordan, when a voice from heaven declared, "this is my beloved son" etc. This statement is made, of course, from a Christian perspective, in which the divine speech at the baptism forms a first and direct revelation of Christ's divine nature: Matt 3:13–17, Mark 1:9–11, and Luke 3:21–23. The many divine addresses to humans in the Old Testament/Hebrew Bible are discounted in this statement.

63. Gen 3:19.

64. Gen 3:7. Adam's luminous garments are discussed in annotation 13, following the present one.

65. Gen 3:19.

66. Gen 3:18. The connection here is somewhat unclear.

7. Of the guarding (or: fasting), ("have you eaten of the tree of which I commanded you not to eat?").[67]

8. Then, from the enjoyment; it says ("He drove out the man; and at the east of the garden of Eden").[68]

9. Then, the demonstration of hatred ("lest he put forth his hand").[69]

10. From the kingdom. ("Man cannot abide in his pomp; he is like the dumb beasts that perish").[70]

11. From the priesthood, for he was not able to offer a sacrifice in his lifetime.[71]

12. Then the (power of) prophecy fell silent, for no longer was a word shown as a memorial of his glory.

Annotation 13. Luminous Garments

The luminous garments that Questionnaire attributes to Adam draw upon a complex of ideas with its roots partly, at least, in the Bible. Over the centuries, Jewish and Christian exegetes developed certain ideas about Adam's garments, which drew on biblical antecedents, both as to their luminosity and as to the nature and material of the garments themselves. Within the limits of the present study, we can explore in a certain measure of detail only some of the ways these ideas functioned, particularly as they relate to Questionnaire and in some other facets of Armenian tradition. Certain other ideas, however, we can only indicate in short order in this context.

The idea of humans' glory is referred to already by Ps 8:5–6(6–7): "5 Yet thou hast made him little less than God,[72] and dost crown him with glory [כבוד] and honor [הדר]. 6 Thou hast given him dominion over the

---

67. Gen 3:11.
68. Gen 3:24.
69. Gen 3:22. It is unclear how this phrase, referring to Adam, shows hatred. Is this divine speech taken out of context as referring to Cain's murder of Abel?
70. Ps 49:12 (48:13).
71. This and also the reason offered in the next case are not biblical citations.
72. Adam is seen as equal, or almost equal, to angels in 2 En. 30.10 and, later, in many Armenian sources, such as Łewond, text 4 in Stone 2013, 318 and Aṙakʻel Siwnecʻi, *Adamgirkʻ* in Stone 2007a, 37, 48, 55, 90–91, 145, 215, 271–72, 280–83, 287. The glory of Adam's robe is mentioned by Hamam (ninth century): see Thomson 2005, 183. Much of interest in this connection is also to be found in Murdoch 1967, 377–78, who discusses the similarity of Adamic and angelic garments. See also Bunta 2007, 147 and further in n. 78 below. Witztum 2011, 93–106 examines the Qurʾanic

works of thy hands; thou hast put all things under his feet." In the verse preceding this, we read: "What is man (or: a human) that thou art mindful of him, and the son of man (or: an Adamite) that thou dost care for him?" As it stands in that verse, in the second hemistich "son of man," (or Adamite) simply means "human being," a view confirmed by the use of the word אנוש "human" as its parallel in the first hemistich. In Jewish exegesis, אדם here was sometimes taken to mean Adam, and often Christians read the second hemistich as referring to the Son of Man.[73]

In the phrase "little less than God" in Ps 8:5, the English word "God" renders Hebrew אלהים, which, indeed, is usually translated as "God" in the RSV, the Bible version customarily quoted here. However, in this very verse of Psalms, the LXX renders אלהים as ἀγγέλους "angels," and, following the LXX, as is its general custom, the Armenian Bible (Arm) reads զհրեշտակս քո, "your angels." If the verse is understood as the LXX and Armenian Bible do, it speaks of humanity, or Adam, as almost angelic in quality, saying in the Armenian: "Yet thou hast made him little less than your angels."

Another exegetical issue arising from these two verses of Psalms is the phrase, "(thou) dost crown him with glory [[כבוד and honor [הדר]." The words "dost crown him" translate Hebrew תעטרהו. That verb (עטר) can signify "to surround" and, in the *pi'el* form, "to crown, surround the head with something." What is being described appears to be that Adam's head is surrounded by "glory and honor," rather like a halo.[74] This crowning brightness indicates his high status in the created order.[75] Indeed, the idea of radiance and luminosity as being a characteristic of beings of elevated status is already well rooted in the Old Testament/Hebrew Bible and Ps 8 is just one example of it.[76]

---

traditions about Adam and Eve's clothing and their affinities and possible origins in Jewish or Christian Syriac sources.

73. This designation of Christ has a very complicated *Vor-* and *Nachgeschichte* that is richly documented and discussed in scholarly literature.

74. "Crown" here does not carry the overtones of "crown as king" and does not refer to the granting of a *royal* crown.

75. Note that in the blessing of Adam in Gen 1:28, "and God said to them, 'Be fruitful and multiply, and fill the earth and subdue it; and have dominion,'" neither the verb "subdue" nor the verb "have dominion" derives from the root מל״ך which designates "king, royalty," "reign over," but are from the roots כב״ש "to conquer" and רד״ה, which means, "to have power over, rule over."

76. There exist further instances of such a function of brightness and glory.

The idea of human beings endowed with luminosity or glory definitely occurs in Wisdom of Joshua ben Sira (early second century BCE), the Greek translation of which work says at the end of the passage called "Praise of Fathers of Old": "Shem and Seth were honored [ἐδοξάσθησαν] among men, and Adam above every living being in the creation" (Sir 49:16). The RSV translation of Ben Sira, which I have quoted at this point, is presumably based on the Greek version. However, the Hebrew text in Genizah MS B reads somewhat differently: "And Shem and Seth and Enosh died and more than all living beings (was) the glory [תפארת] of Adam."[77]

In the Dead Sea Scrolls, the righteous are said to have "all the glory of Adam," or alternatively "of humans," that is, were very glorious humans.[78] That Qumran occurrence of Adam's glory has figured in scholarly discussions in recent decades.[79] Another clear example is to be found in 4Q504 8, 4, The Words of the Luminaries, which reads: "] and our [fat]her you fashioned in the image of your glory [." This passage certainly expresses the idea of Adam's physical appearance being a likeness of the celestial.[80]

---

77. Genizah manuscript B reads: ושם ושת ואנוש נפקדו ועל כל חי תפארת אדם. Shlomi Efrati remarks to me that נפקדו, the reading of manuscript B from the Cairo Genizah, may be taken to mean "went missing" and so "died." This reading, embodied in my translation here, seems very plausible to me and strengthens the point of the verse; even the great antediluvian figures Shem and Seth died, and yet Adam's glory exceeds that of all humans.

78. See 1QS IV, 22–23, 1QH[a] IV, 15–16; CD III, 19. Fletcher-Louis (2002, 96–97) regards these passages as showing that Adam had divine glory. See also his further discussion on pp. 100–102. Indeed, the word דמות ("image") in 4Q504 is that which is used in Gen 1:26, and there it is usually translated "likeness." Orlov (2007, 327) has discussed this passage in some detail. The relevant verses of Genesis are also considered in Lambden 1992. Barzilai (2007, 11–12, 16–17) suggests that some Qumran texts say that Adam was created in the image of angels in order to avoid the anthropomorphism that might be inferred from Gen 1:26. Rabbinic sources speak both of Adam's luminosity and of his loss of it; see Gen. Rab. 12.6; Tanh. Ber. 6.2; Num. Rab. 13.12. See further on Adam's brilliance, Mekhilta de Rashbi, Baḥodeš 6; Pesiqta of Ten Commandments 3 (Pesiq. Rab. 23, fol. 118a; Efrati 2019, 2:42–43); y. Ber. 8:5, 12b. See also the Romanian version of Testament of Abraham as discussed in detail by Bunta 2007, 144–48. He explores the complex tradition of the luminosity of Adam or his garments.

79. See the overview articles on glory by Davies in *IDB* 2:401–3 and on δόξα by Kittel (1974). Another interesting study is by Golitzin 2003, 275–308. Worthy of note also is Orlov 2007, 327–29; see further also Orlov 2019; Annus 2011, 7.

80. See Orlov 2007, 329. On God's glory, see Ps 104(103):2 "who coverest thyself

Given the connections set forth above, this "likeness" most probably involves brightness or light. The term *honor* or *glory*, Hebrew תפארת, which is used by Ben Sira in 49:16, resembles Armenian փառք, which is in turn comparable with the Iranian *x^{v}arena*. All three words carry a strong association of luminosity or effulgence.[81] Indeed, Adam was often accorded royal status, which related to his naming of the animals, and his glory (փառք) was regarded as a royal characteristic.[82]

Adam lost his luminosity and royal status when he sinned, an idea that was exegetically anchored to Gen 3:10, in which the verse "I was naked" is understood to mean "I became naked."[83] This language of

---

with light as with a garment"; Dan 7:9 "his (the Ancient of Days') raiment was white as snow"; 1 En. 14.20 refers to God as "like the appearance of the sun and whiter than much snow." See on God's raiment a particular tradition referred to in Gen. Rab. 3.4, which also offers the temple as a possible source of light. According to that midrash, God robed himself in light and that light was visible throughout the whole of creation. An alternative tradition argues that light was created from the place of the temple, thus highlighting this idea's priestly connection. Second Enoch is relevant but not completely similar, when in 22.1–2 the author writes: "On the tenth heaven, which is called Aravoth, I saw the appearance of the Lord's face, like iron made to glow in fire, and brought out, emitting sparks, and it burns. Thus in a moment of eternity, I saw the Lord's face, but the Lord's face is ineffable, marvelous and very awful, and very, very terrible." Golitzin 2003 compares the Qumran "glory of Adam" with the light that the contemplative will achieve, as is discussed in the pseudo-Macarian *Homilies* (dated to 534 CE at the latest) and some further, related sources. In these early Byzantine writings, light plays a central role as an expression of enlightenment. Orlov (2002) discusses this as well. These connections, however, go far beyond what is implied in Questionnaire.

81. Duchesne-Guillemin 1962, 214, 339, etc. Observe that in the Pseudo-Epiphanian *Homilies*, Adam is called փառակից ("sharer of glory") with God, and Armenian փառ- is cognate with Iranian *xvar*. See Dorfmann-Lazarev 2020a, 313 on which page Adam's glory is also discussed.

82. This idea is also to be found in *Adamgirkʻ* 1.21.6 (Stone 2007a, 206). See Toepel 2012, 312. This is also discussed by Maguire 1987, 363–65, 369. His evidence is not unambiguous. The idea that Adam was luminous before his sin is also to be found in rabbinic sources. See, e.g., Mekilta de R. Išmael, Baḥodeš 7; Gen. Rab. 11.2; Pesiqta of Ten Commandments 3 (Pesiq. Rab. 23, fol. 118a; Efrati 2019, 2:42–43); Pesiqta deRav Kahana, Parah 4; Deut. Rab., Ve-Zot Haberakah 3; y. Ber. 8:5, 12b. See also Kuehn 2019, 173–74. In certain Muslim sources, Adam is pictured as sitting on a throne, flanked by hosts of angels (Kuehn 2019, 183–86). See also Stone 2007b.

83. Or even, as Sebastian Brock suggested, "I had become naked"; see part 97 and 99 below. On Adam's being stripped naked, see also CT 4.17–18 (*MOTP* 1:543) and other sources that are discussed in the text here immediately following. See further

"stripping, becoming naked" is often used for Adam's fall, and when he sinned, he became naked of glory, of royal status, and so, it was inferred, of his heavenly garments, which were luminous. This idea is common in Armenian and other Christian texts.[84] Adam's loss of royalty is associated in Ephrem Syrus's Syriac *Comm. Gen.* 2.14–15 (CSCO 152) with his loss of Edenic glory and that might be the case in Questionnaire here, though it is not explicit.[85] Indeed, Lucas van Rompay has remarked incisively that Adam's glory has most frequently been mentioned in connection with his loss of it.[86] In the passage being discussed here, Questionnaire is basically oriented toward the details of protology, as is the discussion at the present juncture, so I will defer consideration of the eschatological dimension of garments of glory to below.

Lambden 1992, 77. On Adam's garments as royal robes, see Anderson 2001, 104–5 and compare CT 2.17–18, 20–25 (*MOTP* 1:541–42). See also Badalanova Geller 2021a, especially 36–40. Later, in iconography, this is expressed by Adam's being represented wearing a crown. See, for example, the miniature in J1667 of 1529 CE, fol. 58v. Concerning this manuscript, see: Połarean (Bogharian) 1971, 5:519–22. The same is shown on a painted ceramic tile of ca. 1720 in the Chapel of S. Ejmiacin in Jerusalem; Narkiss and Stone 1976, 133, fig. 174. See also manuscripts Erevan, M6420 of the year 1604 fol. 28a (1604 CE) and Musée arménien de France PA56, a Hymnal of 1591.

84. Among the Armenian apocrypha we read in Adam Story 2 §5, "and they both were stripped of their former glory" and see also §8 of that work. Other instances may be observed in Creation and Transgression §§18–19 (Lipscomb 1990, 111, 121); Adam, Eve and the Incarnation §2; and n. 83 to this annotation. Outside Armenian literature, the Greek PH 4.7 (*MOTP* 1:601) says that Adam and Eve were stripped of divinely-woven raiment: see also PH 5.1. For many further references to this motif, see Murdoch 1967, 376 n. 15; Brock 1979a, 212–32. On p. 217, Brock suggests that this tradition has Jewish roots. On that idea, see moreover, the words of Cumont 1956, 125–26 and Bousset 1960. Targum pseudo-Jonathan to Gen 3:7 reads, "they were stripped of the garments of nail," taking up the rabbinic midrash that their garments of glory resembled finger-nail.

85. Similar ideas and language occur in 3 Bar (Greek) 4.16–17: "Adam was condemned and stripped of the glory of God." The same language in Ephrem's *Commentary on Genesis* is cited in Bucur and Ivanovici 2019, n. 14. In Frik's *Poem on Adam*, there is a nice instance of light—nakedness—dark faces; see Tirayr 1952, 522 ll. 8–12. Apparently, it is Satan and the serpent that received the dark countenances, see l. 16 of that poem.

86. Rompay 1993, 556. Observe that Orlov (2011) discusses in detail not just the correspondence of Adam's garments and angelic garb, but also their being transferred to Adam from Satan.

Adam's initial clothing, then, resembled angelic garb, and it was glorious and luminous, not only a sign of Adam's Edenic state and kingly status but also of his being created in the image of God's glory. Adam's connection with the angels is very close, and Jewish and Christian exegetes understood that, prior to their sin, Adam and angels were not very dissimilar.[87] As has been noted, Adam and Eve were stripped of that initial clothing because of their sin.[88]

In the Bible, the clothing of angels is mentioned in Dan 10:5, where the angel was dressed in linen and "loins girded with gold of Uphaz."[89] Other descriptions of angelic luminous garb are Dan 12:6—linen; Matt 28:3—white as snow; John 20:12—white[90]; Acts 1:10—white; and Rev 15:6—pure bright linen. Reference to angelic, Edenic, and eschatological luminescence is made in 2 Bar. 51.5—the splendor of angels; 51.10—the redeemed will be changed "from light into the splendor of glory"; Gen. Rab. 21.5—glory[91]; *Apoc. Mos.* (Greek LAE) 20.2—Eve was clothed with glory. In Apoc. Zeph. 8.1–4, the prophet says, following a lacuna in which

---

87. The idea that, to quote Ps 8:6, "you have made him a little less than angels" (אלהים; see the immediately preceding exposition) finds expression in 1 En. 69.11, "For humans were not created to be different from the angels, so that they should remain pure and righteous." In 2 En. 30.12, one reads "I placed him on earth, a second angel, honorable, great and glorious, and I appointed him as ruler to rule on earth." Adam's royal characteristic is discussed below, on p. 96 n. 107 and see p. 90, above. Adam's quasi-angelic features are considered by Murdoch 1967, 377–78. These passages mention the similarities existing between angels and Edenic humans.

88. Ephrem frequently speaks of Adam and Eve as "clothed in glory"; see Murdoch 1967, 377 and n. 18. Adam and Eve's garments of glory are, of course, mentioned in many Armenian writings. A substantial number of instances are to be found gathered in Stone 2013, 11–175, §§1.1.5 and 4.2.3. Of considerable interest among these many sources is the use of the idea of glory and brightness, which is interwoven throughout the *Adamgirk'*, the Adam epic composed by Aṙakʻel Siwnecʻi (1356?–1422?); see Stone 2007a, 214 n. 697 and index, s.v. "glory."

89. Both Theodotion and Armenian Daniel, in their translations of that verse, follow the MT and differ from the LXX, which has καὶ τὴν ὀσφὺν περιεζωσμένος βυσσίνῳ, καὶ ἐκ μέσου αὐτοῦ φας.

90. White men symbolize angels in the Animal Apocalypse of 1 En. 87.2, 89.9 and a few other verses. 1 En. 66.8 describes the righteous as white in color. Angels have shining faces according to 2 En. 1.6, 19.1; they are glorious according to 2 En. 19.1, and these references could be multiplied manyfold. I have assembled examples and discussed the meaning of shining faces in Stone 1990a, 244–45, 254, 326–27. Eschatological glory, expressed in 2 Bar. 3–10 is discussed by Bucur and Ivanovici 2019.

91. On Adam's splendor, see Ginzberg 1909, 5:112, n. 104.

an ascent vision was probably described, "I, myself, put on an angelic garment."[92]

The history of Adam and Eve's clothing and the concomitant terminology of garments proved to be a most fertile source of ideas and speculations, some of which we are exploring here.[93] According to the embroidered biblical narrative, Adam and Eve, having transgressed, were stripped (of the Edenic luminous apparel) then made themselves aprons of fig-leaves (Gen 3:7); subsequently, God made Adam and Eve garments of skin (Gen 3:21) and expelled them from the garden (Gen 3:21).[94] In Genesis, the issue of Adam and Eve's garments, moving from their consciousness of their nakedness to human-made aprons and, finally, to God-made garb, is intriguing indeed. These divinely manufactured garments of skin subsequently became the subject of many rabbinic and early Christian exegeses and stories.[95] Targum pseudo-Jonathan refers to the garments of skin as לבושין דיקר ("garments of glory"). This might reflect, at one remove, a Hebrew paronomasia בגדי אור / בגדי עור "garments of skin / garments of light." In Gen. Rab. 20.12, the reading "garments of light" is mentioned, which evidently stood behind the translation in Targum Pseudo-Jonathan of Gen 3:21, and Genesis Rabbah attributes it to a Torah scroll associated with R. Meir (second century).[96] This understanding is

---

92. On the apocryphal Apocalypse of Zephaniah, see Schürer 1987, 803–4; and Kuhn 1984, 915–26.

93. See Ricks 2000. A fine presentation of the uses of the garment terminology in Syriac tradition was written by Brock 1982. He provides a most useful collection of relevant textual extracts, and he shows the importance of clothing in the Semitic Syriac tradition. See also his somewhat earlier paper, Brock 1979a, 221–23. Various matters that are dealt with in the present annotation are illuminated by Orlov 2011. A further study along this line is Kowalski 1982, who deals with Syriac usage of "glory of Adam." Concerning ancient Near Eastern attitudes to clothing, see Vogelzang and van Bekkum 1986. See also Bucur and Ivanovici 2019, and for early Muslim sources see Kuehn 2019, 176.

94. Ricks (2000) gives a survey of Jewish, Christian, and Muslim views of Adam's garments, a subject that has attracted much attention; see also CT 3.14 (*MOTP* 1:542). In 3 Bar. 4.16, the tree and not Adam is said to be stripped of glory. Some rabbinic interpretations of these garments are considered and analyzed by Reuling 2006, 251–59.

95. See Ginzberg 1909, 5:103–4 n. 93.

96. Gen. Rab. 20.12. Also compare TM 5.2, Deut. Rab. 11.3, and Odes Sol. 11.11 (in a different context). See the "luminous garment" in the list of The Twelve Gifts in §9 above. See also Orlov 2002 and Anderson 2001, 101–43. There is further discussion of Adam's and Moses's glory in Orlov 2007, 328–30.

difficult to sustain at the point in the narrative at which Gen 3:21 occurs. Therefore, Sebastian P. Brock suggested that some ancient interpreters took the verb "made" in a pluperfect sense, "had made."[97]

The rabbis have the same idea that, because of Eve's sin, the protoplasts were deprived of their glorious clothing, and thus, one can infer that before that, they wore luminous clothing.[98] This notion, of course, is based on an exegesis of Gen 3:7, which reads, "Then the eyes of both were opened, and they knew that they were naked." As I noted earlier, "they were naked" is taken by various exegetes to mean "they had become naked" or "they were stripped naked," that is, of the Edenic or luminous garments. Interestingly, as Brock remarked, the reverse idea was current in late antiquity outside Jewish and Christian tradition, that during its ascent through the heavenly spheres, the soul strips off the body, as one would a garment.[99]

God, Gen 3:21 says, made garments for Adam and Eve from skins. This immediately raised the question—whence the skins? Did he slaughter an animal and use its skin? If not, how is skin to be understood? So, the ancient exegetes asked. An example of a later attempt at a literal understanding of skin is that according to CT 4.22 (*MOTP* 1:543), the skin from which God made their garments was taken from trees.[100] The author thought of bark or some other such vegetal material, which notion reflects the *aporia* about the source of the skin mentioned in Gen 3:21, from which God made the garments. A different solution to the same difficulty is brought forward by other sources that claim it was the skin

---

97. Brock 1982, 14. See n. 83 above.

98. See Schäfer 1986, 74. There Schäfer also discusses the heavenly benefits that they lost.

99. Brock 1982, 28 n. 6. Brock remarks, and I have noted below in n. 113, that, according to the reverse idea, which was current in late antiquity, the soul strips off the body during its ascent through the heavenly spheres. See further on this in Minov 2016b, 137–62. In this paper, Minov primarily discusses the idea that paradise was located on a mountain, concerning which, see n. 46 to annotation 16 in the present volume. Lewy (1956, 413–17) discusses the idea of the ascent and descent of the soul through the seven heavenly spheres, and Lewy's work was reedited by Michel Tardieu in 2011 with additional notes. The number seven of the spheres to which Lewy refers is constituted of six for the planets and one for the fixed stars. The idea of the sublunar sphere is discussed at the end of annotation 22.

100. On this East Syrian tradition, see Brock 1982, 17–18.

9. Adam and Eve in the Garden

of a serpent or the Leviathan.[101] After all, such reptiles shed their skins, which thus become available without killing any creature. In a variant on this theme, according to Pirqe R. El. 20.3, Adam and Eve had coats of glory from serpent's skin. If we adhere to the apocryphal expansions of the narrative line of Genesis, then these garments of skin are clearly to be distinguished from the luminous clothing with which the protoplasts were endowed at the time of their creation.[102]

To these various speculations about the skin from which God made the protoplasts' clothing, we may add a Muslim tradition adduced by Stephen D. Ricks, which relates that down to the expulsion Adam and Eve were covered with hair which formed a hairy garment. They shucked it at the time of the expulsion.[103] This idea has penetrated an early modern Greek folk-tale about the Cheirograph of Adam, one assumes from Muslim sources.[104]

According to the Syriac CT 3.5 (*MOTP* 1:542), a further variant on this theme is that Satan too, being an angel, had glorious garments which he lost when he fell and that he subsequently disguised himself as an angel to deceive Eve.[105] The apocryphal Struggle of the Archangel Michael with Satanel, which exists in Greek, Slavonic, and Romanian is focused on Satanel's having stolen his celestial, glorious garments from heaven. By his fall, he had lost the right to wear them, and the archangel Michael was tasked with recovering them from him and returning them to heaven.[106]

---

101. See Ricks 2000, 204–5 for many further references. See also Orlov 2023.
102. Special eschatological clothing is also referred to in 3 Ezra 2.11, 45 as well as in Herm. Sim. 8.12–14 and Ascen. Isa. 1.5, 3.25, 4.16–17, 9.14, 26. On baptismal dress as these Edenic garments, see Toepel (2012), 313–14. This subject is very substantial and is beyond the scope of the present Annotation.
103. Ricks 2000, 206–7, 210. Badalanova Geller 2017b, 275–77 deals with hairy garments in South Slavonic legends and parallels to them. Many more reformulations of Gen 3:21 could be culled from the apocryphal Adam literature.
104. Stone 2002, 102; Megas 1928, 100.
105. Observe that, in LAE 9.1, Satan is said to "transfigure himself into the brilliance of an angel" (Latin) or "took on the form of a cherub with splendid attire" (Armenian) and similarly in the other versions. See Anderson and Stone 1999, 11–11E.
106. See Miltenova 1981. Edward Jeremiah is preparing an edition of the Greek text of this work. The Slavonic and Romanian versions are being edited by Alexander Kulik and Emanouela Timotin respectively as part of the same project. This legendary formulation may be related to the idea forwarded by Orlov 2011, who discusses in

Garments of Glory and Priestly Vestments

The glorious garments are sometimes associated or identified with priestly garb and vestments.[107] Stephen N. Lambden suggests that the complex garments described in Ezek 28:13 are attributed to Adam in Eden because of his priestly character: compare the elaborate description of the high priest in Sir 49:16, 50:11.[108] It is also very likely that the glory of the priestly vestments and the glory and brilliance of the divine presence are related. After all, the priests alone could enter the holier parts of the temple and, on certain occasions, even the adytum or holy of holies; some texts say explicitly that the priests are like angels.[109] This sacred place was thought to be filled with the divine presence; see, for example, Isa 6:1. For a related view concerning the tent of meeting, see Exod 34:34–35. It seems clear, therefore, considering the discussion above, that Adam's glory is related to the priestly glory.

At the beginning of book 2 of the Samaritan biblical poem Tibat Marqe, there is an eulogy to the spring of Eden, which is striking in terms

---

detail not just the correspondence of Adam's garments and angelic garb, but also their being transferred to Adam from Satan.

107. See Ricks 2000, 212–14 and Lambden 1992, 79. The glory of the priesthood is also celebrated in Samaritan sources, see TM 2.13. I will discuss this priestly dimension further below. Adam's partaking of royal, priestly and prophetic characteristics is a common theme in Armenian ancient and medieval literature; see Stone 2013, index, s.v. "Adam, royal characteristics of." This is, of course, also connected with the Old Adam–New Adam typology, and Christ is also endowed with these same three functions. Observe that according to Armenian Pseudo-Epiphanius, *Homilies*, on his expulsion from Eden, Adam received both priesthood and kingship (Dorfmann-Lazarev 2020b, 323). Adam's priestly function is also recorded in CT 5.27 (*MOTP* 1:544), which refers to "the first priest, Adam." On Adam's priestly characteristics, see Toepel 2012, 313.

108. See the detailed study of this chapter in Mulder 2003. Many details there are relevant to the present annotation; note particularly the description of the vestments (pp. 125–26); the use of the special garments (pp. 147–49); and the discussion of כבוד and תפארת (pp. 147–48). Schneider (2012) deals with many of these issues in very considerable detail. Orlov (2011) discusses the connection of Adam's garments with the garments of the high priest in the Yom Kippur ceremonies. Garments of light also play a role in some gnostic texts such as Gos. Phil. 69, 90, 107.

109. Barzilai 2007, 14. See Anderson 1988, 202 on Eden as temple and Mazor 2012, 167–70.

of the Ezekiel text quoted above and also of Zech 14.¹¹⁰ Of course, here and in other places where Tibat Marqe is cited, one should remember that it is a Samaritan work, and the nature of its relations with Jewish and also with Christian parabiblical material is not yet deeply understood. I give the references to this work basically as parallels rather than as instances of the same ideas, but it is possible that it may eventuate that this practice of mine is too cautious.

Eschatological Brilliance

The Edenic and heavenly luminosity will be restored to the saints at the eschaton, or else it will be granted to prophets or seers when they come into the presence of the Godhead.¹¹¹ This is the meaning of the white garments of the saints according to Rev 7:9, 13 and 2 En. 66.8. Furthermore, 1 En. 62.15–16 reads:

> 15 And the righteous and the chosen will have arisen from the earth,
> and have ceased to cast down their faces,
> and have put on the garment of glory.
> 16 And this will be your garment, the garment of life from the Lord of Spirits.
> and your garments will not wear out,¹¹²
> and your glory will not fade in the presence of the Lord of Spirits.

---

110. TM 13, 157. It is worth bearing in mind that the prophetic books are not included in Samaritan scriptures.

111. Golitzin (2003) compares the Qumran "glory of Adam" with the light that the contemplative will achieve and the notions of the pseudo-Macarian *Homilies* in which light plays a central role as a manifestation of enlightenment. This concept can be seen an expression of a mystical interiorization of eschatology. Also compare Orlov 2002. Additional bibliography can be found in Rubin and Kosman 1997. Rubin and Kosman investigate the significance of priestly clothing and the concurrent demand for purity. They analyze the significance of special clothing both on a vertical axis that opposes heavenly and earthly garb and on a horizontal axis from primordial clothing to eschatological, providing a useful analytic perspective. Their examples are drawn from rabbinic literature. A particularly explicit and striking instance is the statement in Tanh. Toledoth 12, that Adam is to wear high priestly garments in Eden. Thus, the priestly is tied with the protological and the protological with the eschatological. See further n. 80 above.

112. The miraculous nature of clothes "that do not wear out" is already to be observed in Deut 8:4.

In this section, the eschatological garment of glory is also called the "garment of life." Compare this passage with 2 Cor 5:1–4, which speaks of the reversal of nakedness by means of a heavenly tent = body.

In Ascension of Isaiah, these eschatological garments are called "garments of the saints." One interpretation regards the body as the garment of the soul and maintains that the soul will be restored to its celestial character (it is an image of God, of course) by being stripped of its bodily garment.[113] In Ascen. Isa. 9.9, we read, "And there I saw Enoch and all who were with him, stripped of the garments of the flesh, and I saw them in their garments of the upper world, and they were like angels." This details exactly the same concept.

In more general terms, light in the eschatological state is tied into the light of "the seven days" in Isa 30:27, which reads, "moreover the light of the moon will be as the light of the sun, and the light of the sun will be sevenfold, as the light of seven days"[114] when Israel is restored. An ancient exegete could readily understand this to refer to the seven days of creation and the brightness of Eden.

Moses's Shining Face

Another aspect of shining countenances already appears in the Pentateuch. Although it has nothing to do directly with Adam's Edenic luminosity, the transformation of Moses's countenance described in Exod 34 exhibits the same underlying concept that proximity to the Deity causes luminosity. Exodus 34 describes Moses's second ascent of Mount Sinai.[115] There he remained for forty days and received the commandments. They were revealed to Moses in a theophany, vividly described: God says to him (33:22–23): "And while *my glory* passes by I will put you in a cleft of the rock, and I will cover you with my hand until I have passed by; then I

---

113. De Conick and Fossum 1991. That perception influenced the gnostic Gospel of Thomas and other early Christian writings. See also 2 En. 66.8. Above, Brock's rather similar characterization of the ascent of the soul in the Hellenistic-Roman world was discussed; see n. 99 to this annotation.

114. RSV reads "seven days," though the Hebrew has the definite article, "the seven days."

115. Note that the historical-critical issue of the precise dating of the Pentateuchal accounts is not relevant to our analysis, nor are other aspects of the historical study of the Pentateuch. From the perspective of Questionnaire, the Pentateuch contains true accounts of the history of the remote past.

9. Adam and Eve in the Garden 99

will take away my hand, and you shall see my back; but my face shall not be seen." As a result of this vision of God, so Exod 34:29 says, when he descended from Mount Sinai, "Moses did not know that the skin of his face shone[116] because he had been talking with God." As a result of his theophanic encounter with God, Moses's face is said to be shining[117] and glorious; the people cannot bear to look at him, so he wears a veil. In this incident, the revelation of God results in the insupportable brilliance of Moses's countenance.[118] Also compare the imagery in 2 Cor 5:2–4. By the way, it is interesting to observe that §26 of the Armenian work Of Moses and Aaron reads: "For, from the revelation of God, Moses's face shone with the brilliance of the life to come and with that which Adam had in

---

116. Hebrew קָרַן, a famous *crux interpretationis*, of which "shone" is clearly one possible understanding. On the interpretation of this crux in iconography, see Mellinkoff 1970, 1–2 and *passim*. Compare 1 En. 14.24, where God speaks to Enoch "with his own mouth." There is, moreover, a seeming inner contradiction in Exodus. In Exod 33:20, we read, "you cannot see my face; for man shall not see me and live," and similarly, in v. 23 of the same chapter, God hides his face from Moses. In Exod 33:11, however, the text says the opposite, that "thus the LORD used to speak to Moses face to face, as a man speaks to his friend." See the discussion of this tension by Sanders 2002, 401–2.

117. The Samaritan poetic work Tibat Marqe celebrates the brightness of Moses's face (TM 2.40), and the same work says in 5.35 that Moses wore the ray of light all his life (see Exod 34:29–30). Moses played a particularly exalted role in Samaritan belief. Furthermore, in TM 5.33 we read that Moses's glory was that which Adam had cast off in Eden and that his face shone until the day of his death; see also the discussion in Tal 2019, 509. This is not the only text that connects Adam's and Moses's glory, and above note was taken of lines of affiliation between these two figures (see p. 93).

118. Sanders 2002, 402 says: "Divine contact has changed Moses, and this change is manifest in the way he looks." Observe the brightness that accompanies the visions of the divine in Ezek 1:26–28 and Dan 7:9–10. On Moses shining face, see also Golitzin 2001, 132. The shared brightness strengthens, of course, the priestly connections of garment of glory (see above, pp. 96–97, text section 3). The symbolic understanding of the various parts of the priestly vestments is shown forth by a quite different use of the word "garment" that may be observed in LAB 20.2. That passage speaks of Joshua's transformation when, after Moses's death he puts on Moses's "garment of wisdom … girdle of knowledge." With this description in LAB compare the "breastplate of understanding" and the other significant items listed in the passage describing the vesting of Levi as a priest in T. Levi 8.2. Brightness is not mentioned in this connection. It appears, therefore, that in antiquity a symbolic exegesis of the various parts of the high-priestly vestments was cultivated.

Eden."[119] Here the three are tied together, Moses after his vision of the Divine, Adam's protological luminosity, and eschatological glory.

The temple was thought to be filled with the divine presence and thus was associated with brightness.[120] The brightness in the tent of meeting is implied by Exod 34:34–35. Both draw upon the idea that brightness is a predominant feature of the Divine epiphanies. That idea occurs often in the Bible; see, among many texts, 2 Sam 22:13, Isa 60:19, Ezek 1:4, 1:27, and Rev 1:16, 10:1. In the transfiguration, Jesus's "face shone like the sun and his garments became white as light" (Matt 17:2, Mark 9:2–3).[121]

Transformed Nebuchadnezzar

Matthias Henze points out and analyzes parallels between the falls of Adam and Nebuchadnezzar. These two falls, moreover, are related to the fall of Hellel ben Shachar in Isa 14:11–14 and 19, which passage is applied to Nebuchadnezzar's fate.[122] Henze finds the connection between Adam and Nebuchadnezzar to be their loss both of glory and of their royal status.

Is it fanciful to see a similarity in Adam's bodily changes when he was expelled from the garden to those that Nebuchadnezzar undergoes in Dan 4, transforming from a human, royal state to a lesser, bestial state and then back again to royal standing after penitence?[123] I think this resemblance rather likely. In Syriac sources, Henze points out, the type of the "hairy ascetic"[124] is applied to the transformed Nebuchadnezzar, and we are drawn to compare the ascetic's successful penitence with the Babylonian king's repentance and restoration to royal splendor.

Partly overlapping is the tale of Abraham's coming to the hairy Melchizedek, according to various Melchizedek apocrypha,[125] cutting his

---

119. *Arm Apoc* 6:148.
120. On the temple as pertaining to heavenly reality, see Otzen 1984, 199–215; in particular, see pp. 201–3.
121. Bucur and Ivanovici 2019, at n. 41 argue that Jesus, in his transfiguration, is actually evoking Adam's glory, and Mount Tabor is a "new Sinai." S. Efrati suggests in oral communication that this may be related to Moses's face according to Exod 34.
122. Henze 2001, 556–62
123. See Henze 2001, 567.
124. On this figure, see Williams 1925.
125. Concerning Armenian Melchizedek apocrypha and on possible Greek sources of some of these traditions, see *Arm Apoc* 3:5–12 and several texts published in that volume. The Melchizedek tradition is very rich, and several interesting and

hair and nails and bathing him.[126] Thus we read in the Story of Terah and of Father Abraham §§47–48: "When the day came, he set forth and proceeded to the place and found (him), that his appearance was unlike a human appearance. But he was dressed, and the hair of his head descended as far as his knees. And his spine (back) was like a tortoise's spine and his nails were a span long."[127]

Cutting his hair and nails and bathing him are all preparations for his taking on priestly function and robes.[128] The actions by which Abraham domesticates Melchizedek are readily comparable with Dan 4:30, where it says of Nebuchadnezzar's undomestication, his taking on the characteristics of the "wild man, hairy ascetic," that "his hair grew as long as eagles' feathers, and his nails were like birds' claws." This coincidence is not random. If this process is, in turn, related to the priestly robes as garments of glory (which I have discussed above on pp. 96–97) and to Eden's temple-like purity (see part 7, n. 4), we have traveled a complete circle. Melchizedek has returned from his wild state and been garbed with priestly robes,[129] just as Adam lost his luminous robes on sinning, and they will be restored to the righteous in the eschaton.[130]

The notion of the eschatological temple conceived of Eden also illuminates the importance of the understanding of Adam's glorious clothing as high-priestly vestments.[131] The same theme occurs in Ezek 28, the oracle against the king of Tyre. Here, too, the prophet associates Eden

---

learned studies of it have been written recently. See Dochhorn 2004; Böttrich 2010; 2012; Piovanelli 2012.

126. For this detail, also found in the *Palaea*, see Flusser 1971, 58.

127. See *Arm Apoc* 3:143 and 162. A similar description is found in Concerning Abraham's Hospitality §46, in Stone, *Arm Apoc* 3:46, 175.

128. See The Story of Terah and of Father Abraham §§47 and 54 in *Arm Apoc* 3:162, 165, and index, s.v. "Melchizedek, priestly function of." See also Concerning Abraham's Hospitality §§46–48 in *Arm Apoc* 3:175–76.

129. Story of Terah §54. Satran 1989, 119–20, follows up another ramification of the unchecked growth of fingernails and hair, which also develops from Dan 4.

130. On the relationship of the temple and the garden of Eden, see Ratzon 2018. On p. 16, she remarks on Edenic imagery connecting with the imagery of the temple. See particularly n. 4 on that page. The Eden language in biblical literature is the subject of the detailed study of Stordalen 2000.

131. The priesthood is included in the list of Things Adam Lost; see above table 2 on pp. 83–84.

with the temple, an association that includes elements of priestly garb.[132] Thus, Eden and the temple are connected, and consequently, one may assume that a relationship between Adam's glory and the high priestly robes exists, the more so since Adam's priestly function was well established in the tradition.[133] This is another entrancing aspect of this fecund garment imagery.

Prophetic Commissioning and Priestly Purification

In two relevant passages, the prophetic literature narrates the commissioning of a prophet and a high priest before the heavenly court.[134] In these instances, in the books of Zechariah and of Isaiah, the heroes, who are respectively a high priest, Joshua, and a prophet, Isaiah, are purified from earthly dross as an essential part of accepting the divine summons. It is noteworthy that Isaiah's commissioning before the heavenly court takes place in the holy place inside the temple.

Most strikingly, Zech 3 presents this purification as a change of garments. In that chapter, the prophet sees the high priest Joshua standing before an angel in the heavenly court, "clothed with filthy garments."[135] The angel orders his garments to be replaced with "rich apparel" and "a clean turban" (3:3–5), using terminology that refers specifically to priestly vestments. This change of clothing is symbolic of his being cleansed from sin and his renewed consecration to his priestly function, which is understood to promise well for the future.[136] Here, the new vestments play the same role as the angel's cauterizing of Isaiah's mouth in his call vision, in Isa 6:7. Isaiah relates that, in his vision received in the temple, the angel

---

132. Himmelfarb 1991, 66; see also Stordalen 2000, 394–96. Both scholars adduce persuasive demonstrations that the temple spoken of as Eden.

133. On Adam's priestly function and Eden viewed as temple, see Anderson 1988, 202–3, 206–8.

134. The literature on the divine court is extensive. See Cross 1973, 186–90 on the early period. These ideas were revived at Qumran which shows how deeply embedded such concepts were in ancient Jewish culture; see Ben-Dov 2016.

135. See Orlov 2011, 6–7. On p. 8, Orlov argues for the Adamic background to the crucial passage in Apoc. Abr. 13.14 referring to Adam's garments. Since Abraham's role, according to him, is priestly, its possible connection to an Adamic arrière-fond is indeed intriguing. Also compare 2 En. 22.

136. This is the more intriguing because of the language of the body as a garment, which I discussed above; see n. 99.

takes a burning coal from a brazier, "and he touched my mouth and said: 'Behold, this has touched your lips; your guilt is taken away, and your sin forgiven.'" The prophet is then able to answer the divine summons (Isa 6:8). Jeremiah, too, undergoes a divine touch on his lips in his call vision in Jer 1:9, which has the same function of making the prophet's lips worthy of bearing and pronouncing the divine word.[137]

In Zech 3, the incident related after Joshua's consecration is that the angel indicates to Joshua that, if he observes the divine commandments, he will have "right of access among those who are standing," that is, the angels standing in the divine court before God.[138] His new, clean apparel signifies that he has this angelic status *in potentia*.[139] This quite strikingly resembles 2 En. J 22.8 in a passage, the dynamic of which recalls that Zech 3.

> And the Lord said to Michael, "Go, and extract Enoch from [his] earthly clothing. And anoint him with my delightful oil and put him in the clothes of my glory." … 8 and so Michael … anointed me and he clothed me. And the appearance of that ointment is like … the rays of the glittering sun. 10 And I looked at myself and I had become like one of his glorious ones, and there was no observable difference.[140]

---

137. On the meanings of "change of garments" in Christian, baptismal contexts, see Meeks 1972, 183–86; this is also related to Adam's tale (Meeks 1972, 187–89). The newly-baptized catechumen was garbed in a white robe, which relates to the eschatological angelic robe of the righteous; see also, for example, Rev 3:5, 18, 4:4.

138. Does "standing" indicate those who can stand in the Lord's presence? The expected position might be prostration. "Those standing," then, might then resemble the angels of the presence, those archangels that serve directly before the divine throne.

139. In some texts, explicitly, the clothing is the clothing of the soul, that is, the body. The ascent to the heavens involves stripping the soul naked of the body. Does the high priest Joshua's new apparel thus indicate that he is to receive a celestial body. This is discussed in part 9, n. 99 above.

140. See Golitzin 2001, 131. On the heavenly oil, see Stone, 1979. Of course, anointing with fragrant oil is part of the ceremony of consecration of priests and, naturally, of kings. It is not by chance that the recipe for the oil is one of the subjects dealt with by Questionnaire in part 17. See Exod 30:25, 35:8, Lev 8:12, 30, and elsewhere for priestly anointing. On the anointing of kings, see 1 Sam 10:1 (Saul) and 16:3 (David) and 1 Kgs 1:39, 2 Kgs 9:3, etc.

Another instance of an almost angelified prophet is found in Apoc. Zeph. 8. In the heavenly scene described there, myriads of angels bow down to the prophet, who is clothed in angelic garb.[141]

The passage in Zech 3 speaks not just of clean garments but makes it explicit that these are *priestly* garments. The special, beautiful ceremonial robes of the high priest are lauded in sources from the Second Temple period. Perhaps the best-known passages are the descriptions of the high priest in Sir 50 (early second century BCE) and in Philo's (lived ca. 25 BCE–ca. 50 CE) *Spec.* 1.66-97 and *QE* 11.51-124.[142] In Ben Sira, this description of the high priest forms the climax of the long passage called "Praise of the Fathers of Old," which invokes biblical heroes of the past. Ben Sira 50:6-11 graphically conveys the impression that the vested high priest made upon the people. I have marked the words that draw on the semantic fields of glory, brilliance, and wonder.

> 6 Like the *morning star* among the clouds, like the moon when it is full.
> 7 like the *sun shining* upon the temple of the Most High, and like the *rainbow gleaming in glorious clouds.*
> 8 Like roses in the days of the first fruits, like lilies by a spring of water, like a green shoot on Lebanon on a summer day;
> 9 like *fire* and incense in the censer, like a vessel of *hammered gold* adorned with all kinds of *precious stones*;
> 10 like an olive tree putting forth its fruit, and like a cypress towering in the clouds.
> 11 When he put on his *glorious robe and clothed himself with superb perfection* and went up to the holy altar, *he made the court of the sanctuary glorious.*[143]

Nearly three centuries later, the priest, general, and historian, Josephus, in his *A.J.* 3.151-180 (first century), gave a very detailed description of the high priestly garb and of his vesting, emphasizing once more his glorious

---

141. The preceding two pages of the unique manuscript of Apocalypse of Zephaniah are missing but presumably related an ascent vision or experience of which this part of the climax survives. On Apocalypse of Zephaniah, see n. 92 above. The scene of Enoch's acceptance in the divine court is also described in 1 En. 71.
142. On the temple and vestments, see van den Hoek 1988, 116-47.
143. See further on this passage, Bucur and Ivanovici 2019, n. 25. At n. 28, they draw attention to the image of Aaron as high priest in the Dura Europos synagogue, and particularly to the vestments he wears. There is a reproduction of the fresco in their work.

appearance. Moreover, Josephus gives an interpretation of the vestments as representing the cosmos.[144]

In these instances—Isa 6, Jer 1, and Zech 3—a purification of the hero, high priest, or prophet from earthly dross is described. As already noted,[145] Exod 34:29 describes a similar transformation of Moses after his experiencing the theophany on Mount Sinai. That verse says that, "when Moses came down from Mount Sinai, with the two tables of the testimony in his hand…, Moses did not know that the skin of his face shone because he had been talking with God."

In Rev 6:11, 7:9, et cetera, the righteous in heaven are said to wear white robes. In the ceremony of the vesting of an Armenian Christian priest who is going to celebrate the Mass, we read the following: "with wonderful power didst thou create Adam in a lordly image and didst clothe him with gracious glory in the garden of Eden, the abode of delights" (trans. Brightman). Through Christ's suffering, man "hath again been made immortal, clad in a garment that none can take from him."[146] The word "again" indicates that this refers back to Adam, who lost immortality. While the choir sings the text just quoted, the priest in his prayer says: "at this hour when I make bold to draw nigh to the same spiritual service of thy glory, to be stripped of all mine ungodliness which is the garment of filthiness and be adorned with thy light."[147] Here then, the priest being vested is likened unto Adam who wears a garment of glory.[148] All these connections between Adam and the Priest, between Eden and the temple, buttress the idea that Adam's luminous Edenic clothing was (also?) high priestly vestments.

Future Glory

An eschatological dimension of the celestial or Edenic glory is, of course, implied by many of the texts we have discussed. In the future, Adamic glory, which is the angelic and the heavenly glory, will be restored to the

---

144. Observe above, n. 118 to the present part, where I discuss the symbolic meanings attributed to the various vestments.
145. See pp. 99–100 above.
146. Brightman 1896, 412–14.
147. Brightman 1896, 413. The liturgy at this point is influenced by the language of Zech 3:3–4.
148. For another translation, see Nersoyan 1984, 4–5.

righteous. This idea is, of course, implied by the well-known saying: τὰ πρῶτα ὡς τὰ ἔσχατα (see Barn. 5.13). This correspondence of the protological and the eschatological glory is very striking in some Qumran texts, probably the most famous being 1QS IV, 22–23. In that passage, the upright are promised access to divine and angelic wisdom and "all the glory of Adam." Similarly, in CD III, 20, the same "glory of Adam" is promised to first adherents of the covenant. The basic idea is that the eschatological righteous, or alternatively duly vested and officiating priests, were clothed in (garments of) glory that are a restoration of the Edenic luminous garments of Adam.[149] Their clothing, in turn, is sometimes spoken of as the clean, white heavenly garments of the angels or "glorious ones" (cf. 2 En. 22.8-10). This idea is widespread in Armenian sources, though its origin was not there, as may be seen most explicitly from the passage Zech 3:4–5, which I have discussed on pages 102–4 above.

In Ascen. Isa. 9.9, we read: "And there I saw Enoch and all who were with him, stripped of the garments of the flesh, and I saw them in their garments of the upper world, and they were like angels, standing there in great glory," and the passage of 2 En. 22.8-10 that I quoted above on page 103 relates the same. Moreover, the verses from Ascension of Isaiah clearly talk of the body of flesh as a garment.[150] The same clothing metaphor is observed in the discourse of comfort extended to Jerusalem in Bar 5:1–3, which applies it to the ruined city and the hope for its restoration.

> 1 Take off the garment of your sorrow and affliction, O Jerusalem, and put on forever the beauty of the glory from God. 2 Put on the robe of the righteousness from God; put on your head the diadem of the glory of the Everlasting. 3 For God will show your splendor everywhere under heaven.

Of course, the language of investment with glory or splendor endows this passage with future hope. The use of this language in Baruch, together with that in Zech 3 discussed above, shows the currency of this terminol-

---

149. See the description of the eschatological glory of the righteous in 2 Bar. 51.3–10. See Bucur and Ivanovici 2019, n. 33.

150. De Conick and Fossum 1991, esp. 124–28. They discuss stripping of the garment, like in Gosp. Thom. 37, as belonging in a baptismal context. See also Maguire 1987, 363–73. See above, nn. 102 and 137. Here, the Hellenistic idea that the bodily garment is stripped from the ascending soul is incorporated into Christian understanding of the ascent of the soul.

ogy during the last half-millennium BCE. Later, under the influence of body—spirit dualism, which became current in the Hellenistic period and later, the idea that the body is the garment of the soul appears.[151]

---

151. See succinctly Brock 1982, 21–23 and 33–34 dealing with with Hellenistic body-spirit concepts. That idea of Brock's is discussed in part 9, n. 99.

Parts 10–18
Noah to Exodus, the Oil of Anointing,
and Prophets' Names

10

Expulsion from Eden up to the Flood

The subjects of this section of the text of Questionnaire arise from consideration of the biblical text as it relates the story of the first human generations, but the subjects discussed here are not actually drawn from the Genesis narrative itself. Such parabiblical issues include certain aspects of Adam's progeny, Cain and Abel and their descendants down to Noah, together with the beginnings of the story of the Sethites and Cainites. The tale of the Sethites and the Cainites, together with the incident of the sons of God and the daughters of humans (Gen 6:1–4), explain the human wicked conduct that brought about the flood.

TEXT

M682 / fol. 7b.17–fol. 7g.9

10.1/ Հարց: Կային ընդէ՞ր սպան զԱբէլ:

Պատասխանի. Վասն Բ.(2) նախանձու. նախ՝ զի Աբէլ ընդիրն ի խաշանց մատոյց պատարագ, Աստուած հաճեցաւ: Իսկ Կային հողագործ գյողին գործենոյ մատոյց, եւ ոչ ընդունեցաւ, այլ ասաց Աստուած. «Ուղիղ մատուցեր, բայց ուղիղ ոչ ընտրեցեր. առ քեզ լիցի դարձ նորա:»

Եւ Բ.(2) նախանձն, զի Կային դրախտոս եւ ծառս դարմանէր եւ նովաւ ուրախանայր, իսկ Աբէլ ցանկայր դրախտին Աստուծոյ. լուեալ ի հօրէն. զԿայենին արհամարհէր:

10.2/ Հարց: Ո՞րք են Է.(7) յանցանքն Կայենի:

Պատասխանի. Պատարագն անարժան. նախանձ եղբօրն, խաբել ի զրոսանս, սպանանել, առաջին սպանող՝ եղբայրասպան, եւ ստեցն

Աստուծոյ թէ՝ Ո՛չ գիտեմ։ Վասն որոյ է.(7) պաժտիժ¹ ընկալաւ յԱստուծոյ։ Նախ՝ Անիծեալ լիցիս. Բ.(2) յերկրի. Գ.(3) գործել հանապազ, Դ.(4) երկիր պտուղ ոչ տացէ: Ե.(5) երերալ մարմնով, Զ.(6) տատանել հոգով, Է.(7) կօտօշն:

10.3/ Հարց: Քանի՞ ամաց էր Աբէլ:
Պատասխանի. Երեսուն ամաց Աբէլ էր, եւ Կ.(60) զԿային, զի Լ.(30) ամին ծնանէր Եւայ Ա.(1) ուստր եւ Ա.(1) դուստր, զի Ձ. (900) տարին Լ.(30) փոր ծնաւ. յետին դուստր առաջի տղային առնոյր կին:

10.4/ Կային ծնաւ զԵնովք, նա՝ զԳայերիդադ, նա՝ զՄայէլ, նա՝ զՄաթուսադայ: նա՝ զՂամեք, որ սպան զԿայէն:

Եւ թէ՝ էր սպան:
Չի ազգին իւրոյ նախատինքն բառնի յաշխարհէ:

10.5/ Ղամեք ծնաւ զԱդդա, եւ նա՝ զԹոբէլ որ է հայր այնոցիկ որք անասնաբոյծք են եւ վրանօք շրջին, եւ Յուբալ եղբայր նորին երգս եւ քնարս արար: Եւ քոյր նոցա Նոյեմ արար զարդս կանանց, գծարիր եւ գանգոյր.

10.6/ Ադամ յետ Աբէլի, ծնաւ զՍէթ եւ այլսն եւ մեռաւ ՋԼ. (930) ամաց:² / fol. 7c / Սէթ ծնաւ զԵնովս եւ մեռաւ ՋՀ. (970) ամաց: *blank, approx. 15 letter spaces.*

10.7/ Սա մարգարէացաւ թէ՝ Ի բազմանալ մեղացն շնչելոց է Աստուած զաշխարհս: Եւ արար Բ. (2) սիւն՝ Ա. (1) պղնձի³ եւ միւսն ադիսի եւ գրեաց զանցս ժամանակին եւ զանուանս կենդանեաց, զորս Ադամ անուանեաց. «Չի թէ հրով անցցէ, ասէ, պղինձն այրի եւ ադիսն մնաս, եւ թէ ջրով՝ ադիսն ապականի եւ պղինձն մնաս»:

10.8/ Սա յուսացաւ կոչել զանուն Տեառն Աստուծոյ եւ մարգարէացաւ, թէ՝ Դարձեալ մտանելոց եմք ի դրախտն: Սա ծնաւ զԿայնան եւ մեռաւ ՋՀ. (970) ամաց: Կայնան ծնաւ զՄադադիէլ, եւ մեռաւ ՊՃ. (850) ամաց: Մադադիէլ ծնաւ զՅարեդ, եւ մեռաւ ՊՂԵ. (895) ամաց: Յարեդ ծնաւ զԵնոք եւ մեռաւ ՋԿԲ. (962) ամաց:

10.9/ Ենովք ծնաւ զՄաթուսադայ, եւ վերափոխեցաւ ՅԿԷ. (367) ամաց: Մաթուսադայ ծնաւ զՂամեք եւ մեռաւ ՋԿԲ. (972) ամաց: Ղամեք ծնաւ զՆոյ եւ մեռաւ ՇԿԳ. (763) ամաց:

---

1. Sic!
2. This is the last word on the folio. A small coronis takes up some blank space on the line.
3. For the orthographical alternation of ծ/ձ, see Stone and Hillel 2012, 439, index, no. 300.

Translation

10.1/ Question: Why did Cain kill Abel?

Answer: On account to two envies:[4]

— the first (envy), because Abel offered the choicest of the sheep as a sacrifice God was pleased. But Cain, the farmer, offered the worst of the wheat and it was not accepted. Then God said, "You have made the offering correctly, but you did not select (the sacrifice) correctly, and you shall have its recompense."[5]

— And the second envy: for Cain cared for the garden and trees and was gladdened by that, but Abel desired the garden of God, having heard (of it) from his father. He (God) despised Cain's (offering).[6]

10.2/ Question: Which are Cain's seven transgressions.

Answer: unworthy offering, envy of (his) brother, deceit in playing, killing, (being) the first murderer,[7] fratricide, lying to God (by saying),[8] "I do not know."[9] On account of this, Cain received seven punishments from God: First, you shall be cursed;[10] second, from the earth/land;[11] third, to

---

4. See annotation 14 below.

5. This is one of two reasons suggested for Cain's fratricide; see also Abel and Cain §7. The phrase "and you shall have its recompense" is taken from Gen 4:7. There, however, its meaning is "its desire will be for you," while here in Questionnaire it means, apparently, "It, or its outcome, is returned to you." The same phrase is also taken up in History of the Forefathers §6. In §4 of that work, the overall phraseology is very similar to that here, particularly in God's reproach of Cain. See *Arm Apoc* 2:184. On Cain's envy, see also TM 4.36, 6.12.

6. The text apparently puts forward the notion that Cain cared for his own garden while Abel pined for the garden of Eden. See Minov 2020, 57–76, §6 on p. 71. Such a story as is found in this Syriac composition is not even hinted at in our text, though a variation on it may be observed in CT 5.22 (*MOTP* 1:544); compare also T. Adam 3.5.

7. It is not quite clear to me what the difference is between "killing" and "(being) the first murderer" that would make them count as two different transgressions.

8. For ease of understanding, I add "by saying."

9. Gen 4:9.

10. Gen 4:11–12. The numerals after "first" are cardinal digits in the Armenian text, but for the sake of English style, I have translated them as ordinals. This is frequently the situation in Armenian manuscript documents. The first two curses take up sequential phrases from Gen 4:12. The third and fourth summarize the next phrase of that verse. On varying lists of Cain's punishments, see the discussion in *Arm Apoc* 4:18–19.

11. Gen 4:11.

work always; fourth, the earth will give no fruit;[12] fifth, trembling of the body; sixth, affliction of the soul; [13] seventh, the horn.[14]

10.3/ Question: How many years old was Abel?

Answer: Abel was thirty years old, and Cain (was sixty).[15] For Eve bore one son and one daughter every thirty years. For in nine hundred years, she gave birth in thirty pregnancies.[16]

She would take the later daughter for the former son.[17]

10.4/ Cain begot Enoch, he—Gayeridrad, he—Mehujael, he—Methusael, he—Łamech who killed Cain.[18]

And why did he kill (him)? So that the shame of his family should be removed from the world.[19]

10.5/ Lamech begot Adda[20] and he, T'obēl,[21] who is the father of those who raise cattle and wander around with tents.[22] And Jubal, his brother

---

12. Gen 4:12.

13. Gen 4:11–12. RSV has "fugitive and wanderer." Armenian Gen 4:12 has երերեալ եւ տատանեալ, "shaking and trembling," deriving from LXX, which reads στένων καὶ τρέμων, "groaning and shaking." This is the text that is the basis of curses numbers five and six. It is a translation that took the Hebrew differently from the RSV.

14. The seventh, the horn, is one of the standard interpretations of the "sign" or "mark of Cain" in Gen 4:15. See Ginzberg 1909, 5:141 n. 28.

15. That is, at the time of the fratricide, Abel was thirty years old and Cain sixty. We have supplied the apparently elided words. On the significance of the age of thirty years, see the preceding part 9 n. 14 and below in the exegetical remark on Abel's age.

16. See the exegetical remark following the translation of §10 for the twin sisters.

17. See the discussion in the exegetical remarks immediately following. There are traditions of Cain being jealous of Abel, who had married his (Cain's) twin sister: see again annotation 14, below.

18. See Gen 4:17, 23. The following are the Armenian forms of the names: "he—Kayeridad, he—Maayel, he—Matʻusała, he—Łamekʻ." See my remarks following the translation concerning this incident.

19. See *Arm Apoc* 6:261, 274. Similar reasoning may be observed in History of the Forefathers §§15–16; Abel §5.3; and the same notion is once again to be found in Armenian Pseudo-Ephrem, *Commentary on Genesis* seen in the translation of Mathews 1998, 55.

20. This agrees neither with the LXX nor with the MT. According to Gen 4:19, Adda (Adah) is one of Lamech's wives, who bore Jubal (4:20). Considering the formulaic character of §§18–19, the Armenian author of Questionnaire may have thought Adda to be Cainite Lamech's son and the father of Tobēl; compare Gen 4:20. Conceivably, the same Armenian text might be translated "Adda and she" though this seems forced.

21. Gen 4:20; and there, the name is Jabal, for which Arm Genesis has Յուբէլ,

10. Expulsion from Eden up to the Flood

made songs and lyres.[23] And their sister Noyēm[24] made women's ornaments, and rouge.[25]

10.6/ Adam, after Abel, begot Seth and the others, and he died at 930 years. Seth begot Enosh and died at 970 years.[26]

10.7/ And he prophesied that with the increase of sins, God is going to destroy this world. And he made two pillars, one of copper and the other of brick, and he wrote (on them) the passage of time and the names of the animals that Adam had named. "For if it[27] passes away by fire," he said, "the copper will be burned up and the brick (will) remain, and if (it passes away) by water, the brick will be destroyed, and the copper (will) remain."[28]

10.8/ He hoped to call the name of the Lord God[29] and prophesied that we are going to enter the garden again.[30] He begot Kaynan (Kenan),

---

Yovbēl. As far as I know, Յուբալ, "Yubał," here seems to be an idiosyncratic variant of Questionnaire.

22. That is, nomads: see Gen 4:20.

23. See the same idea also in Sethites and Cainites §10 (Stone 2021c, 205).

24. The name of Noah's wife is Noyem Zara, deriving ultimately from the name Amzara found in Jub. 4.33, 1QGenApoc VI, 7, in both instances (with slight variation). Amzara, which may derive from Hebrew אם זרע, "mother of seed," is also witnessed in the tenth-eleventh century Syriac text published by Minov 2020, 70. In the Armenian tradition, Noah's wife is called Noyem Zara. That name is composed of E(A)mzara to which "Noy = Noah" has been prefixed: so, Wives of the Patriarchs (*Arm Apoc* 2:90–91, 97—manuscript J1529); History of the Forefathers to Abraham §11 and M2182 (*Arm Apoc* 4:58–59, 62) elsewhere. However, Noyem, Jubal's sister in the Armenian tradition, is not the same person. She is mentioned in the Bible as Naamah (Gen 4:22).

25. This section evokes the teachings of the Watchers. See below in the subsection on "Descent of the Sethites from the mountain" on p. 142.

26. MT, LXX, and Arm have 912 years (Gen 5:8). This is also the reading of various chronological texts in *Arm Apoc* 4:29, 45, 61. The origin of the age of 970 for Seth's death is unclear.

27. That is, the world.

28. The two pillars tradition is discussed in the exegetical remarks directly following this text.

29. Gen 4:26. Here, as would be expected, the Armenian version of Genesis follows the LXX Greek version of this verse and so reads "hoped." The History of the Forefathers §§34–41 (*Arm Apoc* 2:196–199) gives as many as seven interpretations of this word.

30. On the Enoch figure, see Fraade 1984, 1998.

and he died at 970 years.³¹ Kaynan begot Małaliēl, and he died at 850 years. Małaliēl begot Jared, and he died at 895 years. Jared begot Enoch, and he died at 962 years.

10.9/ Enoch begot Methuselah, and he was translated at (the age of) 367 years.³² Methuselah begot Lamech and died at 972 years. Lamech begot Noah and died at 763 years, after the translation of Enoch to heaven.

Exegetical Remarks

§10.2. Seven Punishments of Cain

The number seven of Cain's punishments is presumably derived from Gen 4:15, "If anyone slays Cain, vengeance shall be taken on him sevenfold," particularly when that verse is compared with Gen 4:24, "If Cain is avenged sevenfold." The idea of compiling a list of punishments is shared by many sources. Jacob of Edessa (seventh century) lists Cain's seven sins and seven punishments in the fragment published by Dirk Kruisheer (1977, 192–93); see further T. Benj. 7.2–5. Another instance occurs in the Greek fragments of Philo's *Quaestiones et solutiones in Genesin*,³³ but no list is provided there. Also observe the long discussion in Pseudo-Ephrem, *Gen.* 3.³⁴ According to PH 11.1 (*MOTP* 1:603–4) as well, Cain committed seven sins. The number seven for his punishments also occurs in Repentance of Adam and Eve §§50–58; Yovhannēs Tʻlkurancʻi, *Rhymed History* 243–253; and History of the Forefathers §§20–21; as well as in PH 10.9–11.2 (*MOTP* 1:603–4), also with a list.

§10.2. Cain deceives Abel

This section considers the embroidery that relates that Cain tricked Abel into going to the field, and thus Abel became a victim through a decep-

---

31. This was also Seth's age when he died, according to Questionnaire.

32. His age is in accordance with Gen 5:23, except that there his life is 365 years long. This may be another instance of the commonly found confusion of five and seven, probably because of Armenian numerical notation, according to which these digits are graphically very similar. See part 14 n. 5, below on this variant and see Stone and Hillel, 42, index, no. 77. See also *Arm Apoc* 1:87.

33. Paramelle 1984, 45.

34. See Mathews 1998.

tive game. This is, in turn, a development of the reading of Arm. Gen 4:8, which reads, following the LXX: եկ երթիցուք ի դաշտ, "Come let us go to the field (or: plain)." The MT does not include this phrase, but immediately afterwards, it reads בהיותם בשדה, "while they were in the field." History of the Forefathers §§20–23 is a passage very close to Questionnaire here.[35] Indeed, the whole story, as related in History of Cain and Abel §§5–44,[36] is based on this understanding of the biblical text. The detail that, because Abel was the stronger, Cain had to overcome him by a trick during a game is not familiar outside the Armenian tradition. [Rabbinic sources transmit a tradition that Abel was stronger than Cain, and the latter overcame him through treachery, not as part of a game but rather during their deadly fight.–S.E.][37]

§10.3. On Abel's age

The idea that, in each of her numerous pregnancies, Eve bore twins and that each pair of twins was composed of one son and one daughter was widely known in rabbinic literature.[38] The same tradition is also found in other early Jewish sources and doubtless came about through the need to account for the wives of Cain and Abel, without whom they could not have had descendants.[39] It is noteworthy that, in 4 Ezra 10.43, the barren woman, symbol of Jerusalem, bore a child after thirty years. Moreover, according to the gospels, Jesus was about thirty years old when he was baptized (see Luke 3:23). Clearly, the number thirty was auspicious.[40]

It is, moreover, intriguing to observe also that the Greek and both the Armenian versions of LAE 1.1 report, with some variation, that eighteen years and two months after the expulsion, the twins Cain and Abel were born. This is a quite different tradition. However, manuscript B of Greek Life of Adam and Eve (Apocalypse of Moses) replaces that phrase with ἦσαν πενθοῦντες χρόνους τριάκοντα, "(Adam and Eve) were mourning for

---

35. See *Arm Apoc* 2:189–90. See on this, Kim 2001, 72–73.
36. Lipscomb 1990, 143–52, 158–67.
37. See Gen. Rab. 22.5 and further references in Ginzberg 1909, 5:139 n.19; Lipscomb 1990, 97.
38. See Gen. Rab. 22.2, b. Yevam. 63a; Ginzberg 1909, 1:108; 5:134–35, 138, 145.
39. See §10.3 above.
40. One possible explanation is that a generation was considered to be thirty years in length. See part 12, n. 21 for this idea.

thirty times," thus also showing familiarity with the tradition of thirty years.[41]

Both Armenian and other sources regularly say that Eve delivered twins every thirty years (see Abel and Cain §4; Repentance of Adam and Eve §§28–29, 79). Similarly, in History of the Forefathers §29, we read that after the birth of Seth: "he (that is, Adam) begot sons and daughters, thirty pregnancies (and) sixty children."[42] This information is echoed in History of the Forefathers §27, which mentions both thirty years' mourning and then the birth of Cain and his twin and, after another thirty years, Abel and his twin. We find the same in Abel and Other Pieces §1,[43] which agrees with the many Armenian texts that say that Cain was born thirty years after the expulsion and Abel thirty years later. Such is History of Adam and His Grandsons §1–3 and see commentary there.[44] Both Yovhannēs Tʿlkurancʿi, *On the Creation of the World* 229–232 and Mxitʿar Ayrivanecʿi (thirteenth century), *The History of the Armenians* 24 have the same information.[45] This rich subject is worthy of a fuller treatment separately. In addition to these Armenian sources, there are similar traditions in PH 16.3 (*MOTP* 1:605), and that text speaks of sixty sons of Adam who were thirty androgynes, likely a development of the idea of twins. In this context, it is notable that according to Gen. Rab. 8.1, the first human was created androgynous.

§10.4. Lamech killed Cain

The story of the Cainite Lamech who killed Cain arises from Gen 4:24 and is rather highly developed in Armenian.[46] The question posed in the second part of §10.1, "why did he kill him?," is actually a subsidiary question within a question. The idea that Lamech killed Cain to remove the shame from his family is found elsewhere in Armenian parabiblical

---

41. The origin of the time span of eighteen years and two months remains quite obscure.

42. see *Arm Apoc* 2:195. Adam's thirty begettings are discussed with parallels in *Arm Apoc* 2:92, where many sources are adduced.

43. On the twin sisters and their names, according to Ethiopian sources, see Witakowski 2017, passim.

44. *Arm Apoc* 2:92–93.

45. Stone 2005 and James Russell 1987, 182. See Ēmin 1860.

46. See Asya Bereznyak's excursus on the Cainite Lamech traditions in *Arm Apoc* 4:92–93. See for this event Tanh. Berešit 11; CT 8.7 (*MOTP* 1:547), and PH 13 (*MOTP* 1:604–5, respectively).

sources; see Questions and Answers from the Holy Books §14 in *Arm Apoc* 6, which says that Cainite Lamech killed Cain: "because of the dishonor of his family."

§10.7. The Two Pillars

The tradition of the two pillars is old, documented at least as far back as Josephus, *A.J.* 1.67–71. It is found in Greek and Armenian sources and discussed at length in History of the Forefathers §§41–44.[47] In that passage, the phrase "passage of time," which denotes that which was written on the pillars and probably indicates the course of history, is not to be found.[48] Other Armenian sources include this tradition, such as Abel §4.4 (*Arm Apoc* 2:151). The flood of fire is discussed in detail in annotation 23 below.

§10.7. The Names of the Animals

The corruption of the Adamic names of the animals is related in History of the Forefathers §42–43 published in *Arm Apoc* 2:199.

> And the writings on the two stelae told the names of all things, for he knew that by lispers, stutterers and stammerers the language was destined to be corrupted. 43 And they confused and changed the names of the objects that had come into being, which Adam had named and fixed them.

Naming was seen as an integral part of creation, and there were various attitudes toward this naming.[49] Hebrew was often viewed as the language in which creation took place.[50]

---

47. *Arm Apoc* 2:199–200.
48. *Arm Apoc* 2:151, 199–200. Observe that in History of the Forefathers §41, in this context the invention of writing is attributed to Seth (*Arm Apoc* 2:199). A quite developed Western legend of the two stelae, Seth, Enoch, and Solomon is to be found in an appendix to the Latin Life of Adam and Eve: Anderson and Stone 1999, 96E = Latin §52; in Jub. 8.1–4 a partly parallel tradition relates the discovery of ancient writing containing, inter alia, astronomical knowledge and omens. On the reception history of the two stelae tradition, see also Orlov 2001; Marie-Fritz 2004.
49. See Dorfmann-Lazarev 2022, 314–16. See also Badalanova Geller 2021b, 325–26. See also Stone 2007b on the function of naming.
50. See Jub. 12.27, which verse says that Hebrew was the language of creation. CT 24.10–11 (*MOTP* 1:558) claims that Syriac was the language from Adam to the

§10.8. Enosh's Prophecy

I know of no further occurrence of the idea that Enosh delivered a prophecy of return to Eden; such is lacking, for example, even from the long passage on Enosh in History of the Forefathers §§35–45 referred to in the preceding remarks. That passage and that cited in note 30 to this part do not call him a prophet. However, medieval Armenian usage is often to refer to Old Testament authors and certain other biblical characters as prophets. The general idea of Enosh foretelling Eden is to be found in History of the Forefathers §35, which exegetes Gen 4:26 in the Armenian Bible version. The idea comes from the latter half of the verse in Armenian, which reads նա յուսացաւ կոչել զանուն Տեառն Աստուծոյ, "he hoped to call (upon) the name of the Lord God." This phrase of Armenian version follows the Septuagint, which reads οὗτος ἤλπισεν ἐπικαλεῖσθαι τὸ ὄνομα κυρίου τοῦ θεοῦ, and it differs from the Hebrew text that is reflected in the RSV translation: "At that time men *began to call upon* the name of the LORD."[51] The point of History of the Forefathers §§35–41 is that Enosh "demonstrated the renewal of the corrupted image of humans" in several ways, underpinning the future hope by his example.

ANNOTATION 14. CAIN'S MOTIVE FOR FRATRICIDE

Questionnaire 10.1 raises the question of the reason for Cain's envy. His envy is not made explicit in the biblical text, which talks specifically of his anger and resentment, while his envy was, it seems, inferred from these two qualities. Moreover, the name Cain was, in postbiblical times, sometimes interpreted as deriving from the Hebrew root קנ"א, "to envy." This is unlike Gen 4:1, where the biblical name-etiology derives Cain from קנ"י, "to get, create" (compare T. Benj. 7.5).[52] Both etymologies are given in

---

tower and denigrates Hebrew. The same is to be found in Levene 1951, 86. The subject is a large one and of much interest, and considerable discussion of it is to be found in Badalanova Geller 2021b.

51. The variant arises from two different parsings of the Hebrew verb in this phrase.

52. See also PH 9.1 (*MOTP* 1:603). The same is found in Philo, *QG* 1.58, *Sacr.* 2.2, Eusebius, *Praep. ev.* 11.6.3 and Pirqe R. El. 21. See the many sources assembled in Hollander and de Jonge 1985, 433 in their remarks on T. Benj. 7.5. The sources they cite include 1 Clem. 4 (end of the first century CE), where Cain is described as envious, but the connection with his name and its etymology is not made (see below).

Pseudo-Clementines, *Hom.* 3.25 and in the Onomastica Sacra, the Armenian text of which reads for the name "Cain": "Կային. ստացուած կամ նախանձ։ Cain. possession or envy."[53] The "envy" etymology is widespread in Armenian parabiblical works.

The phrase, "its return will be to you"[54] found in the Armenian version of Gen 4:7, referring to Cain and sin, is also taken up in History of the Forefathers §6. Furthermore, §4 of that work contains phraseology that is very similar to Questionnaire here, particularly in God's reproach of Cain,[55] according to which he says, "You did not make me a just offering and you did not make a just division." The two sources are dependent on Gen 4:7, of which they share an interpretation.

Jubilees does not state that it was envy that moved Cain to fratricide, and while this might be taken as implied by Wis 10:3, "But when an unrighteous man departed from her (wisdom) in his anger, he perished because in rage he slew his brother," that writing does not use the word "envy," but says ἐν ὀργῇ αὐτοῦ, "in his anger." Anger is said to be Cain's motive by Josephus, *A.J.* 1.55. In 1 Clem. 4.7, however, "jealousy and envy" are mentioned. In the Armenian pseudepigraphon Third Story of Joseph §15, in a homiletic context, we read that "wicked and hateful envy made Cain a brother-killer."[56]

Tiranun vardapet (2009, 957–97, C10) speaks of Cain's envy and of Satan's envy that caused the fratricide.[57] In the thirteenth century, Vardan Arewelc'i says:

---

53. Wutz 1915, 902. The same is given in PH 9.1; see further PH 10.3 (both in *MOTP* 1:603).

54. In RSV, it is translated: "its desire is for you."

55. See *Arm Apoc* 2:184. This might suggest a relationship between these two writings. For a perceptive overview of the exegesis of the story of Cain and Abel, see Kugel 1990.

56. *Arm Apoc* 4:205. This envy is said, in some sources to arise from Cain's desire to marry Abel's twin sister, whom Abel married; see Pirqe R. El. 21, though that text speaks of anger rather than envy. See further n. 70 below dealing with the pattern of marriage of Adam and Eve's children.

57. See Stone 2013, 397. Satan's responsibility for sin through his envy is maintained by Grigor Aknerc'i (thirteenth century), *History of the Nation of the Archers* who says, "But the Devil, Satan, on account of his evil envy, continually taught men to do unfitting things, such as the fratricide of Cain" (quoted in Stone 2013, 469). On Satan standing behind Cain in scenes of the murder, see Kuyumdzhieva 2016, 385–86.

Վասն որոյ ի կարծիս եղեալ Կայէն վասն Աբէլի, թէ առնու զսա ի դրախտն Աստուած վասն ընդունելի պատարագին, եւ նախանձու վառեալ սպան զսա:

Therefore, Cain supposed, concerning Abel, that God would receive him into the Garden because of his acceptable offering; and inflamed with jealousy, he slew him.[58]

Genesis 4:5 is silent about why God accepted Abel's sacrifice and rejected Cain's. This is exactly the sort of issue that intrigued ancient exegetes.[59] Angela Y. Kim (2001, 69–70) considers that the silence of Genesis, which made God's action seem capricious, was a major issue for early readers of the story of Abel and Cain. I wish to suggest a somewhat different formulation. On the face of the matter, the problem is that Genesis offers no reason for God's rejection of Cain's offering.[60] Kim maintains that this issue was resolved in the exegetical tradition by highlighting this incident as the inception of envy. That very issue of the rejection of Cain's offering is on center stage in §10.2 here. Highlighting the inception of envy does not explain what was wrong with Cain's offering or why it was rejected.

The two explanations of Cain's envy offered arise from the brevity and nonspecificity of the narrative in Genesis, and both these explanations are based on the notion that Cain's sacrifice was in some way inferior to Abel's.[61] The first recorded exegetical strategy marshalled to justify God's rejection of Cain's offering was employed by Philo in *Sacr.* 20, 52–54, 88 and *QG* 1.60. He maintains that Cain's sacrifice was rejected because he brought "fruits" and not the special "first-fruits." He deduces

---

Thus, Grigor Aknerc'i, while not giving a specific reason for Cain's jealousy, does attribute it ultimately to Satan.

58. Stone 2013, 480–81.

59. In Abel and Cain §§10–12, it is related that the rejection of Cain's sacrifice was signaled by a black cloud, and the acceptance of Abel's by illumination of his face; see Lipscomb 1990, 148. On blackness of face, see Stone 2013, 179–80 and Stone 1990a, 257. This is set in obvious contrast to Abel's shining face. On Adam's luminosity, see annotation 13.

60. Kim defines the issue arising from the biblical text as it stands. Because no reason is given, she says, God's behavior in rejecting Cain's offering seemed capricious. I would maintain that the problem is precisely that the rejection is not explained, and consequently an explanation is sought. This is the exegetical problem, and I prefer to focus on it rather than on theological issues arising from its implications.

61. Observe a similar idea in Gen. Rab. 22.5; Tanh. Berešit 9; Pirqe R. El. 21. Further references are to be found in Ginzberg 1909, 5:136–37 n. 12.

this from the language of Gen 4:3–4, which relates that Abel brought "the firstlings," that is, the firstborn of his flock, while Cain brought an unspecified "offering."[62] Indeed, so special was this firstborn lamb that an Armenian legendary tradition developed concerning it and its role in the *historia sacra* and that is presented here in annotation 15. In that annotation, traditions that developed concerning this firstborn of Abel's flock are assembled. Abel's lamb is the beast that Abraham slaughtered and served to the three men (Gen 18:7). It was, the story goes, subsequently restored to life.[63]

The same interpretation, that Cain did not offer the first-fruit of his crop, is proffered by the Samaritan work TM 4.32. That Cain's offering was inferior is also the view of Josephus, though he differs as to why, seeing agriculture as less desirable than herding animals: *A.J.* 1.54–55. It is noteworthy that, according to the Slavonic version of LAE 33–34.3, Satan is the (temporary) lord of this world and so the owner of the land Adam sought to plough. Therefore, Satan says to Adam, "If you want to become mine, then, by all means, till the earth,"[64] and Adam tricks him with an ambiguous reply. This Satanic connection between the earth and agriculture is surely related to the curse of the ground in Gen 3:17.[65]

The second, more general explanation is that while Abel offered the choicest beasts of his flock, Cain's sacrifice was of the least valuable produce of his fields. This constatation remains at a nonspecific level. Such a view is to be found in John Chrysostom, *Inan. glor.* 39.[66] In the Armenian tradition, this approach is well summarized in the poem, *On the Creation of the World* by Yovhannēs Tʻlkurancʻi (1320?–1400?) in stanzas 120–121:

120 Abel offered a sacrifice, it was acceptable to God.
Cain, too, made an offering, not a good one, and it was not pleasing.
121 Abel, the choicest of the lambs, with eager, willing intent,

---

62. Brichto 1976; Hess 1992, 9, among others.
63. See pp. 128–29 for the sources for this incident concerning Abel's sheep.
64. Anderson and Stone 1999, 6–6E.
65. See further on this, Stone and Timotin 2023, 77–78 and index, s.v. "agricultural story." Badalanova Geller (2017b, 279) remarks that in the Balkans, "agriculture is considered to be the archetypical marker of manhood/fatherhood." In Romanian frescos, Adam is shown tilling the ground and Eve spinning—each doing the work typical of their gender and indeed, as observed, at that time the earth was thought to be Satan's; see Stone and Timotin 2023, 118, fig. 13.
66. See also Alexandre 1988, 350; consult in addition PH 8.3 (*MOTP* 1:603).

But Cain, the vilest of the produce, useless, unfitting.⁶⁷

Moreover, this explanation occurred in the Armenian tradition before the time of Yovhannēs Tʻlkurancʻi and may also be observed in the writings of Vardan Arewelcʻi (1200?–1271).⁶⁸

A different explanation of Cain's hatred is offered by Pirqe R. El. 21, and an explanation also found in the Samaritan work Asaṭir.⁶⁹ It is as follows: Cain and Abel were married to their twin sisters. Cain wanted to marry Abel's sister, who was Abel's wife, and that was the cause of his envious hatred of Abel and ultimately the reason that Cain killed Abel.⁷⁰ This is, is, of course, against the explicit prohibition of incest in Lev 18:16, 20:21 and Pirqe de Rabbi Eliezer discusses the question of incest and concludes that, in this instance, it was permissible because there were no other women whom they could marry.⁷¹

According to Pirqe de Rabbi Eliezer, then, the envy or hatred was not caused by the acceptance or rejection of sacrifices or competing desires of Cain and Abel but was over Cain and Abel's twin sisters.⁷² At the end of its narrative of this incident, Pirqe de Rabbi Eliezer adds: "R. Ṣadoq says: Great envy and malice entered Cain's heart because Abel's sacrifice was accepted. Moreover, Abel's twin was most beautiful. He (Cain) said, 'I will kill my brother Abel and take his wife.' As it says, 'and when they were in

---

67. Stone 2005, 71. A similar view is voiced in the Armenian apocryphon History of the Forefathers §4, where God says his sacrifice was not ուղիղ, "straight, upright," and "you did not make a just (or: righteous) offering." This passage is cited on p. 121. On the sacrifices, see also Hayward 2009, 102–6. Aptowitzer 1922, 39–41 writes about the affinities of this tradition unit.

68. See Stone 2013, 433 and Abel and Cain §7.

69. This is discussed by Tal 2021, 263–64.

70. See this passage in the translation by Friedlander 1981, 154. See also for another instance of this idea, Witakowski 2017, 526. In general, there are two views, according to which they were to marry their own sisters or to "cross-marry," that is, to marry each other's sisters. According to both variants, Cain is said to be envious of Abel and to have desired the sister whom Abel was to marry.

71. This is, of course, reminiscent of the incident of Lot and his daughters related in Gen 19:31–32.

72. Pirqe R. El. 21. On the brothers' rivalry over Abel's twin sister, see further Aptowitzer 1922, 19–23. See also b. Sanh. 58b and y. Yevam. 11:1, 11d = b. Yevam. 62a. Relating to a different corpus of texts, Witakowski (2019, 458) suggests that the motif of the envy over the sisters in the Ethiopic composition that he is studying originates in Cave of Treasures.

the field, (Gen 4:8).' The field is a woman, who was likened to a field, as it says, 'humans are the trees of the field.' (Deut 20:19)."[73]

The idea that Cain's jealousy arose over Abel's twin sister, which we observed in Pirqe de Rabbi Eliezer, is also found in an eight–ninth century Syriac *Tabula Gentium* by Dawid bar Pawlos.[74] Yoram Erder (1994, 125) remarks on the Karaite view that this was the earliest practice and, though usually forbidden, was permitted to early generations. According to CT 5.21 (*MOTP* 1:544), Cain and Abel were to marry each other's sisters, and this is also the view of Questionnaire as is explicit in §10.3 and in the note to that section.[75]

The Murder Weapon and the Murder

Pirqe de Rabbi Eliezer continues to relate that Cain took up a stone and killed Abel with it. This idea that the murder weapon was a stone also occurs in Abel and Other Pieces §3.3, History of the Forefathers §23 ("a heavy stone"), Repentance of Adam and Eve §36, and CT 5.29 (*MOTP* 1:544). In erotapocritic form, Abel and Other Pieces §3.3 says, "And by which thing was Abel killed, for a sword did not yet exist? Some say that (Cain) strangled (him), but God said, 'The voice of your brother's blood.' They say[76] with a flint stone." In Abel and Cain §27, it is also a flint, which is described as "sharp as a razor." Likewise, it was also specifically described as a flint according to Abel and Other Pieces §3.2 and in Repentance of Adam and Eve §36. Indeed, many centuries earlier than these Armenian works, the idea of a stone as the murder weapon occurs in Jub. 4.31, though

---

73. My translation. Compare Friedlander 1981, 154. In Deuteronomy, of course, the statement is a (rhetorical) question, but it is repurposed by Pirqe de Rabbi Eliezer here.

74. See Minov 2020, 71. Thus, it would not be surprising to find this view in Armenian sources, but, in fact, I have not yet encountered it.

75. See also Tal 2021, 264.

76. In contexts like this in Armenian texts, the phrases "some say" and "they say" are signs of scholastic learning, usually invoking differing patristic authorities or traditions. Here, the point of the alternative tradition marked by "they say" is that strangling would not let blood, and since blood is mentioned in Gen 4:10, his death must have involved bleeding. On the other hand, the tradition quoted by Questionnaire infers from "voice" to neck, and so to strangling.

not specifically a flint stone. The sharpness of the stone perhaps explains its identification as flint, which was noted in the preceding exposition.[77]

Flint, as a knife, is already mentioned by the Hebrew Bible in connection with circumcision in Exod 4:25 and Josh 5:2–3. Apparently, in ancient Israel, this sort of knife was used for circumcision, which must have been an archaic tradition. One might perhaps wonder at the specification of flint in Armenian texts, written in a country with rich deposits of volcanic glass, obsidian, from which neolithic people did make tools, including knives, that are to be observed readily as surface finds in Armenia. But, in fact, according to *NBHL*, բայլախաք, the word translated as "flint," might just designate a sharp stone, which could, inter alia, be a sharp piece of obsidian. This is, of course, speculative. The text of the Armenian apocryphon Brief History of Joshua §33, speaking of the events of Josh 5:2–3, says: "And He commanded to circumcise them with a flint because its incision is easier than a wound (caused by) iron, and heals more quickly than the wound of iron." This is obviously, of course, a postfactum etiology.[78]

There is a developed story in Armenian texts that relates that Cain did not know how to kill, and Satan sent ravens to teach Cain how to do the deed.[79] One form of it occurs in Abel and Cain Recension 2 §27, where we read: "Then Satan came in the form of two ravens, and the one took a sharp stone, struck the other with it in the throat, and killed him. The stone was sharp as a razor."[80] At this point, Issaverdens (1934) quotes the *Commentary on Genesis* of Vardan vardapet Arewelcʻi (1200?–1271),

---

77. See further Abel and Cain §34 and the discussion in *Arm Apoc* 5:95–96.

78. See the discussion in *Arm Apoc* 5:92 and in n. 139 there.

79. In CT 5.27, Satan is said to possess Cain so that he killed Abel. History of the Forefathers §23 presents the same story discussed in the text here as one possible answer to the question how Cain learned to kill (*Arm Apoc* 2:192). On demons disguised as ravens, see *Arm Apoc* 2:148 and pp. 127, 165–66 below. A similar story is to be found in the Qurʾan al-Māʾidah 5:32, where ravens show Cain how to bury Abel; on this, see Witztum 2011, 115–22. Much related information is to be found in Muslim commentaries and exegetes on this passage; see the overview by Roberto Tottoli 2023. Indeed, the raven is a black bird and black is a satanic color; see Stone 2013, 179–80. Compare, for instance, the episode in b. Sanh. 107a, where Satan is said to have disguised himself as a bird to tempt King David. Ravens and other birds of prey represent rulers of the Persian period in the Animal Apocalypse in 1 En. 90.2, 9–10, etc.

80. Lipscomb 1990, 164 n. 11, p. 273; Issaverdens's translation is to be found in Issaverdens 1934, 56. See also *Arm Apoc* 1:35, note to lines 11–13, and the reference

which transmits a similar tradition. In History of the Forefathers §25, we read similarly to the above ideas: "Satan disguised himself in the likeness of two ravens, and the one cast the other to the ground and slaughtered (it) with a flinty stone. Thus Cain did to Abel and killed him."[81] The same may be observed in Abel and Other Pieces §3.4.[82] [The legend about Cain learning from ravens how to kill his brother also appears in a Targumic expansion to Gen 4:8-7, of an unknown date,[83] and in Muslim sources, where the killing bird is actually Satan (Iblis) in disguise.[84] These legends are related to, and may have developed from, an attested tradition about Cain, or Adam and Eve, learning from ravens (or other birds) how to bury Abel's corpse or conceal it. We find this in various Jewish, Eastern Christian, and Muslim sources,[85] and its earliest datable version appears to be in the Qur'an Al-Ma'idah 5:31. The relationship between these sources is debated.[86] –S.E.]

Thus, we see that in Hebrew and in Armenian texts, Satan is said to use ravens to mime sinful actions in order to teach them to humans.[87]

---

given there to a parallel Georgian legend in Lüdtke 1919, 156. Ravens are also discussed in Stone 2021c.

81. *Arm Apoc* 2:193.

82. Ravens or crows are frequently mentioned in Abraham texts because of the incident of Abraham and the ravens. See, for example, *Arm Apoc* 3, index s.v. "ravens," and Brock 1978. It may also be observed that ravens and other birds of prey and certain other living creatures are among the creatures utilized to represent rulers of the Persian period in the Animal Apocalypse in 1 En. 90.2, 11, etc.

83. Klein 1986, 1:12–5. The language of this expansion is mixed and seems to reflect the artificial, literary use of Aramaic. See Witztum 2011, 118 n. 27.

84. See, for example, the source quoted in Witztum 2011, 122 n. 40; Grattepanche 1993, 138, where however Satan is not said to have appeared as a bird.

85. For the Jewish sources see Pirqe R. El. 21 and Tanh. Berešit 10. For Christian traditions, see, for instance, the interpolated passage in 2 En. 7.36 (long recension; see Andersen 1983, 1:208–9). See the comprehensive surveys in Rüger 1981 and Böttrich 1995, 78–114; and the important critical reassessment in Witztum 2011, 115–22.

86. Geiger 1898, 80–81, argued the Qur'anic tradition derives from Pirqe deRabbi Eliezer; Sidersky 1933, 18 claimed it derives from Midrash Tanhuma. Yet these scholars assumed rather than proved the dependence of the Qur'anic passage on the Jewish (or Christian) legends. Witztum 2011, 122, concludes more cautiously: "Is it possible that the midrashic sources reflect *tafsīr* [Qur'an exegesis. –S.E.] traditions in this instance? Perhaps."

87. See also Badalanova Geller 2017b, 288 with instances involving a dove or a raven.

The choice of this technique, it may be supposed, is due to the blackness of ravens and their rough cawing, which were suggestive of a Satanic or demonic quality.[88] Darkness and blackness were regarded as Satanic in medieval Armenian texts.[89]

ANNOTATION 15. ABEL'S SHEEP

Genesis 4:4 says that Abel offered "the firstlings of his flock and of their fat portions." In embroidered biblical stories, this firstborn lamb of Abel's offering became a parade example of a desirable beast. In Abraham, Isaac, and Mamre §32, as Isaac lay bound upon the altar, ready to be sacrificed, we read concerning the ram caught in the thicket: "the marrow of this ram is the sweet oil with which they anointed you. And this ram was Abel's ram that the Lord accepted as Abel's offering … and Heaven accepted the ram whole, and it was preserved until Sahak's (Isaac's) birth, whom Abraham promised to God." This is the direct speech of the angel speaking to Abraham. It is somewhat unclear to which event the sweet oil and the anointing of Abraham refer, but the special character of Abel's ram is obvious.[90] Rabbinic literature also knows of the special character of Isaac's replacement ram. It was one of the things prepared in the twilight of the sixth day of creation.[91]

In Concerning Abraham's Hospitality §28, in the context of the preparation of food for the three angelic visitors, the text says, "For a calf had been born to Abraham that resembled Abel's lamb." This is the calf that was slaughtered for the meal that Abraham set before the three men, according to the narrative in Gen 18:2–16. Abraham, Isaac, and Mamre says that when Abraham slaughtered this calf, he was careful not to break any of its bones, which is in accordance with the biblical prescriptions concerning the Passover sacrifice.[92] Then, in §29, we read the following:

---

88. Compare concerning ravens and for the negative evaluation of blackness, part 12, annotation 19, "On the Raven."
89. See Stone 2013, 164, 179–80. I have discussed this on several occasions above.
90. See *Arm Apoc* 3:14 for further comments on the marrow. In 2 En. 22.8–9, Enoch is anointed with fragrant heavenly oil that transforms him into the likeness of an angel. Similarly, when Adam died, his body was anointed with sweet oil and clothed in linen garments according to LAE 40.1–2. 3 Ezra 2.12 also refers to the fragrant oil of the tree of life.
91. See Pirqe R. El. 31.
92. See Exod 12:46, Num 9:12 on not breaking bones of special sacrifices.

"Night fell, the cows came, and one cow was lowing. Christ asked, 'Why does that cow low?' 'Behold,' Abraham said, 'it was that cow's calf that was slaughtered.' Our Lord, Jesus Christ, commanded Abraham and said, 'Gather that calf's bones and cast (them) into (its) skin and bring (them).' And Abraham did that which the Savior commanded, and Christ made the sign of the cross, and he resurrected the calf." Now, the raising up of this calf is already found in T. Abr A 6.5. The Palaea (PH 49.8 [*MOTP* 1:619]) also recounts this miracle, but more briefly.[93] One suspects that a more detailed tradition or traditions may be behind this complex of ideas relating to Abel's sheep, and it may well come to light in the course of time.

---

93. See Adler 2015, 4. On the Palea text of this incident, see Flusser 1971, 60.

11
The Sethites and the Cainites: Beginnings

In this section, the narrative of events eventually leading to the flood commences. The first episode is related in Gen 6:1–4, the incident of the sons of God and the daughters of humans, and it gave birth to the story of the sons of Seth and the daughters of Cain. This reading of Gen 6:1–4 originates in Byzantine sources, in which it explained, or rather explained away, the exegetical difficulties of that pregnant biblical passage. As will become evident below, those verses, which speak of intercourse between the sons of God (probably understood as angels or some other celestial beings) and human women, raised conceptual and exegetical difficulties, primarily due to various differing views about such beings.

The tale here in Questionnaire is a shortened and variant form of the same story about the Sethites and Cainites recounted in Concerning the Good Tidings of Seth.[1] Other forms of this tradition that include the detail that the Sethites withdrew to a mountain may also be observed.[2] Sergey Minov (2016b, 141) notes that certain Syriac sources say that the Sethites' only occupation was "to praise and glorify God, with the angels," as they could hear the "voices of the angels who were singing praises in paradise."[3]

---

1. See Lipscomb 1990, 172–205.

2. *Arm Apoc* 2:176–78, 205–6. For details on the mountain, see annotation 16, n. 46. See on pp. 12, 19–20 above for a discussion of the idea that the primary function of angels is to sing the praise of God.

3. The idea of joint human and angelic praise of God is a concept found at several points in the Questionnaire.

Text

M682 / fol. 7g.9–19/

11.1/ Յետ վերանալոյն Ենովքայ յերկինս՝ որդւոցն Սէթայ, ԵՃ. (500) այր լուան թէ որ ոք սրբութեամբ մնա, կարէ ի դրախտն մտանել։ Ելին յանապատ եւ միանձնական մինչեւ Շ. (500) ամա. ապա ձանձրացեալք դարձան յաշխարհի, զի կանայս առցեն, բայց ազգն նոցա ոչ ետուն նոցա կանայս այլ անարգեցին եւ ի միջոյ իւրեանց վարեցին. ուխտապանց եւ ուրացող կոչելով։

11.2/ Իսկ նոքա յարեցան ազգն Կայենի եւ անտի առին կանայս եւ կռիեցին զիրամանն Աստուծոյ. զի Աստուած պատուիրեաց Սէթայ ընդ ազգն Կայենի մի խառնիլ. վասն որոյ եղեւ խռովութիւն ի մէջ Բ.ուց (երկուց) ազգացն։ Եւ կացուցին որդիքն Կայենի իւրեանց թագաւոր զՍամիրոս, եւ որդիքն Սէթայ՝ Աղորոս։

Սա եզիտ գթիւս մոլորակաց եւ աստեղաբաշխութեան, որ եւ քաղդեացիք անուանեցան։

11.3/ Այս եղեւ սկիզբն խռովութեան եւ սպանութեան, եւ խառնակումն ընդ դստերսն Կայենի զազիր պղծութեամբ, մինչեւ բարկացեալ Աստուծոյ, ասաց. «Մի մնասցէ հոգի իմ ի դուա վասն լինելոյ դոցա մարմին. զղջացայ զի արարի զմարդն։» վասն որոյ հրամայեաց Նոյի շինել տապան, զի աւերելոց է աշխարհի.

Translation

11.1/ After the translation of Enoch to the heavens, 500 men <of> the sons of Seth[4] heard that whoever remains pure,[5] can enter the garden. They went forth to a desert[6] (and) lived celibately until the five hun-

---

4. Apparently, the preposition ի (յ-) has been lost, a not uncommon error: see Stone and Hillel 2012, 295, index s.v. The tale that follows here is a shortened and variant form of the story recounted in Concerning the Good Tidings of Seth (see Lipscomb 1990, 172–205). Other forms of this tradition, with the Sethites withdrawing to a mountain, may be observed in *Arm Apoc* 2:176–78, 205–6. On the number 500 of the Sethians, see n. 44 below.

5. That is, virgin or celibate.

6. The Armenian word անապատ as well as meaning "desert," may also signify an isolated monastery or monastic cell. Here, that sense of it might well be in the background.

dredth year. Then they grew weary[7] (and) returned to the world so that they might take wives, but their (own) people[8] did not give them wives but despised them. They lived in their (people's) midst, being called oath-breakers and apostates.

11.2/ Then they joined with the people[9] of Cain and took wives from them[10] and trampled upon the commandment of God. For God had commanded Seth[11] not to be mixed with the people of Cain. Because of this, there was dissension between the two peoples. And the sons of Cain set up Samirōs[12] as a king for themselves, and the sons of Seth, Alōros.[13] He[14] discovered the number of the planets and of astronomy, who[15] were called Chaldeans.

11.3/ This became the beginning of dissension and murder and abominably filthy intercourse with the daughters of Cain until God became angry and said, "Let my spirit not remain in them because they are body. I regret that I made humans."[16] On account of this, he commanded Noah to build an ark, for he was going to destroy the world.

---

7. That is, of the celibate life.

8. uqq properly may also designate "kin-group, family" as well as "people." Here it designates the sons of Seth.

9. I have translated uqq here as "people," but one must bear in mind that the word implies familial relations between its members.

10. Or: from then on.

11. "Seth" here designates presumably both the patriarch and "sons or descendants of Seth, Sethians." In CT 6.7–14 (*MOTP* 1:545), Adam gives this commandment to Seth on his deathbed.

12. A name unknown elsewhere. Phonetically it resembles Semiramis (Armenian: *šamiram*); see Movsēs Xorenacʻi, *History of the Armenians* 1.15 (see Thomson 2006, 93–99). However, Semiramis is a familiar, albeit legendary, female figure and of postdiluvian vintage. See the section on the *Chronography* of Michael the Syrian below.

13. These names are not mentioned in the texts referred to in nn. 4, 12 above. Movsēs Xorenacʻi, *History of the Armenians* 1.4 says that Ałovros (Ałōros) ruled for thirty-six thousand years, not as a king of the race of Seth, but as a mythical king of Babylon (see Thomson 2006, 68).

14. Apparently, Ałōros.

15. That is, perhaps, the Sethites. Astronomers or astrologists were often called "Chaldeans" in ancient texts because of the fame of Babylonian astronomical learning (see Dan 2:2, etc.). The sentence has grammatical anomalies, but the overall sense is clear. It seems to have been shortened.

16. The author here draws on Gen 6:3 and 6 in the context of the last verses of Gen 5.

Annotation 16. The Sons of God, the Sons of Seth, the Watchers, and the Giants

In this part, we find the next stage of the story of the sons of God and the daughters of humans, which is based upon the passage Gen 6:1-4: "the Sons of God saw that the daughters of men were fair; and they took to wife such of them as they chose" (Gen 6:2). The earliest postbiblical interpretation of this is in the Book of the Watchers (henceforth: Watchers), one of the works incorporated into the apocryphal book of Enoch, which is also known as 1 Enoch. In that book, as in Second Temple Jewish sources in general, "the Sons of God" are said to be angels. They were members of a high angelic rank called "Watchers"; see, for example, Dan 4:10, 14, and 20.

The publication of the Aramaic Dead Sea Scrolls fragments of 1 Enoch and the particularly early date (third century BCE) of some of the manuscript evidence for, and consequently of the composition of, the first part of the Book of the Watchers have attracted a good deal of scholarly attention in recent decades.[17] This has been intensified by bringing to bear the prior discovery that the Manichean Book of the Giants is an adaptation of an earlier Jewish Enochic work, extant in Aramaic fragments from Cave 4 at Qumran.[18] This is not the place, however, to present that particular scholarly discourse, for my aim is another, to see what the Armenian tradition made of the incident related in Gen 6:1-4.

The background of this development of the Genesis pericope is the following. Early in the Second Temple period, this passage of Genesis was taken to be about the fall of angels or some sort of celestial beings.[19]

---

17. In the Book of the Watchers, the sons of God are interpreted as angels, and the Gen 6 passage is read as a story of their fall (see Stone 2023, 399–422). In recent times, there has been a torrent of scholarly writing on the Watchers, who are fallen angels. Here is not the place to survey it. An up-to-date bibliography is maintained by the Orion Centre for the Study of the Dead Sea Scrolls at the Hebrew University: http://orion-bibliography.huji.ac.il/.

18. See Reeves 1992. This is an excellent study of the Book of Giants, which writing has been the object of intensive attention in recent years. The suggestion that, in their Book of Giants, the Manicheans adopted an older Jewish work was first made by Walter B. Henning (1934; 1943). Jozef T. Milik (1976, 57–58) identified the work at Qumran. Concerning the Qumran fragments, see Stuckenbruck 1997a.

19. For the mythological background to Gen 6:1-4 and its treatment in Judaism and early Christianity, see, among others, Alexander 1972.

Moreover, that understanding is indeed the reading of this verses found in an impressive list of witnesses to the LXX, including Codex Alexandrinus, Philo, and Josephus.[20] For "sons of God" in the Hebrew text of Gen 6:2, all these witnesses read "angels of God," or the like. The crucial, relevant passage in the Book of Watchers reads:

> 1. When the sons of men had multiplied, in those days, beautiful and comely daughters were born to them. 2. And the watchers, the sons of heaven, saw them and desired them. And they said to one another, "Come, let us choose for ourselves wives from the daughters of men, and let us beget children for ourselves."
> 3. And Shemiḥazah, their chief, said to them, "I fear that you will not want to do this deed, and I alone shall be guilty of a great sin." 4. And they all answered him and said, "Let us all swear an oath, and let us all bind one another with a curse, that none of us turn back from this counsel until we fulfil it and do this deed."
> 5. Then they all swore together and bound one another with a curse. 6. And they were, all of them, two hundred, who descended in the days of Jared onto the peak of Mount Hermon. And they called the mountain "Hermon" because they swore and bound one another with a curse on it. (1 En. 6.1–7)[21]

Observe three important points here: the name Shemiḥazah for the leader of the fallen Watchers; the fixed number two hundred for the fallen Watchers;[22] and the site of the descent and the oath, which is specified as Mount Hermon, the highest mountain in the land of Israel (2,814 m.).[23] Indeed, Book of the Watchers, the first part of the work called 1 Enoch, supplies a name aetiology for this mountain that is based on the story of the

---

20. See Wevers 1974, ad loc.
21. Cited according to Nickelsburg and VanderKam 2012, 23–24. For the history of this tradition, see Reed 2005, 318 and the works cited in nn. 17 and 18 above.
22. On this number, two hundred, which was very early in the tradition, see Reeves 2014, 106–7. See also Badalanova Geller 2021c, 15–16.
23. On the role of Mount Hermon in the early Jewish parabiblical texts, perhaps reflecting a more ancient sanctity, see Nickelsburg 1981. It is also discussed in Stone 2004. It is very likely that Mount Hermon, and not the traditional Mount Tabor, was the high mountain of the transfiguration. Clermont-Ganneau (1971, 1:329–37) long ago remarked on ancient cult sites on this mountain. Mount Hermon certainly served as a major cult centre from antiquity and on through the Roman period. See further Aliquot 2008 and Dar 2022. This last article deals with earlier material as well.

fallen angels in verse 6:5: "And they called the mountain 'Hermon' because they swore and bound one another with a curse on it." This aetiology is founded upon a word-play in Aramaic, the name חרמון ḥrmwn "Hermon" being connected with the root חר״ם ḥrm, meaning "to curse, to ban," with associations of sacrality. These narrative details also survive in part in the Aramaic Enoch fragments preserved among the Dead Sea Scrolls.[24]

The ideas that I have mentioned were subsequently taken over through various channels of transmission and largely reinterpreted in different texts down to the twelfth-century *Chronography* of Michael the Syrian (lived 1126–1199), of which composition two reworked Armenian versions exist.[25] One might propose that subsequently, they passed thence and into the Armenian apocrypha, including Questionnaire. The latter, however, speaks of five hundred fallen Sethites.[26] Of course, this might not have been the only line of transmission, and several other possibilities could be suggested.

In other Jewish sources from the Second Temple period, the interpretation of the Watchers as angels is sustained. This identification, however, raised difficulties, for how could heavenly beings, that is, angels, have intercourse with human women? It is that problem that is addressed in a passage in T. Reu. 5.5–7, which work probably reached its present form in the second century CE.[27] This writing attempts to resolve the difficulty by positing some kind of mental and not fleshly sexual intercourse of the Watchers with the human women. The relevant passage reads:

> 5. Flee, therefore, impurity, my children, and command your wives and daughters that they do not adorn their heads and faces, because every woman who uses these wiles has been reserved for eternal punishment.[28] 6. For thus they bewitched the Watchers before the Flood:

---

24. It is also possible that the descent of the Watchers was set in the generation of Jared (Yered), Enoch's father because the Hebrew rood ירד means "descend."

25. On this material in the various sources, see Hilkens 2018, 58–61. On the two Armenian recensions, see Andrea B. Schmidt 1996; 2013. See further annotation 17 below.

26. Two hundred is the number in Short History of the Forefathers §19 (*Arm Apoc* 4:171).

27. The date of the Testaments of the Twelve Patriarchs has been greatly debated. For a detailed discussion of the scholarly controversy, see Hollander and de Jonge 1985, particularly the introduction.

28. This theme has been noted already in the consideration of §10.5 above.

as these looked at them continually, they lusted after one another, and they conceived the act in their mind, and they changed themselves into the shape of men, and they appeared to them when they were together with their husbands. 7. And they, lusting in their mind after their appearances, bore giants: for the Watchers appeared to them as reaching unto heaven.[29]

In this writing, the Watchers are still super-terrestrial, heavenly beings.

The issue of how the intercourse of Watchers with human women could have taken place is not raised in 1 Enoch, as we have seen. This mixed union of heavenly beings with human women resulted, it is said, in the conception of giants. The giants are exegetically derived from Gen 6:4: "These (that is, the children of the angels and human women) were the mighty men that were of old." "Mighty men" is translated γίγαντες by the LXX. Thus, Jub. 5.1 (a work of the second century BCE) tells the same story in the following fashion:

> When mankind began to multiply on the surface of the entire earth and daughters were born to them, the angels of the Lord—in a certain (year) of this jubilee — saw that they were beautiful to look at. So, they married of them whomever they chose. They gave birth to children for them, and they were giants.[30]

In Byzantine texts, the term *sons of God* in Gen 6:2 was taken euhemeristically.[31] According to that rationalizing interpretation, the sons of God were not heavenly beings, a specific class of celestial angels but instead an exalted race of men, the descendants of Seth.[32] This interpretation was

---

29. Cited according to Hollander and de Jonge 1985, 101–2. The idea is analogous to that behind the biblical story of Jacob and Laban's sheep in Gen 30:37–38.

30. This is quoted from Vanderkam 1989, 31–32. Another tradition contributing to this idea of the giants was the Greek mythological view of the Titans. Thus, the Gizeh Greek text of 1 En. 9.9 reads "Titans" for the word "giants." On this development, see Bremmer 2004, 56–61. See also Badalanova Geller 2021c, 16–17.

31. This development is laid out in an admirable fashion by Adler 1989, 114–22. It is also discussed in some detail by Annette Reed (2014, 162–69), who notes that this euhemeristic approach became widespread in Christian exegesis.

32. According to Sermon Concerning the Flood §3, as well as the sons of Seth, the sons of God also include those of Enosh. Noah was one of their number according to Short Story of the Holy Forefathers §29. He alone maintained his virginity (see annotation 18 below). The view that the children of Sethite men and Cainite women were

apparently first mentioned in the third century CE by the chronographer Sextus Iulius Africanus, whose work survives only in fragments.[33]

This view was certainly bolstered by the special role that was ascribed to Seth in many circles in late antiquity.[34] The euhemeristic strategy resolved the issue that had arisen earlier of the inappropriateness, even for fallen angels, of corporeal intercourse with human women.[35] We have seen in Testament of Reuben one attempt to resolve this conundrum. The solution offered in Byzantine texts is even more radical, maintaining that the sons of God were exalted humans and not heavenly beings at all. This development had very considerable ramifications, which are well laid out by William Adler. These include the idea that the first kings of Babylonia were descendants of these mighty men, the sons of God. This was important for those interested in the succession of legendary kings and chronology, as were the Byzantine, Syriac, and Armenian chronographers.[36]

An Old Armenian Tradition about the Watchers

The oldest Armenian tradition about the Watchers is to be found in Agathangelos §290, 295 (dating from the fifth century CE).[37] Although this author's text gives no details, it does refer to Sethites and Cainites and the prohibition of mixing. The Sethite-Cainite tradition we are discussing here seems to lie in its background, and we can conclude that it was familiar in fifth-century Armenia. Agathangelos states as follows:

- §290 God commanded Sethites not to mix with Cainites.
- §295 Nonetheless, Sethites did mix with Cainities, leading to fornication and eating of abominations.

---

giants was strongly supported by Ephrem Syrus in his hymns (see Kronholm 1978, 164, 167–71 for Ephrem's views on this matter).

33. See Spurling and Grypeou 2007, 225–26; Adler 2007, 48–49, F23. In Question §6, the separation of Sethites from Cainites is mentioned and 11 Periods §3 adds that it took place after Adam's death.

34. See the following studies, which are a sampling of modern investigations of Seth's special role: Klijn 1977; Stone 1981b; Pearson 1988a; Toepel 2006a. There exist many more studies of Adam's son, Seth.

35. See Adler 1989, 114–15.

36. See pp. 145 and 174 below.

37. Thomson 2001, 77, 79.

11. The Sethites and the Cainites: Beginnings

Chronography by Michael the Syrian (Twelfth Century)

Adler points to the presentation of the sons of God passage in the Syriac *Chronography* of Patriarch Michael the Syrian (1126–1199 CE), also known as Michael the Great (Rabo). The Syriac text of the whole *Chronography* and an annotated French translation were published by Jean-Baptiste Chabot (1899). The sons of God passage in the *Chronography* presents an elaborated view of the interpretation of Gen 6:1–4, integrated into patriarch Michael's retelling of world history.[38]

The *Chronography* was translated into Armenian soon after the author's death.[39] The Armenian translation was made in Hṙomkla in the Cilician Armenian kingdom in 1246/48 at the order of the Catholicos of Cilicia, Constantine Barjrberc'i (1221–1267). The translators were a learned *vardapet* called Vardan Arewelc'i or Vardan the Easterner (d. 1271) and the Syrian scholar Isho'/Yeshu' of Hasankeyf (d. 1247). They translated the *Chronography* from Michael's autograph. In fact, there are two recensions of the Armenian translation, made one after the other in the middle of the thirteenth century and extant in very old manuscripts. Recension I was published by the Sts. James Press in Jerusalem in 1870[40] and Recension II, also by the same press in Jerusalem, in 1871. The Armenian texts differ quite a lot from the Syriac original, and in addition, the two recensions diverge considerably from one another. They present a detailed form of the tradition of the Sethites and Cainites exhibiting certain very important features. A précis of it follows.

Division of Cainites and the Sethites, according to Michael the Syrian

After Adam, Seth ruled, and in his time, Adam's children divided into two groups: (1) those who married and lived on a plain—the Cainites, and (2) the Sethites, descendants of Seth, who ascended the mountain of paradise or Mount Hermon and lived there acting righteously and remaining celibate.[41]

---

38. See nn. 11–13 on the translation of section 11.2 above.
39. For details of the Armenian versions, see the very clear and helpful article by Schmidt 2013.
40. Langois's (1867) French translation of the first Armenian version was made from late manuscripts. The 1871 Jerusalem version, that is, Recension 2, is available to me and is used in the present work.
41. The "plain" mentioned here is the "field" of Gen 4:8, where Arm also has դաշտ "field" and the LXX read τὸ πεδίον. See Brock 1979a, 217, who points out that Peshitta

Other texts speak of a mountain "opposite Paradise," see Question §6 and Sethites and Cainites §9. Moreover, Question §9 says that Seth and the Sethites were giants, and Sethites and Cainites §5 says that, in this, they resembled Adam.[42] For that reason, they were called sons of God (Gen 6: 1).[43]

In parts 11 and 12.1, Questionnaire refers to the two hundred or five hundred ascetics who came in from the desert.[44] These are the sons of Seth, who separated themselves completely from the sons of Cain so as to remain pure.[45] Usually they are said to live on a mountain, as is written Michael's *Chronography*,[46] but here the *Questionnaire* author's empha-

---

to Gen 4:8a has "valley." The tradition of paradise upon a mountain widespread in Syriac sources. See n. 46 in this part below. See also Spurling and Grypeou 2007, 227.

42. See part 7 n. 18 above, where Adam's great size is implied.

43. See Abel §4.2. However, in Abel §4.5, we read: "And they were called 'true sons of God' because God loved them before they fornicated." This brief phrase, of course, implies the existence of the whole of the Cainite-Sethite tradition.

44. The figure of five hundred sinning Sethites, found in Questionnaire §11.1, is unusual. The number two hundred is more commonly encountered: 1 En. 6.6 speaks of two hundred fallen sons of God. Short Story of the Holy Forefathers §29 also mentions two hundred Sethites, including Noah; see also Sermon on the Flood §3 and part 12 n. 22 below. See further concerning two hundred fallen angels or sinning Sethites: Michael the Syrian, *Chronography*; two hundred righteous Sethites are mentioned in the Armenian parabiblical work History of the Forefathers. Similarly, Yovhannēs Erznkacʻi (1230–1293), in his poem *On the Creation of the World*, mentions two hundred righteous who subsequently sinned. Translations of all these texts may be found in the preceding annotation. A third tradition is that there were 520 celibate anchorites; that occurs in Concerning the Good Tidings of Seth §§18, 20.

45. In Sermon on the Flood §2, this separation is said to be at divine behest. Indeed, that work stresses the purity of the sons of Seth and of Enosh and that, initially, they went forth pure. They took an oath to remain virginal until their death, according to Sermon on the Flood §3. Such emphases on ascetic behavior are to be found quite often in Armenian parabiblica. See annotation 27.

46. They are said to live around a mountain opposite paradise in Question §6 and Sethites and Cainites §9. According to Sermon on the Flood §3, they went to Mount Ahermon, and Short Story of the Holy Forefathers §29 says that they climbed Mount Hermon, which mountain is the highest in the land of Israel (2814 m.). Hermon is already mentioned rather early in connection with the fallen sons of God in 1 En. 6.5. Some discussion of Mount Hermon in the Armenian tradition is to be found in Stone 2004. Mount Hermon is specified in connection with the Sethites in Sermon on the Flood §3 and Short Story of the Holy Forefathers §29.

Paradise was on a mountain according to various sources. This might well be related to the idea of a tall mountain connecting heaven and earth, on which, in some sis on asceticism led to their being considered to come from a desert, the quintessential habitat of ascetics.[47] Furthermore, the Armenian word անապատ, "desert," is also glossed in *NBHL* as "a monastery of celibates some distance from a city," which confirms that particular emphasis. It is noteworthy that the same appetite for the ascetic life is expressed by Noah's claimed five hundred years of virginity in Questionnaire 12.1 below.

In Question §5,[48] the Sethites are said to go forth around the mountain of paradise. In the Armenian version of the *Chronography* of Michael the Syrian, they are said to be on Mount Hermon,[49] and in other sources, on Mount Ahermon, "Ahermon" being apparently a variant of "Hermon." Thus, though the desert in this context instead of the mountain is quite unusual, nonetheless, its origin is clear. The same incident is related in CT 12 (*MOTP* 1:549-50). The Armenian parabiblical works, Question §6, and Sethites and Cainites §9 say that the Cainites lived in a plain or a field, both being possible translations of Armenian դաշտ, the word used in Gen 4:8. Below, in this annotation, several texts dealing with the number of years of their heroes' ascesis are mentioned.

---

cultural traditions, the gods lived. Gary Anderson (1988) has written a most interesting study of the Syriac idea of a cosmic mountain and it mythical roots. In Greece, Mount Olympus played this role. In the ancient Near East, the idea of a mountain upon which the gods reside is present already in the Ugaritic epics of the second millennium BCE. The notion of paradise on a mountain is prominent in the Syriac tradition. See Minov 2016b, 137-62; there, on p. 144, Minov speaks of "the notion of the Garden of Eden as a cosmic mountain." This, he remarks, is characteristic of the Syriac Christian tradition, giving prominence to an idea very likely already reflected in Ezek 28:1. The same mountain seems to be implied by Jub. 8.19-20: "19 And he knew that the garden of Eden is the holy of holies, and the dwelling of the Lord, and Mount Sinai the center of the desert, and Mount Zion -the centre of the navel of the earth: 20 these three were created as holy places facing each other." On this passage see Mazor 2012, 30. Moreover on pp. 13-14, she discusses this idea as it occurs in the Hebrew Bible. See for biblical sources, Mazor 2012, 5-6. Also observe the interesting remarks of Otzen 1984, 202-3. The mountain of paradise and its ancient Near Eastern background is also discussed by Annus 2011, 10-15.

47. On this emphasis on the desert, which is found in Syrian monastic ideals, see Henze 2001, 550-71. The role of the desert is highlighted throughout Chitty 1966, note esp. p. 6. In Prescott 1958, there are many descriptions of the desert as experienced by a fifteenth-century pilgrim from Ulm, Germany, called Felix Fabri. See there, index, s.v. "desert." Literature on this theme is very extensive.

48. Published in *Arm Apoc* 2:120.

49. See, for example, *Arm Apoc* 4:173.

Descent of Sethites from the Mountain

In the fortieth year of Jared, the Sethites, who were two hundred in number, or five hundred according to Questionnaire 11.1, grew impatient with their celibacy and descended from Mount Hermon and took Cainite women as wives.[50] Jared was Enoch's father. His name could be understood as deriving from the Hebrew root יר״ד, "descend." It was, therefore, connected with the descent of the Sethites from the mountain or alternatively, with the descent of the sons of God, lusting after human women. Genesis 5 traces the descendants of Adam down to Noah. Genesis 6 opens with the events leading to the flood, the first of which, according to the sources being considered here, was the descent (יר״ד) of the sons of God. Again, the connection with an etymology of the name Jared, Enoch's father, provides a hook for the inner-biblical chronology.

The number of years of Sethite ascetic celibacy is put at eight hundred in Question §8 and Sethites and Cainites §8. However, the latter work, Sethites and Cainites, also has a doublet tradition in §9, which speaks of intercourse between the Sethites and Cainites starting in the five hundredth year. In the six hundredth year, moreover, the Cainite women went to the mountain and seduced the Sethites (Sethites and Cainites §7). They begat giants. It was not merely the Sethites' impatience but the very intent of the wicked Cainite women to corrupt the righteous Sethites that is mentioned in several Armenian sources. Several of the variant versions of the story say explicitly that the corruption of the Sethites was the work of Satan. This may be observed in Question §7, and in §10 the same text says: "And having pushed (instigated), he (that is, Satan) cast the giants, sons of Seth, into the pit of sins." Other Armenian parabiblical texts say that the Cainites envied the Sethites their purity, so Sermon on the Flood §40. Moreover, Short Story of the Holy Forefathers §29 reports that they envied the Sethite appellation "sons of God." The envy is surely connected with the name etymology of Cain, discussed above, pages 120–21.

Sermon on the Flood §3 says that the Cainite women made braids and coiffures and donned antimony and rouge. Notably, the use of "antimony and rouge," mentioned also in several other sources in connection with the Cainite women's use of cosmetics, is regarded as a Satanic teaching. The

---

50. On Mount Hermon and the mountain on which some traditions place the garden of Eden, see n. 46 above.

words "antimony" and "rouge" are rare lexemes, being technical names for specific cosmetic materials. Sermon Concerning the Flood §4 also has the same two words in the same context, as also does Short Story of the Holy Forefathers §29. These two terms also occur in Yovhannēs T'lkuranc'i's poem *Concerning the Creation of the World*, again in the identical connection.[51] This phrase, of course, is an embroidery of Gen 4:21–22.

While other inventions attributed to the Cainite line, such as musical instruments, are mentioned in the early part of Genesis, the women's ornaments, coiffures, and cosmetics are not there. Many centuries earlier than Questionnaire, the Book of the Watchers, a part of 1 Enoch, and which was written in the third century BCE, attributes two materials, one of which is antimony, to the teachings of the fallen angels. Thus, we read in 1 En. 8.1, expanding upon Gen 6:2–4: "He (Asael) showed them metals of the earth and how they should work gold to fashion it suitably, and concerning silver, to fashion it for bracelets and ornaments for women. And he showed them concerning *antimony and eye paint* and all manner of precious stones and dyes."[52]

Many texts say that the use of cosmetics and dancing accompanied by instrumental music are the wiles by which the Cainite women seduced the Sethite men. Questionnaire ties these two inventions of cosmetic materials into the cultural history attributed to the descendants of Cain, and combined with music, they are transferred to the offspring of the sons of God, interpreted as the Cainites. This is a memory of textual material with which we are familiar more than a millennium earlier than Questionnaire, and it is used in the same context in the parabiblical text Questionnaire. Observe how long some of these parabiblical materials persisted!

The culture-hero facet of the Cainite line is already prominent in Genesis. Thus, after Cain went away to the land of Nod, Enoch, son of Cain, built the first city (Gen 4:17). Cainite Lamech was his fifth-generation descendant (Gen 4:18). Lamech's children by Ada were Jabal, father of nomadic herders (Gen 4:20), and Jubal who invented the lyre and the pipe, that is, musical instruments (Gen 4:21). Zillah, Lamech's second wife, bore Tubal-Cain, who taught humans copper-working and iron-working (Gen 4:22). These very skills, according to 1 En. 8.1, were taught to humans by

---

51. See 2000a, 167–213.
52. See Nickelsburg and VanderKam 2012, 25.

Asael, one of the fallen angels. That passage specifies, among other skills taught, iron smithery and metals, the making of women's ornaments, and the use of antimony and eye paint. In Short Story of the Holy Forefathers §29, it is Satan who defined minstrels.

In general, drawing on the Bible's attribution of the discoveries of a series of cultural arts to the Cainite line (Gen 4:17–22), the Armenian parabiblical sources present the idea that the Cainites invented those arts and that by using them the Cainite women entrapped the descendants of Seth. In addition, according to a variant tradition recorded in Death of Adam §3–4, in the context of culture origin stories, the skill of smithery was taught to Adam by an angel, and subsequently, it was taught by Tobel. That text puts the time of smithery's invention before the birth of Cain, which conflicts with the chronology implied by Gen 4:22 and various apocryphal sources. Two relevant observations may be made. First, as noted, according to Death of Adam, smithery as an Adamic skill predates the birth of Cain to whose descendant Tubal Cain, the invention of that skill is usually attributed, following Gen 4:22. Second, the working of iron is considered by book of Enoch to be one of the illicit teachings of the Watchers. It is not found in the other texts examined here, and perhaps it is significant that in its heading, Death of Adam says that it is a work that was translated from the Paralipomena of the Greeks, though no Greek form of it has yet come to light.

Kings of the Cainites mentioned in Questionnaire 11.2

The king whom the Cainites set up for themselves was called Samarios. This form of the name is found in the Armenian version of Michael the Syrian's *Chronography*, while in Questionnaire it has become "Samiros." However, the name as it occurs in the original Syriac of Michael's *Chronography* is "Semiazos."[53] That is suggestive of a Graecized form of the name Shemḥazai or Shemiḥazah (1 En. 6.3), chief of the Watchers according to Book of the Watchers as may be read in the passage quoted in extenso above on page 135 above. Andy Hilkens writes to me: "Samiros, however, is a post-diluvian king mentioned by Andronikos, and a mistake here for Semiazos or Semeiazes, one of the pre-diluvian Chaldean kings from the

---

53. For the Syriac text, see Chabot 1899, 1:5–6.

Chronography of Annianos of Alexandria."[54] In rabbinic texts, Shemḥazai is often paired with Azazel as two demonic princes.[55]

At this point, then, Questionnaire is dependent either directly or indirectly on the Armenian version of the *Chronography* of Michael the Syrian.[56] Indeed, this fact is notable also since it contributes to the dating of Questionnaire. We can now say that, as far as we know today, Questionnaire as it stands must be later than the Armenian translation of Michael the Syrian's *Chronography*, that is, later than the middle of the thirteenth century.[57]

The tradition about the Sethite king Ałoros[58] mentioned by Questionnaire also occurs in Michael the Syrian's *Chronography* in both the Syriac and the Armenian versions. The Armenian of Michael's *Chronography*, but not the Syriac, credits Ałoros with the discovery of astronomy and planetary movement; compare 1 En. 8.3 where these branches of knowledge are taught by the fallen angels.[59] Questionnaire adds to this the information that the practitioners of these skills were called Chaldeans.[60] This feature is also absent from the Syriac text of the *Chronography* and is

---

54. Dr. Andy Hilkens most kindly communicated this information privately (autumn 2022). Hilkens also observed that "Enanos" is mentioned in this passage of Michael's *Chronography*, and he is, apparently, Annianos the Chronographer (fifth century CE).

55. Azazel does not appear in the Armenian texts I have quoted.

56. An alternative explanation might regard both Questionnaire and *Chronography* as partaking of a shared, earlier tradition, but Occam's razor tells against this possibility unless further evidence appears to support it.

57. See introduction, p. xxviii above on the date of Questionnaire.

58. Movsēs Xorenacʻi, *History of the Armenians* 1.4 says that Ałovros ruled for thirty-six thousand years. Xorenacʻi does not mention him as a king of the race of Seth but instead as a mythical king of Babylon (see Thomson 2006, 68). See also Eusebius, *Chronicle* in Aucher 1818, 21–22.

59. Badalanova Geller (2021c, 19–20) observes that the teaching of illicit knowledge is absent from 2 Enoch. This work preserves further Enoch traditions, differing from those in 1 Enoch, Jubilees, etc. See, for more information, the recent collection of essays: Boccacini, Orlov, and Zurawski 2012.

60. As noted above (n. 15 to this part), "Chaldeans" was a name for astronomers or astrologers in texts of late antiquity. The early Armenian usage of this term is discussed in some detail by Thomson 1992, 306–7. On 309–311, Thomson deals with a list of terms for magic, divination, astrology, and the like. The relevant Armenian sentence of Questionnaire exhibits grammatical anomalies. It seems to have been abbreviated, but the overall sense is clear.

discussed above in the note on the text at this point.⁶¹ The occurrence of "Ałoros the astrologer" and the reference to the Chaldeans are shared by both Questionnaire and by the Armenian of Michael's *Chronography* but are not found in Michael's original Syriac. This clinches the dependence, direct or indirect, of Questionnaire on the Armenian version of Michael's work or the less likely close adherence of both to a common source tradition (see n. 57). It has not been found so far elsewhere in the Armenian references to the story of the Sethites and the Cainites.⁶²

Michael the Syrian and his translators did not invent this tradition, but he reworked the Byzantine reinterpretation of the story of the giants, and, in turn, the translators of his *Chronography* into Armenian embellished it even further. In this story, as presented by Michael, there survive elements of the older tale of the fall of the Watchers (angels), which, as I have noted, is first related in the sources known to us from the third century BCE work, 1 En. 6.1–7.⁶³

Another complex Syriac form of this tradition is to be found in CT 11–12 (*MOTP* 1:548–49). Already CT 7.18 (*MOTP* 1:546), giving an intimation of what is to come, reports Adam's admonition to his descendants not to descend from the mountain of paradise.⁶⁴ Some highlights of this tradition about the subsequent generations are CT 11.4 (*MOTP* 1:548) where demons are mentioned as stimulating the invention of musical instruments, and in chapters 11–12, Cave of Treasures stresses the role of music and dance in the debauchery and fornication that the Cainites initiated. The tradition in Cave of Treasures is much richer and

---

61. See n. 15.

62. Of course, arguments e silentio are never completely convincing. Likewise, we cannot infer that the tradition did not yet exist in the tenth century from its absence from *Magnalia Dei*, the first biblical epic composed in Armenian, which was written by Grigor Magistros, who lived 990?–1059 CE. See for the most recent edition and translation of that biblical poem: Terian 2009.

63. In the Syriac tradition, the identification of the sons of God with angels is strenuously opposed by Ephrem Syrus (306–373); see Kronholm 1978, 163–71. See the table and analysis of the use of 1 En. 6.1–6 in Hilkens 2018, 58–61. He discusses the identification of the sons of God.

64. Observe the idea that Adam gave a prophetic testament to Seth, which is to be found in the second fragment of Testament of Adam in Kmosko 1907, 1339–54. There exists a similar document in Armenian called, Words of Adam to Seth. See Stone 1992, 104; Yovsēp'eanc' 1896, 331–32; Issaverdens 1934, 73–74; Lipscomb 1990, 206–9, and *Arm Apoc* 1:12–13.

11. The Sethites and the Cainites: Beginnings

more detailed than that preserved in the Armenian sources surveyed and shows no distinctive connection either with Michael's *Chronography* or with those Armenian traditions.

The Sethites in other Armenian Sources

I shall now systematically present the material at present known to me as witnessing the occurrence of this narrative of the descent of the Sethites in Armenian sources other than Questionnaire. Some of these passages have been mentioned already, but drawing all of them together in one place helps us to make the overall shape of the tradition evident. These tales are particularly widely diffused in the Armenian apocryphal Adam literature. The cases set out below, among others, refer to the tradition of the descent of the Sethites and, in addition, certain other features of the legend of the Sethites and Cainites that were mentioned above. Some of these instances are mere glancing allusions, which by their nature demonstrate that the readers were familiar with the full story and would not be at a loss to understand such brief references. Unfortunately, all these instances in the apocryphal Adam literature are preserved in relatively late copies, while the Armenian translation of Michael's *Chronography* dates from the mid-thirteenth century.[65] The existence in Armenian of the Watchers tradition in the mid-thirteenth century is also confirmed by the references in the poetry of Yovhannēs Erznkacʻi Pluz (1240?–1293) and, in the early fourteenth century, of Yovhannēs Tʻlkurancʻi (1320?–1400?).

The story circulated in different forms. That closest to the *Chronography* of Michael is found in Questionnaire, while an alternative form is found in some medieval Armenian poetry and in Armenian apocryphal Adam literature. This second form, extant already in the thirteenth century, differs from the version found in Michael's *Chronography* and is of comparable age.

1. Eleven Periods in M9100 (1686 CE)[66]

§3 In the third period, God separated the family (race) of Seth from the family (race) of Cain.[67]

---

65. See the discussion *Chronography* by Michael the Syrian in part 11 on this work.
66. The dates in parentheses are those of the copying of the manuscripts cited.
67. *Arm Apoc* 2:139.

2. Descendants of Adam M4231 (fifteenth century)[68]

In the unfortunately lacunose work titled Descendants of Adam, reference is made to an illicit mixing and the making of magical potions (ll. 1–6). This last subject does not occur in any other of the passages discussed in the present section but is encountered in much older, non-Armenian passages dealing with the sons of God as fallen angels (see, for example, 1 En. 7.1, 8.3, 9.8). From the surviving Armenian text, it is unclear whether Descendants of Adam referred to illicit mixing of Watchers with humans, or of Sethites with Cainites. It is also noteworthy that this text is preserved in a fifteenth-century manuscript, while nearly all the other apocryphal documents discussed are in even later manuscripts. This is most probably a matter of the happenstance of preservation and not an indication of the date of the traditions, yet it is intriguing that I have encountered no further copies of Descendants of Adam in the four decades since I first published it.[69]

> 1[.]were beloved, for they were full of demons and 2 [.] Sons of God did not [.] with the daughters of m[en] 3 they invented and learned from Satan potions of love and potions of hate. And by this they were dec[eived and] were mixed.

3. Question[70] from M9100 (1686)

While the texts called Periods[71] have only an allusion to the story, a full version of it occurs here in Question. This includes dates not found in Michael the Syrian's version. However, it preserves neither the name of the chief of the Watchers nor the reference to Mount Hermon, but it does incorporate details about the Cainites drawn from Genesis, notably Gen 4:21, independently of the story found in Michael's *Chronography*. Moreover, it reflects a tradition that the Sethites were the giants, the "mighty men" mentioned in Gen 6:4, who were punished (§§3, 10). This notion,

---

68. *Arm Apoc* 4:39.
69. *Arm Apoc* 1:84–85.
70. *Arm Apoc* 2:119–20. See Stone 2006, 239 where the tradition cited in Question is discussed.
71. *Arm Apoc* 4:38–41. The document is preserved in manuscript M2036 (seventeenth century).

which is discussed at the end of the present Annotation, introduces some confusion into the story. The following are the relevant paragraphs of Question in which the elements of this narrative occur.

> §3 The Sethites were giants.
> §4 In the three-hundredth year, the Cainites wanted Sethites' daughters as wives.
> §5 In the eight-hundredth year, fornication was spread by Cainites from fratricide.[72]
> §6 The separation of Cainites and Sethites.
> §7 Craftsmen from the line of Cain invented music. (This assertion depends on Gen 4:21.)
> §6 Sethites were around the mountain of paradise[73] and Cainites in "the field" or "plain," the դաշտ of Gen 4:8 (compare Sethites and Cainites §9, below).
> §8 In the eight hundredth year, fornication, sodomy, and bestiality became rampant (compare §5 above and Sethites and Cainites §§8 and 9, below).
> §9 of Question relates that in the nine-hundredth year, Satan brought the Sethites to the Cainite daughters.

The dates for these events are even more complex in Sethites and Cainites §6 below. That work sets the initial relations of the Sethites and Cainites after five hundred years; the brazen conduct of the Cainite women a hundred years later and in §7 relates that subsequently fornication increased, and giants were begotten. Short Story of the Holy Forefathers §30 simply says that the Cainites went to a mountain and seduced the Sethites.

> §10 The giant Sethites were cast into a pit of sins.

---

72. This formulation is unclear; apparently, the sin of fratricide was considered to have brought all the other corruption in its wake, though just how this happened is not described. Alternatively, it is an obscure reflex of the story of Cain's envy of Abel's sister discussed above.
73. See n. 46 in this section.

4. Sethites and Cainites M10320 (seventeenth century)[74]

This work is part of a larger composition, The Cycle of Four Works.[75] It depends on Question as I have shown elsewhere[76] and transmits various elements of the story. The Cycle of Four Works takes up the tale of the Sethites and Cainites in the Work named Concerning the Good Tidings of Seth §§18–33.[77] These traditions were also transmitted with some variants in Sethites and Cainites §§6–12.[78] They include:

- §5 Seth was born a giant (so Question §3).
- §6 The mixing of Sethites and Cainites (so Question §9).[79]
- §7–8 In the six-hundredth year promiscuity increased; in the eight-hundredth year there was yet more fornication, Cainites spread homosexuality and bestiality that stemmed from the fratricide (so Question §§5, 8).
- §8 and destroyed divinely established order.[80]
- §9 After Adam's death, the Sethites ascended mountains near the garden while the Cainites remained in the plain where Cain had killed Abel (Gen 4:8). This detail is also found in Question §6.[81]
- §11 In the five-hundredth year of the second millennium, Sethite men and Cainite women fornicated and begat giants. This resembles but is not identical with Question §1.

5. Abel and other Pieces M10200 (1624, 1634, 1666)[82]

This source has the basic story-line but omits very many associated details, such as the mountain. Observe the item of medical lore in §6.2 and note

---

74. *Arm Apoc* 2:204–6.
75. *Arm Apoc* 2:102–4.
76. See Stone 2006, 239 and parallels there.
77. Lipscomb 1990, 193–97; Yovsēpʻeancʻ 1896, 319–24; Issaverdens 1934, 63–70.
78. *Arm Apoc* 2:118–22, 204–6.
79. This is said to happen in the five hundredth year and not in the nine hundredth year as in Michael's *Chronography*.
80. Note the parallel to this remark in the descriptions of the Sodomites in Supplication Concerning the Sodomites §9 and in Sermon Concerning the Flood §8.
81. See above p. 138. Brock (1979a, 217) points out that Peshiṭta of Gen 4:8a says that Abel was killed in a valley.
82. *Arm Apoc* 2:150–55.

the highlighting of Satan's role in the fall of the Sethites. That is also to be observed in §6.2.

> §4.1 (Implied question:) Scripture says that Sons of God had intercourse with the daughters of men.
> §4.2 God called the sons of Seth "sons of God" (see §4.5).
> §4.5 "And they were called true sons of God because God loved them before they fornicated."[83]
> §6.2 Satan inflamed the giants, sons of Seth, with lust. As a result, the women became infertile; excessive semen from men caused women's death in childbirth.
> §6.3 The children of these unions are also giants whose purpose is to destroy Satan.

In this document, the giants are not simply the sons of Seth but the offspring of their illicit union with the Cainite women. The last remark, that the giants were to destroy Satan, is unique to this text, and its like is not to be found in the other documents discussed here.

6. Sermon Concerning the Flood M5571 (1657–1659)[84]

> §2 God commands Sethites not to mix with Cainites.
> §3 "Some" of the sons of Seth and Enoch, desiring to be pure, went to Mount Ahermon (that is, Hermon) and swore an oath to remain virginal.
> §4 The Cainites became envious that the Sethites were celibate. Cainite women made cosmetics—antimony and rouge.[85]
> §5 They also made musical instruments (Gen 4:21) and went to Mount Ahermon. The tradition about cosmetics and musical instruments clearly does not originate in Michael's *Chronography* but is found already among the forbidden teachings of the Watcher Asael in 1 En. 8.1 and, at least as far as the music is concerned, stemmed from Gen 4:21.

---

83. "They" seems to refer in this context to Enosh, and apparently to his descendants (see *Arm Apoc* 2:151).
84. *Arm Apoc* 2:176–78.
85. These two cosmetic materials are discussed on pp. 142–43, 153.

§6 After two hundred years[86] of ascesis, those women went to Mount Ahermon, seduced the ascetic Sethites who descended from the mountain and had intercourse with them. Here, the initiative is attributed to the Cainite women, while in Questionnaire, it is said to be due to the impatience of the Sethite men. Noah alone kept his oath for five hundred years. Construction of Noah's Ark relates that even at the age of five hundred, Noah did not wish to marry, but eventually, God instructed him to marry "one pure virgin <from the line of Seth who kept her virginity unstained>, whose name is Noemzara."[87]

7. Concerning the Good Tidings of Seth[88] (the Cycle of Four Works 4)

§17 The sons of Adam and Seth, inspired by Enoch's assumption to heaven, live ascetically in mountains, not explicitly asserted to be either Mount Hermon or the mountain of paradise.

§§18, 20 Cain's descendants included a large majority of women. The Sethites separated themselves from the Cainites. There were five hundred and twenty virgin and anchorite Sethite men. This number of the Sethites is found only here in the sources examined. In Questionnaire §11.1, the Sethites are five hundred in number.

§21 The Cainite women invented cosmetics and musical instruments. They used henna on their hands and feet. Henna has not been mentioned in the works cited previously.

§22 Singing and dancing, they seduced the Sethite men, and the consequent fornication took place. Noah was the only exception.

Remarks:

1. The sons of blind Lamech son of Methusael, the person who killed Cain, invented music. The sons were called Yobal and Taliel (see Question §7). The name Jobal comes from Jabal (Gen 4:20). Taliel is unknown elsewhere. Could it be a much-changed form of Tubal-Cain, Lamech's son, by Zilla (Gen 4:22)?

---

86. Here the number two hundred refers to years and not ascetic Sethites. The same number of years is found in Questionnaire §11.1 and in Sermon on the Flood §6.
87. On Noem Zara, see above part 10, n. 24.
88. Cited from Lipscomb 1990, 189–205.

2. The Cainites made musical instruments (Sermon on the Flood §5).
3. The Cainites invented false music, musical instruments, and dance (Sethites and Cainites §9; Satan defined minstrels according to Short Story of the Holy Forefathers §30).
4. They adorned themselves and their women (so Sermon on the Flood §5). Short Story of the Holy Forefathers §29 relates that they adorned women with rouge and antimony.[89]

8–9. History of the Forefathers §45 M2245 (1689) and Short History of the Holy Forefathers §19 M2111 (1652–1679)[90]

Both these writings have much the same passage, and in both it is connected with Enosh. That passage transmits the first three items below. Here the Sethite and Cainite traditions are tied to Enosh and not to Enoch, as in the preceding and following texts.[91] The confusion of these two antediluvian figures with similar names is found elsewhere in Armenian parabiblical literature.

> Enosh preached celibacy to his children.
> Two hundred people "established a covenant for themselves to live purely."
> These were called sons of God.

In addition, Short History of the Holy Forefathers §§29–30 also relates in connection with Enoch that:

> Two hundred Sethites climbed Mount Hermon and lived ascetically. Noah was among them, and they were called "sons of God."
> Cainite women invented cosmetics.

---

89. On these cosmetics, which are distinctive of the Watchers tradition and its ramifications, see §10.5 above and pp. 115, 142–44, 151.
90. *Arm Apoc* 2:200; 4:171, 173. The first work is found in several copies (see Lipscomb 1990, 180).
91. See *Arm Apoc* 1:13; 2:84, 151. See also Reed 2014, 169–72, 174; she argues that the Armenians present the Enoch figure with certain distinctive characteristics that are independent of Syriac traditions.

Under the influence of music and dance, the Sethites ascetics were suborned and became sons of perdition.

10. Yovhannēs Erznkacʻi Pluz. Concerning the Creation of the World, lines 259–305 (thirteenth century).[92]

In this passage, derived from Gen 4:23, the Cainite Lamech appears as the instigator of the seduction, which idea has not appeared in the other texts quoted so far. He encourages his wives to seduce the Sethites.[93] The chief points of Yovhannēs Erznkacʻi's retelling are:

> ll. 263–263⁴: "They took paint and antimony, the women teachers of wickedness, | They fell upon the race of Seth and that which they desired took place."
> l. 299 Two hundred souls were reconciled in the generation of Enoch.
> ll. 300–301 They lived on Mount Ahermon, celibate; later, they descended and …
> l. 302 They fell in with the daughters of men and went about in lustfulness.
> l. 303 They sinned.
> l. 304 "Twenty men copulated with one woman; no semen flowed."[94]
> l. 305 But one was born, tall in height, and his mother choked on the day of birth.
> l. 306 They were giants, forty cubits long.

11. Yovhannēs Tʻlkurancʻi (fourteenth century) Poem no. 14[95]

Here again the seductive power of music is foremost.

> 57 The children of Seth were confounded,
>   They who were eager ascetics.
> They heard the horn and the cymbals,
>   And all came down from the mountain.

---

92. Quoting the translation in James Russell 1987, 183–84. I myself have also translated and published excerpts from this poem in Stone 2006, 149–93.
93. See Asya Bereznyak in *Arm Apoc* 4:92–93.
94. Contrast Abel 6.2 above, where excessive semen is mentioned.
95. Pivazyan 1960, 57–60; James Russell 1987, 78.

The citations that have been given in this section are surely not exhaustive. Nonetheless, they do illustrate clearly how the ideas of Gen 6:1–4 were current among the Armenians and some of the ways in which they developed.

Giants in Armenian Texts about Cainites and Sethites

The idea that there were giants in the antediluvian time was very old and was exegetically based on Gen 6:4. It is already found in Sir 16:7 (early second century BCE), where the Greek translation reads "giants" for "princes of old"[96] (compare also Wis 14:6). Our purpose here is not to explore the views about giants in the ancient world; it is more modest than that, just to look at Armenian sources connecting giants with the Cainites and Sethites.[97] It will be observed just from the short list that follows here that giants had an integral role in a number of Armenian forms of the story of the Sethites and the Cainites. They were always connected with the line of Seth either positively or negatively. The first relevant context is that the children of the sons of God and the Cainite women were giants. They were an unnatural outcome of an unnatural coupling. This context is basically negative. However, Seth, who was a positive figure, was also said to

---

96. See Goff 2010. Goff thinks that the reference is to the Canaanite rulers of the land. However, τῶν ἀρχαίων γιγάντων, "of the ancient giants," is the actual interpretation found in Ben Sira's grandson's Greek of Ben Sira's Hebrew term נסיכי קדם, "princes of old," the reading of the Genizah Hebrew manuscript. There are quite numerous additional references to giants in other works of the Second Temple period. See, for example, 4Q180 1; 4Q201 1 III, 16, Jub. 5.1, 7.22. Later the giants are mentioned in Armenian in Sethites and Cainites §11. Moreover, there are plentiful mentions of giants in other sources, Qumranite, rabbinic, and more. On giants in the Hellenistic world, see Bremmer 2004, 35–61. In the Roman world, supposed remains of giants were celebrated at various places. These might have been fossils, and this interesting matter is discussed by Elisha Fine and Steven Fine (2022).

97. The connection of giants with the fallen angels is to be found particularly in Book of the Giants, a work associated with the Enochic writings. See the bibliography cited in nn. 17, 18 to this part. On the Qumran fragments, see Stuckenbruck 1997a. In Ps-Eupolemus, frag. 2, Abraham is said to trace his ancestry back to the giants, presumably the Sethians; see in the next note. Fragments of this Samaritan work survive in Greek. See Attridge 1984, 165. Note also that Philo wrote a treatise *On the Giants*, another witness to the power of this tradition. The lines of connection between Watchers, demons, and giants are traced by Fröhlich 2016. Other papers in that volume also greatly illuminate this interesting subject.

be a giant and so were his sons, even before the union of the Sethites with the Cainites. There are rabbinic traditions that Adam was of extraordinary size.[98] One wonders whether this is because Seth was thought to be a giant since, according to Gen 5:3, he was in the "image and likeness" of Adam, using the same words as Gen 1:26 uses of Adam's creation in God's image and likeness. Be that as it may, the discussion of giant antediluvian Sethites shows that although giants are not always bad, they certainly originate in the antediluvian age. More specifically, we read that:

1. The children of Sethite men and Cainite women were giants.[99] This idea is found in Sethites and Cainites §11; Abel §6.3;[100] Yovhannēs Tʻlkurancʻi, *Rhymed History* 306–307.
2. The sons of Seth were giants (Question §3, §10; Abel §6.2)
3. Seth was a giant (Sethites and Cainites §5)

Annotation 17. Questionnaire's Position in the Armenian Tradition: Sethites and Cainites

It is clear from the evidence presented above that the tradition of the Sethites and Cainites is deeply rooted in the Armenian telling of the antediluvian history. The numerous texts cited above, when compared with Questionnaire and with the *Chronography* of Michael the Syrian, also serve to highlight the sustained similarities between these two writings in contrast with nearly all the others adduced here. More evidence and further relevant tales and poems almost certainly exist but have not yet come to our attention. Clearly, additional research is needed so as to be able confidently to outline the shape and transmission of the Armenian tradition of the Sethites and Cainites, but to date, two chief variants may be observed. One is the form of the tradition in the *Chronography* of Michael in its Armenian version and the same tradition also is recorded

---

98. See for example, Ginzberg 1909, 5:79 n. 22; 86 n. 37. See further Barzilai 2007, 11–14, who discusses early (predestruction) texts concerning the creation of Adam "in the image of the holy ones" (that is, angels).

99. This, of course, goes back to Gen 6:4. See also Jub. 5.2; and T. Reu. 5.7. It also is to be found in the Syriac original of the *Chronography* of Michael the Syrian (Chabot 1899, 1:5).

100. Compare Abel §7.3, where the depth of the flood is attributed to the giants' height.

with minor variants in Questionnaire. In the various parabiblical Adam and primordial history materials, a second variant of this tradition is to be found, which differs from that in the *Chronography* and Questionnaire, as shown above.

12
Noah and the Building of the Ark

The subjects of this part include Noah's virtue, particularly his five-hundred-years' celibacy,[1] as well as the birth of his three sons and then the birth of their descendants. It takes as a given the separation of the pure Sethites who went to the desert from the evil and licentious Cainites and the eventual seduction by lascivious Cainite women of all the Sethites but Noah.[2] Then, the division of the earth among Noah's four (sic!) sons is given, based on the Tabula Gentium in Gen 10. Next in this section, Gen 6:1–4—that is, the incident of the sons of God and the daughters of men—is taken to describe the corruption of the Sethites and their illicit mixing with the Cainite women. From this forbidden union, there issued the events that led to great wickedness and consequently to the building of the ark and the flood and eventually to the tower of Babel. The continuation of the legendary history with which this part ends is the subject of the next chapter, part 13, below.

TEXT

M682 / fols. 7g.20–7d.24/

12.1/ Եւ եղեւ Նոյ այր արդար եւ հաճոյ Աստուծոյ.[3] զի Շ. (500) արքն[4] որ յանապատէն դարձան եւ խառնակեցան ընդ դստերսն Կայենի, միայն Նոյ պահեաց զկուսութիւն իւր.

---

1. Also compare CT 14.2 (*MOTP* 1:550) among many sources for this feature.
2. See annotations 16 and 17 to part 11 above.
3. This sentence is adapted from Gen 6:9.
4. One would expect a partitive ablative here.

12.2/ վասն որոյ ասաց Աստուած. «Մեղք մարդկան բազմացաւ,[5] եւ լցաւ երկիր անիրաւութեամբ. ահա ապականելոց է երկիր. զնա՛ եւ առ քեզ կին զի որդիս ծնցես եւ տապան շինեսցես, զի յետ ՃԽ. (140) ամի ջնջեցից զմարդ եւ ամենայն կենդանիս զի ապականեաց, ասէ, ամենայն մարմին զճանապարհի իւր:

12.3/ Եւ էառ կին Նոյ եւ ծնաւ Ճ. (100) ամին որդիս Գ. (3), Սէմ, Քամ եւ զԱբէթ, զի Լ ամին մի անգամ մերձենայր ի կինն: Եւ եւս Աստուած զի օր աւուր առաւելոյր չարութիւն մարդկան զԻ. (20) ամս կարճեաց եւ ետ ջրհեղեղ յետ Ճ. (100) ամին:

12.4/ Եւ շինեաց Նոյ զտապանն ի Ճ. (100) ամս.[6] երկայնութիւնն Յ. (300) կանգուն, լայնութիւնն Ծ. (50) եւ բարձրութիւնն Լ. (30). եւ թէ[7] որշափ է կանգուն, զազի անուն է պարսիցն Բ. (2) թիզ է: հայոցն Դ. (4), հոռմոցն Գ. (3), եւ փռանկացն Ը. (8):

12.5/ Եկն անձրեւ ջրհեղեղին Խ. (40) տիւ եւ զԽ. (40) գիշեր եւ բարձրացաւ ջուրն Ձ. ամիս եւ նստաւ ի Ձ. (6) ամիսն. ի բոլոր տարին ի ներքս մնացին. եւ ապա արձակեաց զագռաւն այլ ոչ դարձաւ, յորինակ սատանայի. եւ արձակեաց զաղաւնին եւ դարձաւ, յորինակ հոգւոյն սրբոյ, որ դարձեալ ետ բնութեանս Քրիստոս. եւ տապանն օրինակ եկեղեցւոյ:

Translation

12.1/ And Noah was a righteous man and pleasing to God,[8] since (of) the five hundred[9] men who returned from the desert[10] and had intercourse with the daughters of Cain, Noah alone preserved his virginity.[11]

---

5. In the instance of this verb, բազմացաւ the *pluralis tantum* մերք is treated *ad sensum* as a singular. The second word of the section is illegible.

6. A locative, that is, ամին would be expected.

7. Following թէ is a much-blotted word, which, judging from its outline, seems to be a dittographic թէ.

8. Gen 6:9.

9. The figure of five hundred sinning Sethites, found in Questionnaire §11.1 and here, is unusual. More commonly, the number is set at two hundred. Concerning the Good Tidings of Seth §§18, 20 has a third tradition that there were 520 celibate anchorites. See part 11, n. 44 above.

10. See part 11, n. 47 above on p. 141.

11. This is, of course, based on Gen 6:8–9. That Noah's "righteousness" was virginity is a Christian reading of the biblical text also found in other Armenian sources;

12. Noah and the Building of the Ark

12.2/ On account of which God said, "The sins of humans have increased[12] and the earth is full of unrighteousness.[13] Behold, the earth is going to be corrupted.[14] Go and marry a wife so that you will have children, and you will build an ark,[15] for, after 140 years,[16] I will destroy humans and all animals, for all flesh,"[17] he said, "has corrupted its path."[18]

12.3/ And Noah took a wife and begot three sons in the hundredth[19] year, Shem, Ham, and Japheth.[20] For a man would draw near to his wife

---

see annotation 18 to part 12 below. Also compare the treatment of Isaac's virginity in part 15 n. 33 and annotation 27.

12. See Gen. 6:5.
13. Gen 6:11. The next phrase is also taken from this verse.
14. Or: is corrupted. This is the verb used in Arm Gen 6:11.
15. This is derived from Gen 6:12–14.
16. The origin of this number of years is unclear. In Gen 7:11, the flood is said to begin in "the six hundredth year of Noah's life, in the second month, on the 17th day of the month." His sons, Shem, Ham and Japheth were born in his five hundredth year (Gen 5:32), so the figure 140 cannot be derived from the biblical text. A typical presentation of Noah's chronology is in History of the Forefathers to Abraham and Their Years. In §11 of this work we read: "Noah, being 500 years old begat Shem, Ham, and Japheth from Noyem Zara his wife. And he lived another 100 years and the flood came and after the flood <he lived> for 350 years and died at 950 years" (*Arm Apoc* 4:62). [The number 140 must be a mistake: The following section claims that God shortened the time span by twenty years to one hundred—so the original time was 120 years. This number arises from Gen 6:3 "His days shall be 120 years." This line of interpretation, taking 120 years as the time left until the flood, is already attested in a composition found in Qumran, known as "Commentary on Genesis A," 4Q252 I, 1–3: "[In the] 480th year of Noah's life, their end (or: time) came to Noah. And God said: 'My spirit shall not dwell with man forever, their days shall be cut off [ויחתכו ימיהם] at 120 years, until the time of the waters of the flood." A similar interpretation is found in Targum Onqelos to Gen 6:3: "A prolongation shall be given to them, 120 years, (to see) if they should repent." See further references in Ginzberg 1909, 5:174–75 n. 19. –S.E.].
17. That is, fleshly beings.
18. Or: ways.
19. It should be "five-hundredth," and the apparently first digit, the preceding numeral "five," has fallen out.
20. The birth of Noah's sons is mentioned in Gen 5:32 and 6:10, but no date is given in those verses. Later, in Gen 7:6 and 11, the flood is put in Noah's six hundredth year. Noah is said in Gen 5:32 to be five hundred years old when the children are born, and his virginity up to the age of five hundred is inferred from that. The comment about shortening a thirty-year period by twenty years fits with the idea of thirty years between each of the three births plus an additional ten years, though it is not clear where the additional years were thought to come, presumably after the birth

once in thirty years.[21] And when God saw that day by day the wickedness of humans increased, and he shortened (that time) by twenty years (see Gen 6:3) and brought[22] the flood after a hundred years.

12.4/ And Noah built the ark in one hundred years: its length (was) 300 cubits, its breadth (was) 50, and its height (was) 30. And what is the measure of a cubit? it is called a gazi[23]; it is two spans of the Persians, 4 of the Armenians, 3 of the Byzantines, and 8 of the Franks.[24]

12.5/ The rain of the flood came for forty days and for forty nights, and the water rose for six months and receded[25] in six months. For a whole year, they remained inside; then he sent forth the raven, a symbol of Satan, but it did not return; then he sent the dove, and it returned, as a symbol of the Holy Spirit, which again He gave to this nature, Christ,[26] and the ark (is) a symbol of the church.[27]

---

of Japheth. On this, see S. Ephrati's remarks at the end of the note 16 above. It is also inferred from Noah's age of five hundred years when his children were born according to Gen 5:32. See Philo, *QG* 2.49. See further Minov in Stone, Amihai, and Hillel 2010, 238–41. There, he discusses also Afrahat, *Demonst.* 13.5–6 and Ephrem's views as they are expressed in his *Comm. Gen.* 8.17–18. See above part 10.

21. Similarly, in the Armenian apocryphal traditions, the births of Adam and Eve's children were thought to be thirty years apart (see Stone 2013, 91, n. 67, where the subject is treated at length and part 9, n. 14 of the present work). In the antediluvian genealogies in the Bible, Shelach, Peleg, and Serug all begat sons when they were thirty years old (Gen 11:14, 18, 22). It is not surprising, therefore, that intercourse was said to take place every thirty years. Thirty years was thought to be the ideal age of life of males. According to Luke 3:23, Jesus began his ministry at the age of thirty. Likewise, Adam was considered to have been created like a man of thirty years of age, so Anania Širakacʻi (Stone 2013, 44–45); Aṙakʻel Siwnecʻi, *Adamgirkʻ* 1.22.35 (Stone 2007a, 212); Dawitʻ Ganjakecʻi Canon 85 (Stone 2013, 411). Thirty years are reckoned a generation according to Philo, *QG* 4.5 (see Paramelle 1984, 162–63).

22. Literally: gave.

23. *gaz* is a Persian measurement sometimes said to be an ell. Here, it is said to be a cubit.

24. The mention of "the Franks" betrays the high medieval date of the composition.

25. Literally: sat.

26. The reference is to the descent of the Holy Spirit at the baptism of Christ in the form of a dove (see Matt 3:16, Mark 1:10, Luke 3:22, and John 1:32). "Nature" refers to the human body, one possible meaning of the Armenian word, and so this expression has to do with the incarnation.

27. These symbolic understandings of the raven, the dove, and the ark are found elsewhere. They are discussed in brief in Gutmann 1977. See also Stone 2021c, 344–57. The raven, some traditions maintain, did not return to Noah because it was a carrion

Annotation 18. Noah's Virginity

That Noah alone of the Sethites was virtuous and was thought to have remained a virgin until he reached the age of five hundred years has been noted above. His virginity is often remarked upon or discussed in Armenian apocryphal sources, such as Descendants of Adam §1.30, Sermon Concerning the Flood §10, Construction of Noah's Ark §4, Concerning the Good Tidings of Seth §§26, 30, Q&A from the Holy Books (both versions) §17, Short History of the Holy Forefathers §26, and Form and Structure of Noah's Ark §4. See also Minov on Afrahat, *Demonst.* 13.5–6 (and his discussion of the matter) and also Biblical Paraphrases 1.[28]

Annotation 19. The Raven

The raven in the Noah story has attracted considerable exegetical interest. Genesis 8:6–7 only tells us that Noah sent it forth and that it did not return: "At the end of forty days Noah opened the window of the ark which he had made and sent forth a raven; and it went to and fro until the waters were dried up from the earth." Why did it not return? What did it do? These lacunae in the story naturally raised questions in the minds of readers and exegetes through the centuries.

Before going on to look at answers that have been given to those questions, however, I must make some general remarks and examine the attitude toward ravens in the biblical sources, a subject upon which I have already touched.[29] The raven is a common bird in the northern hemisphere and is a hunter and a scavenger. Its striking black feathers that have an almost burnished sheen mark it out as a comparandum serving to describe the beloved's hair in Song 5:11. The raven is an intelligent bird, and it makes a distinctive croaking sound called cawing. Both the male and the female participate in feeding the chicks.

In the Bible, it is listed among birds of prey and carrion-eaters that are forbidden for human consumption (see Lev 11:15; Deut 14:14). It is also mentioned as a typical denizen of desolate places by the prophets Isaiah and Zephaniah (Isa 34:11; Zeph 2:14). The raven is well known for

---

eater and stayed away to eat corpses (Pirqe R. El. 23). See further, Lewis 1984. See further below on this.

28. Stone, Amihai, and Hillel 2010, 238–39; *Arm Apoc* 1:86–87.
29. See part 10 n. 79.

its care of its young. The young ravens calling for food, which is provided, as I said, by both the male and female, are reflected in Ps 147:9: "He gives to the beasts their food, and to the young ravens which cry." This is also referred to by Job 38:41, "Who provides for the raven its prey, when its young ones cry to God, and wander about for lack of food?" The ravens' activity in the feeding of their young also inspired the imagery in Luke 12:24. The ravens' feeding of their chicks makes them the appropriate instrument for Elijah's miraculous sustenance in 1 Kgs 17:4, 6.[30]

In Jub. 11–12, we read the story called "Abraham and the Ravens," which relates that ravens attacked the Babylonians' fields and vineyards, and Abraham managed to chase them away with the help of God. This tale is also familiar both in Syriac and in Armenian parabiblical and associated writings.[31] It is witnessed quite early in Armenian, already appearing in the *Commentary on Genesis* perhaps to be attributed to Stepʻanos Siwnecʻi, which is likely to be dated to around the eighth century.[32] According to the story in Jubilees, the ravens are sent to the fields in Babylon by Mastema as a punishment. Abraham prays to God to remove the ravens, and the ravens disappear. Thus, he comes to recognize God. In Syriac writings, including the *Chronography* of Michael the Syrian, and in the Armenian apocryphal texts, these ravens are sent by God and not by Mastema or Satan.

The idea that the raven is a Satanic bird is, however, explicit in §12.5 above, which says, "the raven, a symbol of Satan." This association surely arises from the ravens' color and their hoarse croaking call.[33] Indeed, this view is found as early as Philo, who, in his discussion of Gen 8:7 in *QG* 2.35 says that "the raven is a blackish and reckless and swift creature, which is a symbol of evil." In the story of Noah and the ark as it is related in Sib. Or. 1.217–282, Noah twice sends doves and then a "black-winged

---

30. Ravens and crows differ but belong to the same biological family, the corvidae. However, the names are often used interchangeably in ancient texts. In Armenian and Hebrew, for example, one word, ագռաւ and עורב, respectively, may translate both "crow" and "raven."

31. On this story in Syriac, see Brock 1978; Hilkens 2018, 75–81. For Armenian forms of the story, see *Arm Apoc* 3:18–20, 42–43, etc. See part 10, n. 82. Anecdotally, I have myself observed large flocks of ravens feeding on newly ploughed ground in Armenia, a few kms. north of Erevan.

32. See Michael E. Stone 2021b, 18–21, §2.1.6–8.

33. Edgar Allen Poe's famous poem, "The Raven," of course, also ascribes an ill-omened character to this bird and evokes the same feeling.

bird," and the latter, unlike the dove, alighted on dry ground and did not return.³⁴ While this statement is neutral as regards the raven and its connection with evil, which feature does not occur in the biblical sources, Philo knows that connection very well.

Jewish sources of the late Hellenistic period show some differences from the biblical narrative. This is the case in the Sibylline Oracles, just mentioned. In 4Q254ᵃ 15 4 as well, we read that after Noah exited the ark he sent a raven off, and it returned. The context, as so often in the Dead Sea Scrolls, is broken, and the returning raven is said to be a sign for the future, but no more is preserved.

In the Armenian Adam literature, the question is raised how Cain learned to kill Abel, and an interesting recital is found in recension 2 of Abel and Cain, where we read:³⁵

> 26 Now Cain was walking here and there, but he did not know with what he must kill him (that is, Abel). 27 Then Satan took on the form of two ravens, and the one took a sharp stone, and it struck the other with it in the throat and killed him, and the stone was sharp as a razor. 28 And Cain learned from Satan, and he took the stone and leapt upon his brother.

Another version of the same story is related in Abel and Other Pieces §3.4, which reads:

> 4 And whence did he know how?³⁶ Two demons in the form of ravens quarreled, and one, taking the flint, slaughtered his fellow. From this (Cain) learned, and having found (a stone), he slaughtered him bloodily. And he was buried by his parents.³⁷

---

34. This order of birds is found in certain ancient, extrabiblical sources. See the remarks by John J. Collins in *OTP* 1:340 n. t on this matter. See *DSSE* 1:508–9. On this passage see Peters 2008, 162 n. 49. She talks of a supposed Jewish belief in the ability of doves and ravens to see into the future. In my judgment, this view needs a more convincing demonstration, but that the raven was seen in many cultures as a bird of (usually ill) omen cannot be disputed.

35. Cited from Lipscomb 1990, 272–73. We choose to quote the second recension because there is a textual corruption in the first recension at this point, as remarked by Lipscomb 1990, 164. This material is also discussed in annotation 14.

36. That is, how to kill Abel.

37. See *Arm Apoc* 2:148; the same tradition occurs also in Vardan *vardapet* Arewelc'i's *Commentary on Genesis* (see Issaverdens 1934, 56); a Georgian variant is

In this version of the story, it was two demons who became ravens, rather than Satan himself turning into two ravens. Demons are typically represented in Armenian manuscript paintings as being black.[38] Yovhannēs Ĵułayecʻi (1643–1715) likens Satan to a raven, and further sources could be quoted that illustrate the Satanic association of this bird in medieval Armenia.[39]

The same negative association of the raven already occurs in the Animal Apocalypse in 1 En. 90.2 and 11, where the ravens are listed together with eagles and vultures as birds that symbolize the enemies of Israel. Another biblical textual hook for a variant negative understanding of raven is to be exemplified in the Samaritan work TM 1.54, which quotes Exod 8:20 but reads the Hebrew word ערב, translated "flies" by RSV, as עורב, "ravens." According to this reading, the text says, "A great darkness was seen there, with exceedingly many ravens" (TM 1.54). This very interpretation shows, once more, a negative view of the raven. Finally, the same negative characterization of the raven or crow as the Jewish people may be found in the Christian work, Physiologus §31.2–4, where we read, "The Physiologus says about the crow … (that) it was the Jewish people, that killed the celestial Word."[40]

In the text called Noah and the Cheirograph,[41] the following occurs:

> 3. Question: What happened to the raven?
> Answer: Some say that it was drowned in the water, conceiving through (its) mouth by its partner, or it remained on a corpse of an animal. And others say that the builder of the Ark named Nersēs had built a house upon the Ark without God's command. He was killed, and the raven ate his corpse.

---

mentioned in Lüdtke 1919, 156. The same incident is found both in Abel and repeated in History of the Forefathers §§23–25 (*Arm Apoc* 2:148, 193). See also Stone 2013, 180. Compare the Mandean exegesis of the raven in Right Ginza §18: Edmundo Lupieri 2002, 210–12.

38. This, of course, is scarcely surprising. Acts of Thomas 64 mentions demons in the form of black humans. See N. Stone 2011, where the blackness of demons is discussed.

39. Stone 2013, 672 §4. See also part 10 n. 79 in this volume and Stone 2021c, 344–57.

40. See Muradyan 2005, 135–36, 160–61. Ravens and crows differ but belong to the same biological family, the corvidae.

41. Stone 2021c, 348.

12. Noah and the Building of the Ark

Figure 10. M5523, 1414 (The Harrowing of Hell Showing Black Demon)

In the present annotation, the reasons for the nonreturn of the raven are being enumerated. The idea that it drowned while mating has no known parallels. However, the view that it was busy scavenging and devouring carrion is found quite widely. See Pirqe R. El. 23 and PH 22.4 (*MOTP* 1:608), among other sources.[42]

---

42. This matter is dealt with also in Stone 2021c, 353. The same reason is given in the Mandean Book of John (Lupieri 2002, 202), which says that, being busy eating corpses, the raven forgot the task given it by Nu (Noah). Further discussion of its being a carrion-eater is to be found in Lewis 1984, 47, 146; Ginzberg 1909, 1:164; Gatch (1975) deals in considerable detail with the raven and the carrion-eating explanation in early English art and texts. Gutmann (1977) talks of the Eastern and early Christian iconography showing the raven eating human bodies, while European sources often have it eating the corpses of beasts. See also PH 22.4 (*MOTP* 1:608), which explains

This story of Nersēs, Noah's helper, is known to me only from one other Armenian document: The Form and Structure of Noah's Ark §4.[43] The full story about him remains unknown, pending further discoveries.

---

the raven's failure to return saying that "after finding the bodies of the deceased, it fed on them." See Lupieri 2002, 202.

43. This is published as no. 8 in *Arm Apoc* 6:45–51.

13
Peoples of the Sons of Noah

One of the points of interest within this thirteenth part of Questionnaire is that a list, probably drawn from an independent document, is embedded in it at §13.1. This is a shorter form of a text bearing the same name, Peoples of the Sons of Noah, that I published some decades ago from manuscript M533 of the year 1660.[1] These two parallel passages are examples of lists of nations, going back ultimately to Gen 10, where Noah's offspring are listed and treated as ancestors of various nations.[2] In the other manuscript, M533, the list of peoples is followed in each case by a short geographical description of their territory. Those territorial descriptions are not found in M682. Other than that, the two texts show the following substantial differences:

պարսիկք] omit M533 | մակեդոնացիք] + Մադացիք "Medes" M533]
| աղուանք "Caucasian Albanians"] ալանք "Alans" M533.

A third particular tradition presented by Questionnaire deals with Maniton, Noah's apocryphal fourth son, his activities after the flood, and his cultural, geographical, and ethnographical roles. This tradition is discussed in detail in annotation 21. Finally, in §13.4, the postdiluvian disposal of Adam's remains is taken up again. This matter has been discussed in annotation 6 above.

---

1. See Stone 1981a, 224–27. Of course, the Tabula Gentium tradition found here is much older than that text or, for that matter, than the present document, Questionnaire.
2. Scott 2002 dealt with this material, which formed the basis of several ethnographic and geographic lists in various early Christian sources, as is discussed in n. 33 below. See also Scott 1997a; 1997b. See further concerning such lists in Syriac, Minov 2020.

Text

M682 fol. 7g.31

13.1/ Այս են ազգ³ որդւոցն Նոյ.

Սեմայ. Եբրայեցիք, փռանք, Պարսիկք, եւ այլք:

Եւ Աբեթի ազգ. հայք, մակեդոնացիք, յոյն, լատինացիք, ադուանք եւ վրացիք:

Իսկ Քամայ ազգ. եգիպտացիք, հնդկացիք, հեթացիք, յեբուսացիք, հապաշք որ են քուշացիք, ամուրհացիք, գերգեսա/ fol.7d /ցիք, արուադացիք, քաղդեացիք որ են ասորիք:

13.2/ Եւ յետ ելանելոյ ի տապանէն ծնաւ Նոյ որդի մի Մանիդոն անուն եւ դուստր մի Աստղիկ անուն: Եւ եկաց Նոյ այլ եւս ՃԼԵ. (135) ամ, որ լինի ամենայն ամք կենաց նորա ՋԾ. (950).

13.3/ Եւ բաժանեաց զաշխարհս որդւոց իւրոց.

բաժին Սեմայ է ի միջերկրեայս,⁴ Պարսից աշխարհ, եւ Ասորոց եւ Պաղեստին.

բաժին Աբեղի, հիւսիսոյ կողմ աշխարհի ի Տիգրիս գետէ,

բաժին Քամայ զիարաւ Եգիպտոս եւ Հապաշստան:

Եւ բաժին Մանիտոնի ծովու այն կողմն եւ Աստղիկ դուստրն յԱրաբիայ է:

13.4/ Իսկ նշխարքն Ադամայ <եւ>⁵ Եւայի, անդրանկին իւրոյ Սեմայ ետ Նոյ եւ նա թաղեաց իւրում երկրին ի Պաղեստինէ, Ադամայն ի Գողգոթայ եւ Եւային ի Բեթղահէմ. բայց յետոյ Քանանու որդիքն բռնութեամբ տիրեցին երկրին, վասն որոյ ասաց Աստուած Աբրահամու թէ «ձեզ տաց զերկիրն Քանանու, զվիճակ ժառանգութեան ձերոյ», զի Աբրահամ ի Սեմայ է, որպէս ասէ ազգահամարն. Սեմ, Արփաքսաթ, Կայնան, Սաղայ, Եբեր. սա էր աշտարակի շինողաց տանուտերանց. Փաղեկ, Ռագաւ, Սերուք, Նաքովր. Թարայ, Աբրահամ:

13.5/ Հարց: թէ ուստի՞ սկսաւ կռապաշտութիւն:

Պատասխանի. Առաջին թագաւորն զոր եդին որդիքն Սէթայ առաջ քան զՆոյ, նա եղեւ աստղաբաշխ: Եգիտ զթիւս կենդանակերպիցն եւ զկարգ նոցա: Յետոյ Մանիտոն որդին Նոյի

---

3. That the plural ազգք is required is clear. On the loss of the final -ք following a palatal, see Stone and Hillel 2012, index, nos. 333, 334.

4. եՕ above the line, p.m.

5. Presuming that եւ was lost through haplography with the first syllable of Եւա "Eve."

13. Peoples of the Sons of Noah

յաւելաւ աստեղագիտութիւնն եւ զհմայութիւն: Եւ Արփաքսաթ որդին Սեմայ բազմացոյց զԹաղդեացւոց մոլորութիւնն, եւ կախարդելն եգիտ եւ եցոյց բախտ եւ ձակատագիր ըստ աստեղաց ընթացից, եւ մոլորակաց ընթացք:

13.6/ Վասն որոյ որդիք նորա իբրեւ զաստուած համարեցին. կանգնեցին նմա պատկեր ի կենդանութեան իւրում: Այս եղեւ սկիզբն պատկերապաշտութեան, վասն որոյ յարարածապատումն Մովսէս ոչ յիշէ զսա:

13.7/ Եւ յետ աշտարակին թազաւորեաց քաղդեացւոցն որ եւ Նեբրովթ, եւ աստուած քարոզեաց զինքն.[6] Եւ Հայկ որ էր մի ի տանուտէրանց աշտարակին ոչ դաւանեաց զնա աստուած եւ եկեալ Բէլայ ի վերայ Հայկին պատերազմել, եւ հարեալ զնա Հայկն նետիւ սպան զԲէլ:

13.8/ Յետ Բէլայ թազաւորեաց Կամբիւրոս. սա արար ոսկեհան եւ արծաթագործութիւն: Յետ սորա Ամիրոս. սա բազում քաղաք շինեաց եւ հաստատեաց կշիռս եւ չափս եւ գոյնս ներկուածոյ խայտածս եւ նկարս տաձարաց. գդրամս գկնիքս. կազմագործութիւնս եւ պատկերս ի կռաւս:

Չի ասեն թէ Գ. (3) աչք ունէր եւ եղջիւր եւս. զի հսկայ էր եւ ուժեղ: Ոմանք Յոբ յայսմ ժամանակի ասեն:

Translation

13.1/ These are the peoples of the Sons of Noah:
of Shem (are) Hebrews, Franks, Persians, and others;
of Japheth (is) this descent (these nations): Armenians, Macedonians, Greeks, Latins, Albanians,[7] and Georgians;

---

6. ն2° is in red ink and above the line. Perhaps it is a correction of a mistake observed by the scribe while rubricating this text. Some diacritical signs in red ink are also to be found on this folio, suggesting that they were also added during the same process.

7. The reference is to the Caucasian Albanians (Armenian: Ałuankʻ), who were the third Christian nation of the Caucasus in antiquity, together with the Armenians and Georgians. They do not survive today as a separate ethnic group. In annotation 20 on part 13 below, devoted to the Tabula Gentium, as well as in the introductory remarks to this section, I discuss several Armenian perceptions of ethnography and geography.

then of Ham (are these) peoples: Egyptians, Indians, Hethians (Hittites), Jebusites, Habashians who are Cushites,[8] Amorites, Gergasites, Aruadites,[9] Chaldeans who are (As)Syrians.

13.2/ And after the going forth from the ark, Noah begot one son, Maniton by name, and one daughter, Astłik by name.[10] And Noah lived for <350>[11] more years, which makes all the years of his life 950 years.

13.3/ And he divided this earth among his children:

Shem's portion is in the mid-terran (region),[12] the land of the Persians and of the (As)Syrians and Palestine.

Japheth's portion is from the northern region of the world up from the Tigris River.

Ham's portion is the south, Egypt and Ethiopia.

Maniton's portion is the other side of the sea, and (Noah's) daughter Astłik's is in Arabia.[13]

---

8. That is, Ethiopians.

9. The Amorites and the Gergasites are two of various peoples that are mentioned in Gen 10:16–18 as descendants of Canaan. The Aruadites are also mentioned in that connection, and, in addition, the name occurs as one of the families of the tribe of Simeon in Num 26:17 (MT), which is 26:2 (LXX). Arm Num 26:17 has Արուադացի, a hapax legomenon in the Bible.

10. See annotation 21 to part 13, below, concerning Maniton and Astłik.

11. The number ՃԼՃ in the Armenian text is confused and does not make sense. Digit for digit it is 100 30 50. According to all the versions of Gen 9:28, it should be 350, and those Armenian digits could produce 3.100.50, which might have been behind the corruption in Questionnaire. Noah's total length of life here agrees with Gen 9:29. We have amended this reading in the translation.

12. Or literally: medi-terran. However, in fact, this seems to refer to Palestine, which was considered to contain the center of the earth. This idea has been discussed in annotation 6, p. 47. The actual center of the earth is said to be Jerusalem, or the temple, or Gologotha as is set forth in that annotation. This idea is widespread; see, for instance, the texts translated in Hilkens 2018, 109. There, Persia and (As)Syria are made explicit.

13. This section is also abbreviated from the work, Peoples of the Sons of Noah, which is discussed in the introductory remarks to this present part 13 and in detail in an annotation 20 following the part. The tradition developing from Gen 10, the so-called Tabula Gentium, is also discussed there. Maniton also appears in a secondary position in Peoples of the Sons of Noah, while Astłik is not mentioned there at all. These two apocryphal children of Noah are discussed in annotation 21 to part 13 on Maniton, below.

13.4/ Then, Noah gave the remains of Adam <and> Eve to his firstborn, Shem,[14] and he buried (them) in his land, in Palestine, those of Adam on Golgotha and those of Eve in Bethlehem.[15] But afterward, the sons of Canaan conquered the land by force,[16] on account of which God said to Abraham, "To you I will give the land of Canaan as the portion of your inheritance,"[17] for Abraham is of (the descendants of) Shem, as the genealogy says: Shem, Arpachshad, Kaynan,[18] Sałay,[19] Eber—he was (one)

---

14. See the Armenian apocryphon, Repentance of Adam and Eve §§98–103, about Shem and the remains of the protoplasts (Lipscomb 1990, 232–33).

15. The history of the remains of Adam and Eve is a substantial complex of tradition. It is discussed more extensively in annotation 6 to part 7 above. Here, it suffices to observe that, according to Repentance of Adam and Eve §99 as well, Adam's coffin was carried in Noah's ark. The idea that Adam was buried on Golgotha developed from the idea that, when Christ's cross was set up, it was on the spot of Adam's burial and the blood of the New Adam washed clean the sin of the Old Adam; see CT 49.10 (*MOTP* 1:579). This, in turn, was bolstered by the established etymology of Golgotha as "skull" (Matt 27:33, Mark 15:22), which was then taken as referring to Adam's skull. In a parallel way, Eve was said to be buried in a cave near Bethlehem, which is the place of the nativity; see further discussion and bibliography in annotation 6 to part 7, above. The same traditions are also present in the Armenian text known as The Bones of Adam and Eve (Stone 2000b). The illustration of the burial of Eve in the grotto at Bethlehem is discussed also in Hakobyan 2020, 524–25.

16. The author had to account for the name Canaan given both to the land and to Ham's son and reads "to you I will give Canaan's land (that is, the one he unjustly conquered)." He does this by having Canaan take the land of Palestine by force from the portion of Shem, which led to its renaming and consequently, he is forced by this argument to use the name "Palestine" for the holy land, so he can make his point. The name "Palestine" is quite rare in Armenian apocryphal texts; see one instance in Stone 2013, 81, 97 (with an onomastic etymology). See on this material, Hilkens 2018, 73. Here the author tries to understand the gift of the land to Abraham and his descendants. That was a problem for some authors of Armenian apocrypha who apparently had difficulties with the promise of the land to Abraham. See Stone 2018, 85 and note there.

17. This idea occurs connected with Abraham "for an everlasting possession" in Gen 12:7, 15:7, 18, 17:7, etc. It is given to Israel "for an inheritance," according to Deut 4:21 and similarly in many other places.

18. This list agrees with that in 1 Chr 1:24–27, except that it introduces Kaynan (קינן, Kenan, Cainan), the son of Arpachshad (cf. 1 Chr 1:2). This is not Kenan, son of Enosh, father of Mahalalel of the antediluvian age mentioned in Gen 5:9, but it is the second Cainan mentioned as the father of Shelah in Luke 3:36–38. The same individual is mentioned in the LXX of Gen 10:24, 11:12–13, in Codex Alexandrinus of 1 Chr 1:18, and in Jub. 8.2. A complex tradition about him exists, which relates that he found antediluvian writings carved on the rock; see in detail Jub. 8.1–5. On the Jubi-

of the builders of the tower, the heads of households[20]—Peleg, Reu, Serug, Nahor, Terah, Abraham.[21]

13.5/ Question: whence did idolatry begin?

Answer: The first king whom the sons of Seth, before Noah, appointed was an astrologer. He discovered the number of the constellations and of the planets and their order.[22] Afterwards, Maniton, Noah's son, increased astronomy and divination. And Arpachshad, son of Shem, compounded the error of the Chaldeans and learned magic, and he demonstrated chance and fate according to the paths of the star and the paths of the planets.

13.6/ On account of this, his sons esteemed (him) like a god.[23] They set up an image to him while he was alive.[24] This was the beginning of idolatry, concerning which Moses, who wrote about creation, does not mention.[25]

---

lees passage, see Bauckham 1991; Fry 1992. Thus, Jubilees regards him as a tradent of forbidden astronomical and divinatory teaching. See also Jacobus 2009, 208–9.

19. This is transliteration of the name Shelah (Hebrew שלח, Greek Σαλα, Arm Սաղա). Shelah is mentioned in Arm Gen 10.24, 11:12 (13) as Սաղա Saɫa, etc.

20. Many traditions exist in the Armenian apocrypha about the building of the tower. A number of these were published in *Arm Apoc* 1:91 and several further Tower Texts were assembled and published in *Arm Apoc* 6:52–72. Indeed, Armenian apocryphal texts speak of seventy-two heads of families who united to build the tower; see below n. 27 and annotation 23.

21. This list resembles that in 1 Chr 1:24–27.

22. This passage, indeed many aspects of part 13, draw heavily on the thirteenth-century *Chronography* of Michael the Syrian according to which the Sethites who came and mixed with the Cainite women, established a king, in imitation of Semazios who was king of the fallen "Sons of God." Michael's text, in the Armenian translation found in the 1871 edition, reads: եւ եղին եւ նորա իւրեանց թագաւոր ի Քաղդեացւոց երկրին՝ զԱղորոս. Նա եգիտ զաստեղագիտութիւնն եւ զթիւս կենդանակերպից եւ մոլորակաց եւ շրջմունս նոցա: "And they (the Sethites), too, set up a king for themselves in the land of the Chaldeans, Aɫoros. And he discovered astronomy and the number of constellations and planets, and their orbits" (my trans.). See Sawalaneancʻ 1871, 7. See further in annotation 16 to part 11, above.

23. Or: "like God"; grammatically, this is a possible translation, but the sense demands "like a god."

24. Compare the euhemeristic explanation of the origins of idolatry in Wis 14:15–18. Here the author absolves Hayk, eponymous ancestor of the Armenians (*Hay* is the Armenian self-designation) from any suspicion of idolatry. The story of Hayk and Bel is to be found in Movsēs Xorenacʻi, *History of the Armenians* 1:10–11, translated in Thomson 2006, 82–85.

25. Here, our author accounts for the fact that this story is not mentioned by Genesis. This shows that he regarded his legendary exegetical tradition as being authori-

13.7/ And after the tower, a certain Nebrovtʻ[26] ruled the Chaldeans, and he proclaimed himself a god. And Hayk, who was one of the heads of the families of the tower,[27] did not profess him to be a god, and Bēl came to do battle against Hayk, and Hayk smiting him with an arrow, killed Bēl.[28]

13.8/ After Bēl, Kambiwrōs ruled as king. He made[29] gold mining and silver working.[30] After him (was) Amirōs. He built many cities and established weights and measures and dyed spots of colors,[31] and pictures on temples, money, seals, furniture-making and images on linen.

---

tative, despite the matter not being mentioned in Genesis. Otherwise, he would just have dismissed it.

26. Nebrovtʻ is an Armenian form of the name Nimrod; see Arm Gen 10:8–9, transliterating Greek Νεβρωδ (Armenian ոււ is the regular transliteration of Greek ω); it is *nmrwd* in Syriac. See Gen 10:9–10; n. 44 below, and annotation 22 to part 13 about Nimrod. See PH 25 (*MOTP* 1:609), where the connection between Nimrod and idolatry is blatant: "From that point [that is, Nimrod's days] they began to practice idolatry, and humankind began to worship created things." There we discuss the tradition that Nimrod, king of Babylon, learned astrology from Noah's fourth son, Maniton. The tradition of Maniton's knowledge of astrology and divination is discussed in annotation 21 to part 13.

27. There is an Armenian tradition that seventy-two heads of families or householders united to build the tower of Babel. For this reason, so it says, when they were scattered and the languages were confused, there came to be seventy-two languages. See Biblical Paraphrases; Story of Noah §9 (*Arm Apoc* 1:91–93). The significance of the number seventy-two is discussed by Badalanova Geller 2021b, 336–37, compare her n. 49 on p. 336 with the discussion here. See also Badalanova Geller 2017b, 280 where she notes that in Slavic apocryphal sources seventy-two was the number of diseases brought upon humans by the fall. Observe the shift between seventy and seventy-two of the afflictions or strokes brought upon Adam according to Life of Adam and Eve—Latin and Armenian have seventy; Greek and Slavonic have seventy-two: Anderson and Stone 1999, 38–38E. We would maintain that, as the tradition developed, seventy and seventy-two were first connected to the Tabula Gentium, and the idea of seventy-two princes is an embroidery of that. See about this in detail in annotation 24, below.

28. This is related by Movsēs Xorenacʻi, *History of the Armenians* 1:10–11 (see Thomson 2006, 82–85). Apparently, the text identifies Nebrovtʻ (Nimrod) with Bēl.

29. That is, invented or discovered.

30. These ancient kings and culture heroes are not drawn from biblical traditions. Perhaps Amirōs is to be identified with Samiros, a mythical king of Babylon, mentioned by Michael the Syrian (Chabot 1899, 1:22). Kambiwros is surely Qumbaros, mentioned before Samiros in a list of the kings of Babylon embedded in the same source, p. 28.

31. Compare Stone and Timotin 2023, 88 n. 70 on the malefic character of dyers

For they say that he had three eyes and, moreover, a horn, for he was a giant and strong. Some say that Job (lived) at that time.[32]

ANNOTATION 20. PEOPLES OF THE SONS OF NOAH

As already observed in the introductory remarks to part 13, in this part, a copy of the short text entitled Peoples of the Sons of Noah has been embedded.

This embedded text represents an interpretation of the Tabula Gentium, the record of the division of the lands among Noah's three sons and their descendants, of which the oldest form is to be found in Gen 10. A relatively early interpretation of Gen 10 is to be found in 1QGen Apoc 16–17 (cf. Jub. 8.10–18).[33] There is nothing in those texts directly explicitly bearing on Armenia proper, but Japheth's portion does reach the sources of the Euphrates, the headwaters of which lie in Armenia.[34] The idea that there were seventy or seventy-two languages or nations is connected with the division of the lands among Noah's sons.

The very oldest Armenian reference to the seventy-two tongues or nations is in Agathangelos §612 and, consequently, is of the fifth century CE. Lists of the seventy-two nations are widespread in Armenian manuscripts. The oldest such lists we have encountered in surviving manuscripts are in M2679 of the year 981 CE, fols. 331r–332r, and M5254 (1280 CE), fol.192r.[35] The Syriac text of David bar Pawlos (eighth or ninth

---

in Western tradition. See also 1 En. 8.1 where dyes were taught by the fallen angel, Asael.

32. Although there is some ambiguity, it seems that this sentence is referring to Nimrod, of whom the Bible uses both the attributes, "giant, mighty man" and "strong, mighty" in Gen 10:8–9. The details of his appearance given here are not familiar from any other source. The biblical book of Job provides no date for its events. Various approaches were used over the centuries to set Job within the chronology of biblical events. In b. B. Bat. 15a–15b, several differing views of Job's time are given; see Ginzberg 1909, 5:381. The earliest proposed date for Job that Ginzberg mentions would makes him a contemporary of Abraham.

33. This passage is discussed in some detail by Eshel 2007. She deals with Japheth's portion of the lands of the earth on pp. 114–15. See further Scott 1997b, 295–323. On the Tabula Gentium, see further Scott 2002 and Minov 2020.

34. See 1QGenApoc 16:9 and Eshel 2007, 115; and compare CT 24.16-22 (*MOTP* 1:558–59).

35. Matʻevosyan 1997, 86–87. One form of this list has been published in *Arm Apoc* 1:158–63. Much information on the latter and allied texts, including manuscript

century) studied by Sergey Minov speaks of seventy-two peoples and of fifteen Japhethite nations, six of which know writing systems. "There are fifteen languages in the generations of Japheth, and six writings: Greeks, and Iberians, and Romans, and Armenians, and Medians, and 'Alpāyē, who are interpreted thus: Alans instead of 'Alpāyē. And Arabians, who ceased to exist, together with their writing."[36] The Syriac lists of literate nations, designed to give pride of place to the Syriac language, are analyzed in detail by Andy Hilkens (2020a, 20–21, 24), who gives tables of the literate peoples, organized according to Noah's three sons.[37] These traditions of the division of the earth among the nations and of the literate peoples are worthy of further investigation and will grant insight into the ethnographic, linguistic, and geographic notions of the author and his contemporaries

Both the descent of the nations from Noah and their genealogy played a role in the Armenian people's self-understanding; they viewed themselves as Noah's direct descendants through Japheth and their ancient and distinguished origins were thus seen to be confirmed by the Bible.[38] This biblical claim occurs in many Armenian sources[39] and the Armenian tradition sees the biblical generations of Japheth set out in Gen 10:2–4 to be seven in number: Gomer, Magog, Madai, Javan, Tubal, Meshech, and Tiras.[40] These also had sons, who, like their fathers also lived "in

sources is to be found in Anasyan 1959, 1: cols. 299–303. This tradition is much developed in Armenian, and texts associated with the lists of seventy-two peoples and languages also deal with the qualities attributed to languages and, like the Syriac texts discussed here, with the literate nations, writing systems, etc. The latter subjects are not discussed in Gen 10 and 11:7–9.

36. See Minov 2020, 65–66.

37. See also Hilkens 2018, 110 for a table of the literate nations, and on pp. 68–72 he discusses the parallel forms of the diamerismos and their interrelationship.

38. So, for example, Movsēs Xorenacʻi, *History of the Armenians* 1.5 and see Thomson 2006, 72; see further Sebēos, *Primary History of Armenia*. This section is not included in Thomson, Howard-Johnston, and Greenwood 1999. The same idea is expressed in Aṙakʻel Siwnecʻiʼs poetic *Book of Paradise*; see Tēr Nersēsean 1956, 2: stanzas 13–14.

39. Valentina Calzolari (2010) demonstrates how the same urge to show that the Armenians are the chosen people informs certain central New Testament Apocrypha. Badalanova Geller (2017b, 253–54) describes an analogous movement among the Slavs.

40. Michael the Syrian says, "les tribus [descendant] de Japhet furent au nombre de quinze," and counting Japheth himself that makes sixteen. Armenians were descendants of Japheth (Chabot 1899, 1:15).

their own lands, each with his own language, by their families, in their nations (tribes)" (Gen 10:32). Movsēs Xorenacʻi, *History of the Armenians* 1.72 gives the genealogy of the Armenians' ancestors listed as follows: (1) Yaphet, (2) Gomer, (3) Tʻiras, (4) Tʻorgom, (5) Hayk, (6) Armaneak, (7) Aramayis, (8) Amasya, (9) Gełam, (10) Harmay, (11) Aram, (12) Ara the Handsome.[41] Xorenacʻi's list is constructed based on Gen 10 combined with some preexisting Armenian traditions. Tʻiras, the third generation according to Movsēs Xorenacʻi's list, is the eighth and last in the list in Gen 10:2. The rest are of varied origins. Tʻorgom is most likely Japhetite Togarma, son of Gomer (Gen 10:3).[42] One wonders at the name Aram, drawn from the Shemite Genesis genealogy (Gen 10:22), which is second last in Movsēs's list. The inclusion of this name and its position in Movsēs's list remain unexplained. The other names are not biblical; they fill the lacuna following Togarma.

A second biblical connection for the Armenians was the toponym Ararat, first mentioned in connection with Noah's ark ("mountains of Ararat" in Gen 8:4). From Hellenistic times, the mountains of Ararat were generally said to be in Armenian lands, and these mountains connected Armenia with Noah and his ark and thus, with the reestablishment of humanity after the flood.[43] This topographical view served to bolster the genealogical claim.

Annotation 21. Maniton, Noah's Fourth Son

The words in §13.5 concerning astronomical and divinatory knowledge correspond to the Syriac text of Michael's *Chronography* as published by Chabot (1899, 13). Note the order of discovery given in §13.5: first, knowledge of the constellations and the planets was discovered by the unnamed king appointed by the Shemites; then next, astronomy and divination were increased by Maniton; then, Arpachshad, Shem's son, invented augury and foretelling by the movements of the stars and the planets and their orbits, that is, astrological divination.

Similarly, we read in the Armenian composition called Question §§16–17: "Maniton received God's gift of wisdom, such as the skill of

---

41. See Thomson 2006, 72.
42. See Cardona 1966.
43. See Stone and Topchyan 2022, 1–18; Garibian de Vartavan 2021; Stone 2010. An interesting older study is Inglisian 1935. See further Mellink 1962; Petrosyan 2016.

astrology. 17. Nebrovtʻa (Nimrod) went to him. He received a secret from him. This Nebrovtʻ first ruled over the earth." The connection between Maniton and Nimrod seems to bespeak a more complex story, which is being alluded to here but, for the moment, remains largely obscure.

It is noteworthy that the tradition that we have cited in the preceding paragraph concerns Maniton, Noah's fourth and apocryphal son, who was born to Noah after the flood. He is also familiar to us from Syriac sources as Yonṭon. The story presented by Questionnaire deals with him and his activities after the flood. In various sources, we find the following information about Maniton (or Yonṭon), which I assemble here in some detail.

Stephen Gerö wrote an integrative article about the Maniton or Yonṭon tradition with which he was familiar from Syriac sources, and I myself have also discussed Maniton elsewhere.[44] He had a sister named Astłik, which in Armenian means "star, little star." In the Armenian sources with which I am familiar, the following passages bear on this figure.

1. Question §§1.3–1.7

In this section, Question is drawing on the Apocalypse of Pseudo-Methodius, a Syriac composition that became widely influential.[45] We have already had occasion to refer to Question in connection with Nimrod, whom it links with Maniton:

> 1.3 In the 900th year, Noah begot a son according to his likeness. And he called him Maniton. 1.4 And he gave to his son Maniton some things

---

44. Stephen Gerö (1980, 325–26), assembles traditions about Ionton (Maniton), Noah's fourth son, and his instruction of Nimrod in astrology. For my work, see *Arm Apoc* 2:116–17. Maniton or Yonṭon played a considerable role in the *Apocalypse* attributed to Pseudo-Methodius, concerning which influential Syriac work see Reinink 1993; on the Armenian version, see Topchyan 2014; he discusses its origin in Greek on p. 368. This Armenian version does not contain the "legendary history" that includes the Nimrod material (see Topchyan 2014, 364–65). Concerning knowledge of the idea of Noah's fourth son in medieval Jewish sources, see the article published online by Amihai 2022.

45. On Question and its use of Pseudo-Methodius, see *Arm Apoc* 2:114–15. As was noted there, Stepʻanos Ōrbelian's *History of the Province of Sisakan* is considerably indebted to Pseudo-Methodius. On the role of Pseudo-Methodius in Armenian literature, see Topchyan 2014, 362–78.

when he was 100 years (old). And he sent him to Ovēayn.... 1.6 But Maniton <went to> Ovēayn[46] up to the sea, which is called the region of the sun.[47] In this place, Canaan went forth, and he dwelt there. This Maniton received God's gift of wisdom, such as the skill of astrology.

2. History of Adam and His Grandsons §16

16 And after the flood, he lived another three hundred and fifty years. And Noah begot one son, Maniton by name, and one daughter Astłi<k>[48] by name.

Although Maniton is most often referred to alone, he is sometimes, as in this document, said to have a sister called Astłik. In Questionnaire, she also figures, as is obvious from the next extract.

3. Questionnaire §§13.5–6

In the context of the inception of idolatry, we read the following euhemeristic explanation.

13.5/ Afterwards, Maniton, Noah's son, increased astronomy and divination. And Arpachshad, son of Shem, compounded the error of the Chaldeans and learned magic, and he demonstrated chance and fate according to the paths of the stars and the paths of the planets. 13.6/ Because of this, his sons esteemed him like a god. They set up an image

---

46. [The Syriac and Greek versions of Pseudo-Methodius say that Noah sent Yon(i)ton "to the (land of the) east." The strange Armenian name, Ovēayn, is probably a mistransliteration of the Greek ἑῴας, "to the East," which might have yielded Armenian *(Ե)ՈՎԱՍ, with a graphic corruption of Ս to Ն. Concerning that graphic corruption, see Stone and Hillel 2012, index no. 65. The Latin version, too, transliterated this word as "Eoas" instead translating it (see Aerts and Kortekaas 1998, 1:80–81 [texts], 2:68 [comment]). Topchyan argues that the Armenian Pseudo-Methodius goes back to an early Greek translation of the original Syriac (see Topchyan 2014, 362–78). –S.E.] See below, p. 182 on Otros.

47. [Thus, also the Greek and Latin translations of Pseudo-Methodius. The Syriac version has "Fire of the Sun" (ܢܘܪܐ ܝܘܡ). The Greek and Latin versions, as well as Questionnaire, perhaps reflect an early Syriac variant ܝܘܡ "region" instead of ܝܘܡ "fire." See Reinink 1993, 26; Aerts and Kortekaas 1998, 2:7; Su-Min Ri 2000, 324–27. –S.E.]

48. The manuscript is damaged. I read: "Astłik" for his sister's name, which I have drawn from other sources, and which is compatible with the surviving marks on the manuscript.

to him while he was alive. This was the beginning of idolatry,⁴⁹ concerning which Moses does not mention (anything) in Genesis.

4. Questionnaire §13.4

This section of Questionnaire forms a part of the tradition of the Tabula Gentium and the division of the earth among Noah's sons, based on Gen 10. That tradition is the main theme, of course, of Peoples of the Sons of Noah, which I have already discussed in the preceding annotation 20. It was an accepted truism of Armenian historiography that the Armenians descended directly from Noah's son Japheth.⁵⁰ In Questionnaire §13.3, we read:

> 13.3/ And he divided this earth to his sons (children):
> Shem's portion is in the mid-terran (region),⁵¹ the land of the Persians and of the (As)Syrians and Palestine.
> Japheth's portion is from the northern region of the world up to the Tigris River.
> Ham's portion is the south, Egypt and Ethiopia.
> Maniton's portion is the other side of the sea⁵² and his (Noah's) daughter's is Arabia.⁵³

This geographical information is parrelleled by information found in manuscript M10720 (eighteenth century):

---

49. This is a euhemeristic explanation of the origins of idolatry; see n. 24 above. An early example of this technique is to be found in Wis 14:14–21.

50. A clear example is Movsēs Xorenac'i, *History of the Armenians* 1.5, which combines the biblical genealogy of Japheth with Armenian traditions and produces the sequence: Yapheth > Gamer > Tiras > Torgom > Hayk > Ameneak > Aramayis > Amasya > Gełam > Harmay > Aram > Ara the Handsome. Compare Thomson 2006, 72. See also pp. 175–76 above.

51. Or: Mediterranean region, but the lands specified are not on the Mediterranean Sea but Palestine, in particular, which was considered to be at the center of the world.

52. No mention of a specific sea precedes this passage, and the exact meaning here, as it stands, is unclear.

53. This section is also abbreviated from Peoples of the Sons of Noah as I noted in the introductory remarks to section 13 above. Maniton also appears in a secondary position in that text, while Astłik is not found there at all. Of course, the Tabula Gentium tradition occurring here is much older than Peoples of the Sons of Noah. See also Scott 2002.

Նոյի որդիքն. սեմ. քամ յաբեթ. եւ կնոջն Նեեմ զարայ. եւ հարսներուն՝ Զանազան. Զամրանազան. Արեզնազան: Ի տապանին յետեւն Բ որդիդ ծնաւ Մանիտոն անուն տդայ. եւ Աստղիկ անուն աղջիկ:
The sons of Noah: Shem, Ham and Japheth. And his wife, Neem Zara,[54] and his various daughters-in-law, Zanazan, Zamranazan, Aregnazan.[55] In the ark, subsequently, he begat two children, a boy named Maniton and a girl named Astłik.[56]

So, in Questionnaire, Noah's fourth son, Maniton and "his daughter," doubtless meaning "his daughter Astłik," are listed as receiving portions of the world, just as Noah's other three sons did. In Question §6, the name of Maniton's portion is Ovēayn (see above), but no portion is listed in that passage for Astłik, and Questionnaire is the only source ascribing territory to her, namely, Arabia. Incidentally, the names of Noah's sons' wives are to be found in variant forms, Zanazan, Zarmanazan, and Yereknazan, in Concerning the Construction of the Ark §§38–39.[57]

Cave of Treasures

In the Syriac Cave of Treasures, Maniton, or Yonṭon as he is called in the Syriac tradition, is not mentioned in the division of the earth among Noah's sons in chapter 24, but a quite detailed passage concerning him occurs in chapter 27 in connection with his role as Nimrod's teacher (*MOTP* 1:560–61). We read there:

> 27.7 When he (Nimrod) reached the sea Otros[58] he found Yonṭon the son of Noah there. 8 … Then he drew near and worshipped Yonṭon. 9

---

54. As early as Jub. 4.33 and 1QGenApoc 6.7, her name is Noyem Zara. That form of the name occurs also in Armenian. This matter is considered in greater detail in part 10, n, 24.

55. These names are unfamiliar outside Armenian sources. See n. 60 below for some variant forms of them.

56. In the Mandean Right Ginza, we read of "Nu (Noah), the man, and Nuraita, his wife, and Sum (Shem), Iam (Ham), and Iapit (Japheth), the sons of Nu" (Lupieri 2002, 200). Nuraita, the name of Noah's wife here in Right Ginza, is surely cognate with her name Norea found in gnostic texts. See Pearson 1975, 143–52; 1988b, 265–75. A revised form of Pearson's 1977 article is to be found under the same title in Pearson 1990, 84–94.

57. *Arm Apoc* 5:14.

58. [The Syriac manuscripts attest the forms ܐܘܩܪܘܣ (Okro/as, *mutatis mutandis*)

Yonṭon said to him, "You are a king, and you worship me?" 10 Nimrod told him: "It is because of you that I came down here." 11 He stayed with him for three years, and Yonṭon taught Nimrod wisdom and a book of oracles.⁵⁹ Then he told him: "Do not come back to me again."

The same is to be found in the Armenian work, Question §1.7. That composition relates that Nebrovtʻa (Nimrod), who first ruled over the earth, went to Maniton and received a secret from him. Intriguingly, the mysterious name of the sea is "Otros" here and "Ovēayn" is a region that reaches up to the sea according to the writing called Question cited above. Scholars have independently suggested that both names are derived from Ocean.⁶⁰ It seems to me that this passage of Cave of Treasures is drawn from a different source than that utilized by chapter 24 of the same work concerning the division of the earth. In all likelihood, in Syriac, there once existed a fuller form of the traditions of Yonṭon/Maniton and perhaps of Astłik, and, of course, it may exist to this day, lying undiscovered in a Syriac or, for that matter, an Armenian manuscript.

Yonṭon/Maniton is known from the Syriac Apocalypse of Pseudo-Methodius, which is a source of the relevant part of Stepʻannos Ōrbelian's *History of the Province of Sisian*, as well as of the Armenian text bearing the title Question to which we have referred above.⁶¹ It also seems to be the source of the Maniton (Yon[i]ṭon, Ionṭon, Monētōn) material in the Armenian version of the *Chronography* of Michael the Syrian.⁶²

Hilkens (2020b) proposes a connection between Noah's descendant Yon(i)ṭon and Gandoubarios, an Indian astronomer.⁶³ He concludes that

---

and ܐܛܪܣ (Atras), whose derivation is far from clear. Su-Min Ri 2000, 324–25, suggests to derive them from "Ocean" (ܐܘܩܝܢܘܣ), but this is tenuous. This reading is also proposed in *MOTP* 1:560, n. b, without any explanation. –S.E.]

59. See Gerö 1980, 325–26. His speculations on the origin of this tradition are given on pp. 328–29, and he notes points in the history of the Yonṭon material in Latin on pp. 326–27. See also Toepel 2006b.

60. Efrati suggests that it could be a graphic mistake in Armenian: ՕՎԵԱՅՆ > ՕՎԵԱՅՆ; or perhaps in Syriac, ܐܘܩܝܢܘܣ > ܐܘܩܢܘܣ (but cf. n. 46 above). This seems quite likely. However, the connection between Otros and Oceanos is less obvious and seems less convincing.

61. See the discussion in *Arm Apoc* 2:115 for Stepʻanos Ōrbelean and on pp. 116–17 concerning Maniton.

62. On the *Chronography*, see n. 22 above.

63. Indeed, he argues on pp. 138–39 that this is an East-Syrian tradition and that the West Syrian tradition does not make this identification.

the Yon(i)ton tradition already circulated in Mesopotamia in the sixth or early seventh-century CE.[64] He also presents the debate about the origins both of Yon(i)ton and of the positive view of Nimrod, both traditions connected with the origins of astronomy, while astrology was attributed to Zoroastrian and other contexts.[65] Hilkens's sources do not mention Noah's daughter called Astłik ("Star"), who figures, as we have seen, in some Armenian tellings of these events.[66]

The acute remark of I. Dorfmann-Lazarev, in his translation of extracts from the Armenian version of the *Homilies* of pseudo-Epiphanius of Salamis, should be noted. Dorfmann-Lazarev remarked on the phrase "he (Noah) divided this quadrangular world between his three sons" and observed that, in fact, the addition of a fourth son would correspond to the four corners of the earth. Indeed, Adam's name was explained as an acrostic of the initial letter of the Greek words for the four directions.[67] This hypothesis is attractive, but unfortunately unprovable.

The Maniton tradition connects with a further tradition complex concerning the protoplasts, that is, the narrative of the vicissitudes of the bodies and relics of Adam and Eve. Of course, the question of what happened to their bodies during and after the flood was sure to arise, and it became the focus of lively interest in the Armenian parabiblica, and some elements of this tradition have already been discussed in the present volume.[68] The narrative of the fate of the protoplasts' relics climaxes with the successful burial of Eve's remains in the Grotto of the Nativity in Bethlehem. Eve was said to have arisen at the time of the nativity to care for the Christ child, and she is sometimes represented in paintings of Christ's birth. Adam's body, in contrast, was interred on Golgotha, where Christ's cross was said to have been erected upon Adam's skull or grave. It was often shown in paintings of the crucifixion.[69] Adam's skull thus provided

---

64. The Apocalypse of Pseudo-Methodius probably took this tradition from Cave of Treasures (see Minov 2016a, 135–36).

65. Minov (2016a, 134) dates CT based on the Yonṭon tradition to before 690. Against Gerö 1980, who proposes a Jewish origin for this tradition, Hilkens argues strongly that it originated in a Christian milieu.

66. See above, §13.2 and note there.

67. See Dorfmann-Lazarev 2020c, 296. See also above p. 48.

68. See annotation 6 above and see also Stone 2000b.

69. This is well discussed by Dorfmann-Lazarev 2020b, 272–77. See above, pp. 46–56, on these burial places of Adam and Eve and pp. 51–52 on Eve's role in the nativity.

an aetiology for the name Golgotha, which means "skull" in Aramaic, or else the name Golgotha itself attracted the notion that Adam's skull was interred there. Eve was said to have arisen at the time of the nativity to care for the Christ child. The tradition in Question §14, as seen in light of the Armenian form of the *Chronography*, relates that Noah gave Maniton some of Adam's relics (see *Arm Apoc* 1:116–17).

There probably once existed a fuller form of the traditions of Yonṭon/Maniton and perhaps of Astłik, his sister in Syriac. Of course, the full story may still be extant, still undiscovered in a manuscript.[70]

Regardless of this speculation, Yonṭon/Maniton is known from the Syriac Apocalypse of Pseudo-Methodius (late seventh century), which is a source of the relevant part of the *History of the Province of Sisian* by Stepʻanos Ōrbelean (1250/60–1304) and also of the Armenian text bearing the title Question to which we have referred above. It also seems to be the source of the Maniton (Yon[i]ṭon, Ionṭon, Monētōn) material in the Armenian version of the *Chronography* of Michael the Syrian.

ANNOTATION 22. NIMROD

Nimrod is mentioned four times in the Bible, twice in the primaeval history in Gen 10:8–11, once in 1 Chr 1:10, and once in the prophecy of Mic 5:5.[71] In Gen 10:8–9 we read:

> 8. Cush became the father of Nimrod; he was the first on earth to be a mighty man.[72]
> 9 He was a mighty hunter before the LORD; therefore, it is said, "Like Nimrod, a mighty hunter before the LORD."[73]

---

70. See the discussion in *Arm Apoc* 2:115 for Stepʻanos Ōrbelean and on pp. 116–17 concerning Maniton.

71. On the biblical Nimrod figure and its antecedents and its vicissitudes in postbiblical Jewish and Christian sources, see van der Toorn and van der Horst 1990, 1–16. This article casts light on nearly all aspects of the development of this figure that are discussed in the present annotation.

72. Nimrod is also mentioned with similar characteristics in 1 Chr 1:10 quoted here. This denotation recurs in LAB 4.7, which adds: "he began to be proud before the Lord."

73. Minov (2020, 67), in his study of David bar Pawlos, quotes: "(he) began to show upon the earth mighty deeds through the weapons of war and hunting of animals."

According to 1 Chr 1:10, "Cush was the father of Nimrod; he began to be a mighty one on the earth." According to these sources, which agree with one another, Nimrod, a mighty man, perhaps a giant, is a grandson of Ham, the son of Ham's son, Cush. Movsēs Xorenacʻi, *The History of the Armenians* 1.5 adds a person named Mestrayim (an onomastic form perhaps derived from the Hebrew name for Egypt—miṣrayyim) in the genealogy between Cush and Nimrod.[74] Nimrod is characterized as a hunter in Gen 10:9, and Gen 10:10–12 attributes the founding of the Mesopotamian kingdoms of Babylon and Assyria to him. Indeed, the expression, at the start of Gen 10:10, "The beginning of his *kingdom*," served as a textual hook for attribution of the role of king to him.

> 10 The beginning of his kingdom was Babel, Erech, and Accad, all of them in the land of Shinar. 11 From that land, he went into Assyria and built Nineveh,[75] Rehoboth-Ir, Calah, and Resen between Nineveh and Calah; that is the great city.

From this passage or the tradition reflected in it, the prophet Micah's reference to Nimrod undoubtedly derives, for in Mic 5:6, "land of Nimrod" is parallel to "land of Assyria." Clearly, some more extensive legend lies behind these references to him as a monarch, founder of kingdoms, and a mighty man and hunter. The expression "mighty man" in Gen 6:4 was traditionally taken to refer to giants, the offspring of the union of the sons of God (usually understood as angels) and humans, and so Nimrod, who also is called a גבור, "a mighty man," by the Hebrew Bible, became considered a giant. Indeed, in the LXX, in the translations of the passages in Genesis and Micah, he is called γίγας. The present passage in Questionnaire is the first occasion in the Armenian apocryphal texts studied so far on which the epithet "giant" is applied explicitly to Nimrod.

Nimrod plays a considerable role in Armenian and Syriac apocrypha. Nimrod was king of Canaan,[76] and those apocryphal traditions preserve the well-known narrative that Nimrod cast Abraham into fire for refus-

---

74. Movsēs claims the authority of a "learned and erudite Syrian" (Thomson 2006, 72–73).

75. Minov 2020, 74–75 studied a Syriac text attributed to David bar Pawlos that gives generations as Nimrod, Belus, and then Ninus. Ninus, he claims, "built Nineveh and called it after his name" (p. 67). This differs from Gen 10:10 quoted here.

76. "King of Canaan." This is a change both from the biblical story and from many parabiblical traditions, where he is king of a Mesopotamian realm.

ing to worship idols. Abraham was saved by the archangel Gabriel who turned into water and extinguished the fire.[77] According to some East Syriac sources, Canaan was an ancestor of Nimrod, and Melchizedek was his descendant.[78] This tradition, which dates from the ninth century, regards Melchizedek as a descendant of Nimrod and contrasts with the wider-spread view that associates Melchizedek with Shem b. Noah. In Armenian, Movsēs Xorenacʻi, *The History of the Armenians* 1.7 identifies Nimrod with Bēl in the story of Hayk and Bēl about the origins of the Armenian people. He says that "the one called Kronos and Bēl is Nimrod."[79] Nimrod was king of Babylon and was killed when the divinely sent wind destroyed the tower, so Michael the Syrian relates.[80] Movsēs Xorenacʻi also notes, drawing most likely on Eusebius's *Chronicle*, that the Egyptians consider Hephaistos to be Ham and connect him with the invention of fire.[81]

Nimrod's association with fire is very close and occurs in diverse contexts, though it is not mentioned in the biblical sources. The Syriac work, CT 27.1–4 (*MOTP* 1:560), conveys an unusual tradition that was apparently excerpted or summarized from some older extrabiblical Nimrod narrative. It relates that fire appeared on the earth and that Nimrod

---

77. See Gerö 1980, 321–30. There are also legends about Abraham and Nimrod in the Ethiopian Beta Israel work, *Teʾezāza Sanbat* (see Leslau 1951, 6, 9, and 27–28). The Samaritan work Asāṭīr also knows the story that Nimrod cast Abraham into a fire (see Tal 2021, 271).

78. Nimrod's role in East Syriac traditions is discussed by Minov 2010, 731–33. In general, one might remark that Nimrod was important for Syriac Christians because he was seen as the founder of the Mesopotamian kingdoms.

79. Also see n. 28 above.

80. In Josephus, *A.J.* 1.4.2, Nimrod is said to lead the tower builders, and presumably that passage was the source from which Michael's *Chronography* ultimately drew. Sawalaneancʻ 1871, 16 reads: զկնի ջրոյն, առաջին թագաւորեաց ի Բաբելոն Նեբրովթ եւ ի քառասուն ամին Ռագաւայ թագաւորեաց Նեբրովթ ... եւ մեռաւ Նեբրովթ սպանմամբ աշտարակին զարկուցանէ, եւ են ժամանակք թագաւորութեան նորա վաթսուն եւ ինն ամ, "After the water, (that is, the flood,) Nebrovtʻ was the first to reign in Babylon. He became king in Reu's fortieth year.... And Nebrovtʻ died in the killing connected with the tower, and the times of his rule lasted 69 years." See also Minov 2020 concerning Nimrod. That document as cited on p. 67 of Minov's article says, "*And the beginning of his kingdom was Babel*, that is, he built it first, and began to reign in it." See also Badalanova Geller 2021b, 335–36.

81. See Thomson 2006, 1, 200.

studied it and then created the cult of fire that passed to the Persians.[82] Thus, Nimrod is credited with the inception of Persian "fire worship," a common polemical designation for Zoroastrianism. Moreover, Nimrod is connected with fire in various other ways as well. This is evident in the rabbinic legend mentioned above that, because Abraham refused to worship fire, Nimrod tested his faith with an ordeal, and he cast him into a fiery furnace. [83]

In addition to the Jewish sources, certain early Christian sources are also familiar with the story of Nimrod casting Abraham into a fiery furnace from which he emerged unscathed.[84] This is found as a Jewish tradition transmitted in Jerome, *Qu. heb. Gen.* 11:28.[85] The Syriac Chronicle of 1234 likewise knows this story.[86] As we observed, the story is reminiscent of (perhaps structured on) Dan 3. In the Bible, the testing of the righteous is oft times compared with the smelting of ore in a furnace to eliminate the dross. See for this imagery Isa 1:22, 25; Ezek 22:18, 19; and Prov 25:4. Moreover, Prov 17:3 reads strikingly, from the perspective of our discussion: "The crucible is for silver, and the furnace is for gold, and the LORD tries hearts."[87] One might ask whether the ordeal by fire is related to this image.

---

82. [In the Pseudo-Clementine literature, Nimrod is the founder of the Persian fire cult. See *Recogn.* 1.30; *Hom.* 9.4 = *Recogn.* 4.28–30. In the latter source, Nimrod and Ham switch roles, and one wonders whether this form of the tradition could somehow have contributed to Xorenacʻi's confusion between Ham and Hephaistos as the inventor of fire. See Ginzburg 1909, 5:200–201 n.83. –S.E.]

83. Shades of Dan 3! The legend that Nimrod cast Abraham into a furnace of fire (unconnected to fire worship) is very common in rabbinic sources (see, for example, b. Pesah. 118a; Targum Neophiti and Pseudo-Jonathan to Gen 11:28; further references in Ginzberg 1909, 5:200–201 n. 83 and 212–13 nn. 33–34); cf. Gen. Rab. 44. Rabbinic and other early Jewish literature on Nimrod is presented in van der Toorn and van der Horst 1990, 16–29. They also document his association with fire worship as well as his relationship with Zoroaster. See further, Badalanova Geller 2021b, 337–38. This story is also known to the Qur'an, Al-Ankabut 29.23–24: see Heller n.d.

84. See *JE* 9.309–310.

85. See Hayward 1995, 108–9. Compare John Chrysostom, *Hom Gen.* 13:14. See also Kamesar 1993, 141–44. Both Jerome (b. 347) and John Chrysostom (b. 347) are fourth-century sources.

86. See the references in Hilkens 2018, 46; compare also Gen. Rab. 39:3 on Gen 11:28 and the Targum Pseudo-Jonathan to Gen 11:28. On the latter, see Bowker 1969, 187–89.

87. See the allied concept in Prov 17:3, 17. Compare Ephrem, *Exp.* 1.105, 2.78 in Egan 1968, and many other sources.

Eusebius in his *Chronicle* says that Bēl, whom Questionnaire identified with Nimrod, is Aramazd—a later form of the name of Ahura Mazda, the chief Zoroastrian deity, whose cult relates to fire.[88] In addition, rabbinic sources also preserve an onomastic tradition about Nimrod, connecting the name with the Hebrew root מר״ד meaning "rebellion."[89]

When discussing the division of Alexander's empire, Michael the Syrian reports that Seleucus, at Alexander's order, rebuilt Edessa (Uṙha), which Nimrod had built and Sennacherib had destroyed.[90] Nimrod's connection with building is first to be found in Gen 10:11–12 where he is named as the builder of Nineveh and some other cities. His construction of Edessa is congruent with his role as a builder of cities. An early reference to this connection is Josephus, *A.J.* 1.114–117, where Nimrod is the initiator of the building of the tower and its leader.[91] In other sources, different roles are assigned to him.[92] According to one rabbinic tradition, he built the tower of Babel as an act of rebellion against God.[93] Also in the Armenian version of the *Chronography* of Michael the Syrian, he is involved in the building of the tower of Babel.[94] Indeed, the connection of Nimrod with the builders of the tower of Babel is prominent in the corpus of Armenian texts relating to its construction.[95]

Nimrod was renowned as a hunter as far back as Gen 10:9, which verse says that he was a "mighty hunter." What is more, Armenian legend,

---

88. Aucher 1818, 1:25. On Bēl and Nimrod, see here part 13 n. 28 on §13.7 above.

89. See "Nimrod" in *JE* 9.309–311 and b. Ḥag. 13a, b. Pesaḥ. 118a. This is also the view in TM 269.

90. Michael the Syrian reports that "Seleucus (re)built Uṙha (Edessa) at Alexander's command, which Nimrod had built, and Sennacherib had destroyed" (Sawalaneanc 1871, 420).

91. So also Asāṭāir (see TM 215).

92. See Badalanova Geller 2021b, 335–36. Observe that according to Josephus, his motivation was to be revenged on God for those drowned in the flood. This resonates with the hubristic attitudes of the builders, which is evident already in Genesis.

93. b. Avod. Zar. 53b. See, for example, Gen. Rab. 23:7; b Ḥul. 89a; Pirqe R. El. 24. Thus, already in Josephus, *A.J.* 1.4.2–3. Further references Ginzberg 1909, 5:201 n.88.

94. Sawalaneancʻ 1871, 13. This connection is also found in rabbinic sources (see b Ḥul. 89b and *JE* 9.309).

95. I have published and translated all such compositions known to me to date, a small corpus of Tower Texts, in *Arm Apoc* 6:52–72. See also Badalanova Geller 2021b, 331–33. It should be noted further that in the early Georgian historiographic tradition, Nimrod features as a rather positive hero-king and becomes an ancestor of the royal house. This is discussed by Rapp 2014.

as well as the *Chronography* of Michael, relates that he fed the builders of the tower with the game he hunted.[96] Later midrashic sources relate that his hunting prowess (Gen 10:9) resulted from his wearing Adam's garment made by God (Gen. Rab. 63:13, Pirqe R. El. 24). The other person whose skill as a hunter the Bible celebrates is Esau (Gen 25:27). There he too is said to be "a man of the field," and rabbinic legend relates that later Esau also received the special garments from Nimrod. Those garments were made in Eden, and it was them that Jacob wore to deceive his father, Isaac.[97] Thus, Nimrod and Esau were associated in a variety of ways, and both were understood as negative figures.

In general, the Armenian tradition about the tower of Babel is rather developed. It tells that seventy or seventy-two heads of families united to build the tower and they were led by "Lamsur of the family of Shem, Hayk of the family of Japheth, and Bēl of the family of Ham, their hunter."[98] This "Bēl of Ham, the hunter" was identified with Nimrod and thus

---

96. See Tigran Sawalaneancʻ1871, 13: ի սկիզբն աւուրցն Ռագաւայ, սկսան շինել զաշտարակն յերկիրն Սենաար։ Եւ Նեբրովթ հսկայ որսայր շինողաց որս, եւ կերակրէր զնոսա, "In the beginning of the days of Reu they began to build the tower in the land of Shinar. And Nimrod (Nebrovtʻ) the giant hunted game for the builders and fed them."

97. See further Tanh. Toledot 12; Targum pseudo-Jonathan to Gen 25:27; and the article in *JE* 5:206–8.

98. Questionnaire did not know the form of the tradition found in LAB 6, according to which twelve men refused to participate in the building and Abram was one of their number. In that version of the story, the unnamed ruler flung them into a fiery furnace.

The name "Lamur" in *Arm Apoc* 6:56 is a misprint for "Lamsur." Hilkens, in a personal communication, informs me that Lamsur is associated with Haik and Nimrod in the 1870 recension of the Armenian version of the *Chronography* of Michael the Syrian. The same names are also found in a very similar sentence in Tower Text 1 in *Arm Apoc* 6:56–58.

The story of Hayk and Bel, which deals with Armenian ethnogenesis, is referred to in Questionnaire here and Bēl is identified as Nimrod. These figures play important roles in early Armenian heroic history. The claim for Japhetic descent is a crucial feature of Armenian Christianization of the story of their national origins; see *Arm Apoc* 5:380–91 on the function of this splicing of the Armenians into biblical genealogy. See also Stone 2023, 229–43. This is discussed further in n. 40 to this part.

In the Bible, it is Nimrod who is characterized as a hunter (Gen 10:9). Here, Bēl is the hunter who will bring them food and he is identified in various sources as Nimrod, see above n. 28. This passage is cited from Tower Text 2 in *Arm Apoc* 6:56–57. The various elements of this interesting tradition are discussed in the same place.

received the epithet "the hunter," for of Nimrod it was said that "he was a mighty hunter before the LORD," whose skill is specifically noted in Gen 10:9. The individual called Lamsur is unknown from any other context but as a builder of the tower. So, he was identified according to the *Commentary on Genesis* by Vardan Arewelcʻi, the 1870 Armenian recension of the *Chronography* of Michael the Syrian, and the Tower Texts.[99]

There exist quite a lot of other documents referring to Nimrod. Here are some examples.

1. The Palaea Historica, a Greek composition dated between the ninth and twelfth centuries CE, has a portion of the Nimrod story in chapter 25 (*MOTP* 1:609):

   After this Nimrod became king, a giant of a man who founded Babylon the great and reigned over it for eighty-five years. This Nimrod measured all the universe, both the land and the sea, and he discovered the middle of the world in Palestine.[100]

Similarly, in CT 27.7–10 (*MOTP* 1:560–61), Nimrod is given instruction "in all wisdom" by Yonṭon/Maniton, including particularly knowledge of the stars.[101]

2. The Syriac CT 24.24–26 (*MOTP* 1:559) presents a tradition that adds one more Nimrod incident to those noted so far. That passage reads:

   24. In Reu's days, in his 130th year, the hero Nimrod reigned as the first king upon the earth. He ruled for sixty-nine years, and the capital of his kingdom was Babylon. 25 Once, he saw something like a crown in the sky and then called the weaver Sisan, who wove a similar one for him and put it upon his head. 26 Because of this, it is said that the crown came down from heaven.

---

99. See Matenadaran MS M1267 (fifteenth century), fol. 47v of Vardan Arewelcʻi, *Commentary on Genesis*. Arm Apoc 6:57, 63.
100. See Lüdtke 1919. Flusser (1971, 54) suggests that the PH may have used sources originally written in Syriac.
101. See the preceding annotation 21, which is devoted completely to Maniton, Noah's fourth son.

The role and function of this tradition in Syriac national culture is quite considerable, though the number of textual witnesses is not very large.[102]

---

102. Compare the crown woven of prayers referred to in part 2, n. 11. See Desreumaux 2021. On pp. 195–96, Desreumaux points out the importance of Nimrod for Edessan Syrian identity.

14
Concerning the Construction of the Tower

This part is concerned with two chief tradition complexes or tales, the story of the tower of Babel and the seventy-two tongues. Each of these complexes is dealt with in its broader context in detail in a separate annotation below. In Questionnaire, we encounter first the narrative of the tower of Babel, its building, and its destruction (Gen 11:1–9). This is followed by the confusion of tongues, from which emerged the idea that there were seventy-two languages.[1] This latter notion is quite extensively developed in Armenian, and it came to include several rather striking and unusual details.

Text

M682 fol. 7d.24–32/

14.0/ Վասն աշտարակի շինութեան:[2]
14.1/ Էյի՞նչ պատճառ շինեցին:
Չի յետ Նոյի Շէե. (525) ամին դարձեալ ամբարշտեցան մարդիկք.[3] եւ յիշեցին գշրհեղեղն թէ վասն մեղաց եղեւ, բայց դրախտն Ադամայ ոչ եհաս ջուրն, զի բարձր է լեառն դրախտին եւ մօտ ի լուսնական գօտին.
14.2/ վասն որոյ ասեն. «Եկայք շինեսցուք աշտարակ եւ բարձրացուսցուք մինչեւ ի գօտին լուսնական, ի չափ դրախտին. զի թէ այլ գայցէ, ոչ հասցէ անդ:»
14.3/ Եւ բարձրացուցին մինչեւ Ժ. (10) ամսոյ ճանապարհի, Ե. (5) ամիս ի գնալն եւ Ե. (5) ի գալն: Եւ տեսեալ Աստուծոյ գչար

---

1. An early Armenian occurrence of the idea of seventy-two languages is in Agathangelos §612 (see Thomson 2001, 196).
2. The sign over the abbreviation of -ութեան has been omitted.
3. On this form, see part 13, n. 3.

միաբանութիւնն, ինչեաց հողմ սաստիկ եւ եղեւ շարժումն խիստ եւ փլոյց զաշտարակն։

14.4/ Եւ յահէն գրուեցան մարդիքն. եւ {ապա ուշաբերեալ⁴ սկսան այլ եւ այլ լեզուս խօսել։ Եւ բաժանեցաւ մի լեզու ՀԲ. (72), վասն որոյ գրուեցան իւրաքանչիւր աշխարհի եւ խաղաղացան։

Translation

14.0/ Concerning the building of the tower.

14.1/ For which reason did they build?

Because 525 years[5] after Noah, again, men acted impiously. And they remembered the flood, which took place on account of sins, but its water did not reach Adam's garden, for the mountain of the garden[6] is high and close to the lunar zone.[7]

14.2/ On account of this, they said, "Come, let us build a tower and let us raise it up to the lunar zone, to the measure of the garden. If another (that is, flood) comes, it will not reach there."[8]

---

4. ապա ուշաբերեալ means "then remembering," which does not make sense here. I venture to suggest that the two words ապա ուշ are corrupt for ապուշ "astounded," and that the verb "to carry, bear" followed it. However, *NBHL* does not record an expression ապուշ բերել. I do not venture emend the text itself because of this lack of corroboration, though the meaning seems clear from the context.

5. According to Robert H. Charles's calculation of the dates in the book of Jubilees, the period was 336 years. However, in Armenian chronological texts, 525 is the usual number. See *Arm Apoc* 4:30, 32, no. 2.2; 60–63, no. 2.7; see *Arm Apoc* 1:82–83, though this text gives 527 years, which is a result of the common confusion of ե/է, that is of 5 and 7, on which see part 10 n. 32 above. Although I published some chronological texts in *Arm Apoc* 4, such material in parabiblical books needs to be seen in light of the broader tradition of Armenian chronological and calendary learning. Fascinating examples of this tradition may be observed in Eynatyan 2002.

6. Or: paradise. See annotation 23 and part 11 n. 46.

7. The lunar zone is the first level of heaven in this text's cosmography. See further annotation 23. Anderson 1988, 204 remarks: "As each generation rebels against God, it moves farther and farther from the peaks of the cosmic mountain range where Eden lies. Finally, with the flood, the location of Eden is lost forever." Here the stepped peaks relate to cosmic zones.

8. This motivation, explained in §14.1, is intriguing, and, moreover, it implies clearly that Eden was on a mountain; see annotation 11 n. 46. The extraordinary height of the tower is emphasized by speaking of it in terms of ten months' journey.

14. Concerning the Construction of the Tower

14.3/ And they heightened (it) until (it was) a ten-months' journey, five months going and five, coming.[9] And God saw the evil agreement,[10] a terrible wind blew, and there was a great earthquake, and it knocked the tower down.

14.4/ And humans scattered from fear and, <being astounded> they began to speak various languages.[11] And one language was divided into seventy-two. Because of this, they were dispersed, each to their own land, and they were at peace.[12]

Annotation 23. The Tower

The tower of Babel narrative is found in Gen 11:1–9. In the biblical text, as it stands, this story fulfils the function of explaining the multitude of languages spoken by humans. By a Hebrew word-play, the Bible takes the existence of many languages to explain the name of the city of Babel (Babylon), which was in Mesopotamia. Thus, the story serves to answer two questions: that of the variety of languages and that of the significance of the toponym Babylon.

Indeed, in Gen 11:4, the builders describe their purpose, saying: "Come, let us build ourselves a city, and a tower with its top in the heavens, and let us make a name for ourselves, lest we be scattered abroad upon the face of the whole earth." This verse says that the purpose of the tower was to reach the heavens, which involves a crossing of the boundary between human and celestial. It also implies a need to preserve the solidarity of humans; observe the use of the pronouns "us" and "ourselves." God reacts to this illegitimate boundary crossing by saying (Gen 11:6): "this is only the beginning of what they will do; and nothing that they propose to do will now be impossible for them." The issue, according to

---

9. The various details of the height and breadth of the tower are discussed in annotation 23 on the tower at the end of this part.

10. That is, that they had agreed to do evil.

11. The confusion of tongues, based naturally on Gen 11:9, is mentioned in many sources, of which the earliest is Jub. 10.23–26. Concerning the restoration of the single primordial language as part of the eschatological good things, see Eshel and Stone 1993.

12. This is, therefore, a statement of the situation after the dispersal of the peoples and languages that resulted from God's scattering of the builders of the tower.

the biblical text, is quite explicitly the hybristic desire to cross the boundary between the human or mundane and the celestial.[13]

The motivation of the building, as it is explained by Questionnaire 14.1, is different from the Bible's and intriguing. Humans, the document says, knew they were sinning, and they feared a second flood. This, itself, is odd, for God had said to Noah, in Gen 9:11, "I establish my covenant with you, that never again shall all flesh be cut off by the waters of a flood, and *never again shall there be a flood* to destroy the earth" (emphasis added). Thus, if they expected the second flood to resemble the first and be of water, they were assuming that God would break his own promise.[14] Were this second deluge to be a flood of fire and not of water, that difficulty would be avoided.[15] A flood of fire is not known in the Bible but is familiar from later texts.[16] Interestingly, from the Hellenistic period on, there was an expectation of a future flood of fire (see Jub. 36.10; perhaps 1 En. 102.1; Josephus, *A.J.* 1.70–71a, and LAE 49.3). The expectation of two future floods, one of fire and the other of water, also occurs in other Armenian sources in addition to this possible reference in Questionnaire. In Abel and Other Pieces §4.4, it is Enosh who utters this prophecy, and it also occurs attributed to Enosh in History of the Forefathers §41–44 in connection with the discovery of two antediluvian stelae.[17] It also occurs, intriguingly, in a number of short texts relating the incident of the tower of Babel.[18] Moreover, at the very end of a work called Short History of the Holy Forefathers, the author

---

13. Badalanova Geller (2021b, 332) observed that overweening ambition was involved in building the tower with its top in the heavens. The same pride, she remarks, was also expressed in the use of baked bricks rather than the easier sun-dried ones.

14. This is the case because Gen 9:11 explicitly refers to a flood of water.

15. Mansfeld (2017) deals with the end of the world in ancient philosophy; see particularly pp. 94–96 on the role of fire in this event.

16. See Ginzberg 1960. In Armenian texts, the two floods are often mentioned in connection with the two stelae or pillars bearing primordial knowledge. See §10.7 and the remark on that section on p. 119. For further references, see Kister 2018–2019; Eshel 2018–2019; and Ben-Dov 2018.

17. See for discussion of stories of the discovery of stelae or hidden tablets or other ancient writings containing special knowledge, Speyer 1970, 111–19. He deals with such stories in relation to Egyptian, Mesopotamian, Greek, and Jewish sources. See also Ginzberg 1909, 5:149. A different perspective on the stelae is forwarded by Ben-Dov 2021.

18. See *Arm Apoc* 6:52–72. Most of those texts assume that there are two floods, one of water and the other of fire.

or a copyist adds a prayerful wish, "Through him (that is, Noah) may the Lord God save us from the fiery flood, through his prayers. Amen."[19] This seems to indicate that the idea of the flood of fire at the eschaton had become common coinage among medieval Armenians.[20]

The developed Armenian tower story, then, starts with seventy-two householders banding together to build a tower. This specific formulation is to be found not only in all three recensions of text 1 and in text 2 of Concerning the Tower, but also in Biblical Paraphrases, 2 Story of Noah §9,[21] and in other works. The tower was built in order to escape a second flood. A high tower was needed, as inferred from the ideas that the first flood did not reach the garden of Eden and that the garden of Eden is on a mountain.

The phrasing in §14.2, then, clearly implies that the mountain upon which Eden was situated reached from the earth to the height of the moon. That is, it was the axis and center point of the world.[22] In Gen 11:4, the tower builders' motivation seems to be the hubristic desire to reach heaven. That was to cross a boundary and is the reason for the destruction of the tower, the scattering of its builders, and the separation of the languages. In the Armenian form of the tower tradition, humans built it to avoid the punishment of a future flood that they feared would be brought about by their iniquity.[23]

In the pre-Copernican earth-centered understanding of the cosmos, as among the Greeks and very clearly in Aristotle, the sphere of the moon was the first sphere encountered in the ascent from the earth. Thus, sublunary denotes the earth, and the first layer of the heavens is high as the moon. That sphere was constituted of the four elements: fire, air, water, and earth.

---

19. *Arm Apoc* 4:174. The manuscript is M2111 dated to 1652–1679 CE, so it is quite late.

20. The idea, as found in earlier Jewish texts, is often linked by scholars to the Stoic concept of *empyrōsis*, a cyclical conflagration that reverted the world to its beginnings. See *Stanford Encyclopedia of Philosophy*, article by Baltzly 2023.

21. *Arm Apoc* 1:91–93.

22. On the idea of paradise on a mountain and its ramifications, see annotation 11, n. 49 above

23. The second flood stands in contradiction to God's promise to Noah in Gen 8:21, as noted above, on p. 196.

Annotation 24. The Seventy-Two Languages and Nations

The idea that there were seventy-two languages is clearly related in the Armenian tower story to the embroidery that seventy-two heads of families banded together to build the tower. Thus, when God scattered them and made them speak different languages, then seventy-two languages came into being. In ancient Jewish and Christian texts, the number of seventy languages is more common and may be observed in a very wide range of sources, such as Targ Pseudo-Jonathan to Gen 11:8; Epiphanius, *Pan.* 1, 2.11; and later in Jeraḥmeel 4.3, just to mention a selection out of many sources.[24] Seventy (= 10 x 7) and seventy-two (= 12 x 6) are both typological numbers, and in various contexts they alternate. It has been suggested that the difference noted here is due to there being seventy descendants of Noah according to the Hebrew text of Gen 10 but seventy-two in the Septuagint's version. However, it is to be remarked that, as I show in the following paragraphs, the difference between seventy and seventy-two also occurs in contexts having no relationship to the tower incident or to the number of the descendants of Noah. Hence, it seems that it is more likely that their interchange was a result of their numerological significance.

In PH 24.9 (*MOTP* 1:609), the number of languages is seventy-two, and that composition sets forth the connection between that number and twelve: "And there was given to them the understanding of the twelve tribes, that is of the seventy-two languages." The Syriac text of David bar Pawlos (eighth or ninth century CE) also enumerates seventy-two peoples and fifteen Japhethite nations, six of which know writing systems.[25] Quite similar is the number of the translators of the Septuagint (which name actually means "seventy") as set forth in the Armenian texts associated with Epiphanius of Salamis, *De mensuris et ponderibus*, there often explicitly said to be six men from each of the twelve tribes of

---

24. For Jeraḥmeel 4.3, see Yassif 2001, 127. It is found at 31.1 in other editions. Ginzberg discusses the number of languages, seventy or seventy-two, in Ginzberg 1909, 5:194 and cites numerous rabbinic sources. See also vol. 7:429, which contains indexes, under the lemmata: "seventy nations," "seventy-two nations," "seventy languages," and "seventy-two languages."

25. See Minov 2020, 65–66. The remark concerning the Arabians is odd. See further on this passage on p. 172 above.

14. Concerning the Construction of the Tower

Israel.[26] Furthermore, in various sources there is uncertainty between seventy and seventy-two as the number of Christ's disciples.[27]

In Cave of Treasures, the existence of seventy-two languages and peoples is asserted, and then the children of Japheth are enumerated (CT 24.17 [MOTP 1:558–59]). So, we read: "From Japheth's seed there were thirty-seven nations and kingdoms: Gomer, Javan, Madai, Tubal, Meshech , and Tiras, and all the kingdoms of the Alans: those are the children of Japheth." The geographical spread of the Japhethites is then briefly outlined and in a fashion apparently differing from 1QapGen ar.[28]

The Syriac lists of literate nations, designed to give pride of place to Syriac, are analyzed in detail by Hilkens, who gives tables of the literate peoples, organized according to Noah's three sons.[29] These traditions of the division of the earth among the nations and of the literate peoples are worthy of further investigation and will provide insight into medieval Armenian ethnographic, linguistic and geographic notions.

The oldest Armenian reference to the seventy-two tongues or nations, which is the usual number in Armenian, is in Agathangelos §612 (fifth century), and it occurs again in the *Chronography* of Philo of Tirak (late seventh century) §56.[30] This is related to the idea that seventy-two princes built the tower. The oldest known manuscript with a Tower Text is to be found in manuscript M8531 of the fifteenth century.[31]

In Armenian manuscripts, a list of seventy-two languages or nations circulates as a separate work. One copy of the list has been published from a late manuscript, and a good number of others exist.[32] The oldest such lists

---

26. See Ervine and Stone 2000, 83 and 93; on p. 101 tension between seventy and seventy-two may be observed.
27. Metzger 1959. For lists of disciples, see Schermann 1907, 107–221.
28. Concerning the seventy-two nations and the tower of Babel in the Armenian tradition, see *Arm Apoc* 6:52–70, nos. 9.1–9.5 and above in the present volume in note 27 on §13:7.
29. Hilkens 2020a, 20–21, 24. See also Hilkens 2018, 110 for a table of the literate nations and pp. 68–72 for a discussion of the parallel forms of the diamerismos and their interrelationship.
30. See MH 5.906.
31. Some of these texts are published in *Arm Apoc* 6:52–72.
32. *Arm Apoc* 2:161–63; manuscripts that I have observed include, J1171 fols. 103-04; M605 fol. 77v; M2036 fols. 242r–v; M8494 fol. 215r; M10200 196v–198v; M10725 fols. 204r–v; and a substantial number of further copies exist. A recent study

encountered in surviving manuscripts are in M2679 of the year 981 CE, fols. 331r–332r, and M5254 (1280 CE), fol.192r.[33] Both the Syriac and the Armenian texts of the *Chronography* of Michael the Syrian have seventy-two as the number of languages.[34] Badalanova Geller rightly remarks that the loss of the primordial single language was a sort of fall, parallel in several ways to the fall of Adam.[35] The confusion of tongues is another loss of the innocence that had preceded it.[36]

An important implication of the existence of seventy-two languages emerged when this idea was laid alongside Deut 32:8–9:[37]

> When the Most High gave to the nations their inheritance, when he separated the sons of men, he fixed the bounds of the peoples according to the number of the sons of [God]. For the Lord's portion is his people, Jacob his allotted heritage.

In fact, the text above, taken from the RSV, includes a portentous emendation of the Hebrew text. The last words of Deut 32:8 are "sons of Israel" in the Masoretic Text, not "sons of [God]." In the Septuagint, as well as in one of the Qumran copies of Hebrew Deuteronomy, indeed, the words "angels" or "sons of God" are found where "sons of Israel" stands in the Masoretic Hebrew. In the Armenian Deuteronomy, in Cox's edition as

---

of the question of the origin of languages and of their confusion or differentiation is Badalanova Geller 2021b, 324–63.

33. Matʻevosyan 1997. One form of this list has been published in *Arm Apoc* 2:158–63. Much information on this and allied texts, including manuscript sources, is to be found in Anasyan 1959, 1: cols. 299–303.

34. Chabot 1899, 1:19; Sawalaneancʻ 1871, 13. For the Ethiopic tradition, see Cowley 1988, 20–24.

35. Badalanova Geller 2021b, 331. An analysis of the falls encountered in the Urgeschichte is given in Stone 2023, 399–422. In Syriac texts, the primordial language was usually considered to be Syriac, while in some other textual traditions, it was Hebrew. See for Syriac CT 24.10 (*MOTP* 1:558), CT 53.21 (*MOTP* 1:583), and Minov 2020, 74, among other sources. Hebrew was considered Adam's tongue according to a Qumran text published in Eshel and Stone 1993 and, of course, many other sources; see also Jub 12.25–26.

36. I have developed the idea that, in the parabiblical Embroidered Bible tradition, the tower was the fifth in a series of falls that started with the fall of Satan (see Stone 2023).

37. On this passage see Ben-Dov 2016, 13–15, 18–20.

14. Concerning the Construction of the Tower

well as in Zohrabean's of 1805, the text reads որդւոց Աստուծոյ, "sons of God," with a marginal reading հրեշտակաց, "of angels."[38]

Through this analysis, we have come to understand that the Armenian people viewed themselves as Noah's direct descendants through Japheth and their ancient national origins were thus seen to be confirmed by the Bible. This biblical claim is to be found in many Armenian sources and is deeply embedded in the Armenian national tradition.[39] For instance, Xorenacʻi's list of the descendants of Japheth is based on Gen 10 combined with some pre-existing Armenian traditions of varied origins.[40] Xorenacʻi's presentation of the nation's origins has been extremely influential over the centuries.

In addition to Japhetite descent, a second clear biblical connection to the Armenians is prominent in the toponym Ararat, first mentioned in connection with Noah's ark ("mountains of Ararat" in Gen 8:4), and the name apparently derived from "Urartu." From Hellenistic times on, the biblical mountains of Ararat were believed to lie in Armenian lands, and these mountains connected Armenia with the story of Noah and his ark.[41]

Probably in Syriac and perhaps in Armenian, a fuller form of the traditions of Yonṭon/Maniton and perhaps of Astłik once existed, which still lies somewhere undiscovered. This tradition unit reinforces the geographical and ethnographic concepts that form a basis of the "biblicization" of the Armenians' self-understanding.

The Armenian tradition, as other Christian sources, interpreted Deut 32:8–9 as referring to the tower event, and it is, therefore, taken as a statement of the situation after God's dispersal of the peoples and languages that resulted from the building of the tower.[42] Christ's seventy-two disciples were sent to these seventy-two nations, resulting, in the end, in the reversal of that confusion of tongues and peoples.

---

38. Cox 1981, 205. See further on this topic the analogous material adduced by Ben-Dov 2016, 14–16. The old, but still standard edition of the Armenian Bible (faute de mieux), is that of Zohrabean 1805.

39. See Thomson 2006, 72 for Movsēs Xorenacʻi's version of the Japhethite genealogy.

40. For full detail on this subject, consult annotation 20 above.

41. See above, part 13, n. 43 and the bibliography cited there.

42. The numbers seventy and seventy-two may well come from different calculations of the number of the peoples mentioned in Gen 10, as I have noted.

15
Concerning Abraham and His Sons

This part deals briefly with several genealogical traditions relating to Abraham, Isaac, and Jacob and their spouses. Its title constitutes the last line on fol. 7d of the manuscript, and the text itself occurs following it, on the upper part of fol. 8r. After the end of this Abraham genealogical text, still on fol. 8r, a blank area has been left that continues onto fol. 8v. Of course, without a reason given explicitly by the scribe for this phenomenon, only conjecture is possible. One explanation, however, might be the following. Considering the structure of the Armenian parabiblical traditions that constitute the Embroidered Bible, it seems most likely that the blank was left for a text dealing with Joseph. In that tradition, Joseph is the next major figure after Abraham.

Joseph's great significance for the Armenian tradition, partly arising from a christological interpretation of the figure of this patriarch, is evident from the substantial number of Joseph texts produced and circulating in Armenian (see *Arm Apoc* 6:242 n. 26 for a list thereof, which list is not necessarily complete). Such a Joseph document was apparently lacking from the literary resources that stood at the author's disposal or, even more likely, was physically missing from the scribe's *Vorlage*. Of course, the scribe or the author might have intended to draw it from a different source and never have done that due to some circumstance. This, of course, might serve as evidence that the document Questionnaire is an autograph and was not copied from an earlier, complete manuscript. However that may be, this nonextant Joseph text is, in any case, only hypothetical.

The Abraham passage included in M682 is called Concerning Abraham and His Sons. It constitutes §15 of Questionnaire, and it is another version of part of Genealogy of Abraham, a text which has already been published.[1] A comparison of the two documents shows that the first sections of the two texts are rather similar and the text of the Genealogy of Abraham overlaps §§1–5 of the present document. Concerning Abraham and His Sons has a longer form of §5 and some scattered additional phrases elsewhere. Concerning Abraham and His Sons §§5–6, then, preserve a rather different form of the corresponding material in Genealogy of Abraham.[2] Next, in §10 of part 15, Concerning Abraham and His Sons transmits a distinctive tradition concerning Abraham's brother Haran. It retails the narrative of Haran's death that is known to other Abraham texts but not formulated by them in the way it is presented here.[3]

In presenting this part 15, I give the text and translation of our document, Questionnaire, and compare it in the discussion with the corresponding material in Genealogy of Abraham. In addition to the above-noted parallel sections, the list of Abraham's ten trials that occurs in Concerning Abraham and His Sons §2 is also embedded in Genealogy of Abraham §2. The list of trials also occurs in several other manuscripts as an independent document, and I published it as such some years ago under the title The Ten Trials of Abraham.[4] Thus, it is evident that Concerning Abraham has a quite complex literary historical *Vorgeschichte* and incorporates preexisting lists and similar narrative units. These compositional practices have already been noted elsewhere in the present work.

Text

M682/ fols. 7d.33–8r.23/

15.0/ Վասն Աբրահամու և որդոց նորա

15.1/ Թարայ հայրն Աբրահամու ծնաւ զՆաքովր զԱռան և զԱբրահամ։ Եւ ի ժէ. (18) ամին Աբրահամ ճանաչեաց զԱստուած. և

---

1. *Arm Apoc* 3:78–85 from MS Galata 154, which is close to the present writing and which dates from the seventeenth century.

2. The section divisions in Questionnaire §15 are not identical to those in Genealogy of Abraham.

3. Compare with Abraham Texts §4.6 and §10.9 in *Arm Apoc* 3:58 and 64, 125–26. For a variant form of the story, see Flusser 1971, 53. As he observes, the Haran story occurs as early as Jub. 12.12–14 and had ramifications in the Byzantine chronographic tradition.

4. *Arm Apoc* 3:204–5.

15. Concerning Abraham and His Sons

ի Կ. (60) ամին ասաց Աստուած ելանել յերկրէն որ եւ բնակեցան, ի Խառան. Եւ Հէ. (75) ամին դարձեալ ել ի Խառանայ եւ յքնտանեցան, եւ պանդխտեցաւ ի Պաղեստին, եւ Ժ. (10) փորձանաց դանդիպեցաւ:

15.2/ Նախ՝ ելանելն յերկրէ եւ բնակիլն ի մէջ օտարաց:

Բ. (2)՝ քարշիլն Սառայի փարոնի:

Գ. (3)՝ բաժանիլն Ղովտայ:

Դ. (4)՝ ոչ ինչ առնուլն յաւարէն Սոդոմայ:

Ե. (5)՝ քարշիլն Սառայի Աբիմելիքայ:

Զ. (6)՝ ի ծերութեան թլփատիլն:

Է. (7)՝ տալ զՀագար ի ձեռն Սառայի:

Ը. (8)՝ ի բաց հանել Հագարայ:

Թ. (9)՝ աւետեացն Աստուծոյ ոչ երկմտելն:

Ժ. (10)՝ որդին պատարագել:

Վասն այսց հաձոյ եղեւ Աստուծոյ եւ արար զնա հայր բազմաց:

15.3/ Ի ՁՁ. (86) ամին ծնաւ զԻսմայէլ ի Հագարայ. ի ՂԹ. (99) ամին թլփատեցաւ. ի Ճ. (100) ամին ծնաւ զԻսահակ ի Ղ. (90) ամին Սառայի. եւ մեռաւ Սառայ ՃԻԷ ամաց:

15.4/ Եւ էառ կին Աբրահամ զՔետուր, յորմէ ծնաւ որդիս Զ. (6). Մինն զմինն եսպան եւ այլք լցին զերկիր, որոց մի են Թուրք, որ եւ Պալհաւունիք կոչին, Պահլ քաղաքին անուամբ եւ Արշակունիք յաղագս Արշակայ քաջին. եւ մեռաւ Աբրահամ ՃՀԵ.(175) ամաց:

15.5/ Իսահակ էառ կին զՌեբեկայ, թոռն Նաքովրայ, եղբօրն Աբրահամու. Խ. (40) ամին իւրոյ առաւ, բայց ոչ մեձեցաւ մինչ ի Ի. (20) ամն. եւ ի Կ. (60) ամին Իսահակայ, ծնանի Ռեբեկայ զՅակոբ եւ զԵսաւ: Եսաւ էր վայրագ, զազանավիտ, անասնաբարոյ, մարդատեաց, որովայնամոլ, անձնասէր եւ ոչ աստուածասէր. վասն որոյ զանդրանկութիւն վաճառեաց Յակոբայ:

15.6/ Եւ Յակոբ փախեալ յԵսաւայ գնաց ի Խառան եւ էառ զերկուսին դստերն Լաբանայ քեռոյն իւրոյ, Բ. (2) նամշտօքն: Այս են ծնունդքն Յակոբայ՝ Ռուբէն, Շմաւոն, Ղեւի, Յուդա, Իսաքար, Զաբուղոն, եւ Դի<ն>ա[5] քոյր նոցա ի Լիայէ կնոջէն. Դան եւ Նեփթաղիմ Զելփայէ աղախնոյ նորին. Գաղ եւ Ասեր ի Բալլայէ աղախնոյն Ռաքելի. Յովսէփ եւ Բենիամին ի Ռաքելայ: Եւ մեռանի Իսահակ ՃՁ. (180) ամաց:

---

5. The same omission of the -ն- may be observed in MS Galata 154 (see *Arm Apoc* 3:79). Genealogy of Abraham §6 in that manuscript continues to resemble Questionnaire closely in this section. Here, however, the text of Questionnaire is somewhat shorter.

15.7/ Բայց թէ էր ասաց Գիրն թէ ՚մեռաւ Առան եղբայրն Աբրահամու առաջի հօր իւրոյ Թարայի, վասն զի ոչ էր մեռեալ որդի յառաջ քան զհայրն յԱդամայ⁶ հետև, եւ սա զի ծնունդ չորրդ արար, վասն որոյ բնութեան սահմանի ոչ մեռաւ այլ յառաջ քան զհայրն:

Translation

15.1/ Terah, Abraham's father begot Nahor, Aṙan,⁷ and Abraham. And Abraham recognized God in his 18th year. And in his 60th year God told him to go forth from the land where they dwelt, to Haran.⁸ And in his 75th year again he went forth from Haran and from his family,⁹ and he sojourned in Palestine, and he encountered ten trials.¹⁰

15.2/ First, going forth from (his) land and dwelling amid strangers.
(2) Sarah's being dragged away to Pharaoh.¹¹
(3) The separation of Lot.¹²
(4) Taking nothing of the booty of Sodom.¹³
(5) The dragging away of Sarah to Abimelech.¹⁴
(6) Being circumcised in old age.¹⁵
(7) Delivering Hagar into Sarah's power.¹⁶

---

6. This word is damaged in the manuscript.
7. This is the usual Armenian spelling of the name Haran. Haran was Abraham's brother. This incident is also included in other Armenian Abraham texts (see *Arm Apoc* 3, index s.v. "mule"). The Samaritan work *Asāṭīr* raised the same difficulty about the reason for Haran's early death but offers Haran's insolence to Abraham as the reason (see Tal 2021, 271–72).
8. Gen 11:31. According to Jub. 11.38, Abraham was fourteen years old when he recognized God.
9. Gen 12:4–5; and many sources, see, for example, CT 28.5 (*MOTP* 1:561). Jub. 12.12 says that he was sixty when he went forth.
10. Gen 12:1. The expression "trial, test" is derived from Gen 22:1: "God tested Abraham." The ten trials continue to refer to biblical incidents that took place up to Gen 22:13. Jacob Licht (1973) wrote on the issue of trials or testing in the Hebrew Bible. More Armenian copies of lists of the ten trials of Abraham exist, see *Arm Apoc* 3:204–5.
11. Gen 12:15–20. փարոնի is a misspelling of փարաւոնի, "to Pharaoh."
12. Gen 13:11.
13. Gen 14:22–23.
14. Gen 20:2–18.
15. Gen 17:24.
16. Or, hand: see Gen 21:12.

(8) Expelling Hagar.[17]
(9) Not doubting God's announcement.[18]
(10) Sacrificing his son.[19]

Because of these (acts), God was pleased with him and made him a father of many.[20]

15.3/ In the 86th year he begot Ishmael from Hagar.[21] In his 99th year he was circumcised,[22] and in his 100th year he begot Isaac, in Sarah's 90th year.[23] And Sarah died at the age of 127.

15.4/ And Abraham took Ketura as wife, from whom he begot six sons.[24] The one killed the other, and the others filled the earth.[25] One of them is the Tʻurkʻ[26] who were also called the Palhavunis after the city Pahl and (another was called) the Aršakunis on account of valiant Aršak.[27] And Abraham died at the age of 175.[28]

---

17. Gen 21:14.
18. That is, of Isaac's birth. This is related in Gen 15:1–6 and Gen 18:1–16.
19. Gen 22:2–13.
20. This sentence, referring to Gen 17:4–6, is not found in MS Galata 154.
21. Gen 16:16.
22. Gen 17:24.
23. Gen 23:1.
24. Gen 25:1–2. This section seems dependent on Movsēs Xorenacʻi, whose aim at this point was to trace the Noachic ancestry of the Armenians (see Movsēs Xorenacʻi, *History of the Armenians* 2.1 and Thomson 2006, 128).
25. We have not found this statement elsewhere. Movsēs Xorenacʻi, *History of the Armenians* 2.68 (see Thomson 2006, 211–12) does refer to conflicts between their descendants.
26. Apparently, as indicated by the plural verb "were," this word is taken as a nominative plural, so one might have translated "Tʻur-s." However, Movsēs Xorenacʻi, *History of the Armenians* 2.8 mentions an individual called Tʻurkʻ, a grandson of the eponymous ancestor of the Armenians, Hayk. Our author apparently has taken the -kʻ of Tʻurkʻ to be a plural ending and perhaps identified Tʻurkʻ with the Turks. That is not appropriate.
27. This sentence also seems to be dependent on Movsēs Xorenacʻi, whose aim at that point was to highlight the Noachic descent of the Armenians (see Movsēs Xorenacʻi, *History of the Armenians* 2.1 and Thomson 2006, 128).
28. This whole section is a rewriting of Gen 25:1–4. Abraham's death is mentioned in Gen 25:7–8.

15.5/ Isaac[29] took Rebecca as wife, the granddaughter of Nahor, Abraham's brother.[30] She was taken as wife when he was 40,[31] but he did not draw to near her for 20 years.[32] And in Isaac's 60th year Rebecca bore Jacob and Esau.[33] Esau was fierce, brutal, bestial, misanthropic, gluttonous,[34] self-loving and not God-loving. On account of this, he sold (his) right of primogeniture to Jacob.[35]

15.6/ And Jacob, fleeing from Esau,[36] went to Haran, and he took (that is: married) the two daughters of his uncle Laban with their two handmaidens.[37] These are the descendants of Jacob:

Reuben, Simeon, Levi, Judah, Issachar, Zebulun and Di<n>a their sister from his wife, Leah;

Dan and Naphtali from her handmaiden Zilpah;

Gad and Asher from Bilhah, Rachel's handmaiden;

Joseph and Benjamin from Rachel.[38] And Isaac died at the age of one hundred and eighty.[39]

---

29. Except for a short expansion, this section is word for word identical with Genealogy of Abraham §5: *Arm Apoc* 3:79. The expansion highlights Isaac's celibacy, a theme observed elsewhere in Questionnaire. See below, annotation 27.

30. Gen 24:67.

31. Gen 25:20.

32. Apparently, for twenty years after they married.

33. The idea of Isaac's continence for twenty years is based on the following biblical verses: Gen 25:20 relates that Isaac married Rebecca at the age of forty, and Gen 25:26 says that she bore Esau and Jacob when Isaac was sixty years old (see *Arm Apoc* 3:121). The tendency to attribute sexual continence to various biblical figures may be observed as relates to Noah and Enoch in §11.1 above. It reflects Christian values and has been discussed in *Arm Apoc* 6:49, 274, and 290. Indeed, Isaac was sometimes seen as a type of Christ (see, for example, *Arm Apoc* 3:54 and index, s.v.), as was Joseph.

34. He was attributed this characteristic because of the incident of the lentil stew, Gen 25:29–34. Literally, the word որովայնասէր means "crazy for his belly."

35. See Gen 25:31–33. The text omits the story of Isaac's blessing and Jacob's deception.

36. Compare Gen 35:1.

37. All this genealogical material is in accordance with Genesis. Similar genealogical summaries are to be found in Gen 35:23–26 and in many later sources. Of the latter, see, as an example, Stepʻanos Siwnecʻi, *Commentary on Genesis* 2.2.118–120.

38. This passage is based on Gen 35:23–26 and Exod 1:1–4 (*Arm Apoc* 6:112).

39. Gen 35:28.

15.7/⁴⁰ But, why did Scripture say that Abraham's brother Haran died before his father, Terah? Because since Adam,[41] no son (child) had died before his/her father, and he (died) because he made the breeding of the mule. Because of this, he did not die at the natural time[42] but before his father.

ANNOTATION 25. THE DEATH OF HARAN, ABRAHAM'S BROTHER

Genesis 11:28 reads: "Haran died before his father Terah in the land of his birth, in Ur of the Chaldeans." This verse aroused interest in the minds of ancient and medieval exegetes. "Why did Haran (in Armenian texts also called Aṙan or, rarely, Achan) die before his father, Terah?" and "How did he die?" are the chief *cruces interpretationis* in the tale related here. In Armenian Abraham texts, a clear answer was given to the first question, for example, in Story of Father Abraham §6:

> 6 And Terah built a house of idols in Haran, and Abraham became angry. He wished to burn (it) with fire. Abraham's brother, the father of Lot [that is, Haran], wished to extinguish the fire and having fallen into the temple, he was burnt up and died before his father. For after the flood,[43] no other son died before his father.
> He learned the breeding of the mule (which was) against God's creation, for it was God's will that every sort should bear its own sort. For that reason, it (that is, the mule) does not have offspring, for it is not created by God, but men have learned (its breeding) through the wiles of Satan.[44]

In this passage, which in content resembles several others cited below, there are three distinct but related traditions: (1) Abraham set Terah's idolatrous temple on fire. (2) Haran fell into this fire and died. (3) Haran discovered how to breed mules; this was against God's will, and for that

---

40. This last paragraph of the text found here in M268 does not occur in MS Galata 154 in Genealogy of Abraham. It disturbs the narrative sequence.
41. This could mean "after Adam" and would be correct because, prior to the flood, Cain killed Abel before Adam's death. Alternatively, less precisely, it might be taken to mean "from the time of Adam" in the more general, unspecific sense of "from the very beginning."
42. Literally: border, limit, portion.
43. Of course, before the flood, Abel's death preceded Adam's.
44. *Arm Apoc* 3:43–44.

reason, he died before his father. These events are presented succinctly in Yovasapʿ Sebastacʿi's *Poem on Abraham, Sahak, Melchizedek, and Lot* (*Arm Apoc* 3:86). The same consideration is to be found in Abraham Text §2.6 (see *Arm Apoc* 3:43–44 n. 30 and see also Abraham Texts 4.6 and 10.7 in that book). This miscegenation of the horse and the ass is not mentioned in the Hebrew traditions about this subject. See *Arm Apoc* 3, index, s.v. "mule."

> 1. Concerning the flocks of crows in the fields,
> Who mentioned God on high, and the ravens fled.
> 2. Then there came to his mind the clear thought,
> (That) it is the Creator, God, who does miracles.
> He burnt the house of idols secretly in the night,
> And the inventor of the mule perished with it.[45]

Terah's idolatry is a widely known tradition. Among Abraham texts in Armenian, we observe it in several documents. In *Story of Abraham, Isaac, and Mamre* and elsewhere, it is connected with Abraham's discovery of God.[46] Often, Terah is said to have built an idolatrous temple or to have been a manufacturer of idols.[47]

Haran fell into the fire that Abraham lit in Terah's idolatrous temple and died. This theme is explicit in the passage just quoted and elsewhere.[48] As early as Jub. 12.12–14, Abraham is said to have set fire to an idolatrous temple and Haran to have died while extinguishing that blaze. In the Armenian forms of the tradition, the only substantial difference is that the temple is said specifically to be Terah's.

---

45. *Arm Apoc* 3:89. Little is known about this poem but that it was written by Yovasapʿ Sebastacʿi (ca. 1510–after 1564) and is first published in *Arm Apoc* 3.

46. See *Arm Apoc* 3:112. Concerning the various stories about Abraham's discovery of God, see *Arm Apoc* 3:1, 6–8. The main themes in the Armenian texts connected with this momentous event are: (1) the story of the ravens (*Arm Apoc* 3:41–43, 65, 89, 113, 147–48, 123, 193, 209, 223, and notes); another form of this idea occurs inEłišē's *Commentary on Genesis*, a work of the fifth century, discussed *Arm Apoc* 3:20; (2) Abraham's discovery of God through contemplation of the astronomical order (*Arm Apoc* 3:42, 51–53, 148, 209–10, 224, and notes); (3) his discovery was precipitated by the evident impotence of Terah's idols (*Arm Apoc* 3:113, 147–48, and notes).

47. The idea that Terah was an active idolater is widespread. In addition to the references above, see *Arm Apoc* 3:41, 65, 112, 147, 193, 223, and as a builder of an idolatrous temple, see *Arm Apoc* 3:65, 194, 210.

48. See *Arm Apoc* 3:194, 210.

Haran discovered the forbidden miscegenation that gave birth to the mule. This notion occurs in a number of documents, including Elenchic Abraham Text §9: "On account of the illegal mixing, the son died before the father in Terah's days since Achan (Haran) cross-bred the donkey with the horse."[49] The idea that it is forbidden to mate a donkey with a horse is understood as coming under the prohibition in Lev 19:19, and it is also reinforced by Gen 1:11, 25, where all creatures are said to reproduce each "after its kind." The forbidden nature of this union is witnessed, the Armenian authors tell us, by the sterility of the mule, which cannot reproduce "after its kind." This cross-breeding is not forbidden in the biblical law against mixing kinds in Deut 22:9–11, nor is it mentioned in Jubilees.[50]

Annotation 26. Ten Trials of Abraham

The idea that Abraham was tested by ten trials doubtless originates in Gen 22:1, "After these things God *tested* Abraham," which is the introduction to the story of the binding of Isaac.[51] The idea of the ten systematic trials of Abraham is a rather ancient development of this idea. It is first to be found in Jubilees, which was composed in the second century BCE. There, a partial list of trials appears in 17.17 and 19.8. In 19.3, there is an explicit reference to a tenth, and apparently the last, trial, the burial of Sarah. The idea of testing enters other traditions about Abraham, perhaps the best-known being Nimrod's testing Abraham in a fiery furnace.[52]

---

49. *Arm Apoc* 3:126; variants of the same incident may be found in *Arm Apoc* 3:43, 65, 126, and 194. Note that the text published there on p. 65 reads: "And because he devised the birth of the mule, because of this the Lord killed him" without specifying his mode of death.

50. On Syriac forms of this story, see Brock 1978, 135–52 and Hilkens 2018, 75–81. See annotation 19 on "The Raven." [Mention should be made of rabbinic traditions about the invention of the mule by Ana, the son of Ziv'on, one of the descendants of Esau—a negative figure that creates a negative creature and, eventually, leads God to create a new kind of harmful reptile (though Ana himself is not punished). See y. Ber. 8:5, 12b; Gen. Rab. 82.15; b. Pesah. 54a; Targum Pseudo-Jonathan to Gen 36:24. See further Ginzberg 1909, 5:322–23 n.322; Hayward 2012. –S.E.]

51. The introduction of "tested" here perhaps serves to signal that God's intention from the beginning was not to demand a human sacrifice. [And yet, sacrificing one's own son is a severe test and proof of obedience. –S.E.]

52. This tradition of Nimrod and the fiery furnace is discussed in annotation 22 above.

Lists of the ten trials of Abraham, presented similarly to the one here, are found in various Armenian apocryphal writings. One such list has been published from manuscript M717, fol. 54r. The phrasing and order there differ from Questionnaire §15.2 here.[53] Ten-trial lists are also embedded in Concerning Abraham §2; in Genealogy of Abraham §2; and in the Story of Mamre §120; as well as in the Synaxarium entry for Abraham.[54] In rabbinic texts, the number ten of Abraham's trials is common, but the lists there are far from identical with those with which we are familiar in Armenian.[55] This teaches us that the idea of trials of Abraham is widespread and that somewhat differing lists of ten trials are to be found in Jubilees, rabbinic literature, and Armenian pseudepigrapha. The number appears to be traditional, and no obvious biblical exegetical hook for it has been found, but the actual trials listed, and their order seem to have varied.

Annotation 27. Isaac's Virginity and Fasting

Above in nn. 32–33, I observed that Isaac is said to be celibate for twenty years after he married. This interpretation of the twenty years gap between his marriage and the birth of his offspring is a typical Armenian Christian reading of Genesis's text, a practice that has been observed in Armenian exegesis in other contexts as well.[56] The same understanding of Isaac's celibacy is set forth in detail in The Memorial of the Forefathers §24: "And for twenty years Isaac did not draw near to her on account of his modesty (chastity), for he was a likeness and a type of Christ."[57] Other examples of the attribution of Christian ascetic virtues to Hebrew Bible figures are to be found throughout the Armenian pseudepigrapha. Such are the interpretation of God's command to the protoplasts not to eat of the tree of knowledge, which is seen as an example of fasting. The sons of Seth, in

---

53. *Arm Apoc* 3:204–5.

54. See, respectively, *Arm Apoc* 5:16, 18, no. 2; 3:78–79, 81; 3:23–24; 3:208–10, no. 12.

55. See m. Abot 5:3; Avot R. Nat. A33:2, Yalqut Shim'oni, Lēk lĕka 12, 68; Midr. Teh. 18.25, and Pirqe R. El. 26–30. Licht (1973, 79–88) discusses the rabbinic sources.

56. See the tradition about Noah's virginity, discussed above at annotation 18. [Its prevalence in Christian sources notwithstanding, such a reading is not necessarily Christian in itself. A similar motif is found already in T. Iss. 3.5. –S.E.]

57. *Arm Apoc* 3:69. In n. 92 on that page, further witnesses to Isaac's celibacy and his being a type of Christ are adduced.

the understanding of Gen 6:1–4 promoted in Sermon Concerning the Flood §3, took an oath to remain virginal: the text describes that as ascesis. Abraham's not eating without a guest is described as fasting in the Story of Terah and of Father Abraham §24. In the same work, we read: "And Abraham who by faith, fast, and prayers, by hospitality and feast brought God down from heaven to his house" (§42). Here, the Christian virtues of faith, fasting and prayer are celebrated. Quite numerous other examples could be adduced. A final instance may be observed in Brief History of Joshua Son of Nun §§1–2, where we read of the hero, Joshua, that "through fasts and prayers he worshiped God with untiring ascesis. And he was a holy virgin and immaculate, like the bodiless angels."[58] Joshua, to be sure, shared his name with Christ.

---

58. *Arm Apoc* 5:81–82. Of course, it is because of his name that Joshua is considered a type of Christ.

16
Egypt and Exodus

The text of Questionnaire concludes with discussions of the Israelites in the desert and matters related to the ark of the covenant. The text does not relate these subjects as a narrative but rather enumerates them as a series of appendixes, chiefly in question-and-answer form. Apocryphal or other traditions about Moses do not occur, but lists of the Ten Commandments, the sacrifices, and the festivals of the Jews are included, as well as the ingredients of the oil of anointing.

After these appendixes, in the manuscript, there occur two documents that have been published already: The Ten Plagues of Egypt has been mentioned above.[1] It was published in 2016 from eight copies in two recensions in an edition that includes the witness of M682.[2] These copies are substantially identical, with occasional variations of order and meaning. The second published passage is Jannes and Mambres, which was edited and translated in full with commentary some years ago.[3] Here, it need only be remarked that this story includes some features that also occur in more extensive texts and testimonia to Jannes and Mambres, while other elements of it are unique to Questionnaire.[4] I have not succeeded in finding other Armenian passages on these two Egyptian magicians, rivals of Moses, though such may well exist. Considering that, one might hypothesize that the passage was translated into Armenian, most likely from Syriac or Greek. On fol. 9r of the manuscript, there remain some unpublished questions and answers that bear the title Concerning the Oil of Anointing of Israel.

---

1. Introduction, p. xxix.
2. See *Arm Apoc* 4:254–57.
3. *Arm Apoc* 4:254–61.
4. The Jannes and Jambres traditions are dealt with in detail by Pietersma 1994. See also DiTommaso 2001, 559–63.

As observed in the previous introductory remarks, the published work, The Genealogy of Abraham (*Arm Apoc* 3:78–85), partly overlaps with it. Specifically, the overlap starts with §16.2, Genealogy §9. Genealogy then skips the Jannes and Jambres material and resumes in §10 corresponding to Questionnaire §16.6. Genealogy §11b is equivalent to Questionnaire §16.7b; §12 to §16.8–9; §13b–15 to 16.10a–14. This correspondence is partly word for word. It is not possible to decide whether one work has shortened the material or the other expanded it.

The page is burnt at several places, but apparently, the burn preceded the writing, so in one place we can observe the conjunction զի with the letters separated and a burnt spot between the two letters. Moreover, the scribe made errors of order in copying the plagues and then corrected them by overwriting in one case and interlinear introduction of an indicative numeral in others. This is discussed in the study of this list in *Arm Apoc* 4:254–57. The list has been transcribed here as it stands in the manuscript.

Text

M682 fol.8v.1–9r.22/5

16.1/ Հարց, թէ՛ քանի են հարուածք Եգիպտոսի:
Պատասխանի. Ժ. (10). Ասա զի[6] զիտացից կարգաւ հակիրճ.[7]
16.2/ Առաջինն՝ զշուրն արիւն լինել.
Բ. (2) գորտն.
Գ. (3) մունն.
Զ. (6)[9] կեղ եւ խաւարտ.[10]
Դ. (4)[11] շանաճանճ.

---

5. The bottom third of fol.8r and the first third of fol. 8v are left blank, presumably for a text on Joseph, who is not dealt with in the Questionnaire.

6. The switch to the authorial first person is odd.

7. կ over ճ p.m.

8. Anomalously, this complement bears the *nota accusativi*, a not uncommon phenomenon in medieval Armenian.

9. The numeral Զ has been written over an illegible sign p.m.

10. The word խաւարտ means "vegetables, greens" and must be a corruption by haplography for խաղաւարտ "abscess," which is found in the form of this list published in *Arm Apoc* 4:256. This plague is number 6 and is misplaced from below.

11. This numeral has been written above the Շ in the interlinear space.

16. Egypt and Exodus

Ե. (5) խաշնամահն.
Է. (7)[12] կարկուտն եւ հուր.
Ը. (8) մարախն.
Թ. (9) խաւար շաւշափելի.
Ժ. (10) անդրանկաց մահն.

16.3/ <Հարց>: Եւ թէ ընդէ՞ր ոչ հաւատային նշանացն:
<Պատասխանի>: Այս է պատճառն. Չի Յանէս եւ Յամբրէս որդիք Բարքոբայ քաղդէացոյ կախարդի գողայնային գտդայս քաղդէացոցն եւ գրհէին կռոցն, որ անուն հօրն իւրեանց. գոր գիտացեալ քաղդէացւոցն հալածեցին գնոսա. եւ նոքա գնացին Եգիպտոս.

16.4/ Որ եւ Մովսէս Ժ.ամեայ (տասնամեայ) լեալ, եւտուն ի նոսա ուսումն. Վասն որոյ կախարդութիւն համարէին. ի ԻԲ. (22) ամին Մովսէսի սկաւ կաւագործութիւնն. ԻԸ. (28) ամին իշխան եղեւ, եւ Խ. (40) ամին սպան գչարչարիչն Իսրայէլի եւ փախեաւ:

16.5/ Յետ փախչելոյ նորա. Յանէս եւ Յամբրէս շինեցին գդրախտն դիւագ չարչարանոք որդոցն Իսրայէլի. եւ առին ՋՁ. (980) մանկունս ի նոցանէ եւ գոհեցին դիւագ եւ յայնմ օրէ հնագանդք եղեն դեւք կախարդաց:

16.6/ Հարց: թէ քանի կարք ունէր փարաւոն:
Պատասխանի. վեց հարիւր էր կարքն:
Հարց:[13] Ո՞րպէս պատառեաց Մովսէս գծովս:
Պատասխանի. Զգաւազանն ձգեաց յառաջն եւ ասէ. Այիա այս է Աստուած իմ առաջի իմ. Յաչ կողմս. Շրաիա. դու հաներ մեզ Աստուած. Ձախ կողմս, Ադոնիա. Տէրդ տերանց ընդ մեզ.

16.7/ Յորժամ որբն պաշտեցին կոտորել եւ Մովսէս ի ժողովրդենէն ԳՌ. (3,000) ձեռամբ Ղեւտացւոցն. Օրէնք տրւաւ յետ Ծ. (50) աւուր անցնելոյն ընդ ծովս:
Հարց: թէ գի՞նչ էր Ժ. (10) բան օրինացն:
Պատասխանի. Ես եմ Տէր Աստուած քո որ հանի զքեզ յԵգիպտոսի:[14]
Մի արասցեւ քեզ կուռս:
Մի կոչեսցես անուն իմ ի վերայ սնոտեաց.

---

12. A small diacritical sign precedes this numeral.
13. As noted above, in this section Հարց, "question," is usually abbreviated to Հ and sometimes to Հց. In the present instance, however, inadvertently, the scribe has written Հպ, that is, Հարց Պատասխանի, "question answer" for Հց "question." Lower down on the page in §16.8, he has made a similar mistake, but then subsequently written պ over Հց.
14. An ablative case would be expected.

Պահեա զշաբաթս իմ սրբութեամբ:
Պատուեա զհայր քո եւ զմայր.
այս է յանձնարական:
Դարձեալ՝ մի շնար. մի գողանար. մի սպանաներ. մի սուտ վկայեր:
Մի ցանկար ընչից եղբօր քո.
այս ե. (5) հրաժարական:
16.8/ Հարց: Ո՞րչափ էր տապանակ ուխտին:
<Պատասխանի>:[15] Երկայն Բ. (2) կանգուն եւ կէս. լայնն կանգուն եւ կէս. եւ բարձրն կանգուն եւ կէս:
Հարց: Զի՞նչ կայր ի մէջ տապանակին:
Պատասխանի. Տախտակ օրինացն զոր ետ Աստուած. սափոր ոսկի լի մանանայիւ. գաւազան Ահարոնի որ ծաղկեցաւ. բունուածն որ պղինձ էր եւ եղեւ ոսկի ի ձեռին Ահարոնի:
16.9/ Հարց: Խորանն վկայութեան ե՞րբ կանգեցաւ: / fol. 9r /
Պատասխանի. Յետ ելիցն Ե. (5) ամսոյն սկսաւ եւ Է. (7) ամիսն կատարեցաւ. ի խորհուրդ Է. (7) աւուր արարչութեանն եւ կանգնեցաւ ի սկիզբն երկրորդ ամին յելիցն:
16.10/[16] Եւ էր չափ խորանին Ծ. (50) փեղք, եւ մի փեղքն եւ ԻԸ. (28) կանգուն երկայն, եւ Դ. (4) կանգուն լայն. ի կարմրոյ, ի կապուտոյ, ի բեհեզոյ, ի ծիրանի: Հարտարապետք խորանին, Բեսէլիէլ, Ուրիայ եւ Եղիաբ:
16.11/ Աղաչանքն Մովսէսի առ Աստուած յորժամ կամեցաւ ջնջել զազգն վասն որթոյն:
Գթած ես եւ ողորմած, երկայնամիտ, բազումողորմ եւ ճշմարիտ. այս է [Գ]թաց[17] առ որդիս, ողորմած առ դարձեալսն, երկայնամիտ առ անդարձսն, բազումողորմ առ բազմապար<տ>սն,[18] ճշմարիտ ի հատուցումն բարեաց:
16.12/ Հարց: թէ տօնք քա՞նի էին ի հինն:
Պատասխանի.
Նախ՝ տարեմուտ եւ ամսամուտ.
Բ. (2) բաղարճակերացն եւ ելիցն.
Գ. (3) տօնութեան. որ օրէնքն տուաւ.
Դ. (4) քաւութեան որթոյն.
Ե. (5) տաղաւարահարացն, որ խորանն կանգնեցաւ.

---

15. By error, the scribe wrote hց, "question," instead of պ, "answer."
16. Sections 10–11 have questions and answers without the tags.
17. The colored initial of this word was never entered.
18. So, emending the reading of the manuscript.

16. Egypt and Exodus

վասն որոյ Ե. (5) նաևակատիս կատարեմք ի նորս. այս, Յայտնութիւնն:

Ջատիկն,[19] Վարդավառն. Աստուածածինն, եւ Սուրբ խաչն:

16.13/ Հարց: Պատարագ քանի՞ էր ի հնումփ:

Պատասխանի. Դ. (4) Ջոհն զոհութեան էր որ հեռաւոր գայր. կամ բարի աջողմունք լինէր. Պատարագ փրկութեան որ զբորոտն սրբէր եւ այլ ցաւս փարատէր. վասն մեղացն որ մեղս խոստովանէին եւ զենուին. ողջակէզ կամաւոր, որ Աստուծոյ նուիրէին:

16.14/ Հարց: Համար զօրացն Մովսեսի քանի՞ էր:

Պատասխանի. Վեց հարիւր Ռ. (1,000) Վ. եւ ՈՃ. (600,000, 3,000, 600 եւ 50 = 603,650), ԻԵ. (25) տարէն ի վեր, եւ Կ. (60) տարէն ի վայր. դետւացիքն որ փոխեցիքն անդրանկացն յաւելցան անդրանկացն, ոգիք ՄՀԳ. (273) վասն որոյ զերկդրամեանն տան անդրանիկքն Դետւացւոցն:

16.15/ Ովզ թագաւոր Թ. (9) կանգուն էր եւ Դ. (4) լայն. այս Ովզ եւ Սեհոն էին զոր Մովսես ճանապարհի խնդրեաց եւ ոչ ետուն, վասն որոյ ի սպառ չնչեաց զնոսա Մովսես: Եւ յորժամ Բ. (2) խրատով Բաղամայ մոզին պոռնեցան, կոտորեաց հրեշտակ ԻԴՌ. (24,000) մինչեւ արզել Փենեհէս:

16.16/ Ահարոն մեռաւ ի Հովր լեառն եւ Մովսէս ի Նաբաւ լեառն, եւ ոչ մտին երկիր աւետեաց, վասն զի Ահարոն որթն արարեալ Մովսէս բամբասեաց. իսկ Մովսէս բարկացոյց Տէր ի վերայ ջուրցն հակառակութեան:

16.17/ Այս են ազգք որ չնչեցին յերկրէն աւետեաց. Ամուրհացին, Քետացին, Փերեզացին, Քանանացին, Գերգեսացին, Խեւացին. Յերուսացին:

16.18/ Բաղամու մարգարէութիւն այս էր վասն Քրիստոսի, ծագեցի աստղ Յակոբայ, եւ ելցէ այր Իսրայելէ:[20]

Translation

16.1/ Question: How many are the plagues of Egypt?[21]

Answer: 10. Say (them) so that I may know (them) in order briefly.

---

19. The initial letter of this word and the next are uppercase. Ջատիկ starts with Ջ, which is also the Armenian numeral for 6.

20. Num 24:17.

21. The list of plagues occurs in MS Galata 154, and it was published as a separate document in *Arm Apoc* 4:254–57, no. 10. See introductory remarks to this part.

16.2/ The first: the water becoming blood.
2. Frog(s).[22]
3. Gnat(s).[23]
6. Ulcers and <abscesses>.[24]
4. Fleas.[25]
5. Murrain.[26]
7. Hail and fire.[27]
8. Locusts.[28]
9. Tangible darkness.[29]
10. Death of the firstborn.[30]

16.3/ <Question>: Why were they not believing the signs?

<Answer>: This is the reason: Because Janēs and Jamrēs, sons of Barkʿoba the Chaldean magician, used to steal the boy-children of the Chaldeans and sacrifice (them) to an idol, the name of which was that of their father. When the Chaldeans learned that, they chased them away, and they[31] went to Egypt.

16.4/ They gave Moses, who was ten years old, to them to learn.[32] On account of this, they were considered magic(ians).[33] In Moses's twenty-second year, the brick-laying began.[34] In his 28th year he became a prince, and in his 40th year he killed the torturer of Israel[35] and fled.

16.5/ After his flight, Janēs and Jamrēs built the garden[36] of demons through the sufferings of the children of Israel, and they took 980 of their

---

22. Exod 8:2–13.
23. Exod 8:16–18.
24. Exod 9:10–11, 14–15. See n. 10 above.
25. Literally: dog flies. These are the flies of Exod 8:21–24, 29.
26. Exod 9:3–7.
27. See Exod 9:22–24.
28. Exod 10:4–6, 12–15.
29. Exod. 10:21–22.
30. Exod 11:5, 12:29–30.
31. That is, Janēs and Jamrēs.
32. That is, from them.
33. This appears to be the meaning. The word means "magic," but the context demands "magician."
34. See Exod 1:11–14.
35. See the remarks by Ableman in *Arm Apoc* 6:130–31, where this title is discussed. See On Moses and Aaron §13 in that volume.
36. See Pietersma 1994.

little children and sacrificed (them) to demons and from that day on, the demons became obedient to the magicians.

16.6/ Question: How many chariots did Pharaoh have?

Answer: The chariots were six hundred.

Question: How did Moses split the sea?[37]

Answer: He held his staff out forward and said, "Ayia, this is my God before me; to the right-hand side, "Šraia, God, you brought us forth"; to the left-hand side, "Adonia, you, O Lord of lords are with us."[38]

16.7/ When they worshiped the calf,[39] Moses caused 3,000 of the people to be cut down at the hand of the Levites.[40] The law was given on the 50th day after the crossing of the sea.[41]

Question: Which were the ten pronouncements of the law?[42]
Answer:
I am the Lord your God who brought you out of Egypt.
Do not make idols for yourself.
Do not call my name over worthless things.
Observe my Sabbaths in holiness.
Honor your father and mother.
These five are personal.[43]

Again: Do not commit adultery. Do not steal. Do not murder. Do not bear false witness. Do not covet your brother's possessions.

These are five to be renounced.[44]

16.8/ Question: Of what dimensions was the ark of the covenant?

<Answer>: two cubits and one half long; one cubit and one half wide; one and one half cubits high.[45]

---

37. Exod 14:16, 21.

38. The fourth, reverse direction is missing. It may never have been there, since the Israelites were to go forward. This same incident is related in On Moses and Aaron §34. For further occurrences of this textual unit, see Stone *Arm Apoc* 6:152 n. 129.

39. That is, the golden calf: see Exod 32:4–35.

40. Exod 32:28 also puts the figure at 3,000 and is doubtless the source of our text.

41. That is, the Red Sea. The fifty days relate to the Feast of Weeks, celebrated seven weeks after Passover.

42. See Exod 20:2–17, the Ten Commandments.

43. That is, commandments given to the individual.

44. In other words, the text distinguishes the first five positive commandments from the following five negative ones.

45. These are the measurements given in Exod 37:1. The same measurements and list of the contents of the ark are specified in Stone 2013, 80, 84.

Question: What was inside the ark?

Answer: The tablet of the law that God gave;[46] the golden urn filled with manna;[47] Aaron's staff that flowered;[48] a censer that was copper and that became gold in Aaron's hand.[49]

16.9/ Question: When was the tent of witness[50] erected?

Answer: From the fifth month after the exodus it was begun, and it was completed in the seventh month as a type of the seven days of creation.[51] And it was set up at the beginning of the second year of the exodus.[52]

16.10/ And the measure of the tent was of fifty panels,[53] and each panel was 28 cubits long and 4 cubits wide, from red (material), from blue, from fine linen, from purple. The architects of the tent were Bezalel, Uriah, and Eliav.[54]

---

46. Exod 31:18, 32:16, etc. Their deposit in the ark is explicit in Deut 10:5 and several other places. 2 Chr 5:10 states that only the stone tablets were in the ark.

47. This is stated in Heb 9:4; Exod 16:33–34 only speaks of a "jar" full of manna, and its being golden is not specified. LXX Exod reads: στάμνον χρυσοῦν ἕνα ("one golden jar"). However, Exodus says the jar is placed "before the Lord," not explicitly *inside* the ark.

48. Num 17:23. As in the case of the jar, according to Numbers, the staff is placed "*before* the Ark of the covenant," not inside it. The description in the text apparently depends on Heb 9:4–5.

49. An angel holding a golden censer is mentioned in connection with the heavenly altar in Rev 8:3. Also, copper censers were hammered out to cover the altar in Num 17:4, and Aaron used a censer to stop the plague in 17:11.

50. Referring to the tent of meeting, the tabernacle.

51. This idea is unusual. According to Exod 40:2, the tabernacle was erected in the first month. The reference to the seventh month may be due to confusion between the tabernacle and the Festival of Tabernacles.

52. See Exod 40:17. Compare Genealogy of Abraham §12 in *Arm Apoc* 3:84. Nathan Daniel (written correspondence) adds the following remark: The idea that several months elapsed between the end of the construction and the erection of the tabernacle in accordance with Exod 40:2 can be found in rabbinic sources; see Exod. Rab. 52.2 and Tanh. Pekudei 11.12. The reference to the seventh month is almost certainly due to a confusion between the tabernacle and the Feast of Tabernacles as confirmed by line 16.12. While confirming the proposed connection between the tabernacle and the Feast of Tabernacles, 16.12 creates a discrepancy in the text as two dates are given for the erection of the tabernacle (in both cases, the verb կանգնեցաւ is used).

53. Reading փերը as փեղկ "panel"; this is the word used in Exod 26:3, 7.

54. Neither Uriah nor Eliav is mentioned in Exodus in direct connection with the building of the tabernacle. Uriah was Bezalel's father; see Exod 31:2: "Bezalel the

16.11/ The supplications of Moses to God when he wished to annihilate the people because of the calf,[55] "You are caring and merciful, long-suffering, very merciful and true."[56]

This is (means): caring for children, merciful to the repentant, long-suffering to the unrepentant, greatly merciful to the greatly guilty, true in the recompense of good things.[57]

16.12/ Question: How many feasts were there in the Old?[58]

Answer:

1. New Year and New Moon.
2. Of Eating of Unleavened Bread and of the Exodus.
3. Of Giving, that the Law was given.
4. Of the Lament of Atonement.
5. Of the Huts (Sukkot) on which the Tent (of Meeting) was set up.[59]

Because of this, we carry out five dedications in the new (dispensation),[60] these (are), Epiphany, Easter, Transfiguration, (Feast of) the Virgin Mother of God, and (Feast of) the Holy Cross.

16.13/ Question: How many sacrifices are there in the old[61] (dispensation)?

Answer: 4—the sacrifice of thanks was when one came from afar or when there were good successes;

the sacrifice of redemption that a leper was purified and other pains relieved;

(the sacrifice) for sin, that they would confess sins and would sacrifice;

---

son of Uri, son of Hur." The Armenian "Eliav" developed from the name of Bezalel's coworker Oholiab, mentioned in Exod 36:1–2.

55. That is, the golden calf (see Exod 32:4). Moses's prayer is described in Exod 32:11–13, 31–32, and 33:13–16.

56. Drawn from Exod 34:6.

57. This is a paraphrase of what was presumably an originally liturgical formula found in Exod 34:6–7, Jonah 4:2, Joel 2:13, and Pr Man 7. See the discussion in Stone 1971, 128.

58. That is, Old Testament.

59. These are the chief festivals prescribed in the Torah. The description here shows no knowledge of Jewish practice in addition to what may be gleaned directly from the Hebrew Bible. The five festivals are seen to parallel the five chief Christian feasts listed in the second part of this section.

60. That is, testament.

61. The unusual word hʻunṭfu is quite clear in the manuscript and is apparently derived from hhu, "old."

the voluntary whole burnt offering which they would present to God.

16.14/ Question: How large was the number of Moses's hosts?

Answer: 603,650 from the age of twenty-five up and under sixty. The Levites who replaced the firstborn were added to the firstborn, 273 souls.[62] On account of this, the firstborn used to give a didrachm to the Levites.

16.15/ King Og was nine cubits (high) and four (cubits) wide.[63] This Og and Sihon were those of whom Moses asked for passage, and they did not grant (it). On account of this, Moses annihilated them. And when by the counsel[64] of the magician Balaam they (the Israelites) fornicated, an angel cut down 24,000[65] until Pinḥas (Phineas) prevented it.

16.16/ Aaron died on Mount Hor[66] and Moses on Mount Nebo,[67] and they did not enter the promised land,[68] because Aaron made the calf[69] and Moses slandered (scil. God).[70] Then Moses angered the Lord over the waters of opposition.[71]

16.17/ These are the nations whom they extirpated from the promised land: the Amorites, the Hittites, the Perezites, the Canaanites, the Gergesites, the Hivites, the Jebusites.[72]

16.18/ This was Balaam's prophecy about Christ: a star will shine from Jacob, and a man shall come forth from Israel.

Annotation 28. Jannes and Jambres in Armenian Texts

These are the names of two legendary Egyptian magicians who were the rivals of Moses in wonderworking before Pharaoh. A Greek Christian

---

62. See Num 3:46.
63. According to Deut 3:11, these were the dimensions, not of Og, but of his iron bedstead.
64. The manuscript has բխրատտվէ, which should be understood as a corrupt բ + the instrumental of խրատ "counsel" (following a suggestion of –S.E.).
65. Num 25:9.
66. Num 33:38. Observe that §16.16 is made up of pentateuchal phrases and allusions, documented in the notes here.
67. Deut 34:1.
68. Num 20:24 (Aaron) and Deut 4:21 (Moses).
69. Exod 32:35.
70. Num 20:11–12.
71. Or: Meribah.
72. Num 27:14. Observe that there are seven peoples in this list, which is taken from Exod 3:17.

retelling of their competition with Moses is to be found in PH 75 (*MOTP* 1:630). The two figures are early attested in the Dead Sea Scrolls fragments of the Damascus Document, CD V, 18–19 = in 4Q266 3 II, 6, where they are called "Yaḥneh [יחנה] and his brother."[73] The origins and ramifications of this tradition are beyond our limits here; suffice it to say that they are considerable, and this is a very early example of biblical embroidery.[74]

Armenian traditions about the magicians Jannes and Mambres are discussed in a rich article by James R. Russell.[75] Features of the form of the story presented here are to be found in the Historical Compilation of Vardan Arewelcʻi.[76] Indeed, that thirteenth-century work in §8 contains nearly all the details found in our text; I quote Vardan's text here and underline the shared details. The passage, which is located directly following Moses's flight to Midian (see Exod 2:15), reads as follows:[77]

> <u>Yanēs and Yamrēs</u> took the sons of Israel and led them fifteen days' journey through the desert. <u>They built their garden</u> for fifteen years, and when the work was completed, <u>they took 980 boys</u> from <u>the sons of Israel and sacrificed them to demons</u>. The latter joined them, and they appointed them as guards for the garden. <u>From then on, demons were even more subject</u> to magicians.

For ease of comparison, I present the relevant section of Questionnaire here:

> 16.5/ After his flight, Yanēs and Yamrēs built the garden of demons through the tortures of the children of Israel, and they took 980 of their little children and sacrificed (them) to demons and from that day on, the demons were obedient to the magicians.

---

73. See *DSSSE* 1:585. [Similar names for Moses's Egyptian opponents appear also in b. Menah. 85a: Yohana and Mamre (יוחנא וממרא). –S.E.] No details are given about the two magicians either in the Dead Sea Scrolls or in b. Menahot that might be compared with our Armenian text. For further reference, see Fraade 2021, 50–52.
74. See Pietersma 1994, 31–38 and for bibliography, DiTommaso 2001, 559–63. See also my earlier discussion of this passage in *Arm Apoc* 4:257–61.
75. James Russell 2014–2015. The magicians are discussed on pp. 32–36, and he has assembled several relevant texts in translation on pp. 44–46. Gerö (1995) presents medieval developments of the Jannes and Jambres tradition.
76. See James Russell 2014–2015, 33–34.
77. See the translation in Thomson 1989, 151.

Questionnaire has omitted the garden and the fifteen days and years but otherwise closely resembles Vardan's text. Obviously, the text of Vardan is most likely the source used by Questionnaire; another possibility is that they share a prior, apparently written source. Considering the author's penchant for including preexistent documents in his work, his close dependence on Vardan is not surprising. That would clearly imply, by the way, that Questionnaire was composed after Vardan Arewelc'i's days (1200?–1271).

17
The Oil of Anointing

This part deals with the ingredients of the oil of anointing, which are set forth in Exod 30:23–24. There, they are in a different order, and that passage reads:

> Take the finest spices: of liquid myrrh five hundred shekels, and of sweet-smelling cinnamon half as much, that is, two hundred and fifty, and of aromatic cane two hundred and fifty, and of cassia five hundred, according to the shekel of the sanctuary, and of olive oil a hin.

It will be observed that in Exodus the measures of each spice are given in what is a quite practical regulation. In Questionnaire 17, however, the measures are omitted. Instead, the text provides a rather general geographic origin for each and specifies the apotropaic effect attributed to these substances. They are from far-off, exotic places—Ethiopia, Mount Sinai, Egypt, and Babylon. The recipe and the specific details are presented as an item of learned knowledge. The oil is attributed to the old Israel in a nonexplicit contrast with the new Israel, which is the church, in which the myron or chrismatic oil is the oil of anointing.[1]

Text

M682, fol. 9r.23–33/

17.0/ Վասն իւղոյն օծութեան հինն Իսրայէլի
17.1/ Եւղն առաջին որ[2] օծանէին զեղանս զքահանայս եւ զմարգարէս այս էր. Դ. (4) ծաղիկ հիրիկ, եղէգն, զմուռ, եւ կինամոն:

---
1. Aznaworean 1996.
2. One would expect an instrumental case here.

17.2/ Հի{հի}րիկն³ ծաղիկ ունի զօրութիւն դղեւս հալածելոյ. գտանի ի Հապաշաստան, յեզր Փիսոն գետոյն:

17.3/ Եղեգն նորա սքանչ անուշահոտ է եւ բուժիչ ցաւոց, մանաւանդ զքոս եւ զունկն փարատէ. եւ գտանի ի Սինա լեառն մօտ յԵգիպտոս:

17.4/ Կինամոնն զարմանալի որ ի քունն մարդոյ շրթունսն դնես, զոր ինչ խորհուրդ ի սիրտն լինի ասէ. եւ ինքն ոչ զիտէ. եւ թէ յեռման ջուր հասուցանես ցրտացնէ. գտանի ի Թաբայիթ:

17.5/ Զմուռսն խունկ է որ զմարմինս թաղաւորաց օծանեն ի մեռանելն, զի անապական մնասցէ. եւ դարն է իբրեւ զեղի. բայց թէ քացախով զք իմէ թմրի. այս է զոր եառուն Քրիստոսի ի վերայ խաչին զի թմրեցցի. եւ գտանի ի Բաբելոն: Այսքան ծաղկանց հաւաքեալ վասն որոյ ազնիւ է:

Translation

17.0/ Concerning the Oil of Anointing of Old Israel

17.1/ The first[4] oil, with which they used to anoint the altars, the priests, and the prophets. This was (made of) four flowers: the iris, the calamus, myrrh, and cinnamon.[5]

17.2/ The iris flower has the power to drive off demons. It is found in Ethiopia, on the bank of the Pison River.[6]

17.3/ The calamus,[7] it has a wondrously sweet odour and (is) healing of pains—particularly it disperses scurf and mycotic infections. And it is found on Mount Sinai, close to Egypt.

17.4/ Cinnamon (is) amazing that if you put it on the lips of a sleeping man, he says whatever secrets he holds in his heart and he does not

---

3. Dittography of the first syllable.
4. This may also be rendered "the former oil."
5. These four ingredients are listed in Exod 30:32–34. The terms here are those used in the Armenian translation of Exodus, but their order differs from that in the Bible. The features listed in sections 17.2–5 are not in the Bible.
6. This is not in accordance with other Armenian geographic traditions, which connect the Pison with India: See Stone 2011. However, India and Ethiopia were sometimes confused in late antique texts.
7. Apparently, the sweet calamus is intended. See OED, s.v. That is the plant which is specified in Armenian Exodus by the word խունկեղէգն զանոյշ, called "sweet incense cane" in RSV of Exodus (see above).

know.[8] If you put it into boiling water, it cools (it). It is found in Tʿebayitʿ (the Thebiad).[9]

17.5/ Myrrh is an incense with which they anoint the bodies of kings when they die so (they)[10] should remain uncorrupted.[11] It is as bitter as wormwood, but if someone drinks it with vinegar, he slumbers. This is that which they gave to Christ on the cross so that he might slumber.[12] And it is found in Babylon.

This much[13] was collected from flowers, on account of which it is rare.

---

8. Understand, "that he has said them."
9. A region of Upper Egypt.
10. Literally: it, that is, the body.
11. [It is worth mentioning that the Palestinian Targums to Gen 50:2–3 and 26 render Hebrew חנט, "embalm," with Aramaic בסם, "to make sweet-smelling, to perfume" (also with perfumed ointments). –S.E.]
12. See Matt 27:48, Mark 15:36, Luke 23:36, John 19:29–30.
13. That is: These four flowers.

18
Names of the Twenty-Four Prophets

On fol. 9v the list, Names of the Twenty-Four Prophets occurs,[1] and it is followed by questions and answers about the fall and cursing of Jericho and other biblical topics. We transcribe this material, which takes up the first thirteen lines of fol. 9v. It is followed by a list of Nine Grades of the Church and texts of blessings on relics and on the body of the deceased, which are not included in the present edition.

TEXT

M682 fol. 9v.1–14/

18.0/ Անուանք բսան եւ չորս մարգարէից:

18.1/ Մովսէս, Սամուէլ, Դաւիթ, Նաթան, Գաթ, Եղիա, Եղիշէ, Եսայի, Երեմիա, Եզեկիէլ, Դանիէլ, ԲԺ. (12).[2]

Ովսէ, Ամովս, Միքիա, Յովէլ, Աբդիու, Յովնան, Նաւում, Անբակում,[3] Սոփոնիա, Անգէաս, Զաքարիա, Մաղաքիա, Յովհաննէս մկրտիչ:

18.2/ Երիքով զոր բակեաց Յեսու եւ ասաց, "Անիծեալ որ շինցէ զսա". բայց շինեաց Ազան Բեթելացի հրամանաւ թագաւորին Աքայաբու. բայց ի դնել հիմանն մեռաւ անդրանիկ որդին. եւ յաւարտն կրասերն:

18.3/ Հարց: քանի՞ անգամ գերեցաւ Իսրայէլ:

---

1. For other lists of twenty-four prophets, see *Arm Apoc* 1:174–75 and compare manuscript M5327, fol. 232r.
2. Above line p.m. There are eleven names in the first list.
3. Observe the unusual spelling with the shift of "n" in the usual Armenian spelling of this word to "m."

Պատասխանի. Բազում անգամ մասնաւոր, բայց առաւել, Դ. (4) անգամ.

Նախ՝ Թագլաթ Փաղասար եւ Սաղմանասար ասորիք.

Ապա՝ Դիոկղետիանոս. ապա՝ Անտիոքոս:

Բայց յետ Քրիստոսի, Տիտոս եւ Վեսպիանոս ի սպառ չշեցին եւ զտաճարն թակեցին:

18.4/ Չի Եսայի մերկ եւ բոկ շրջէր, օրինակ գերութեանն ազգի.

Երեմիա անուր երկաթի արկանէր ի պարանոց իւր:

Եզեկիէլ մազ եւ մորուսն գերծէր եւ որմս ծակէր եւ կորիկոր գնայր.

Ովսէ Բ. (2) կին առնէր,⁴ Ա. (1) պոռնիկ եւ Ա. (1) շնացող.

Երինջն Բ. (2) զոր կանգնեաց Յերեբովամ. Ով նա անուանեաց Ա. (1) երինջն ի Դան եւ միւսն ի Բեթէլ:

TRANSLATION

18.0/ Names of the Twenty-Four⁵ Prophets

18.1/ Moses, Samuel, David, Nathan, Gad, Elijah, Ełišē, Isaiah, Jeremiah, Ezekiel, Daniel, 12.⁶

Hosea, Amos, Micah, Joel, Obadiah, Jonah, Nahum, Habakkuk, Zephaniah, Haggai,⁷ Zechariah, Malachi, John the Baptist.⁸

18.2/ Jericho (is the town) which Joshua destroyed and said, "Cursed is he who builds this one." But Azan of Bethel built it at the command of King Ahiab (Ahab), but when he set the foundation, his firstborn son died, and at its completion, the younger one.⁹

18.3/ Question: How many times was Israel exiled?

Answer: Partly, on many occasions, but in addition, four times.

First, Tiglath-pileser and Sałmanasar the Assyrians.¹⁰

---

4. This is a confusion of առնէր, "he did, made," and առնոյր, "he took."

5. Other lists have twelve and twenty-four prophets (see *Arm Apoc* 1:174–75).

6. There are eleven names given in this first part of the list, where twelve would be expected.

7. Note Armenian Անգէաս with Greek or Latin ending. See part 2 n. 3.

8. This second list has thirteen names, so altogether there are twenty-four names.

9. That incident is mentioned to justify including Joshua b. Nun's name as an addendum to a list of prophets. The incident is drawn from Josh 6:26 combined with 1 Kgs 16:34. It also figures in Brief History of Joshua son of Nun §48. Like here, in that text, the builder's name "Hiel" becomes "Azan" for no discernable reason.

10. For Shalmanezer, see 2 Kgs 17:3 and 18:9. For Tiglath-pileser, see 2 Kgs 15:29 and 16:2.

18. Names of the Twenty-Four Prophets

Then Diocletian,[11] then Antiochus.[12]

But after Christ, Titus and Vespasian completely destroyed and ruined the temple.[13]

18.4/ For Isaiah went around naked and unshod, as a symbol of the captivity of the people.[14]

Jeremiah put an iron collar around his neck.[15]

Ezekiel shaved his hair and beard[16] and pierced the wall and went very lowly.[17]

Hosea (had) two wives, one a prostitute and one an adulterer.[18]

The two heifers that Jeroboam set up, whom did he name? One heifer in Dan and the other in Bethel.[19]

---

11. The introduction of Diocletian here is the result of a confusion: he was emperor from 284–305 CE and infamous for his persecution of Christians. The second of these exiles enumerated by the text was actually the well-known Babylonian exile of 587–586 BCE by Nebuchadnezzar. Diocletian, a persecutor of Christians, has entered the list at this chronologically inappropriate point.

12. Here the text refers to Antiochus IV Epiphanes, who desecrated the temple in 168–167 BCE as related in the books of Maccabees. The concept of exile has been broadened to include the destruction of the temple within its focus.

13. The destruction of the Second Temple in 70 CE is intended. Vespasian and Titus relate to the destruction of 70 CE.

14. Isa 20:7. This section reports instances in which prophets engaged in symbolic actions to concretize their prophecy.

15. Jer 28:10.

16. Ezek 5:1.

17. Or: humbly. See Ezek 12:5–7.

18. Hos 1:2 and 3:1

19. See 1 Kgs 12:29–30, Josephus, *A.J.* 8.226, 228. The Armenian is not completely clear here.

Bibliography

Ableman, Oren. 2021. "Excursus: Moses in Ethiopia." Pages 122–33 in *Armenian Apocrypha from Adam to Daniel*. By Michael E. Stone. EJL 55. Atlanta: SBL Press.
Abrahamyan, Ašot G. 1952. "Սամուէլ Անեցւ տոմարական եւ տիեզերագիտական Աշխատութիւնը" [The Calendrical and Cosmological Work of Samuel Anecʻi]. *Ējmiacin* 1952.1:30–37, 1952.2:34–43.
———. 1973. Հայոց Գիր Եւ Գրչութիւն [Armenian Script and Writing]. Erevan: Erevan State University Press.
Adler, William. 1989. *Time Immemorial: Archaic History and Its Sources in Christian Chronography from Julius Africanus to George Syncellus*. Dumbarton Oaks Studies 26. Washington DC: Dumbarton Oaks.
———. 1996. "The Apocalyptic Survey of History Adapted by Christians: Daniel's Prophecy of Seventy Weeks." Pages 201–38 in *The Jewish Apocalyptic Heritage in Early Christianity*. Edited by James C. VanderKam and William Adler. Assen: Van Gorcum; Minneapolis: Fortress.
———. 2007. *Iulius Africanae Chronographiae: The Extant Fragments*. GCS n.s. 15. Berlin: de Gruyter.
———. 2015. "Parabiblical Traditions and Their Use in the Palaea Historica." Pages 1–19 in *Transformation from Second Temple Literature through Judaism and Christianity in Late Antiquity*. Edited by Menahem Kister, Hillel Newman, Michael Segal, and Ruth Clements. Leiden: Brill.
———. 2020. "Observations on the Textual Transmission of the Palaea Historica in Greek." Pages 64–94 in *Von der Historienbibel zur Weltchronik*. Edited by Christfried Böttrich, Dieter Fahl, and Sabine Fahl. Greifswalder Theologische Forschungen 31. Leipzig: Evangelische Verlagsanstalt.

Adler, William, and Paul Tuffin. 2002. *The Chronography of George Synkellos*. Oxford: Oxford University Press.

Aerts, Willem Johan, and Georg A. A. Kortekaas. 1998. *Die Apokalypse des Pseudo-Methodius: Die ältesten Griechischen und Lateinischen Übersetzungen*. CSCO 569–570, Subsidia 97–98. Leuven: Peeters.

Alexander, Philip S. 1972. "The Targumim and Early Exegesis of 'Sons of God' in Genesis 6." *JJS* 23:60–71.

Alexandre, Monique. 1988. *Le Commencement du Livre: Genèse I–V; La version grecque de la Septante et sa réception*. Christianisme antique 3. Paris: Beauchesne.

Aliquot, Julien. 2008. "Sanctuaries and Villages on Mt. Hermon during the Roman Period." Pages 73–96 in *The Variety of Local Religious Life in the Near East*. Edited by Ted Kaizer. Leiden: Brill.

Amihai, Aryeh. 2022. "הבן הרביעי של נח" [Noah's Fourth Son]. https://amihay.wordpress.com/2022/05/19/yonton/.

Anasyan, Hakob S. 1959. Հայկական Մատենագիտութիւն (Ե-ԺԸ դդ) [Armenian Bibliology, Fifth–Eighteenth Centuries]. Vol. 1. Erevan: Academy of Sciences.

Andersen, Francis I. 1983. "2 Enoch." *OTP* 1:91–213.

Anderson, Gary A. 1988. "The Cosmic Mountain: Eden and Its Early Interpreters in Syriac Christianity." Pages 187–224 in *Genesis 1–3 in the History of Exegesis: Intrigue in the Garden*. Edited by Gregory Allen Robbins. Lewiston: Mellen.

———. 1989. "Celibacy or Consummation in the Garden? Reflections on Early Jewish and Christian Interpretations of the Garden of Eden." *HTR* 82:121–48.

———. 2001. "The Garments of Skin in Apocryphal Narrative and Biblical Commentary." Pages 101–43 in *Studies in Ancient Midrash*. Edited by James Kugel. Harvard: Harvard University Center for Jewish Studies.

Anderson, Gary A., and Michael E. Stone. 1999. *A Synopsis of the Books of Adam and Eve*. 2nd rev. ed. EJL 17. Atlanta: Scholars Press.

Annus, Amar. 2011. "The Mesopotamian Precursors of Adam's Garment of Glory and Moses' Shining Face." Pages 1–18 in *Identities and Societies in the Ancient East-Mediterranean Regions: Comparative Approaches; Henning Graf Reventlow Memorial*. Edited by Thomas R. Kämmerer. Vol. 1. AOAT 390.1. Münster: Ugarit-Verlag.

Aptowitzer, Victor. 1922. *Kain und Abel in der Agada, den Apokryphen, der hellenistischen, christlichen und mohammedanischen Literatur*. Vienna: Löwit.

———. 1924. "Les éléments juifs dans la légende du Golgotha." *REJ* 79:145–62.

Attridge, Harold W. 1984. "Historiography." Pages 157–84 in *Jewish Writings of the Second Temple Period*. Edited by Michael E. Stone. Assen: van Gorcum; Philadelphia Fortress.

Aucher, Johannes Baptist Ancyrni. 1818. *Eusebii Pamphili Caesariensis Episcopi Chronicon Bipartitum* [Bipartite Chronicle of Eusebius Pamphilius, Bishop of Caesarea]. Venice: Mekhitarist Press.

Auffarth, Christoph. 2004. "Angels on Earth and Forgers in Heaven: A Debate in the High Middle Ages Concerning their Fall and Ascension." Edited by 192–223 in *The Fall of the Angels*. Edited by Christof Auffarth and Loren T. Stuckenbruck. TBN 6. Leiden: Brill.

Avalachvili, Zurab. 1928. "Notice sur une version géorgienne de la *Caverne des Trésors*." *ROC* 26:381–405.

Aznaworean, Bishop Zareh. 1996. Կանոն Սուրբ Մյուռոնի Օրհնության [Canon of the Blessing of the Holy Miwṙon]. Catholicosate of Sis: Antelias.

Badalanova Geller, Florentina. 2011. "The Sea of Tiberias: Between Apocryphal Literature and Oral Tradition." Pages 13–158 in *The Old Testament Apocrypha in the Slavonic Tradition: Continuity and Diversity*. Edited by Lorenzo DiTommaso and Christfried Böttrich. Mohr Siebeck.

———. 2017a. "Clandestine Transparencies: Retrieving the Book of Jubilees in Slavia Orthodoxa (Iconographic, Apocryphal and Folklore Witnesses)." *Judaïsme ancien / Ancient Judaism* 5:183–279.

———. 2017b. "10. South Slavic." Pages 253–306 in *The Bible in Folklore Worldwide*. Edited by Eric Ziolkowski. Berlin: de Gruyter.

———. 2021a. "The Garments of Paradisical Flesh: Notes on Edenic Anthropology." Pages 33–56 in *Wandering Ideas on the Paths of Humanities, Studies in Folkloristics, Cultural Anthropology and Slavistics*. Edited by Stanoy Stanoev, Vihra Baeva, Vladimir Penchev, Veselka Toncheva, and Irina Kolarska. Vol. 2. Sofia: Bulgarian Academy.

———. 2021b. "Glottogenesis, the Primordial Language and the Confusion of Tongues." Pages 324–63 in *Festschrift Anna-Maria Totomanov*. Edited by Tatiana Slavova, Gergana Totomanova-Paneva, Maria Ganeva, and Diana Atanasova. Sofia: Universitetsko Izdatelstvo "Sv. Klime."

———. 2021c. "Unde malum? The Watchers Mythologeme in *The Slavonic Apocalypse of Enoch*." *Wiener Slavistisches Jahrbuch* n.s. 9:1–45.

Baert, Barbara. 2005. *A Heritage of Holy Wood*. Leiden: Brill.

Bakker, Arjen. 2017. שבח המאורות בספר המשלים ומקבילותיו מקומראן [The Praise of the Luminaries in the *Similitudes of Enoch* and Its Parallels in the Qumran Scrolls]. *Meghillot* 13:171–84.

Baltzly, Dirk. 2023. "Stoicism, Physical Theory." *Encyclopedia of Philosophy*. https://plato.stanford.edu/entries/stoicism/.

Bamberger, Bernard J., Herman J. Blumberg, Benjamin Baude, Jerome S. Gurland, Bernard H. Mehlman, and Leslie Y. Gutterman. 2007. "Angels and Angelology." *EncJud* 1:150–61.

Baronian, Sukias, and Frederick C. Conybeare. 1918. *Catalogue of the Armenian Manuscripts in the Bodleian Library*. Oxford: Clarendon.

Barrois, Georges A. 1962. "Zion." *IDB* 4:959–60.

Barzilai, Gabriel. 2007. "Incidental Biblical Exegesis in the Qumran Scrolls and its Importance for Study of the Second Temple Period." *DSD* 14:1–24.

Bauckham, Richard J. 1991. "More on Kainam the Son of Arpachshad in Luke's Genealogy." *ETL* 67:95–102.

Baumgarten, Joseph M. 1994. "Purification After Childbirth and the Sacred Garden in 4Q265 and *Jubilees*." Pages 3–10 in *New Qumran Texts and Studies*. Edited by George Brooke and Florentino García Martínez. STJD 15. Leiden: Brill.

Baumstark, Anton. 1922. *Geschichte der syrischen Literatur*. Bonn: Markus & Weber.

Beck, Bruce N. 2011. "'When Shall I Come and See the Face of God?' The Exegetical and Historical Genesis of the Trisagion Hymn." *Greek Orthodox Theological Review* 56:347–85.

Bedrossian, Matthias. 1973. *New Dictionary Armenian-English*. Beirut: Librairie du Liban.

Ben-Dov, Jonathan. 2016. "The Resurrection of the Divine Assembly and the divine Title El in the Dead Sea Scrolls." Pages 9–31 in *Submerged Literature in Ancient Greek Culture. Beyond Greece: The Comparative Perspective*. Edited by Andrea Ercolani and Manuela Giordano. Berlin: de Gruyter,

———. 2018. מבול ביער הלבנון. שרידים מיתולוגיים מן הלבנט במגילות מדבר יהודה [Flooding in the Lebanon Forest: Relics of Levantine Mythology in the Dead Sea Scrolls]. *Meghillot* 14:189–204.

———. 2021. "Neo-Babylonian Rock Reliefs and the Jewish Literary Imagination." Pages 345–79 in *Afterlives of Ancient Rock-cut Monuments in the Near East*. Edited by Jonathan Ben-Dov and Felipe Roja. Leiden: Brill.
Bergamini, Laurie J. 1985. "From Narrative to Ikon: The Virgin Mary and the Woman of the Apocalypse in Thirteenth Century English Art and Literature." PhD diss. University of Connecticut.
Betz, Hans D. 1992. *The Greek Magical Papyri in Translation, Including the Demotic Spells*. 2nd ed. Chicago: University of Chicago.
Bietenhard, Hans. 1951. *Die himmlische Welt im Urchristentum und Spätjudentum*. WUNT 2. Tübingen: Mohr.
Boccaccini, Gabriele, ed. 2007. *Enoch and the Messiah Son of Man: Revisiting the Book of Parables*. Grand Rapids: Eerdmans.
Bohak, Gideon. 2008. *Ancient Jewish Magic: A History*. Cambridge: Cambridge University Press.
———. 2019. "Jewish Amulets, Magic Bowls, and Manuals in Aramaic and Hebrew." Pages 388–415 in *Guide to the Study of Ancient Magic*. Edited by David Frankfurter. Leiden: Brill.
Böttrich, Christfried. 1995. *"Die Vögel des Himmels haben ihn begraben": Überlieferungen zu Abels Bestattung und zur Ätiologie des Grabes*. Göttingen: Vandenhoeck & Ruprecht.
———. 2010. "Geschichte Melchisedeks." In *Weisheitliche, magische und legendarische Erzählungen*. JHSRZ n.s. 1. Gütersloh: Gütersloher Verlaghaus.
———. 2012. "'Much to Say and Hard to Explain': Melchizedek in Early Christian Literature, Theology, and Controversy." Pages 411–29 in *New Perspectives on 2 Enoch: No Longer Slavonic Only*. Edited by Andrei A. Orlov, Gabriele Boccaccini, and Jason M. Zurawski. Leiden: Brill.
Bousset, Wilhelm. 1960. *Die Himmelreise der Seele*. Repr. Darmstadt: Wissenschaftliche Buchgesellschaft.
Bowker, John. 1969. *The Targums and Rabbinic Literature*. Cambridge: Cambridge University Press.
Bremmer, Jan N. 2004. "Remember the Titans!" Pages 35–61 in *The Fall of the Angels*. Edited by Christoph Auffarth and Loren T. Stuckenbruck. Leiden: Brill.
Brichto, Herbert C. 1976. "Cain and Abel" *IDBSup* 5:121.

Brightman, Frank E. 1896. *Liturgies Eastern and Western, Being the Texts Original or Translated of the Principal Liturgies of the Church.* Oxford: Oxford University Press.

Brock, Sebastian P. 1978. "Abraham and the Ravens: A Syriac Counterpart to *Jubilees* 11–12 and its Implications." *JSJ* 9:135–52.

———. 1979a. "Jewish Traditions in Syriac Sources." *JJS* 30:212–32.

———. 1979b. "The Queen of Sheba's Questions to Solomon: A Syriac Version." *Le Muséon* 92:331–45.

———. 1982. "Clothing Metaphors as a Means of Theological Expression in Syriac Tradition." Pages 11–38 in *Typus, Symbol, Allegorie bei den östlichen Vätern und ihren Parallelen im Mittelalter.* Edited by Margot Schmidt in collaboration with Carl-Friedrich Geyer. Regensburg: Friederich Pustet.

———. 1997. *A Brief Outline of Syriac Literature.* Moran 'Eth'o 9. Kottayam: SEERI.

Bucur, Bogdan G., and Vladimir I. Ivanovici. 2019. "'The Image of Adam's Glory': Observations on the Early Christian Tradition of Luminosity as Iconic Garment." *Research Institutes in the History of Art Journal* 0224.

Budge, E. A. Wallis, ed. 1886. *The Book of the Bee.* Anecdota Oxoniensia 1.2. Oxford: Clarendon.

———. 1914. *Coptic Martyrdoms etc. in the Dialect of Upper Egypt.* London: British Museum.

———. 1933. *The Alexander Book in Ethiopia.* London: Oxford University Press.

Bunta, Silviu. 2007. "One Man (φως) in Heaven: Adam—Moses Polemics in the Romanian Versions of *The Testament of Abraham* and Ezekiel the Tragedian's *Exagoge.*" *JSP* 16:139–65.

Calzolari, Valentina. 2010. "'Je ferai d'eux mon propre peuple': Les Arméniens, peuple élu selon la littérature apocryphe chrétienne en langue arménienne." *RHPR* 90:179–97.

Cardona, Giorgio R. 1966. "I nomi dei figli di Tôgarmah secondo il Sepher Yôsêphôn," *Rivista degli Studi Orientali* 41:17–27.

Chabot, Jean-Bapiste. 1899. *Chronique de Michel le Syrien.* Paris: Leroux.

Charles, Robert H. 1902. *The Book of Jubilees or the Little Genesis.* London: Black.

———. 1913. *The Apocrypha and Pseudepigrapha of the Old Testament.* 2 vols. Oxford: Clarendon.

Chitty, Derwas J. 1966. *The Desert a City: An Introduction to the Study of Egyptian and Palestinian Monasticism under the Christian Empire.* London: Mowbrays.
Clermont-Ganneau, Charles. 1971. *Archaeological Researches in Palestine during the Years 1873-1874.* Repr. Jerusalem: Raritas.
Conybeare, Frederick C. 1894. "On the Apocalypse of Moses." *JQR* 7:216-35.
Cowe, S. Peter. 1992. *The Armenian Version of Daniel.* UPATS 9. Atlanta: Scholars Press.
Cowley, Roger W. 1988. *Ethiopian Biblical Interpretation: A Study in Exegetical Tradition and Hermeneutics.* University of Cambridge Oriental Publications 38. Cambridge University Press.
Cox, Claude E. 1981. *The Armenian Translation of Deuteronomy.* UPATS 2. Chico CA: Scholars Press.
Cross, Frank L., and Livingstone, Elizabeth A. 1974. *The Oxford Dictionary of the Christian Church.* 2 ed. rev. Oxford: Oxford University Press.
Cross, Frank Moore, Jr. 1973. *Canaanite Myth and Hebrew Epic: Essays in the History of the Religion of Israel.* Cambridge MA: Harvard University Press.
Cumont, Franz. 1956. *The Oriental Religions in Roman Paganism.* New York: Dover Publications.
———. 1960. *Astrology and Religion Among the Greeks and Romans.* New York: Dover Publications.
Dar, Shimon. 2022. "The Israeli Mount Hermon." Pages 94-102 in *Cities, Monuments and Objects in the Roman and Byzantine Levant: Studies in Honour of Gabi Mazor.* Edited by Walid Atrash, Andrew Overman, and Peter Gendelman. Oxford: ArchaeoPress Archaeology.
Daranałcʻi, Grigor. 1915. Ժամանակագրութիւն [Chronography]. Edited by Mesrop V. Nšanean. Jerusalem: Sts. James Press.
Davies, Gwynne Henton. "Glory." *IDB* 2:401-3.
De Conick, April D., and Fossum, Jarl. 1991. "Stripped before God: A New Interpretation of Logion 37 in the Gospel of Thomas." *VC* 45:123-50.
Desreumaux, Alain. 2021. "La Couronne de Nemrod: Quelques réflexions sur le pouvoir, l'histoire et l'Ecriture dans la culture syriaque." Pages 189-96 in *Early Christian Voices in Texts, Traditions and Symbols.* Edited by David H. Warren, Ann Graham Brock, and David W. Pao. BibInt 66. Leiden: Brill.
DiTommaso, Lorenzo. 2001. *A Bibliography of Pseudepigrapha Research 1850-1999.* JSPSup 39. Sheffield: Sheffield Academic.

Dochhorn, Jan. 2004. "Die *Historia de Melchisedech* (Hist Melch)—Einführung, editorischer Vorbericht und editiones Praeliminares." *Le Muséon* 117:7–48.

Dorfmann-Lazarev, Igor. 2014. "The Cave of the Nativity Revisited: Memory of the Primaeval Beings in the Armenian *Lord's Infancy* and the Cognate Sources." Pages 285–320 in *Mélanges Jean-Pierre Mahé*. Edited by Aram Mardirossian, Agnès Ouzounian, and Constantine Zuckerman. Travaux et Memoires 18. Paris: Assn. des Amis du Centre l'Histoire et Civilization de Byzance.

———. 2020a. "Adam in the Church at Ałt'amar (915–921) and a Pseudepigraphical Commentary on Genesis." Pages 306–32 in *Von Historien Bibel zur Welt Chronik*. Edited by Christfried Böttrich, Dieter Fahi, and Sabrina Fahi. Griefswalde Theologishe Forschungen 31. Leipzig: Evangelische Verlagsanstalt.

———. 2020b. "XII Appendix: Eve, Melchizedek and the Magi in the Cave of the Nativity According to the Armenian Corpus of Homilies Attributed to Epiphanius of Salamis." Pages 264–95 in *The Protoevangelium of James*. Edited by Jan N. Bremmer, J. Andrew Doole, Thomas R. Karmann, Tobias Nicklas, and Boris Repschinski. Studies in the Early Christian Apocrypha 16. Leuven: Peeters.

———. 2020c. "XIII Appendix: Annotated Texts." Pages 295–311 in *The Protoevangelium of James*. Edited by Jan N. Bremmer, J. Andrew Doole, Thomas R. Karmann, Tobias Nicklas, and Boris Repschinski. Studies in the Early Christian Apocrypha 16. Leuven: Peeters.

———. 2022. "The Admonitory Exhortations of Dawit' of Ganjak (†1140): The Armenian-Kurdish Contacts in the Kur Valley and the Birth of the Armenian Legal Tradition." Pages 277–321 in *Sharing Myths, Texts and Sanctuaries in the South Caucasus*. Edited by Igor Dorfmann-Lazarev. SECA 19. Leuven: Peeters.

Duchesne-Guillemin, Jacques. 1962. *La Religion de l'Iran ancien*. Paris: Presses Universitaires de France.

Efrati, Shlomi. 2019. "Pesikta of Ten Commandments" [Hebrew]. PhD diss. Jerusalem: Hebrew University.

Egan, George. 1968. *An Exposition of the Gospel by Saint Ephraem*. CSCO 291–292. Scriptores Armeniaci 5–6. Louvain: Peeters.

Elior, Rachel. 2014. "The Garden of Eden is the Holy of Holies and the Dwellings of the Lord." *Studies in Spirituality* 24:63–118.

Ēmin, Mkrtičʻ, ed. 1860. Մխիթար Այրիվանեցի: Պատմութիւն Հայոց. [Mxitʻar Ayrivanecʻi: History of the Armenians]. Moscow: Lazarean Institute Press.
Erder, Yoram. 1994. "Early Karaite Conceptions about the Commandments Given before the Revelation of the Torah." *PAAJR* 60:101–40.
Ervine, Roberta R., and Michael E. Stone. 2000. *The Armenian Texts of Epiphanius of Salamis De Mensuris Et Ponderibus*. CSCO 583 Subsidia 105. Leuven: Peeters.
Eshel, Esther. 2007. "The *Imago Mundi* of the Genesis Apocryphon." Pages 111–31 in *Heavenly Tablets: Interpretation, Identity and Tradition in Ancient Judaism*. Edited by Lynn LiDonnici and Andrea Lieber. JSJSup 119. Leiden: Brill.
———. 2018–2019. "Destruction by Fire in the Genesis Apocryphon and Related Literature" [Hebrew]. *Meghillot* 14:181–88.
Eshel, Esther, and Michael E. Stone. 1993. "The Eschatological Holy Tongue in Light of a Fragment from Qumran" [Hebrew]. *Tarbiz* 62:169–77.
Eynatyan, Juliette, ed. 2002. Հին Հայկական Տոմարը (7-րդ–15-րդ դդ) [The Ancient Armenian Calendar (Seventh–Fifteenth Centuries)]. Translated by Gohar Muradyan and Aram Topchyan. Erevan: Magaghat.
Feydit, Frédéric. 1973. "Les croyances populaires arméniennes." *Bazmavep* 2:227–46.
———. 1986. *Amulettes de l'Arménie chrétienne*. Bibliothèque arménienne de la Fondation Calouste Gulbenkian. Venice: St. Lazare.
Fiensy, David A. 1985. *Prayers Alleged to be Jewish: An Examination of the Constitutiones Apostolorum*. BJS 65. Chico: Scholars Press.
Fine, Elisha, and Steven Fine. 2022. "Rabbinic Paleontology: Jewish Encounters with Fossil Giants in Roman Antiquity." Pages 3–37 in *Land and Spirituality in Rabbinic Literature: A Memorial Volume for Yaakov Elman* ל"ז. Edited by Shana S. Schick. The Brill Reference Library of Judaism 71. Leiden: Brill.
Fletcher-Louis, Crispin H. T. 2002. *All the Glory of Adam: Liturgical Anthropology in the Dead Sea Scrolls*. STJD 42. Leiden: Brill.
Flusser, David. 1971. "*Palaea Historica*: An Unknown Source of Biblical Legends." Pages 48–79 in *Studies in Aggada and Folk-Literature*. Edited by Joseph Heinemann and Dov Noy. Scripta Hierosolymitana 22. Jerusalem: Magnes.

Fraade, Steven D. 1984. *Enosh and His Generation: Pre-Israelite Hero and History in Postbiblical Interpretation.* SBLMS 30. Chico CA: Scholars.

———. 1998. "Enosh and his Generation Revisited." Pages 59–86 in *Biblical Figures outside the Bible.* Edited by Theodore A. Bergren and Michael E. Stone. Harrisburg: Trinity Press International.

———. 2021. *The Damascus Document.* Oxford: Oxford University Press.

Frazer, Margaret E. 1974. "Hades Stabbed by the Cross of Christ." *Metropolitan Museum Journal* 9:153–61.

Frey, Jörg. 2018. "'Mystical' Traditions in an Apocalyptic Text? The Throne Vision of Revelation 4 within the Context of Enochic and Merkavah Texts." Pages 103–27 in *Apocalypticism and Mysticism in Ancient Judaism and Early Christianity.* Edited by John J. Collins, Pieter de Villiers, and Adela Yarboro Collins. Berlin: de Gruyter.

Friedlander, Gerald. 1981. *Pirke De Rabbi Eliezer: The Chapters of Rabbi Eliezer the Great.* 4th ed. New York: Sepher-Hermon Press.

Fröhlich, Ida. 2015. "Stars and Spirits: Heavenly Bodies in Ancient Jewish Aramaic Tradition." *AS* 13:111–27.

———. 2016. "Giants and Demons." Pages 97–114 in *Ancient Tales of Giants from Qumran and Turfan.* Edited by Matthew Goff, Loren T. Stuckenbruck, and Enrico Morano. Tübingen: Mohr Siebeck.

Fry, Virgil R. L. 1992. "Cainan (Person)." *ABD*, 807.

Garibian de Vartavan, Nazénie. 2021. "'On the Mountains of Ararat': Noah's Ark and the Sacred Topography of Armenia." Pages 276–95 in *Apocryphal and Esoteric Sources in the Development of Christianity and Judaism.* Edited by Igor Dormann-Lazarev. Leiden: Brill.

Gaster, Theodore H. 1962a. "Angels." *IDB* 1:128–34.

———. 1962b. "Satan." *IDB* 4:224–28.

Gatch, Milton McC. 1975. "Noah's Raven in Genesis A and the Illustrated Old English Hexateuch." *Gesta* 14:3–15.

Gaylord, Harry E. 1982. "How Satanael lost his '-el.'" *JJS* 33:303–9.

Geiger, Abraham. 1898. *Judaism and Islam.* Translated by F. M. Young. Madras: M.D.C.S.P.C.K. Press.

Gerö, Stephen. 1980. "The Legend of the Fourth Son of Noah." *HTR* 73:321–30.

———. 1995. "Jannes and Jambres: In the *Vita Stephani Iunioris* (BHG 1666)." *Analecta Bollandiana* 113:281–92.

Ghazaryan, D. 2018. "Old-Printed Armenian Amulets in Scroll of the Library of the Dudean Cultural House at Armenian Apostolic Patriarchate of Romania in Bucharest." *Revue des Etudes Sud-Est Européennes* 54:69–99.

Ginzberg, Louis. 1909. *The Legends of the Jews*. 7 vols. Philadelphia: Jewish Publication Society of America.

———. 1960. "מבול של אש. Flood of Fire" [Hebrew]. *Al Halaka ve-Aggada* 205–20.

Goff, Matthew J. 2010. "Ben Sira and the Giants of the Land: A Note on Ben Sira 16:7." *JBL* 129:645–55.

Golitzin, Alexander. 2001. "'Earthly Angels and Heavenly Men': The Old Testament Pseudepigrapha, Niketas Stethatos, and the Tradition of 'Interiorized Apocalyptic' in Eastern Christian Ascetical and Mystical Literature." *DOP* 55:125–53.

———. 2003. "Recovering the 'Glory of Adam': 'Divine Light' Traditions in the Dead Sea Scrolls and the Christian Ascetical Literature of Fourth-Century Syro-Mesopotamia." Pages 275–308 in *The Dead Sea Scrolls as Background to Postbiblical Judaism and Early Christianity. Papers from an International Conference at St. Andrews in 2001*. Edited by James R. Davila. Leiden: Brill.

Govett, Robert. 1880. "Epiphanius on Golgotha." *PEFQ* 12:109–10.

Grattepanche, Johanna. 1993. "Caïn et Abel dans les Légendes islamiques." *Orientalia Lovaniensia Periodica* 24:133–42.

Greatrex, Marina. 2009. "The Angelology in the *Hexaemeron* of Jacob of Edessa." *Journal of the Canadian Society of Syriac Studies* 4:33–46.

Greene, David, and Fergus Kelley. 1976. *Text and Translation*. Vol. 1 of *The Irish Adam and Eve Story from Saltair Na Rann*. Dublin: Dublin Institute for Advanced Studies.

Grigor Tatʻewacʻi. 1993. Գիրք Հարցմանց [Book of Questions]. Repr. Jerusalem: St. James Press.

Gruenwald, Ithamar. 2014. *Apocalyptic and Merkavah Mysticism*. AJEC 90. 2nd rev. ed. Leiden: Brill.

Grypeou, Emmanouela, and Helen Spurling, eds. 2009. *The Exegetical Encounter between Jews and Christians in Late Antiquity*. Jewish and Christian Perspectives 18. Leiden: Brill.

Gutmann, Joseph. 1977. "Noah's Raven in Early Christian and Byzantine Art." *Cahiers archéologiques* 26:63–71.

Hakobyan, Hayarpi. 2020. "Foremother Eve in the Nativity of Christ according to some Armenian Miniature Paintings from the Thirteenth–Forteenth Centuries." *Orientalia Christiana Periodica* 86:519–28.

Hakobyan, Tadevos X., Stepʻan T. Melikʻ-Baxšyan, and Hikar X. Barseɫyan. 1998. Հայաստանի եվ հարակից շրջանների տեղանունների բառարան [Dictionary of Toponymy of Armenia and Adjacent Territories]. Erevan: Erevan State University Press.

Hannah, Darrell D. 2007. "Guardian Angels and Angelic National Patrons in Second Temple Judaism and Early Christianity." *Deuterocanonical and Cognate Literature Yearbook* 2007:413–36.

Harley McGowan, Felicity. 1970. "Death Is Swallowed up in Victory: Scenes of Death in Early Christian Art and the Emergence of Crucifixion Iconography." *Cultural Studies Review* 17:101–24.

Hartenstein, Friedhelm. 2007. "Cherubim and Seraphim in the Bible and in the Light of Ancient Near Eastern Sources." *Deuterocanonical and Cognate Literature Yearbook* 155–88.

Harutʻyunyan, Sargis. 2006. Հայ հմայական եւ ժողովրդական աղօթքներ [Armenian Incantations and Folk Prayers]. Erevan: Erevan State University Press.

Hayward, Robert. 1995. *Jerome's Hebrew Questions on Genesis: Translated with Introduction and Commentary*. Oxford: Oxford University Press.

———. 2009. "What Did Cain Do Wrong? Jewish And Christian Exegesis of Genesis 4:3–6." Pages 101–23 in *The Exegetical Encounter Between Jews and Christians in Late Antiquity*. Edited by Emmanouela Grypeou and Helen Spurling. Jewish and Christian Perspectives Series 18. Leiden: Brill.

———. 2012. "Mules, Rome, and a Catalogue of Names: Genesis 36 and its Aramaic Targumim." Pages 295–314 in *Studies on the Text and Versions of the Hebrew Bible in Honour of Robert Gordon*. Edited by Geoffrey Khan and Diana Lipton. Leiden: Brill.

Heinemann, Joseph. 1977. *Prayer in the Talmud*. SJ 6. Berlin: de Gruyter.

Heither, Theresia, and Christiana Reemts. 2007. *Biblische Gestalten bei den Kirchenvatern: Adam*. Münster: Aschendorff.

Heller, B. n.d. "Namrūd." *Encyclopaedia of Islam*. Edited by P. Bearman, Th. Bianquis, C. E. Bosworth, E. van Donzel, and W. P. Heinrichs. 2nd ed. http://dx.doi.org/10.1163/1573-3912_islam_SIM_5791.

Henning. Walter B. 1934. "Ein Manichäisches Henochbuch." Pages 27–35 in *Der Sitzungsberichten der Preussischen Akademie der Wissenschaften (Phil.-Hist. Klasse)*. Berlin: Akademie der Wissenschaften.

———. 1943. "The Book of the Giants." *BSOAS* 2:52–74.

Henze, Matthias. 2001. "Nebuchadnezzar's Madness (Daniel 4) in Syriac

Literature." Pages 550–71 in *The Book of Daniel: Composition and Reception*. Edited by John J. Collins and Peter W. Flint. Leiden: Brill.

Herbert, Maire, and Martin McNamara, eds. 1990. *Irish Biblical Apocrypha*. Edinburgh: T&T Clark.

Hess, Richard S. 1992. "Abel (Person)." *AYBD*, 9.

Hilkens, Andy. 2018. *The Anonymous Syriac Chronicle of 1234 and Its Sources*. OLA 272. Leuven: Peeters.

———. 2020a. "Language, Literacy and Historical Apologetics: Hippolytus of Rome's lists of literate peoples in the Syriac Tradition." *JECS* 72:1–32.

———. 2020b. "'A Wise Indian Astronomer Called Gandoubarios': Malalas and the Legend of Yoniṭon." Pages 119–42 in *Intercultural Exchange in Late Antique Historiography*. Edited by Marianna Mazzola and Maria Conterno. OLA Bibliothèque de Byzantion 23. Leuven: Peeters.

Himmelfarb, Martha. 1991. "The Temple and the Garden of Eden in Ezekiel, the Book of the Watchers, and the Wisdom of Ben Sira." Pages 63–78 in *Sacred Spaces and Profane Places: the Geographies of Judaism, Christianity and Islam*. Edited by Paul Simpson-Hansly and Jamie Scott. Contributions to the Study of Religion 30. New York: Greenwood.

———. 1993. *Ascent to Heaven in Jewish and Christian Apocalypses*. New York: Oxford University Press.

Hoek, Johanna Louisa van den. 1988. *Clement of Alexandria and His Use of Philo in the Stromateis: An Early Christian Reshaping of a Jewish Model*. VCSup 3. Leiden: Brill.

Hollander, Harm W., and Marinus de Jonge. 1985. *The Testaments of the Twelve Patriarchs: A Commentary*. SVTP 8. Leiden: Brill.

Hovhanissian, Vahan. 2000. *Third Corinthians: Reclaiming Paul for Christian Orthodoxy*. New York: Lang.

Hultsch, Friedrich Otto. 1864. *Metrologicorum Scriptorum Reliquae—Scriptores Graeci*. Leipzig: Teubner.

Inglisian, Vahan. 1935. *Armenien in der Bibel*. Studien zur Armenischen Geschichte. Vienna: Mekhitarist Press.

Issaverdens, Jacques. 1934. *The Uncanonical Writings of the Old Testament Found in the Armenian Mss. of the Library of St. Lazarus*. 2 ed. Venice: Mekhitarist Press.

Jacobus, Helen R. 2009. "The Curse of Cainan (Jub. 8.1–5): Genealogies in Genesis 5 and Genesis 11 and a Mathematical Pattern." *JSP* 18:207–32.

James, Montague R. 1920. *The Lost Apocrypha of the Old Testament: Their Titles and Fragments.* Translations of Early Documents 1. London: SPCK.

Jansma, Taeke. 1958. "Investigations into the Early Syriac Fathers on Genesis," *Oudtestamentische Studien* 12:69–181.

Jellinek, Adolf. 1938. *Bet Ha-Midrasch.* Repr. Jerusalem: Bamberger & Wahrmann.

Kamesar, Adam. 1993. *Jerome, Greek Scholarship, and the Hebrew Bible. A Study of the Quaestiones Hebraicae in Genesim.* Oxford Classical Monographs. Oxford: Clarendon.

Kazazian, Norayr, and Michael E. Stone. 2004. "The Commentary on the Cycle of Four Works." *JAS* 8:46–51.

Kowalski, Aleksander. 1982. "'Rivestiti di gloria' Adamo ed Eva nel commento di San Efrem a Gen 2,25 (Ricierca sulle fonti dell'esegesi siriaca)." *CNS* 3:41–60.

Kim, Angela Y. 2001. "Cain and Abel in the Light of Envy: A Study in the History of the Interpretation of Envy in Genesis 4:1–16." *JSP* 12:65–84.

King, Michael. 2017. "Adam's Skull, Christ, and Golgotha in Pictish Art." Pages 130–37 in *Islands in a Global Context: Proceedings of the Seventh International Conference on Insular Art.* Edited by Conor Newman, Mags Mannion, and Fiona Gavin. Dublin: Four Courts.

Kister, Menahem. 2006. "אחור וקדם: אגדות ודרכי מדרש בספרות החיצונית ובספרות חז"ל" [Before and After: Aggadoth and Midrashic Methods in the Literature of the Second Temple Period and in Rabbinic Literature]. Pages 231–59 in *Higayon L'Yona: New Aspects in the Study of Midrash, Aggadah and Piyyut in Honor of Professor Yona Fraenkel.* Edited by Joshua Levinson, Jacob Elbaum and Galit Hasan-Rokem. Jerusalem: Magnes Press.

———. 2015. "Hellenistic Jewish Writers and Palestinian Traditions: Early and Late." Pages 150–78 in *Tradition, Transmission, and Transformation from Second Temple Literature through Judaism and Christianity in Late Antiquity. Proceedings of the Thirteenth International Symposium of the Orion Centre for the Study of the Dead Sea Scrolls and Associated Literature.* Edited by Michael Segal and Ruth R. Clements. STJD 113. Leiden: Brill.

———. 2018–2019. "יחסים בין תרבויות ופרשנות המקרא" [Intercultural Relations and Biblical Exegesis]. *Meghillot* 14:163–80.

Kittel, Gerhard. 1974. "δόξα." *TDNT* 2:244–46.

Kiwleserian, Babgen Coadj. Catholicos. 1961. Ցուցակ ձեռագրաց Պալաթիոյ Ազգային Մատենադարանի Հայոց [Catalogue of the Manuscripts of the Armenian National Library of Galata]. Calouste Gulbenkian Armenian Library; Antelias: Catholicossate.

Klein, Michael L. 1986. *Genizah Manuscripts of Palestinian Targum to the Pentateuch*. Cincinnati: Hebrew Union College Press.

Klijn, Albertus F. J. 1977. *Seth in Jewish, Christian and Gnostic Literature*. SNT 46. Leiden: Brill.

Kmosko, Mihaly. 1907. "Testamentum Patris Nostri Adam." Pages 1309–92 in *Patrologia Syriaca 2*. Edited by René Graffin. Vol. 2. Paris: Firmin-Didot.

Krauss, Samuel. 1899. *Griechische und lateinische Lehnwörter im Talmud, Midrasch und Targum*. Berlin: Calvary.

Kronholm, Tryggve. 1978. *Motifs From Genesis 1–11 in the Genuine Hymns of Ephrem the Syrian with Particular Reference to the Influence of Jewish Exegetical Tradition*. ConBOT 11. Lund: Gleerup.

Kruisheer, Dirk. 1997. "Reconstructing Jacob of Edessa's Scholia." Pages 187–96 in *The Book of Genesis in Jewish and Oriental Christian Interpretation: A Collection of Essays*. Judith Frishman and Luc van Rompay. Traditio Exegetica Graeca 5. Leuven: Peeters.

Kuehn, Sara. 2019. "The Primordial Cycle Revisited: Adam, Eve, and the Celestial Beings." Pages 173–99 in *The Intermediate Worlds of Angels. Islamic Representations of Celestial Beings in Transcultural Contexts*. Beiruter Texte und Studien 114. Edited by Sara Kühn, Stefan Leder, and Hans-Peter Pokel. Beirut: Orient-Institut Beirut.

Kuhn, Karl Heinz. 1984. "The Apocalypse of Zephaniah and an Anonymous Apocalypse." Pages 915–26 in *The Apocryphal Old Testament*. Edited by Hedley F. D. Sparks. Oxford: Oxford University Press.

Kugel, James L. 1990. "Cain and Abel in Fact and Fable: Genesis 4:1–16." Pages 176–90 in *Hebrew Bible or Old Testament? Studying the Bible in Judaism and Christianity*. Edited by Roger Brooks and John J. Collins. CJA 5. Notre Dame IN: University of Notre Dame Press.

Kulik, Alexander. 2010. *3 Baruch: Greek-Slavonic Apocalypse of Baruch*. Commentaries on Early Jewish Literature. Berlin: de Gruyter.

Kuyumdzhieva, Margarita. 2016. "Imaging Evil in the First Chapters of Genesis: Texts behind the Images in Eastern Orthodox Art." *Studia Ceranea* 6:377–96.

Lambden, Stephen N. 1992. "From Fig Leaves to Fingernails: Some Notes on the Garments of Adam and Eve in the Hebrew Bible and Select

Early Postbiblical Jewish Writings." Pages 74–89 in *A Walk in the Garden. Biblical, Iconographical and Literary Images of Eden.* Edited by Paul Morris and Deborah Sawyer. JSOTSup 136. Sheffield: University of Sheffield Press.

Langlois, Victor. 1867. *Collection des historiens anciens et moderns de l'Arménie.* 2 vols. Paris: Firmin Didot Frères.

La Porta, Sergio. 2008. *The Armenian Scholia on Dionysius the Areopagite: Studies on their Literary and Philological Tradition.* CSCO Subsidia 122. Leuven: Peeters.

Łazaryan, Vigen. 2013. Դիոնիսիոս Արիսպագացի: Աստուածաբանական Երկեր [Dionysius the Areopagite: Theological Works]. Erevan: Nairi Press.

Leonhardt-Balzer, Jutta. 2005. *Fragen Esras.* JSHRZ n.s. 1.5 Gütersloh: Gütersloher Verlagshaus.

Leslau, Wolf. 1951. *Falasha Anthology.* New Haven: Yale University Press.

Levene, Abraham. 1951. *The Early Syrian Fathers on Genesis: From a Syriac Ms. on the Pentateuch in the Mingana Collection; The First Eighteen Chapters of the Ms. Edited With Introduction, Translation and Notes; and Including a Study in Comparative Exegesis.* London: Taylor's Foreign Press.

Lewis, Jack P. 1968. *A Study of the Interpretation of Noah and the Flood in Jewish and Christian Literature.* Leiden: Brill.

———. 1984. "Noah and the Flood in Jewish, Christian, and Muslim Traditions." *The Biblical Archaeologist* 47:224–39.

Lewy, Hans. 1956. *The Chaldean Oracles and Theurgy.* Recherches d'archéologie, de philologie et d'histoire 13. Cairo: Institute francaise d'archéologie orientale.

Licht, Jacob. 1973. הנסיון במקרא וביהדות של תקופת הבית השני [Testing in the Hebrew Scriptures and in Second Temple Judaism]. Jerusalem: Magnes Press.

Lint, Theo M. van. 1999. "Grigor Narekcʻi's *Tał Yarutʻean*: The Throne Vision of Ezekiel in Armenian Art and Literature 1." Pages 105–28 in *Apocryphes Arméniens: Transmission, traduction, création, iconographie.* Edited by Valentina Calzolari Bouvier, Jean-Daniel Kaestli, and Bernard Outtier. Prahins CH: Zèbre.

———. 2014. "Geometry and Contemplation: The Architecture of Vardan Anecʻi's Vision of the Throne Chariot; *Thesis* and the Art of Memory in Armenia." Pages 217–41 in *The Armenian Apocalyptic Tradition: A*

Comparative Perspective. Edited by Kevork Bardakjian and Sergio La Porta. SVTP 25. Leiden: Brill.

Lint, Theo M. van, and Michael E. Stone. 2000. "The Armenian Vision of Ezekiel." Pages 145–58 in *The Apocryphal Ezekiel*. Edited by Michael E. Stone, Benjamin G Wright, and David Satran. EJL 18. Atlanta GA: Society of Biblical Literature.

Lipatov-Chicherin, Nikolai. 2019a. "The Burial of Adam as an Archetypical Case of Sacred Tradition." Pages 31–50 in *Naming the Sacred: Religious Toponymy in History, Theology and Politics*. Edited by Anna Mambelli and Valentina Marchetto. Göttingen: V&R Unipress.

———. 2019b. "Early Christian Tradition about Adam's Burial on Golgotha and Origen." Pages 151–78 in *Origeniana Duodecima: Origen's Legacy in the Holy Land—A Tale of Three Cities: Jerusalem, Caesarea and Bethlehem*. Edited by Aryeh Kofsky, Brouria Bitton-Ashkelony, Hillel Newman, Lorenzo Perrone, and Oded Irshai. BETL 302. Leuven: Peeters.

Lipscomb, W. Lowndes. 1990. *The Armenian Apocryphal Adam Literature*. UPATS 8. Atlanta: Scholars Press.

Loeff, Yoav. 2002. "Four Texts from the Oldest Known Armenian Amulet Scroll: Matenadaran 115 (a. 1428) with Introduction, Translation." MA Thesis, Hebrew University of Jerusalem.

Lüdtke, Willy. 1919. "Georgische Adam-Bücher." *ZAW* 38:155–68.

Luibheid, Colm, and Paul Rorem. 1987. *Pseudo-Dionysius: The Complete Works*. New York: Paulist Press.

Lupieri, Edmundo. 2002. *The Mandaeans: The Last Gnostics*. Translated by C. Hindley. Italian Texts and Studies on Religion and Society. Grand Rapids: Eerdmans.

Mach, Michael. 2000. "Angels." Pages 24–27 in *Encyclopedia of the Dead Sea Scrolls*. Edited by Lawrence Schiffman and James C. Vanderkam. Vol. 1. New York: Oxford University Press.

Madoyan, Arshak, ed. 1989. Առաքել Սիւնեցի: Ադամգիրք [Aṙakʻel of Siwnikʻ: Adamgirkʻ]. Erevan: Erevan State University Press.

Maguire, Henry. 1987. "Adam and the Animals: Allegory and the Literal Sense in Early Christian Art." Pages 363–73 in *Studies in Art and Archaeology in Honor of E. Kitzinger on His Seventy-Fifth Birthday*. Edited by William Tronzo and Irving Lavin. Washington, DC: Dumbarton Oaks.

Maier, Johann. 1990. "Zu Kult und Liturgie der Qumrangemeinde." *JJS* 14:543–86.

Malan, Solomon C. 1882. *The Book of Adam and Eve, Also Called the Conflict of Adam and Eve with Satan.* London: Williams & Norgate.

Malxaseancʻ, Stepʻan. 1944. Հայերէն Բացատրական Բառարան [Armenian Comparative Dictionary]. 4 vols. Erevan: Armenian SSR State Press.

Mansfeld, Jaap J. 2017. "The End of the World in Ancient Philosophy." *Eranos Jahrbuch* 74:91–140.

Martinez, David G. 1999. *P. Michigan XIX. Baptized for Our Sakes: A Leather Trisagion From Egypt (P. Mich. 799).* Beiträge zur Altertumskunde 120. Stuttgart: Teubner.

Matʻevosyan, Artašes S. 1997. Մատեան գիտութեան եւ հաւատոյ Դաւթի քահանայի: Հայերէն թղթեա հնագոյն ձեռագիր; Նմանատպութիւն [Study, Notes and Indexes. Vol. 2 of Book of Knowledge and Belief by the Priest David; the Oldest Armenian Manuscript on Paper, 981 CE]. Erevan: Nairi Press.

Mathews, Edward G. 1998. *The Armenian Commentary on Genesis Attributed to Ephrem the Syrian.* CSCO 572 Scriptores Armeniaci 24. Leuven: Peeters.

Mazor, Leah. 2012. "הקשר הדו-כיווני בין גן העדן והמקדש" [The Correlation between the Garden of Eden and the Temple]. *Shnaton* 13:2–38.

Mellink, Machteld J. 1962. "Ararat." *IDB* 1:194–95.

Mellinkoff, Ruth. 1970. *The Horned Moses in Medieval Art and Thought.* Berkeley: University of California Press.

Meeks, Wayne. 1972. "The Image of the Androgyne." *HTR* 65:165–208.

Megas, George A. 1928. "Das Χειρόγραφον Adams: Ein Beitrag zu Col 2:13–15." *ZNW* 27:305–20.

Metzger, Bruce M. 1959. "Seventy or Seventy-Two Disciples." *NTS* 5:299–306.

Milik, Jozef T. 1976. *The Books of Enoch: Aramaic Fragments of Qumrân Cave 4.* Oxford: Clarendon.

Miltenova, Anissava. 1981. "The Apocryphon about the Struggle of the Archangel Michael with Satanail in Two Redactions" [Bulgarian]. *Старобългарска литература* 9:98–113.

Minov, Sergey. 2010. "Bar Sarōšway on Melchizedek: Reception of Extrabiblical Material in the East Syrian Tradition of Scriptural Exegesis." Pages 718–35 in *The Embroidered Bible.* Edited by Lorenzo DiTommaso, Matthias Henze, and William Adler. SVTP 26. Leiden: Brill.

———. 2015. "Satan's Refusal to Worship Adam: A Jewish Motif and Its Reception in Syriac Christian Tradition." Pages 230–71 in *Tradition,*

Transmission, and Transformation from Second Temple Literature through Judaism and Christianity in Late Antiquity. Edited by Menahem Kister, Hillel Newman, Michael Segal, and Ruth R. Clements. STJD 113. Leiden: Brill.

———. 2016a. "Date and Provenance of the Syriac *Cave of Treasures*: A Reappraisal." *Hugoye* 20:129–29.

———. 2016b. "Gazing at the Holy Mountain: Images of Paradise in Syriac Christian Tradition." Pages 137–62 in *The Cosmography of Paradise: The Other World from Ancient Mesopotamia to Medieval Europe*. Edited by Alessandro Scafi. Warburg Institute Colloquia 27. London: Warburg Institute.

———. 2020. "A Syriac *Tabula Gentium* from the Early Abbasid Period: Dawid bar Pawlos on Genesis 10." *Khristianskij Vostok* 9:57–76.

Montesano, Marina. 2013. "Adam's Skull." Pages 15–30 in *Disembodied Heads in Medieval and Early Modern Culture*. Edited by Catrien Santing, Barbara Beart, and Anita Traninger. Leiden: Brill.

Morgan, Michael A. 1983. *Sepher HaRazim: The Book of Mysteries*. SBLTT 25 Pseudepigrapha Series 11. Chico CA: Scholars.

Mowry, Lucetta. 1952. "Revelation 4–5 and Early Christian Liturgical Usage." *JBL* 71:75–84.

Mulder, Otto. 2003. *Simon the High Priest in Sirach 50: An Exegetical Study of the Significance of Simon the High Priest as Climax to the Praise of the Fathers in Ben Sira's Concept of the History of Israel*. JSJSup 78. Leiden: Brill.

Murad, Frederik. 1905. Յայտնութեան Յովհաննու Հին Հայ Թարգմանութիւն [The Old Armenian Translation of the Revelation of John]. Jerusalem: St. James Press.

Muradyan, Gohar. 2005. *Physiologus: The Greek and Armenian Versions with a Study of Translation Technique*. HUAS 6. Leuven: Peeters.

Muradyan, Kim, ed. 1984. Բարսեղ Կեսարեցի. Յաղագս Վեցաւրեայ Արարածութեան [Basil of Caesarea: Concerning the Six-Day Creation]. Erevan: Academy of Sciences.

Murdoch, Brian O. 1967. "The Garments of Paradise: A Note on the Wiener Genesis and the Anegenge." *Euphorion* 61:375–82.

Murray, Robert. 1990. "Some Themes and Problems of Early Syriac Angelology." Pages 143–53 in *Symposium Syriacum 1990*. Edited by René Lavenant. OrChrAn 236. Rome: Pontifical Institute of Oriental Studies.

Narkiss, Bezalel, with Michael E. Stone. 1976. *Armenian Art Treasures of Jerusalem*. Ramat Gan: Masada Press.

Naveh, Joseph, and Shaul Shaked. 1993. *Magical Spells and Formulae: Aramaic Incantations of Late Antiquity*. 3rd ed. Jerusalem: Magnes Press.

———. 1998. *Amulets and Magic Bowls: Aramaic Incantations of Late Antiquity*. 3 ed. Jerusalem: Magnes Press.

Nersoyan, Tiran. 1984. *The Divine Liturgy of the Armenian Apostolic Church*. New York: Delphi Press.

Newsom, Carol A. 1985. *Songs of the Sabbath Sacrifice: A Critical Edition*. HSS 27. Atlanta: Scholars Press.

———. 1987. "Merkabah Exegesis in the Qumran Sabbath Shirot." *JJS* 38:11–30.

———. 2000. "Songs of the Sabbath Sacrifice." Pages 887–89 in *Encyclopedia of the Dead Sea Scrolls*. Edited by Lawrence H. Schiffman and James C. VanderKam. Vol. 2. New York: Oxford University Press.

Nickelsburg, George W. E. 1981. "Enoch, Levi and Peter, Recipients of Revelation in Upper Galilee." *JBL* 100:575–99.

Nickelsburg, George W. E., and James C. VanderKam. 2012. *1 Enoch 2: A Commentary on the Book of 1 Enoch 37–82*. Hermeneia. Minneapolis: Fortress.

———. 2012. *1 Enoch: The Hermeneia Translation*. Minneapolis: Fortress.

Odeberg, Hugo. 1928. *3 Enoch or The Hebrew Book of Enoch*. Cambridge: Cambridge University Press.

Olyan, Saul M. 1993. *A Thousand Thousands Served Him: Exegesis and the Naming of Angels in Ancient Judaism*. TSAJ 36. Tübingen: Mohr Siebeck.

Orlov, Andrei A. 2001. "Overshadowed by Enoch's Greatness: 'Two Tablets' Traditions from the *Book of Giants* to *Palaea Historica*." *JSJ* 32 (2001):137–58.

———. 2002. "Vested with Adam's Glory: Moses as the Luminous Counterpart of Adam in the Dead Sea Scrolls and in the Macarian Homilies." *Christian Orient* 4:498–513.

———. 2007. "The Moses Tradition." Pages 327–42 in *From Apocalypticism to Merkabah Mysticism*. Leiden: Brill.

———. 2011. "The Garment of Azazel in the Apocalypse of Abraham." *Scrinium* 7–8:3–55.

———. 2019. *The Glory of the Invisible God: Two Powers in Heaven Traditions and Early Christology*. London: T&T Clark.

———. 2023. *Supernal Serpent: Mysteries of Leviathan in Judaism and Christianity.* New York: Oxford University Press.

Otzen, Benedikt. 1984. "Heavenly Visions in Early Judaism: Origin and Function." Pages 199–215 in *In the Shelter of Elyon; Essays on Ancient Palestinian Life and Literature in honour of G. W. Ahlstrom.* Edited by W. Boyd Barrick, John R. Spencer, and Gösta W. Ahlström. JSOTSup 31. Sheffield: JSOT Press.

Paramelle, Joseph. 1984. *Philon D'alexandrie: Questions sur la Genèse II 1–7.* Cahiers d'orientalisme 3. Genève: Cramer.

Pearson, Birger A. 1975. "The Figure of Norea in Gnostic Literature." Pages 200–208 in Geo Widengren. *Proceedings of the International Colloquium on Gnosticism.* Stockholm: Almqvist & Wiksell.

———. 1988a. "The Figure of Seth in Manichaean Literature." Pages 147–55 in *Manichaean Studies.* Edited by Peter Bryder. Lund: Plus Ultra.

———. 1988b. "Revisiting Norea." Pages 265–75 in *Images of the Feminine in Gnosticism.* Edited by Karen I. King. Philadelphia: Fortress.

———. 1990. *Gnosticism, Judaism and Egyptian Christianity.* Minneapolis: Fortress.

Perles, Felix. 1917. "Nachlese zum neuhebräischen und aramäischen Wörterbuch." Pages 293–310 in *Festschrift Adolf Schwarz zum siebzigsten Geburtstage, 15. Juli 1916.* Edited by Samuel Krauss and Victor Aptowitzer. Berlin: Löwit.

Peters, Dorothy M. 2008. *Noah Traditions in the Dead Sea Scrolls: Conversations and Controversies of Antiquity.* EJL 26. Atlanta: Society of Biblical Literature.

Petrosyan, Armen. 2016. "Biblical Mt. Ararat: Two Identifications." *Comparative Mythology* 2:68–80.

Pietersma, Albert. 1994. *The Apocryphon of Jannes and Jambres the Magicians: P. Chester Beatty XVI (with New Editions of Papyrus Vindobonensis Greek Inv. 29456+29828 Verso and British Library Cotton Tiberius B. V F. 87).* Leiden: Brill.

Pivazyan, E., ed. 1960. *Yovhannēs T'lkurancʻi: Taḷer* [Yovhannēs T'lkurancʻi: Poems]. Erevan: Academy of Sciences Press.

Piovanelli, Pierluigi. 2012. " 'Much to Say and Hard to Explain': Melchizedek in Early Christian Literature, Theology, and Controversy." Pages 411–29 in *New Perspectives on 2 Enoch. No Longer Slavonic Only.* Edited by Gabriele Boccaccini, Andrei A .Orlov, and Jason M. Zurawski. Leiden: Brill.

Połarean (Bogharian), Norayr. 1971. Մայր Ցուցակ Ձեռագրաց Սրբոց Յակոբեանց [Grand Catalogue of St. James Manuscripts]. Jerusalem: St. James Press.

Prescott, Hilda F. M. 1958. *Once to Sinai: The Further Pilgrimage of Felix Fabri*. New York: Macmillan.

Preuschen, Erwin. 1900. "Die apokryphen gnostischen Adamschriften, aus dem Armenischen übersetzt und untersucht." Pages 163–252 in *Festgruss Bernhard Stade zur Feier seiner 25 jährigen Wirksamkeit als Professor dargebracht*. Edited by Wilhelm Diehl and Bernhard Stade. Giessen: Ricker.

Quinn, Esther C. 1962. *The Quest of Seth for the Oil of Life*. Chicago: University of Chicago Press.

Rapp, Stephen H. 2014. "The Georgian Nimrod." Pages 188–216 in *The Armenian Apocalyptic Tradition: A Comparative Perspective*. Edited by Kevork Bardakjian and Sergio La Porta. SVTP 25. Leiden: Brill.

Ratzon, Eshbal. 2018. "Placing Eden in Second Temple Judaism." Pages 15–52 in *Placing Ancient Texts; The Ritual and Rhetorical Use of Space*. Edited by Mika Ahuvia and Alexander Kocar. Tübingen: Mohr Siebeck.

Reau, Louis. 1957. *Nouveau Testament*. Vol. 2.2 of *Iconographie de l'Art Chrétien*. Paris: Presses Universitaires de France.

Rebiger, Bill. 2007. "Angels in Rabbinic Literature." Pages 629–44 in *Angels: The Concept of Celestial Beings—Origins, Development and Reception*. Edited by Friedrich V. Reiterer, Tobias Nicklas, and Karin Schöpflin. Berlin: de Gruyter.

Reed, Annette Y. 2005. *Fallen Angels and the History of Judaism and Christianity: The Reception of Enochic Literature*. Cambridge: Cambridge University Press.

———. 2014. "Enoch in the Armenian Apocrypha." Pages 149–87 in *The Armenian Apocalyptic Tradition: A Comparative Perspective*. Edited by Kevork B. Bardakjian and Sergio La Porta. SVTP 25. Leiden: Brill.

———. 2022. "Fallen Angels and the Afterlives of Enochic Traditions in Early Islam." Pages 51–76 in *Early Islam: The Sectarian Milieu of Late Antiquity*. Edited by Guillaume Dye. Brussels: Éditions de l'Université de Bruxelles.

Reeves, John C. 1992. *Jewish Lore in Manichaean Cosmogony: Studies in the Book of Giants Traditions*. Cincinnati: Hebrew Union College Press.

———. 2014. "Resurgent Myth: On the Vitality of the Watchers Traditions in the Near East of Late Antiquity." Pages 94–115 in *The Fallen Angels*

Traditions: Second Temple Developments and Reception History. Edited by Angela Kim Harkins, Kelley Bautch Coblentz, and John C. Endres. CBQ 53. Washington, DC: Catholic Biblical Association.

Reinink, Gerrit J. 1993. *Die syrische Apokalypse des Pseudo-Methodius.* CSCO 540–541 Scriptores Syriaci 220–221. Leuven: Peeters.

Reiterer, Friedrich V., Tobias Nicklas, and Karin Schöpflin. 2007. "Angels: The Concept of Celestial Beings-Origins, Development and Reception." *Deuterocanonical and Cognate Literature Yearbook.*

Reuling, Hanneke. 2006. *After Eden: Church Fathers and Rabbis on Gen 3:16–21.* Jewish and Christian Perspectives 10. Leiden: Brill.

Rickles, Norman. 2002. "An Angelic Community: The Significance of Beliefs about Angels in the First Four Centuries of Christianity." PhD diss., Macquarie University.

Ricks, Stephen D. 2000. "The Garment of Adam in Jewish, Muslim, and Christian Tradition." Pages 203–25 in *Judaism and Islam—Boundaries, Communication and Interaction: Essays in Honor of William M. Brinner.* Edited by Benjamin H. Hary, John L. Hayes, and Fred Astren. Leiden: Brill.

Robbins, Frank E. 1912. *The Hexaemeral Literature: A Study of the Greek and Latin Commentaries on Genesis.* Chicago: University of Chicago Press.

Robinson, Stephen E. 1982. *The Testament of Adam: An Examination of the Syriac and Greek Traditions.* SBLDS 52. Chico, CA: Scholars Press.

———. 1985. "The Testament of Adam and the Angelic Liturgy." *RevQ* 12:105–10.

———. 1989. "The Testament of Adam: An Updated Arbeitbericht." *JSP* 5:95–100.

Rompay, Lucas van. 1993. "Memories of Paradise: The Greek 'Life of Adam and Eve' and Early Syriac Tradition." *Aram* 5:555–70.

Rose, Herbert J. 1958. *A Handbook of Greek Mythology.* 6 ed. London: Methuen.

Rosenthal, Franz, trans. 1989. *From Creation to the Flood.* Vol. 1 of *The History of Al-Ṭabarī.* Albany: SUNY Press.

Rowland, Christopher. 1979. "The Visions of God in Apocalyptic Literature." *JSJ* 10:137–54.

Rubin, Nissan, and Admiel Kosman. 1997. "The Clothing of the Primordial Adam as a Symbol of Apocalyptic Time in the Midrashic Sources." *HTR* 90:155–74.

Rudolph, Kurt. 1957. "Ein Grundtyp Gnostischer Urmensch-Adam-Spekulation." *ZRGG* 9:1–20.

Rüger, Hans P. 1981. "Das Begräbnis Abels: Zur Vorlage von Sure 5,31." *BN* 14:37–45.

Runia, David T. 1986. *Philo of Alexandria and the Timaeus of Plato*. PhA 44. Leiden: Brill.

Russell, James R. 1987. *Yovhannēs T'lkuranc'i and the Mediaeval Armenian Lyric Tradition*. UPATS 7. Atlanta: Scholars Press.

———. 2011. "The Armenian Magical Scroll and Outsider Art." *Iran and the Caucasus* 15:5–47.

———. 2014–2015. "An Armenian Spirit of Time and Place: The *Švot*." *REArm* 36:13–59.

Russell, Jeffrey B. 1981. *Satan: The Early Christian Tradition*. Ithaca: Cornell University Press.

———. 1984. *Lucifer: The Devil in the Middle Ages*. Ithaca: Cornell University Press.

Sanders, Seth. 2002. "Old Light on Moses' Shining Face." *VT* 53:400–406.

Sanjian, Avedis K. 1969. "Anastas Vardapet's List of Armenian Monasteries in Seventh-Century Jerusalem." *Le Muséon* 82:265–92.

Sargsyan, Levon. 2002. "Մյուռոն [Myuṙon]." Pages 750–51 in Քրիստոնյա Հայաստան. Հանդարգիտարան [Encyclopedia of Christian Armenia]. Edited by Hovhannes Ayvazean. Erevan: Armenian Encyclopedia Editions.

Satran, David. 1989. "Fingernail and Hair: Anatomy and Exegesis in Tertullian." *JTS* 40:116–20.

Sawalaneanc', Tigran. 1870. Տեառն Միքայէլի Պատրիարքի Ասորւոյ: Ժամանակագրութիւն [Rev. Michael the Syrian Patriarch: The Chronography]. Jerusalem: St. James Press.

———, ed. 1871. Ժամանակագրութիւն Տեառն Միքայէլի Ասորւց Պատրիարքի [Chronography of Rev. Michael, Patriarch of the Syrians]. Jerusalem: St. James Press.

Schäfer, Peter. 1986. "Adam in der jüdischen Überlieferung." Pages 69–93 in *Von Alten zum Neuen Adam. Urzeit Mythos und Hielsgeschichte*. Edited by William Strolz. Freiburg: Herder.

Schermann, Theodor. 1907. *Prophetarum Vitae Fabulosae Indices Apostolorum Discipulorumque Domini Dorotheo Epiphanio Hippolyto aliisque Vindicata*. Leipzig: Teubner.

Schimmel, Annemarie. 1993. *The Mystery of Numbers*. New York: Oxford University Press.

Schmidt, Andrea B. 1996. "Die Zweifache armenische Rezension der Syrischen Chronik Michaels des Grossen." *Le Muséon* 109:300–319.

———. 2013. "The Armenian Versions I and II of Michael the Syrian." *Hugoye* 16:93–128.

Schneider, Michael. 2012. *The Appearance of the High Priest: Theophany, Apotheosis and Binitarian Theology from Priestly Tradition of the Second Temple Period through Ancient Jewish Mysticism* [Hebrew]. Sources and Studies in the Literature of Jewish Mysticism 30. Los Angeles: Cherub Press.

Scholem, Gershom G. 1954. *Major Trends in Jewish Mysticism*. Rev. ed. New York: Schocken.

Schürer, Emil. 1987. *A History of the Jewish People in the Age of Jesus Christ (75 BC—AD 135)*. Revised by Geza Vermes, Fergus Millar, and Martin Goodman. Edinburgh: T&T Clark.

Scott, James M. 1997a. "The Division of the Earth in Jubilees 8:11–9:15 and Early Christian Chronography." Pages 295–319 in *Studies in the Book of Jubilees*. Edited by Matthias Albani, Jörg Frey, and Armin Lange. Tübingen: Mohr Siebeck.

———. 1997b. "Geographic Aspects of Noachic Materials in the Scrolls at Qumran." Pages 368–81 in *The Scrolls and the Scriptures*. Edited by Stanley E. Porter and Craig A. Evans. Sheffield: Sheffield Academic.

———. 2002. *Geography in Early Judaism and Christianity: The Book of Jubilees*. SNTSMS 113. Cambridge: Cambridge University Press.

Seymour, St. John D. 1922. "The Book of Adam and Eve in Ireland." *Proceedings of the Royal Irish Academy* 36C:121–33.

Sidersky, David. 1933. *Les Origines des légendes musulmanes dans le Coran et dans les Vies des Prophètes*. Paris: Geuthner.

Smith, Morton. 1992. "On the History of Angels." Pages 285–94 in *"Open Thou Mine Eyes …": Essays on Aggadah and Judaica Presented to Rabbi William G. Braude on His Eightieth Birthday*. Edited by Herman J. Blumberg. Hoboken: Ktav.

Speyer, Wolfgang. 1970. *Bucherfunde in Der Glaubenswerbung der Antike*. Göttingen: Vandenhoeck & Ruprecht.

Spurling, Helen, and Emmanouela Grypeou. 2007. "Pirke de-Rabbi Eliezer and Eastern Christian Exegesis." *Collectanea Christina Orientalis* 4:217–43.

Stokes, Ryan E. 2008. "The Throne Visions of Daniel 7, *1 Enoch* 14, and the Qumran *Book of Giants* (4Q530): An Analysis of Their Literary Relationship." *DSD* 15:340–58.

Stone, Michael E. 1971. "Apocryphal Notes and Readings." *IOS* 1:123–31.
———. 1972. "Oil of Life." *EncJud* 12:1347.
———. 1979. *The Armenian Version of IV Ezra*. UPATS 2. Missoula: Scholars Press.
———. 1981a. *The Penitence of Adam*. CSCO 429–30 Scriptores Armeniaci 13–14. Leuven: Peeters.
———. 1981b. "Report on Seth Traditions in the Armenian Adam Books." Pages 460–71 in *The Rediscovery of Gnosticism*. Edited by Bentley Layton. NumenSup 40. Leiden: Brill.
———. 1981c. *Signs of the Judgment, Onomastica Sacra and The Generations from Adam*. UPATS 3. Chico: Scholars Press.
———. 1986–1987. "The Epitome of the Testaments of the Twelve Patriarchs." *REArm* 20:70–107.
———. 1990a. *Fourth Ezra: A Commentary on the Book of Fourth Ezra*. Hermeneia. Minneapolis: Fortress.
———. 1990b. *Textual Commentary on the Armenian Version of IV Ezra*. SCS 34. Atlanta: Scholars Press.
———. 1992. *A History of the Literature of Adam and Eve*. EJL 3. Atlanta: Scholars Press.
———. 1995. "A New Edition and Translation of the Questions of Ezra." Pages 293–316 in *Solving Riddles and Untying Knots: Biblical, Epigraphic, and Semitic Studies in Honor of Jonas C. Greenfield*. Edited by Ziony Zevit, Seymour Gittin, and Michael Sokoloff. Winona Lake: Eisenbrauns.
———. 1996. *Armenian Apocrypha Relating to Adam and Eve*. SVTP 14. Leiden: Brill.
———. 2000a "The Angelic Prediction in the Primary Adam Books." Pages 111–31 in *Literature on Adam and Eve: Collected Essays*. Edited by Gary A. Anderson, Michael E. Stone, and Johannes Tromp. SVTP 15. Leiden: Brill.
———. 2000b. "The Bones of Adam and Eve." Pages 241–45 in *For a Later Generation: The Transformation of Tradition in Israel, Early Judaism, and Early Christianity*. Edited by Randall A. Argall, Beverly Bow, and Rodney A. Werline. Harrisburg: Trinity Press International.
———. 2000c. "Selections from *On the Creation of the World* by Yovhannēs Tʻlkurancʻi: Translation and Commentary." Pages 167–213 in *Literature on Adam and Eve: Collected Essays*. in Gary A. Anderson, Michael E. Stone, and Johannes Tromp. SVTP 15. Leiden: Brill.

———. 2002. *Adam's Contract with Satan: The Legend of the Cheirograph of Adam.* Bloomingdale: Indiana University Press.

———. 2004. "Armenian Pilgrimage to the Mountain of the Transfiguration and the Galilee." *St. Nersess Theological Review* 9:79–89.

———. 2005. "John of T'lkuran, *On the Creation of the World.*" *St. Nersess Theological Review* 10:51–75.

———. 2006. *Apocrypha, Pseudepigrapha and Armenian Studies: Collected Papers.* 2 vols. OLA 144–145. Leuven: Peeters.

———. 2007a. *Adamgirkʻ: The Adam Book of Aṙakʻel of Siwnikʻ.* Oxford: Oxford University Press.

———. 2007b. "Adam's Naming of the Animals: Naming or Creation." Pages 69–80 in *The Poetics of Grammar and the Metaphysics of Sound and Sign.* Edited by Sergio La Porta and David Shulman. Jerusalem Studies in Religion and Culture 6. Leiden: Brill.

———. 2010. "Mount Ararat and the Ark." Pages 307–16 in *Noah and His Book(s).* Edited by Michael E. Stone, Aryeh Amihay, and Vered Hillel. EJL 28. Atlanta: Society of Biblical Literature.

———. 2011. "The Names of the Rivers." Pages 245–56 in *"Go out and Study the Land" (Judges 18:2): Archaeological, Historical and Textual Studies in Honor of Hanan Eshel.* Edited by Aren M. Maeir, Lawrence H. Schiffman, and Jodi Magness. Leiden: Brill.

———. 2012. *Armenian Apocrypha Relating to Abraham.* EJL 37. Atlanta: Society of Biblical Literature.

———. 2013. *Adam and Eve in the Armenian Tradition: Fifth through Seventeenth Centuries.* EJL 38. Atlanta: Society of Biblical Literature.

———. 2015. "The Cedar in Jewish Antiquity." Pages 66–82 *The Archaeology and Material Culture of the Babylonian Talmud.* Edited by Markham J. Geller. IJS Studies in Judaica 16. Leiden: Brill.

———. 2016. *Armenian Apocrypha Relating to Angels and Biblical Heroes.* EJL 45. Atlanta: Society of Biblical Literature.

———. 2017. "Biblical Text and Armenian Retelling." *JSAS* 26:82–87.

———. 2018. "The Armenian *Questions of St. Gregory*. A Text Descended from *4 Ezra.*" *Le Muséon* 131:141–72.

———. 2019. "The Armenian Embroidered Bible." *JSP* 29:3–11.

———. 2021a. *Armenian Apocrypha: From Adam to Daniel.* EJL 45. Atlanta: SBL Press.

———. 2021b. *The Genesis Commentary by Stepʻanos Siwnecʻi (Dub).* CSCO 695 Scriptores Armeniaci 32. Leuven: Peeters.

———. 2021c. "Hidden in Crannies of Noah's Ark." Pages 335–47 in *Tōnagir: Volume in Honour of Levon Ter-Petrossian*. Edited by Vahan A. Ter-Ghevondyan. Erevan: Matenadaran.

———. 2021d. "Sadayēl's Fall from Heaven." Edited by 486–96 in *Historical and Philological Studies in Honour of Zaza Aleksidze*. Vol. 2 of *The Caucasus between East and West*. Tbilisi: Korneli Kekelidze Georgian National Centre of Manuscripts.

———. 2022. "The Armenian Questions of St. Gregory II." *Le Muséon* 135:323–55.

———. 2023. "The Six Falls." *REArm* 41:397–420.

———. 2024. "The Thrice Holy." *MEMAS* 1.1:35–44.

Stone, Michael E., Aryeh Amihai, and Vered Hillel. 2010. *Noah and His Book(s)*. EJL 28. Atlanta: Society of Biblical Literature.

Stone, Michael E., in collaboration with Vered Hillel. 2012. *An Editio Minor of the Armenian Version of the Testaments of the Twelve Patriarchs*. HUAS 11. Leuven: Peeters.

Stone, Michael E., and Manya E. Shirinian. 2000. *Pseudo-Zeno, Anonymous Philosophical Treatise*. PhA 83. Leiden: Brill.

Stone, Michael E., and Nira Stone. 2012. *Catalogue of the Additional Armenian Manuscripts in the Chester Beatty Library, Dublin*. HUAS 12. Leuven: Peeters.

Stone, Michael E., and Emanuela Timotin. 2023. *The Legend of the Cheirograph of Adam: New Texts and Images*. ECCC 1. Turnhout: Brepols.

Stone, Michael E., and Aram Topchyan. 2022. *Jews in Ancient and Mediaeval Armenia: First Century BCE to Fourteenth Century CE*. New York: Oxford University Press.

Stone, Nira. 2011. "The Illumination of Non-biblical Armenian Manuscripts." *REArm* 33:249–79.

Stordalen, Terje. 2000. *Echoes of Eden: Genesis 2–3 and Symbolism of the Eden Garden in Biblical Hebrew Literature*. CBET 25. Leuven: Peeters.

Stroumsa, Gedalyahu G. 1981. "Le couple de l'Ange Divin et de l'Ésprit: Traditions juives et chrétiens." *RB* 88:42–61.

———. 1983. "The Incorporeality of God. Context and Implications of Origen's Position." *Religion* 13:345–58.

Stuckenbruck, Loren T. 1995. *Angel Veneration and Christology: A Study in Early Judaism and in the Christology of the Apocalypse of John*. WUNT 2/70. Tübingen: Mohr Siebeck.

———. 1997a. *The Book of Giants from Qumran: Texts, Translation, and Commentary*. TSAJ 63. Tübingen: Mohr Siebeck.

———. 1997b. "The Throne-Theophany of the Book of Giants: Some New Light on the Background of Daniel 7." Pages 211–20 in *The Scrolls and the Scriptures*. Edited by Stanley E. Porter and Craig A. Evans. Sheffield: Sheffield Academic.

Sumner, Paul B. 1991. *Visions of the Divine Council in the Hebrew Bible*. PhD diss., Malibu CA: Pepperdine University.

Su-Min Ri, Andreas. 2000. *Commentaire de la Caverne des Trésors: Étude sur l'histoire du texte et de ses sources*. CSCO 581 Subsidia 103. Leuven: Peeters.

Tal, Abraham. 2019. *Tibat Marqe: The Ark of Marqe*. SJ 92 Studia Samaritana 9. Berlin: de Gruyter.

———. 2021. "Bridging the Gaps in the Samaritan Tradition." Pages 262–75 in *Apocryphal and Esoteric Sources in the Development of Christianity and Judaism*. Edited by Igor Dorfmann-Lazarev. Leiden: Brill.

Tchekhanovets, Yana. 2018. *The Caucasian Archaeology of the Holy Land*. HdO 1, The Near and Middle East 123. Leiden: Brill

Tēr Nersēsean, Nersēs. 1956. Առաքել Սիւնեցի, Սրախտագիրք [Aṙakʻel of Siwnikʻ: The Book of Paradise]. Treasures of Ancient and Modern Armenian Literature 8. Venice: Mekhitarist Press.

Terian, Abraham. 2009. *Magnalia Dei: Biblical History in Epic Verse by Grigor Magistros*. HUAS 14. Leuven: Peeters.

———. 2016. "Rereading the Sixth-Century List of Jerusalem Monasteries by Anastas Vardapet." Pages 273–88 in *Sion, mère des Églises: Mélanges liturgiques offerts au Père Charles Athanase Renoux*. Edited by Michael Daniel Findikyan, Daniel Galadza, and André Lossky. Semaines d'Études liturgiques Saint-Serge 1. Münster: Aschendorff,

———. 2020. "A Discourse on the Church by Yovhan Mayragomecʻi." Pages 225–41 in *Armenia between Byzantium and the Orient: Celebrating the Memory of Karen Yuzbashyan (1927–2009)*. Edited by Bernard Outtier, Cornelia Horn, Basil Lourié and Alexey Ostrovsky. Leiden: Brill.

Teske, Roland J. 1990. *Saint Augustine on Genesis: Two Books on Genesis against the Manichees and On the Literal Interpretation of Genesis: An Unfinished Book*. FC 84. Washington, DC: The Catholic University of America Press, 1990.

Thackeray, Henry St. John. 1914. "The Song of Hannah and Other Lessons and Psalms for the Jewish New Year's Day." *JTS* 16:177–204.

Theodor, Judah, and Albeck, Chanoch. 1965. *Bereschit Rabba mit Kritischem Apparat und Kommentar*. [Hebrew]. Repr., Jerusalem: Wahrmann & Bamberger.

Thomson, Robert W. 1976. *Agathangelos' History of the Armenians*. Albany: State University of New York Press.

———. 1987. *The Armenian Version of the Works Attributed to Dionysius the Areopagite*. CSCO 488–89 Scriptores Armeniaci 17–18. Leuven: Peeters.

———. 1989. "The Historical Compilation of Vardan Arewelcʻi." *DOP* 43:125–226.

———. 1992. "'Let Now the Astrologers Stand Up': The Armenian Christian Reaction to Astrology and Divination." *DOP* 46:305–12.

———. 1995. *The Syriac Version of the Hexaemeron by Basil of Caesarea*. CSCO 550–551 Scriptores Syri 222–223; Leuven: Peeters.

———. 2001. *The Teaching of St. Gregory*. 2nd ed. Avant. Treasures of the Armenian Christian Tradition 1. New Rochelle: St. Nersess Seminary.

———. 2005. *Hamam: Commentary on the Book of Proverbs*. HUAS 5. Leuven: Peeters.

———. 2006. *Movses Khorenatsʻi. History of the Armenians*. Rev. ed. Ann Arbor: Caravan Books.

Thomson, Robert W., James Howard Johnston, and Tim Greenwood. 1999. *The Armenian History Attributed to Sebēos*. Translated Texts for Historians 31. Liverpool: Liverpool University Press.

Tiranun Vardapet. 2009. "Answer to the Questions of the Kings of Albania Atrnerseh and Pipē." Pages 957–10.997 in *Tenth Century*. MH 10. Edited by Azat Bozoyan. Antelias: Armenian Catholicosate.

Tirayr, Archbishop (Melik Muschkambarian). 1952. Ֆրիկ Շիվան [Poetry of Frik]. New York: AGBU.

Toepel, Alexander. 2006a. *Die Adam- und Seth-Legenden im syrischen Buch der Schatzhöhle*. CSCO Subsidia 119. Louvain: Peeters.

———. 2006b. "Yonṭon Revisited: A Case Study in the Reception of Hellenistic Science within Early Judaism." *HTR* 99:235–45.

———. 2012. "Adamic Traditions in Early Christian and Rabbinic Literature." Pages 305–24 in *New Perspectives on 2 Enoch: No Longer Slavonic Only*. Edited by Gabriele Boccaccini, Andrei A. Orlov, and Jason M. Zurawski. Leiden: Brill.

———. 2013. "Cave of Treasures." *MOTP* 1:531–84.

Toorn, Karel van der, and Piet van der Horst. 1990. "Nimrod before and after the Bible." *HTR* 83:1–29.

Topchyan, Aram. 2014. "The Armenian Version of the *Apocalypse of Pseudo-Methodius*." Pages 362–78 in *The Armenian Apocalyptic Tradition*. Edited by Kevork B. Bardakjian and Sergio La Porta. Leiden: Brill.

Tottoli, Roberto. 2003. "Cain and Abel." *EncIslam*.

Turdeanu, Émile. 1981. *Apocryphes slaves et roumains de l'Ancien Testament*. SVTP 5. Leiden: Brill.

Uluhogian, Gabriella. 1984. "Un Rotolo Manoscritto inedito del Museo Storico di Sofia." Pages 605–14 in *Atti del Terzo Simposio Internazionale di Arte Armena*. Venezia: Mekhitarist Press.

Urbach, Ephraim E. 1979. *The Sages: their Concepts and Beliefs*. Translated by Israel Abrahams. 2nd ed. Jerusalem: Magnes Press.

VanderKam, James C., ed. and trans. 1989. *The Book of Jubilees*. CSCO 511 Scriptores Aethiopici 88. Louvain: Peeters.

Vardanyan, Edda. 2012. "Fragments d'amulettes manuscrites conservés au Musée arménien de France Fondation Nourhan Fringhian: Catalogue et edition." *REArm* 34:333–70.

Vogelzang, Marianne E., and Wout J. van Bekkum. 1986. "Meaning and Symbolism of Clothing in Ancient Near Eastern Texts." Pages 265–84 in *Scripta Signa Vocis: Scripts, Scriptures, Scribes and Languages in the Near East, Presented to J. H. Hospers by His Pupils, Colleagues, and Friends*. Edited by Johannes H. Hospers and Herman L. J. Vanstiphout. Groningen: Egbert Forsten.

Wagner, Thomas. 2006. *Gotttes Herrschaft: Ein Analyse der Denkschrift (Jes 6.1–9.6)*. VTSup 108. Leiden: Brill.

Warren, Andy L. 1994. "A Trishagion Inserted in the 4QSama Version of the Song of Hannah, 1 Sam 2:1–10." *JJS* 45:278–85.

Waterfield, Robin. 1988. *The Theology of Arithmetic Attributed of Iamblichus*. Grand Rapids: Phanes Press.

Watson, Wilfred G. E. 1995. "Helel." Pages 746–50 in *Dictionary of Deities and Demons in the Bible*. Edited by Karel van der Toorn et al. Leiden: Brill.

Weiss, Tzahi. 2020. "Prayers to Angels and the Early Sefirotic Literature." *JSQ* 27:22–35.

Weitzmann, Kurt. 1976. *The Icons*. Vol. 1 of *The Monastery of St. Catherine at Mount Sinai*. Princeton: Princeton University.

Wevers, John W. 1974. *Genesis*. SVTG 1. Göttingen: Van den Hoeck & Ruprecht.

Wilkinson, John. 1977. *Jerusalem Pilgrims before the Crusades*. Jerusalem: Ariel.

———. 1981. *Egeria's Travels to the Holy Land*. Rev. ed. Jerusalem: Aris & Phillips.

Williams, Charles A. 1925. *Oriental Affinities of the Legend of the Hairy Anchorite*. University of Illinois Studies in Language and Literature 10.2, 11.4. Urbana: University of Illinois Press.

Winkler, Gabriele. 2002. *Das Sanctus: über den Ursprung und die Anfänge des Sanctus und sein Fortwirken*. OrChAn 267. Rome: Pontifical Oriental Institute.

Winston, David. 1979. *The Wisdom of Solomon*. AB. Garden City, NJ: Doubleday.

Witakowski, Witold. 2017. "Cain, Abel and Their Sisters in Ethiopian Tradition." Pages 525–49 in *Studies in Ethiopian Languages, Literature, and History*. Edited by Adam Carter McCollum. Aethiopische Forschungen 83. Wiesbaden: Harrassowitz Verlag.

———. 2019. "The Vienna Protology: An Ethiopic Apocryphon on Creation, Adam and Eve, and Their Children." *OCP* 85:453–80.

Witztum, Joseph B. 2011. *The Syriac Milieu of the Quran: The Recasting of Biblical Narratives*. PhD diss., Princeton University.

Wutz, Franz X. 1915. *Onomastica Sacra: Untersuchungen zum Liber Interpretationis Nominum Hebraeorum des Hl. Hieronymous*. TU 41.2. Leipzig: Hinrichs.

Wright, J. Edward. 2000. *The Early History of Heaven*. New York: Oxford University Press.

Xač'ikyan, Levon. 1992. Եղիշէի «Արարածոց Մեկնութիւնը» [Ełišē: The Commentary on Genesis]. Edited by Levon Tēr-Petrosyan. Erevan: Zvartnots Press.

Xač'ikyan, Levon, Yakob Kēosēyan, and Michael Papazian. 2004. Եղիշէ. Մեկնութիւն Արարածոց [The Commentary on Genesis by Ełišē]. Erevan: Magharat.

Yassif, Eli. 2001. ספר הזכרונות הוא דברי ימי ירחמאל [The Book of Memory, That Is, the Chronicles of Jerahme'el]. Tel-Aviv: Tel Aviv University.

Yadin, Yigael. 1962. *The Scroll of the War of the Sons of Light against the Sons of Darkness*. Oxford: Oxford University Press.

Yovsēp'eanc', Sargis. 1896. Անկանոն Գիրք Հին Կտակարանաց [Uncanonical Books of the Old Testament]. Venice: Mechitarist Press.

Zohrabean, Yovhannēs. 1805. Աստուածաշունչ Մադեան Հին Եւ Մաղ Կատակարանաց [The Inspired Scriptures of the Old and New Testaments]. Venice: Mekhitarist Press.

Ancient Sources Index

Hebrew Bible/Old Testament

Genesis
1:1	43
1:3	40
1:3–4	42
1:6–7	40
1:6–8	40
1:7	86, 49
1:7–8	47
1:8	46, 78, 80
1:11	211
1:11–12	78
1:14–18	41
1:16	73
1:17	74
1:19	46
1:20–22	41
1:25	211
1:26	63, 70, 75, 89, 156
1:29	78
3:7	86, 93, 94
3:8 (Arm)	117
3:10	90
3:11	87
3:12	114
3:17	123
3:17–19	73
3:18	86
3:19	73, 86
3:21	93–94
3:22	87
3:24	87
3:26 (Arm)	120
4:1	120
4:3–4	123
4:4	128
4:5	122
4:7	113, 121
4:8	117, 125, 139, 141, 149
4:8a (Peshiṭta)	140, 150
4:9	113
4:10	125
4:11–12	113–14
4:12	114
4:15	114, 116
4:17	50, 53, 114, 143
4:17–22	144
4:18	143
4:19	114
4:20	114–15, 143, 152
4:21	143, 148–49, 151
4:21–22	143
4:22	115, 143–44, 152
4:23	114, 154
4:24	116, 118
4:26	115, 120
5	133
5–6	142
5:3	156
5:6	161
5:8	115
5:9	173
5:10	161
5:23	116
5:32	161, 162
6:1	140
6:1–4	131, 134, 139, 155, 159, 207, 213
6:2	134–35, 137, 143
6:2–4	143

Ancient Sources Index

Genesis (*continued*)

6:3	133, 161–62
6:4	137, 148, 156, 186
6:5	161
6:6	133
6:8–9	160
6:9	159–60
6:10	161
6:11	161
6:11 (Arm)	161
6:12–14	161
7:6	161
7:11	161
8:4	178, 201
8:6–7	162–63
8:7	164
8:21	197
9:11	196
9:28	172
9:29	172
10	159, 169, 172, 176–77, 181, 198, 201
10:2	178
10:2–4	177
10:3	178
10:8–9	175–76, 185
10:8–11	185
10:9	186, 189–91
10:9–10	175
10:10	186
10:10–12	186
10:11–12	189
10:16–18	172
10:22	178
10:24	173, 175
10:32	178
11	161
11:1–9	193, 195
11:4	195, 197
11:6	195
11:7–9	177
11:8	198
11:9	195
11:12	174
11:12–13 (LXX Cod B)	173
11:14	162
11:18	162
11:22	162
11:28	209
11:31	206
12:1	206
12:4–5	206
12:7	173
12:15–20	206
13:11	206
14:22–23	206
15:1–6	207
15:7	173
15:18	173
16:16	207
17:4–6	207
17:7	173
17:24	206–7
18:1–16	207
18:2–16	128
18:7	123
19:31–32	124
20:2–18	206
21:12	206
21:14	207
22:1	206, 211
22:2–13	207
22:13	206
23:1	207
24:67	208
25:1–2	207
25:1–4	207
25:7–8	207
25:20	208
25:27	190
25:29–34	208
25:31–33	208
28:12	6
30:37–38	137
32:27	12
35:1	208
35:23–26	208
35:28	208

Ancient Sources Index

Exodus		36:1–2	223
1:1–4	208	37:1	221
1:11–14	220	40:17	222
1:15	225	40:2	222
3:17	224		
4:25	126	Leviticus	
8:2–13	220	8:12	103
8:16–18	220	8:30	103
8:21–24	220	11:15	163
8:29	220	12:2	46
9:3–7	220	12:2–5	46
9:10–11	220	12:5	46
9:14–15	220	18:16	124
9:22–24	220	19:19	211
11:4	11	20:21	124
12:46	128		
20:2–17	221	Numbers	
26:3	222	3:46	224
26:7	222	9:12	128
29	xxxiii	17:4	222
30:23–24	227	17:11	222
30:25	xxxiii, 103	17:23	222
30:32–34	228	20:11–12	224
31–32	223	20:24	224
31:2	222	24:17	219
31:18	222	25:9	224
32:4–35	221	27:14	224
32:11–13	223	33:38	224
32:16	222		
32:28	221	Deuteronomy	
32:31–32	223	3:11	224
32:35	224	4:21	224
32:42	23	8:4	97
33:11	99	10:5	222
33:13–16	223	14:14	163
33:20	99	22:9–11	211
33:22–23	98	32:8	200
33:23	99	32:8–9	200–201
34	98	34:1	224
34:6	223		
34:6–7	223	Joshua	
34:29	99,105	5:2–3	126
34:29–30	99	6:26	232
34:34–35	96, 100		
35:8	103		

Ancient Sources Index

1 Samuel		Jeremiah	
10:1	103	1	105
16:3	103	1:9	103
		4:31	46
2 Samuel		28:10	233
22:13	100	29:10	27
		31:15	46
1 Kings			
1:9	103	Ezekiel	
1:39	103	1	17
12:29–30	233	1:2	21
16:34	232	1:4	100
17:4	164	1:5	11
17:6	164	1:5–21	21
22:19	5, 10	1:15–21	26
		1:18	17
2 Kings		1:24	21, 27
9:3	103	1:24–25	11
15:29	232	1:26–28	99
16:2	232	1:27	100
17:3	232	3:12	7, 19, 21, 23, 27
18:9	232	3:13	26–27
		5:1	233
Isaiah		10:5	21
6	10, 105	12:5–7	233
6:1	96	28	101
6:2	5, 11	28:1	141
6:2–3	11	28:12	62
6:3	5, 7, 12, 19–21, 23, 27	28:13	96
6:7	102	38:12	47, 82
6:8	103		
14:11–14	62	Hosea	
14:19	100	1:2	233
14:12–14	61–62	3:1	233
14:12–16	62		
14:13	65	Joel	
20:7	233	1:13	223
30:27	98		
34:11	163	Jonah	
40:26	12	4:29	223
42:10	28		
60:19	100	Zephaniah	
66:13	46	1:14	163

Ancient Sources Index

Zechariah
- 1:12 — 8, 27
- 3 — 11, 102–5
- 3:3–4 — 105
- 3:4–5 — 106
- 7:5 — 27
- 14 — 97

Psalms
- 1:8 — 8
- 8:5 — 72, 88
- 8:5–6 (6–7) — 87
- 8:6 — 92
- 19:2 (18:3) — 12
- 24(23):8 — 8
- 29(28):1 — 11
- 29(28):1–2 — 19
- 33(32):3 — 28
- 45(44):7 — 7
- 47(46):7 — 11
- 49:12 (48:13) — 87
- 89(88):6–8 — 10–11, 19
- 90(89):4 — 73–75
- 103(102):20 — 10, 13
- 104(103):1–4 — 43
- 104(103):2 — 89
- 104(103):4 — 10, 13, 43
- 110(109):4–5 — 8
- 145(144):13 — 8
- 147:9 — 164
- 148:2 — 10, 13
- 148(147):3 — 10

Job
- 1:6 — 11
- 25:3 — 26
- 38:7 — 10, 12, 43
- 38:41 — 164

Proverbs
- 18:12 — 62

Daniel
- 1:2 — 133
- 4:10 — 134
- 4:14 — 134
- 4:20 — 134
- 4:30 — 101
- 7 — 5, 10–11
- 7:9 — 90
- 7:9–10 — 99
- 7:10 — 26
- 9:2 — 27
- 9:21–23 — 28
- 9:24 — 27
- 10:5 — 92
- 10:6 — 27
- 12:6 — 92

2 Chronicles
- 5:10 — 222
- 18:18 — 5, 10
- 36:21 — 27

DEUTEROCANONICAL BOOKS

Tobit
- 12:12 — 28
- 12:15 — 28

Wisdom
- 1:23–24 — 63
- 10:3 — 121
- 14:6 — 155

Ben Sira
- 16:7 — 89
- 17:9–10 — 155
- 49:16 — 12
- 50 — 89, 96
- 50:6–11 — 104
- 50:11 — 104

Baruch
- 5:1–3 — 106

Prayer of Manasseh
- 7 — 223

Ancient Sources Index

Pseudepigrapha

Apocalypse of Abraham
- 13.14 — 102
- 18.3 — 17
- 18.12–13 — 17

Apocalypse of Zephaniah
- 8 — 104
- 8.1–4 — 92

Ascension of Isaiah — 12, 106
- 1.5 — 95
- 3.25 — 95
- 4.16–17 — 95
- 7.21 — 10
- 9.9 — 98, 106
- 9.14 — 95
- 9.26 — 95

2 Baruch
- 3–10 — 92
- 21.6 — 41
- 48.10 — 26
- 51.5 — 92
- 51.10 — 92

3 Baruch
- 4.16 — 93
- 4.16–17 (Greek) — 91
- 12 — 31
- 12.1–8 — 28

4 Baruch
- 9.3 — 21

1 Enoch
- 1–36 (Book of the Watchers) — 135, 143
- 6.1–6 — 146
- 6.1–7 — 135, 146
- 6.3 — 144
- 6.5 — 140
- 6.6 — 140
- 7.1 — 148
- 8.1 — 143, 145, 151
- 8.3 — 148
- 9 — 137
- 9.1 — 18
- 9.2 — 28
- 9.8 — 148
- 9.9 — 137
- 9.10 — 18
- 14 — 11
- 14.20 — 90
- 14.22 — 12
- 14.24 — 99
- 20.1 — 18
- 39.12 — 21
- 40 — 26
- 40.1 — 26
- 40.9 — 18
- 54.5–6 — 62
- 54.6 — 18
- 61.10 — 10, 17
- 62.15–16 — 97
- 66.8 — 92
- 69.11 — 92
- 69.22–24 — 10
- 71 — 104
- 71.7 — 17
- 71.8 — 18, 26
- 71.7–9 — 11
- 86.1 — 12
- 86.1–3 — 12
- 87.2 — 92
- 89.9 — 92
- 89.59 — 27
- 90.2 — 127, 166
- 90.11 — 127, 166
- 98.4 — 66

2 Enoch — xxx, 15, 24
- 1.6 — 92
- 2.3 — 42
- 7.36 — 127
- 19.1 — 92
- 20.1 — 10, 16
- 20.3 J — 15
- 20.3–4 — 12
- 21.1 — 12, 21

21.2 J	24	4.33	115
22	102	5.1	137, 155
22.1–2	90	5.2	156
22.3–4	12	7.22	155
22.8 J	103	8.1–4	119
22.8–9	72, 128	8.19–20	141
22.8–10	106	11–12	164
29.2–3	15	11.38	206
29.3	6	12.12	206
30.10	87	12.12–14	204, 210
30.12	92	12.25–26	200
30.13	48	12.27	119
61.10	16	17.17	211
66.8	97–98	19.3	211
		19.8	211

3 Enoch
- 7.25   17
- 40   22

Liber antiquitatum biblicarum
- 20.2   99

3 Ezra
- 2.11   95
- 2.12   72, 128
- 2.45   95

Life of Adam and Eve   117
- 1.1 (Greek and Armenian)   117
- 9.1 (Latin and Armenian)   95
- 9.1–13.5 (Greek)   72
- 12.1–15.01   61

4 Ezra
- 6   81
- 6.2   79
- 6.2–3   79–80
- 6.35–59   39
- 6.44   79
- 7.26–32   76
- 7.80–98   23
- 7.123   81
- 8.21   26
- 8.22   41
- 8.52   79
- 10.43   117

- 13–16   63
- 13.3 (Latin)   58
- 15.3 (Latin)   62
- 20.2 (Greek)   92
- 29   47
- 31   31
- 33–34.3   123
- 35.1–42.4 (Georgian and Slavonic) 72
- 40.1–2   128

Odes of Solomon
- 11.11   93
- 11.16   81

Jubilees
- 2.2   41
- 2.2–3   42
- 2.7   79
- 3.8–9   46, 74
- 3.27–28   73
- 4.31   125

Sibylline Oracles   165
- 1.217–282   164
- 3.26   48

Testament of Abraham   89
- A 6.5   129
- B. 4   12

Testament of Adam		4Q201	
3.5	113	1 III, 16	155
Angelology	13		
Horarium, second hour	22	4Q252	
Horarium, tenth hour	12	I, 1–3	161
Testaments of the Twelve Patriarchs	136	4Q254a	
		15 4	165
Testament of Benjamin			
7.2–5	116	4Q403	
7.5	120	20 II, 3	17
		20 II, 7	17
Testament of Isaac		20 II, 9	17
6.5	12		
6.24	12	4Q504	89
		4	89
		8	89
Testament of Issachar			
3.5	212		
		4Q530	11
Testament of Levi		ii	12
3	10		
3.8	16	4QGenApoc	
8.2	99	VI, 7	115
16.1	27		
		4QSabbath Shirot	16–17
Testament of Reuben	138		
5.7	156	4QSam^a	
5.5–7	136	II, 11–10	21

Dead Sea Scrolls

		CD	
		III, 19	89
1QH^a		III, 20	106
IV, 15–16	89	V, 18–19 = 4Q266 3 II, 6	225
V, 27–28	12		
IX, 29–32	12	Jewish Greek Literature	
1QM		Josephus, *Antiquitates judaicae*	
IX, 14–16	18	1.54–55	123
		1.55	121
1QS		1.67–71	119
IV, 22–23	89, 106	8.226	233
		8.228	233
4Q180			
1	155	Philo, *De confusione linguarum*	
		178–179	66

Philo, *De fuga et inventione*		27:48	229
70	66	28:3	92
Philo, *De opificio mundi*		Mark	
29	42	1:9–11	86
75	66	1:10	162
77–78	79	1:16	41
146	49	9:2–3	100
		11:10	7
Philo, *De sacrificiis Abelis et Caini*		14:62	47
2.2	120	15:22	49, 51
20	122	15:36	229
52–54	122	16:19	47
88	122		
		Luke	
Philo, *De somniis*		1:14	7, 8
1.141	28	3:21–23	86
		3:22	162
Philo, *De specialibus legibus*		3:23	117, 162
1.66–97	104	12:24	164
		19:38	7
Philo, *Quaestiones et solutiones in Exodum*		22:69	47
11.51–124	104	23:36	229
Philo, *Quaestiones et solutiones in Genesin*		John	
1.58	120	1:32	162
1.60	122	19:17	49, 51
2.35	164	19:29–30	229
2.49	162	20:12	92
4.5	162		
		Acts	
Pseudo-Eupolemus		1:10	92
frag. 2	155	17:34	38
NEW TESTAMENT		2 Corinthians	
		5:1–4	98, 99
Matthew		12:2–41	41
1:18	46		
3:13–17	86	Ephesians	
3:16	162	1:21	16
4:18	41	3:10	38
4:21	41	6:10–12	16, 38
17:2	100		
26:64	47	Colossians	
27:33	49, 51	1:16	16, 38

Colossians (*continued*)
 1:18   28

Hebrews
 1:4–8   28
 9:4   222
 9:4–5   222

1 Peter
 3:22   38

Revelation
 1:16   100
 3:5   103
 3:18   103
 4   11
 4–5   21
 4:4   103
 4:8   14, 20–21
 5:11   26
 6:11   105
 7:9   97, 105
 7:13   97
 8:3   222
 10:1   100
 14:2–3   25, 28
 15:6   92

Armenian Parabiblica

Abel
 4.2   140
 4.4   119
 4.5   140
 5.3   114
 6.2   154, 156
 7.3   156

Abel and Cain
 4   118
 27   125
 5–44   117
 (Rec. 2) 27   126

Abel and Other Pieces
 1   118
 3.2   125
 3.3   125
 3.4   127, 165
 4.1–4.2   151
 4.5   151
 6.2–6.3   151

Abraham Text
 2.6   210
 4.6   210
 10.79   210

Abraham, Isaac, and Mamre
 32   128

Adam and His Grandsons
 1   72

Adam Fragments
 1 and 29   72

Adam Story 2   74, 91
 3   55
 5   91
 8   91

Bel and Other Pieces   150

Biblical Paraphrases
 1   163

Bones of Adam and Eve
 1   54

Brief History of Joshua
 1–29   213
 33   126

Concerning Abraham
 2   212

Concerning Abraham's Hospitality
 28, 29   128

Ancient Sources Index

Concerning the Good Tidings of Seth
131–32
4	152
18	140, 160
20	140, 160
26	163
30	163

Conflict of Adam and Eve with Satan
3.20	49

Construction of Noah's Ark
4	163

Creation and Transgression
2	60
3	60
5	65
18–19	91

Creation and Fall
1	15

Creation of Eve and Disobedience
4	82

Cycle of Four Works 150

Death of Adam 144
3–4	144
40	53

Descendants of Adam
1.30	163
ll. 1–6	148

Elenchic Abraham Text
9	211

Form and Structure of Noah's Ark
4	163

Genealogy of Abraham
2	212
5	208

6	205
9	203–4, 216
10	216
11	216
129	216, 222

Good Tidings of Seth
18–33	150

History of Adam and His Grandsons
1–3	118

History of the Discourse
1–29	57

History of the Forefathers
4	113, 121
6	113, 121
11	115
15–16	114
20–21	117
20–23	117
23	125
23–25	166
25	127
27	118
29	118
34–41	115
35–45	120
41–44	119
41	119
42–43	119
45 M2245	153

History of the Forefathers to Abraham and Their Years
11	161

Jeremiah, Susanna, and the Two Elders
29	27

Jonah 1 and 2   53

M10725 (seventeenth century)
fol. 199v	51
fol. 218v	79

Jonah 1 and 2 (*continued*)		102	53
fol. 2104r-v	199		
		Sermon Concerning the Flood	151
Memorial of the Forefathers		2	140
24	212	2–5	151
		3	137, 140, 142
Noah and the Cheirograph	166	4	142–43
		6	152
Of Moses and Aaron		8	150
26	99	10	163
Penitence of Adam	72	Sethites and Cainites	
12–16	62	5	156
14.3	64	6–7	149
		6–12	150
Periods	148	7–9	142
		9	140
Question		11	156
3	156		
3–10	149	Short History of the Holy Forefathers	
4	142	19	136, 153
6	140–41	26	163
7	142	29	137, 140, 142–43
10	142, 156	29–30	153
		30	149
Questions and Answers from the Holy Books		Story of Daniel	
1	13	3	27
14	119		
17	163	Story of Father Abraham	
		6	209
Questions of Gregory Recension I			
24–29	23	Story of Mamre	
42–48	23	120	212
Questions of Gregory		Story of Terah and of Father Abraham	
fol. 237v	82	9	213
		24	213
Repentance of Adam and Eve		42	213
28–29			
36	125	Story of the Holy Forefathers	
50–58	117	30	149
79	118		
97	53	Supplication Concerning the Sodomites	
99–103	54	9	150

Tree of Sabek		22.4	52–53
2–3	53	22.6	49–50, 53
		22.23	49–50
Words of Adam to Seth	72	23.16–17	49–50
		23.18	52
OTHER PARABIBLICAL LITERATURE		24.10	200
		24.10–11	119
Cave of Treasures	124	28.59	206
1.3	16, 18, 42	44.51–55	76
1.4	40	53.21	200
2.6–7	49		
2.15–17	48	Palaea Historica	
2.16	48	3.1–9	58
2.17–18	91	3.6	57
2.20–25	91	3.7	60
2.25	63	4.2	63
3.1	64	4.7	91
3.5	95	5.1	91
3.14	93	8.3	123
4.4	65	9.1	120–21
4.5–11	66	10.3	121
4.17–18	90	10.9–11.2	117
4.22	94	11.1	116
5.1	70	13	118
5.10–12	52	16.3	118
5.18	72	22.4	167
5.22	113	49.8	129
5.27	66, 96, 126, 125	75	225
5.29	133		
6.7–14	133	Saltair na Rann	
6.12	52	4.837–840	15
6.20	53	4.1053–1056	48, 57
6.20–21	53	11.1605–1608	15
7.4	64		
7.18	146	Tibat Marqe	96
8.7	118	1.54	166
11	146	1.66	11
11–12	146	1.78	11
11.4	146	2.4	44
12	141, 146	2.13	96
14.2	159	2.40	99
16.8	73	3.56	11
16.19	53	4.16–17	44
17.20	52	4.32	123
21.11	66	4.36	113

Tibat Marqe (continued)
4.96–97	65
5.2	93
5.31	52
5.33	99
5.35	99
6.12	113
6.19	63
13	97
157	97
503	52

Twelve Fridays, Slavonic	71

Te'ezaza Sanbat (Leslau)
6	187
9	187
25	47, 49
27–28	187

Rabbinic and Other Hebrew Literature

Mishnah, Tosefta, and Talmud

Avot Rabbi Nathan
A33:2	212

m. Abot
5:3	212

t. Berakhot
1:11	22

b. Hagigah
12a	42, 49

b. Sanhedrin
38a–b	47
58b	124
98a–b	75
107a	126

b. Menahot
85a	225

b. Nedarim
8b	41
39b	80

b. Pesahim
51a	80
54a	80, 211

b. Yevamot
63a	117

y. Berakhot
8:5, 12b	77, 89–90, 211
8:5, 12b	
9:1, 13a	28

y. Yevamot
11:1, 11d = b. Yevam. 62a	124

Midrash Rabbah

Genesis Rabbah
1.3	43
3.4	90
5.1	13
6.6	41
8.1	118
8.6	79
11.2	77, 90
11.9	43, 80
12.6	82, 89
15.3	80
19.8	74
20.12	93
21.5	92
21.9	80
22.2	117
22.5	117, 122
78.2	12
82.15	211

Exodus Rabbah
13.12	82, 89
15.22	43

Ancient Sources Index

21.4	28	Pesiqta of Ten Commandments	
52.2	222	1 (Pesiq. Rab. 21, 103a–b)	26
		3 (Pesiq. Rab. 23, fol. 118a)	89–90
Numbers Rabbah		3 (Pesiq.Rab. 23, 118a–b)	77
13.12	82, 89		
		Pirqe de Rabbi Eliezer	125
Deuteronomy Rabbah		3	43, 80
11.3	93	4	6, 43
Ve-Zot Haberakah 3	90	11	47
		14	72
Song of Songs Rabbah		20.3	95
15.22	43	21	120–22, 124, 127
		23	163, 167
Other Rabbinic and Hebrew Works		26–30	212
		31	128

Maimonides, *Mishneh Torah, Sefer Hamada, Yesodei haTorah*
2.7   15

Mekhilta de Rashbi
Baḥodeš 6   89

Mekilta de Rabbi Išmael
Baḥodeš 79   90

Midrash Konen
1.6   80
1.25   43

Midrash Tanhuma
Berešit 1.1   43
Hayye Sarah 3   43
Pekudei 11.12   222

Midrash Tehillim
18.25   212
24.4   43
86.4   43
104.7   43

Pesiqta Rabbati
24   66
46, fol.187b   75

Pesiqta deRav Kahana
Parah 4   90

Seder Gan Eden   80

Sifra Beḥukotai
1:2–6 [110d]   82

Sifre Numbers
42   26

Tana deBei Eliyahu Zuta
3   66

Tanhuma
Berešit 6.2   82, 89
Berešit 9   122
Berešit 10   127
Berešit 11   118
Toledoth 12   97

Targum Onqelos
6:3   161

Targum Pseudo-Jonathan
1:26   43
3:7   91
3:21   93
36:24   211

Targumic expansion
to Gen 3:8–7   127

Targums, Palestinian
   to Gen 50:2–3   229
   to Gen 50:26   229

Yalqut Shim'oni
   Lĕk lĕka 12   212
   Lĕk lĕka 68   212

EARLY CHRISTIAN LITERATURE

Acts of Thomas
   64   166

Aphrahat, *Demonstration*
   13.5–6   162–63
   17.7   79

Apocalypse of Paul
   7   12
   12   32
   16   32

Apostolic Constitutions
   7.35.3   15

1 Clement   22
   4   120–21
   34   22

3 Corinthians
   1.16–17   61

Ephrem Syrus, *Commentary on Genesis*
   91
   2.14–15   91
   8.17–18   162

Epiphanius, *Panarion*
   46.5   50

Eusebius, *Chronicle*
   21–22   145

Eusebius, *Praeparatio evangelica*
   11.6.3   120

Gospel of Bartholemew
   4.53   48
   4.53–55   61

Gospel of Philip
   69   96
   90   96
   107   96

Gospel of Thomas
   37   106

Ignatius, *To the Trallians*
   5   16

Irenaeus, *Adversus haereses*
   1.30.6   61
   5.33.3   81

Jerome, *Epistula* 108
   11.3   52

Jerome, *Liber Quaestionum hebraicarum in Genesim*
   80
   23.2   52

John Chrysostom, *De inani gloria et de educandis liberis*
   39   123

John Chrysostom, *Homily on Genesis*
   13.14   80
   14   47

John Damascenus *Orthodox Faith*
   2.11   80

Origen, *Commentarium in evangelium Matthaei*
   27.33   49

Origen, *De principiis*
   1.6.2   16

Ancient Sources Index

Onomastica Sacra	121	Aṙakʻel Siwnecʻi, *Book of Paradise*	81
Physiologus		Dawitʻ Ganjakecʻi, *Canon 85*	162
31.2–4	166		
		Ełišē, 10	71
Pseudo-Clementines, *Homilies*			
3.25	121	Ełišē, *Commentary on Genesis*	70–71, 73
Pseudo-Dionysius, *Celestial Hierarchy*		Eznik, *On the Sects*	
143–191	6	32–33	64
200C–261D	13, 20	35	65
		51–52	64
Pseudo-Macarius, *Homilies*	90	162–163	79
Shepherd of Hermas, Similitudes		Grigor Aknercʻi, *History of the Nation of the Archers*	121
3.4.01	42		
8.12–14	95		
		Grigor Magistros, *Epistle 11*	81
Theophilus, *Ad Auctolycum*			
2.19	50	Grigor Magistros, *Magnalia Dei*	146
Timothy I of Alexandria, *Discourse on Abbaton*		Grigor Narekacʻi, *Book of Lamentation*	
480	16	4.2.35	59
		64.4.39	59

Other Armenian Sources

		Grigor Taranałcʻi, *Chronicle* 84	82
Agathangelos			
26	61	Grigor Tatʻewacʻi, *Book of Questions* 84	
272	23	144	5, 23
276	11		
278	62–63	Grigor Tatʻewacʻi, *That the Garden Is Incorruptible*	81
290	138		
295	138		
		Hamam Arewelcʻi	87
Aṙakʻel Siwnecʻi, *Adamgirkʻ*	81, 87, 92	Hamam Arewelcʻi, *Commentary on Proverbs*	
1.10.10	15		
1.10.12	15	18:12	62
1.10.12–1.10.20	14		
1.10.16	15	Movsēs Xorenacʻi, *History*	
1.14.1–14.40	78	1.4	145
1.21.6	90	1.15	133
1.21.8	61	2.1	207
1.22.35	162	2.8	207
2.1.54	63	2.68	207

Mxit'ar Ayrivanec'i, *History*
 24   118

Pseudo-Ephrem, *Commentary on Genesis*
 114
 3   116

Pseudo-Epiphanius, *Homilies*   73, 90, 96

Pseudo-Zeno
 1.0.1   40
 1.1.0–1.6.18   40

Step'anos Siwnec'i (dub.), *Commentary on Genesis*
 2.1.6–8   164
 2.2.118–1209   208

Vardan Anec'i, *Poem on Ezek 1*   81

Vardan Anec'i, *Commentary on Genesis*   73, 126
 M1267 5r   15
 M1267, 5v   71, 78
 M1267, 7r   5–6
 M1267, 21v   79
 1:1   78

Vardan Anec'i, *Historical Compilation*   81
 8   225

Yačaxapatum Čaṙk'
 16, 23   65

Yovhannēs Erznkac'i Pluz, *On the Creation of the World*   140, 143
 259–305   154

Yovhannēs T'lkuranc'i, *On the Creation of the World* 19–21   15
 120–121   123
 229–232   118

Yovhannēs T'lkuranc'i, *Rhymed History*
 243–253   117

 306–307   156

Zak'aria Catholicos, *Homily on Life-Giving Passion*
 185   54

Other Sources

Adomnan, *The Holy Places*
 2.9.5   52

amulets
 Cairo Genizah 4.13–14   31
 Ḥorvath Rimmon 10.3–4   31

Aristotle, *Metaphysics*
 1.986a   14, 161

Book of John (Mandean)   167

Book of the Bee (Budge) 9   13

Hesiod, *Theogony*
 52–62   14

Michael the Syrian, *Chronography*   54, 136, 139, 145–46, 156, 164
 (1871) 7   174
 (1871) 16   188
 (1871) 13   189–90
 (Chabot) 1:5   156
 (Chabot) 1:5–6   144
 (Chabot) 1:19   200

Poe, Edgar Allen "The Raven"   164

Qur'an al-Mā'idah
 5:31   127
 5:32   126

Right Ginza (Lupieri) 18   166

General Index

70 and 72, shift between, 175, 198–99
70 or 72 descendants of Noah, 198
70 or 72 languages, 176–77, 193, 198, 200
72 family heads, build tower, 174–75, 197–99
72 languages and nations, 176–77, 198–99, 201
72 languages, origin of, 198
72 afflictions of Adam and Eve, 175
72, significance of, 175
Aaron, 222, 224
   anointing of, xxxiii
   died on Mount Hor, 224
   image of, 104
Abel, 66, 87, 111, 113, 122, 126–27, 165, 208
   age of, 114, 117–18
   killed in valley, 150
   offers firstborn beasts, 123
   sheep or ram of, 123, 128–29
Abimelech, 206
Ableman, O., 220
Abraham, xxxii, 10, 174, 208
   and ravens, incident of, 164
   ascesis of, not eating without guest, 213
   descendant of giants, 155
   discovery of God, themes, 210
   feeds Abel's lamb to three men, 123
   genealogy of, xxxiii, 203
   goes forth, 206
   sets fire to Terah's idolatrous temple, 209
   son of Terah, 206
   ten trials of, 211–12
   trials of, 204, 206

Abrahamyan, A. G., 41, 79
Achan. *See* Haran
acolyte, 36
Adam and Eve
   first twelve hours of, 74
   in garden, xxxii
   intercourse of, 72
   remains of, 51, 53, 184
      Noah gives to Shem, 173
Adam and His Grandsons, work, 72
Adam Books, Armenian, xxiii
Adam Story 2, work, 55, 74, 91
Adam
   acrostic, 48, 184
   and humans, created from the four elements, 48–49
   authority over creatures, 49
   body of
      anointed with sweet oil, 128
      from Babylon, 47
   bones of, 54, 169
   buried
      in cave on mountain, 52
      in center of earth, 53
      in Hebron, 53
      on Golgotha, 49–50, 52, 54–55, 173
      on mountain in Arabia, 50
      on Mount Zion, 53
   coffin of, in Noah's Ark, 173
   created, 45–46
      as thirty-year-old man, 162
      at center of earth, 47
      in Jerusalem, 47, 49
      in the image, 92

Adam: created (*continued*)
    on Golgotha, 48
    on site of temple, 48
    outside Eden, 47
  crowned, 91
  fall of, 100
  garments, glory of, 87, 190
  giant, 140
  glory of, 89, 91–93, 97, 105
  hand of, incised, 51
  head of, from land of Israel, 47
  illness of, 72
  offspring of, xxxiii
  priestly aspect of, 96, 102, 105
  prophetic testament to Seth, 146
  relics of, Noah gives to Maniton, 185
  replaces Satan in heaven, 64–65
  resembles angels, 87, 92
  royal status of, 73, 90, 92
  stripped naked, 90–91, 94
  supernatural size of, 49
  tills ground, 123
  twelve boons/gifts of, 64, 72–73, 82–86
Adamgirkʻ, 14–15
Adda, 114
Adler, W., 9, 27, 46–48, 114, 129, 137–38
Aerts, W. J., 180
Agathangelos, 43, 138, 176, 294
agriculture, inferior to herding, 123
Ahab, king, 232
Ahermon. *See* Hermon
Alans, 177
Albanians, 171
Albeck, Ch., 13
Alexander, king, 134
Alexandre, M., 123
Aliquot, J., 135
Ało(v)ros
  discovered astronomy, 133, 145–46
    king, 133, 145, 174
      of Babylon, 133
      of Sethites, 145–46
    ruled 36,000 years, 133
Amihai, A., 163, 179
Amorites, 172, 224

amulet rolls, Armenian, 28, 30, 61
amulets, codices, 30
Amzara, 115. *See also* Noyem Zara
Anania Širakacʻi, 162
Anastas vardapet, List of, work, 50
Anasyan, H., 200
ancient writings, discovery of, 119
Andersen, F. I., 15, 16, 21, 127
Anderson, G. A., 72, 81, 92, 95–96, 123, 194
Andrew, apostle, 41
androgynes, 118
Andronikos, chronographer, 144
angel
  killed 24,000 in Balaam incident, 224
  speech of, to Abraham, 128
Angelic Hierarchy, work, 13–14
angels, 5–6, 12, 15, 34, 36, 38
  adjuration by, 31
  and stars, 12
  ascending order of, 6, 10
  bow down to Adam, 64
  brigades, choirs of, 13, 24
  classes of. *See* angels: ranks of
  creation of, 41
    day of, xxxii, 39–40, 42–43
  descending order of, 6, 10
  four, of the Presence, 18
  hierarchy of, xxxiii, 5
  liturgy of, 12, 16
  nine, chief, 15
  praise of, 5–7, 10, 12, 17, 19, 23, 25, 28, 131
  prayer of, fixed, 12, 17
  prayers to, 28, 30
  ranks of, 5, 10, 16–17, 23, 42
    eight, 18
    five, 16
    nine, xxxii, xxxiii, 10, 14–16, 20, 33–35
    seven, 16
  rebellion of, 61
  role of, 5
  seven, chief, 15
  twelve, guardian, 31

General Index

angels (*continued*)
  white men symbolize, 92
animals, names of, 46, 115
Annanios of Alexandria, 145
anointing, with sweet, fragrant oil, 128
antimony
  ancient tradition of, 143
  and rouge, paint, 142–43, 151, 154
Antiochus IV Epiphanes, 233
Apocalypse of Moses, work, 59
Apocalypse of Zephaniah, work, 104
Apollonius of Tyana, 22
apostles
  from sea, 41
  twelve, 41
Apotelesmata of Apollonius of Tyana, work, 22
Aptowitzer, V., 48–50, 52, 124
Ara the Handsome, 178, 181
Arabia, Arabians, 172, 181, 198
Aṙakʻel Siwnecʻi, 15, 67
Aram, Japhethite, 178, 181
Aramayis, Japhethite, 178, 181
Aramazd, 189
Aṙan (Haran), son of Terah, 206
Ararat, mountains, 178, 201
archangels, 8, 15, 34, 36
  bring prayers to God, 28
  four, 30
  intercession by, 28
ark of the covenant
  contents of, 222
  dimensions of, 221
ark
  building of, xxxii
  built in one hundred years, 162
  symbol of the church, 162
Armeneak, Japhethite, 178, 181
Armenia, 176
Armenian chronology, 194
Armenian Library and Museum of America, 30
Armenians, 171
  descendants of Noah and Japheth, 177, 181, 201, 207

Arpachshad, 173
  and origin of idolatry, 180–81
  image of, worshiped, 174
  invents augury and foretelling, 178
  learned magic, astronomy, divination, 174, 180
Aršak, Aršakunis, 207
Aruadites, 172
Asaṭir, work, 187
Ascension of Isaiah, work, 12
ascetics, ascetic behavior, 35, 140
Asher, 208
Assyrians, 172, 232
Astłik, 172, 179–80, 183, 185
  portion of, 172
astronomy and divination, 178
Athens, 38
Attridge, H. W., 155
Aucher, J., 189
Auffarth, Ch., 42
Augustine, view of creation, 42
authorities, angelic rank, 15–16
Avalachvili, Z., 16, 18
Azan of Bethel, 232
Azazel, demonic prince, 145
Aznaworean, Z., bishop, xxxiii
Babylonia, kings of, 133, 138, 145, 175, 187
Badalanova Geller, F., xxx, 42, 59, 91, 95, 119–20, 123, 127, 135, 145, 175, 177, 187–89, 196, 200
Baert, B., 72
Bakker, A., 10, 12
Balaam
  magician, 224
  prophecy about Christ, 224
Baltzly, D., 197
Bamberger, B.J., 43
baptized people, as class, 37
Baronian, S., 31
Barrois, G. A., 48
Barzilai, G., 89, 96, 156
Basil of Caesarea, 54
  Commentary on Isaiah, work, 54
  Hexaemeron, work, 39

Bauckham, R. J., 174
Baumgarten, J. M., 46, 74
Baumstark, A., 13
Beck, B. N., 19
Bedrossian, M., 27
Beelzebub, 59, 60
Beersheba, 31
Bekkum, W. J. van, 92
Bēl, Belus, 174, 186, 189
Bēl, Hamite, hunter, 190–91
Beliar, 59, 60
Ben Sira, text, 104
Ben-Dov, J., 11, 102, 196, 200–201
Benjamin, son of Jacob, 208
Bereznyak, Asya, 118, 154
Bergamini, L. J., 41
Bethel
  heifer set up in, 233
  place, 232
Bethlehem, place, 51, 53–54, 173
Betz, H. D., 32
Bezalel, architect of tabernacle, 222
Bietenhard, H., 11, 23
Bilhah, 208
birds, creation of, 41
bishop, office, 36–38
blackness, 128
Boccacini, G., 145
body, as garment, 94, 97, 102–3, 106–7
Bohak, G., 30, 32
Bones of Adam and Eve, work, 54
Book of Adam, work, 59
Book of Giants, work, 11, 134, 155
Book of Paradise, work, 81
Book of the Bee, work, 13–14
Book of the Watchers, text, 134
Böttrich, Ch., 101, 127
Bousset, W., 91
Bowker, J., 188
bowls, magical, 32
boys, Chaldean, stolen by Jannes and Mambres, 220
Bremmer, J. N., 137, 155
Brichto, H. C., 123
brief, in titles of works. *See* short

brigades, angelic, 13
Brightman, F. E., 105
brightness, 90, 100
Brock, S. P., xxvi, 13, 52, 90–91, 93–94, 98, 107, 127, 139 150, 164, 211
Bucur, B. G., 91–93, 100, 104, 106
Budge, E. A. W., 12–13, 16
Bunta, S., 87, 89
Cain, 87, 111, 113, 114, 126–27, 208
  anger, motive for fratricide, 121
  deceives Abel, 116–17
  descendants of, 114, 152
  envy of Abel's wife, 114, 124–25
  envy of, motive for fratricide, 120–22
  God's reproach of, 113
  horn of, 114
  killed Abel with stone, flint, 125
  killed by Cainite Lamech, 119
  name, meaning of, 120
  offering of, defective, unfitting, 113, 121–22, 124
  possessed by Satan, 66
  seven punishments of, 113, 116
  seven sins of, 113
  shaking of, 114
  strangled Abel, 125
Cainan, father of Shelah, 173
Cainite Lamech, instigates seduction of Sethites, 154
Cainite line, culture heroes, 143
Cainite women
  intent to corrupt Sethites, 142
  invented cosmetics and musical instruments, 151–53
  sexual impurity of, 133
  used henna, 152
Cainites, xxxii, 111
  envy of Sethite celibacy, 151
  inhabited a plain, 139, 141, 150
  invented music, musical instruments, dance, 149, 153
  kings of, 144–45
calamus, healing, 228
calf, Abraham's, Christ resurrects, 129
Calzolari, V., 177

General Index

Canaan
 country, 173
 descendants of, 172
 person, 180
 sons of, conquer Palestine, 173
Canaanite(s), 57–58, 155, 224
cane, aromatic, 227
Cardona, G. R., 178
cassia, 227
catechumen, 37
Catholicos, 36–38
Cave of Machpelah, 52
Cave of Treasures, work, 16, 18, 50
caves, four significant, 52
censer, 104, 222
Chabot, J.-B., 139, 144, 156, 175–78, 200
Chaldeans
 astronomers and astrologers called, 133, 145–46, 174
 people and land, 133, 172, 174–75, 209, 220
chariot, God's, xi, 17, 26, 29
Charles, R. H., 15, 47, 194
Cheirograph of Adam, 51, 77, 95, 166
cherubs, 7, 15–17, 19, 22–23, 31, 34, 36, 38, 42
chiliasm. *See* millennarianism
Chitty, D. J., 141
Chrism, Canon of the Blessing of, work, xxxiii
chrismatic oil, xxxiii
Christ, 41, 54, 71, 75, 129, 162
 at God's right hand, 47
 child, 52, 184–85, 212, 229
Christian ascetic virtues, attributed to patriarchs, 87, 137, 152–53, 159, 161, 163, 208, 212–13
Chronicle of 1234, work, 187
cinnamon, qualities of, 227–29
cities, founders of, 53
Clermont-Ganneau, Ch., 135
Collins, J. J., 165
Concerning the Millennia, work, 76–77
Conflict of Adam and Eve with Satan, work, 50

Constantine Barjrberc'i, 139
Conybeare, F. C., 31
copyists, gender of, xxviii
cosmetics and coiffures, 142–43, 151–53
Cowe, S. P., 27
Cowley, R. W., 42, 200
Cox, C. E., 200–201
creatio ex nihilo, xxx
Creation and Fall, work, 15
Creation and Transgression of Adam, work, 60, 65
creation
 first day of, creations on, 40, 42–44
 second day of, 40
Cross, E. A., 78
Cross, F. M., 57–58
crossing, of boundary, 195–96
crown
 descended from heaven, 191
 of glory, 89
 unfading, 81
 woven, 28, 191–92
crows, 164, 166
cubit, size of, 162
Cumont, F., 12, 91
Cushites, 172
Cycle of Four Works, work, xxiv, xxvii, 150, 152
Dan, 208
 place, heifer set up in, 233
Daniel, Nathan, 222
Daniel, prophet, 25–26
Dar, Sh., 135
darkness and light, 60, 65
David bar Pawlos, 66, 176, 185–86, 198
David, king, 103, 126, 232
Davies, G.H., 89
day, God's, one thousand years, 73–75
De Conick, A., 98, 106
deacon, 36, 38
Dead Sea Scrolls, 17–18, 21, 89, 134–35, 165, 255, 238
Death of Adam, work, 53
demon, 30, 59, 62, 148, 165–66, 220, 225, 228

demons
　black, 167
　caused invention of musical instruments, 146
　fallen angels, 61
　representation of, 16
desert, 141
Desreumaux, A., 191
devil, 58–59, 63, 121
Dina, 208
Diocletian, 233
directions, four, 48, 184
DiTommaso, L., 215, 225
divine council, court, 11, 19, 102
divine voice, at baptism, 86
Dochhorn, J., 101
dominions, angelic class, 8, 15–16, 34, 36, 38
doorkeeper, ecclesiastic, 36
Dorfmann-Lazarev, I., 22, 47–48, 52–54, 64, 73, 90, 96, 119, 184
dove, also as symbol of Holy Spirit, 127, 162–65
doxology, 19, 38
Duchesne-Guillemin, J., 90
Dudālēm, land of, 47
Dura Europus, synagogue, 104
dyes, taught by Watcher, 143, 175–76
earth, division of, 159, 176–77, 182–83, 199
Eber, 173
　builder of tower, 174
ecclesiastics, ranks, nine, 35, 37
Eden, xxxi, 57, 71, 80–82
　Adam created in or not, xxx, 45–47
　connected with temple and tabernacle, 46, 90, 96, 101–2, 105
　created
　　before Adam, 80–81
　　before creation, 80
　　from nothing, 78
　　on third day, 79–81
　eschatological temple, 101–2
　fragrance of, 81
　length of time of protoplasts in, xxx, 70, 73–74, 77

Eden (*continued*)
　on mountain, 52, 65, 94, 139, 140–42, 149, 194, 197
　purity of, 46, 74, 101
　Satan's camp, 65
　spring of, 96
　time of creation of, 71
Efrati, Shlomi, xiii, 77, 89–90, 100, 162, 183
Egan, G., 188
Egypt, xxxiii, xxxiv, 172, 181, 186, 220–21, 227–29
Egyptians, 172
Eliav, architect of tabernacle, 222–23
Elijah, fed by ravens, 164
Elior, R., 46
Ełišē, 55
　Commentary on Genesis, 73
Embroidered Bible, xxxiv, xxix, 69
Ēmin, M., 118
empyrōsis, Stoic, 197
enemy, xxx, 58, 70. *See also* Satan
ennead, 14
Enoch, 98–99, 103–4, 106, 116, 119, 128, 132, 136, 142, 151–55, 208
　Cainite, 114, 143
　in Armenian parabiblica, 153
　translation to heaven of, 116, 133
Enosh, 89, 115, 137, 151, 173
　Cainite women made cosmetics, 151
　"hoped to call," 120
　preaches celibacy, 153
　prophecy of, 115, 120, 196
　prophet, 120
　sons of, 137, 140
　two pillars of, 115
envy
　Cain's, of Abel, 113, 120–21, 124, 142, 149
　inception of, 122
　Satan's, of humans, viii, 63, 65
Ephrem Syrus, 92, 138, 162
Epiphanius of Salamis, 49, 198
Epiphanius the Monk, 50
Erder, Y., 125

General Index

Ephrem Syrus, 146
Erevan, xiv, xxvii, 32, 164
erotapokritic form, xxviii–xxix, xxxiii–xxxiv, 9–10
Ervine, R. R., 199
Esau, 190, 208, 211
   hunter, 190
   sells birthright, 208
Eshel, E., 176, 195–96, 200
Ethiopia, 172, 228
eucharistic offering, 53
euhemerism, 137–38, 174, 181
Euphrates River, 17
Eve
   bore twins, 114, 117–18, 121, 124–25
   buried by Noah, in Bethlehem, 53–54, 173
   cares for child Christ, 51–52, 184–85
   garbed in glory, 92
   shown to Adam, second week, 46
   spins thread, 123
   without halo, 52
evil, God did or did not create, xxxi, 64, 66–67
exiles of Isael, 232–33
Exodus, xxxii, xxxiii, 222–23
exorcist, 36–37
Eynatyan, J., 76–77, 194
Ezekiel, prophet, xi, 26, 232
   symbolic acts of, 233
Eznik Kołbacʻi, 64, 79
feasts, Old Testament, 223
   corresponding Christian feasts, 223
Felix Fabri, 141
Feydit, F., 30
Fiensy, D. A., 15
Fine, E., 155
Fine, S., 155
fire
   cult of, 188–89
   upper heavens of, 40
firmament, creation of, 40
firstborn, 123, 128, 173, 220, 224, 232
   Egyptian, 11, 220
Fletcher-Louis, C. H, 89

flint, as knife, 125–27, 165
flood, xxxi, 51–54, 131, 136, 156, 159, 162, 178, 194, 196–97
   and tower, ultimate cause of, 159
   did not reach Eden, 194
   of fire, 119, 196–97
   second expected, 196–97
Flusser, D., 101, 191, 204
fortieth day, Adam enters Eden on, 55, 74
fossil giants, 155
Fossum, J., 98, 106
four corners of earth, 47–48, 184
four elements, 42, 44, 48–49, 197
Franks, 162, 171
Frazer, M. E., 49, 51
free will, angels and humans have, xxx, 64, 66
freeing from hell, 61
Frey, J., 7, 11, 21
Friday
   Adam and Eve sinned on, xxx, 30
   Adam created on, xxx, 41, 70
   role and symbolism of, 71, 74–75
Friedlander, G., 47, 124–25
Fröhlich, I., 12, 155
fruit, of Eden, xxx, 71–72, 75, 78, 81, 86
Fry, V. R., 174
Gabriel, angel, 18, 28, 31, 187
Gad, son of Jacob, 208
Gandoubarios, Indian astronomer, 183
garden of Eden. *See* Eden
Garibian de Vartavan, N., 178
garments
   angelic, 87, 91–93, 96, 104
      Satan steals, 95
   change of, significance, 103
   eschatological, of life, 97–98
   glorious and priestly vestments, 93, 95–97, 99, 101–2, 105
   hairy, 95
   of skin, Edenic, 93–95
   white, 90, 92, 97, 100, 103, 105–6
Gaster, Th., 10, 13, 59
Gaylord, H., 58–59
gaz, gazi, Persian measure, 162

General Index

Geiger, A., 127
Gełam, Japhethite, 178, 181
Genealogy of Abraham, work, 203–4, 215–16
Genizah, Cairo, 31–32
George Syncellus, chronographer, 9, 46–47
Georgians, 171, 177
Gergasites, 172, 224
Gerö, S, 179, 183–84, 187, 225
Ghazaryan, D., 30
giant, giants, 134, 137–38, 142
    40 cubits long, 154
    antediluvian times, 155–56, 186
    origin of, 137
    will destroy Satan, 151
Ginzberg, L., 50, 63, 65, 72, 74–75, 77, 82, 92–93, 117, 122, 156, 162, 167, 188–89, 196, 198
glory. *See also* garments
    celestial and Edenic, 11, 73, 87–93, 90–91, 100, 105–6
    eschatological, 97, 99–100, 106
    of divine presence, 96
    of humans, 87, 89
    of temple, 100
God
    praise of, 10, 12–13, 16, 19, 23, 25, 128, 131
    promise by, to Abraham, 173, 224
    raiment of, 90
gods, war between, 57
Golgotha, 47, 51–54, 172, 184–85
    etymology of, 49, 173
Golitzin, A., 15, 19, 89–90, 97, 99, 103
Gomer, Japhethite, 177–78, 181
good things, eschatological, 63, 195, 223
Govett, R., 50
Grattepanche, J., 127
great, in titles of works, 9
Greatrex, M., xxxi, 6, 60, 62, 65–66
Greeks, 171, 177, 197
Greene, D., 57
Greenwood, Timothy, xxxiv, 177
Grigor Magistros, 81, 146

Grigor Narekac'i, 31, 59
Grigor Tat'ewac'i, *Book of Questions*, work, 5–6, 23, 33, 43–44, 73, 81, 84
Grigor(is) Aršaruni, 12, 55, 71, 74–75
Grotto of Nativity, 51, 54
Gruenwald, I., 12, 21–22
Grypeou, E., 48, 52, 138, 140
Gutmann, J., 162, 167
Habashians, 172
Hagar, 206, 207
Haik, 190. *See also* Hayk
hairy ascetic, 100, 101
Hakobyan, T. X., 173
Ham, 161–62, 172, 182, 186
    identified with Hephaistos, 187
    invented fire and fire cult, 187
    portion of, 172, 181
Hamam Arewelc'i, 62, 87
Hannah, D. D., 31
Haran
    Aṙan, name of, 206, 209
    death of, 204, 209–11
    first bred the mule, 209, 211
    insolence to Abraham, 206
    place, 206, 208
Harley McGowan, 51
Harmay, Japhethite, 178, 181
Harrowing of Hell, image, 167
Hartenstein, F., 18, 22
Harut'yunyan, S., 30
Hayk
    eponymous ancestor, 174
    head of tower family, 175
    Japhethite, 178, 181, 190, 207
Hayward, R., 80, 124, 188
heaven
    gates of, 12
    third, 41
Hebrew, primordial language, 119, 200
Hebrews, 54, 171
Hebron, protoplasts buried in, 52–53
Heinemann, J., 22
Heither, T., 49, 52
hekhalot
    hymns, 22

General Index

hekhalot (*continued*)
  works, 21
hell
  as prison, 61
  Gehenna, 80
Hellel ben Shaḥar, Morning Star, 57–58, 100
Heller, B., 188
Henning, W. B., 134
Henoch, city of, Adam's burial in, 50
Henze, M., 100, 141
Herbert, M., 15
Hermon, Mount, 136, 139–42, 148, 151–52, 154
hexaemeron, 39, 81
Hilkens, A., 136, 144, 146, 164, 172–73, 177, 183–84, 188, 190, 198–99, 211
Hillel, V., 60, 112, 117, 133, 163, 170, 180
Himmelfarb, M., 11, 102
History of the Discourse, work, 19, 57
Hittites (Hethians), 172, 224
Hivite, 224
Hoeck, A. van den, 104
Hollander, H., 120, 136–37
homilies, xxvii
Hor, Mount, Aaron dies on, 224
Horarium, work, 11–12, 22
Horst, P. van der, 185, 188
Ḥorvath Rimmon, place, 31
Hosea, symbolic acts of, 232–33
hour, ninth, 11–12
Hovhanissian, V., 61
Howard-Johnston, J. H., 177
Hŕomkla, place, 139
Hultsch, F. O., 50
humans
  created by God's right hand, 86
  creation of, 41, 49, 71
  fill place of Satan, 58
  free will, xxx, 64, 66
  glory of, 87, 89
  praise God, 8, 12–13, 34
  status of, 89, 92
  tenth heavenly rank, 15, 65
Ialdabaoth, 61

ideograms, 41
idolatry, beginning of, 174–75, 180–81
Ignatius *vardapet*, 15
India and Ethiopia, confused, 228
Indians, 172
Inglisian, V., 178
intercourse, every 30 years, 72, 162
iris, antidemonic, 228
iron working, illicit, Watchers teach, 143
Isaac, 190, 203, 207–8
  binding of, 128, 211
  birth of, 207
  genealogy of, 203
  twenty years' celibacy, 161, 208, 212
  type of Christ, 208, 212
  symbolic acts of, 233
Ishmael, birth of, 207
Isho‘ of Hasankeyf, 139
Israel Science Foundation, xiv
Issachar, 208
Issaverdens, J., xxiii, xxvii, 126, 146, 150
Istanbul, Armenian Patriarchate, xxxi
Ivanovici, V.I., 91–93, 100, 104, 106
Jacob, 12, 137, 190, 200, 203, 208, 224
  genealogy of, 203
  ladder vision of, 6
  twelve children of, 208
Jacob of Edessa, 60, 65
Jacobus, H. R., 174, 247
James, apostle, 41
James, M. R., 47, 50
Jannes and Jambres, 215, 220, 224–26
  garden of demons of, 220
  magicians, 220
  sacrficed 980 children to demons, 220–21
Jansma, T., 42–43
Japheth, 161–62, 171, 176–78, 182
  ancestor of Armenians, 181, 201
  portion of, 172, 176
  territory of, 181
Japhethite nations, fifteen, 176–77, 198
Japhethites, number and spread, 198–99
Jared, 116, 135–36, 142
Javan, 177, 199

Jebusite, 172, 224, 244
Jeremiah, Edward, 95
Jeremiah, Susanna and the Two Elders, work, 27
Jeremiah, symbolic acts of, 233
Jericho, city, 231–32
Jeroboam, sets up heifers, 233
Jerusalem
    Adam created in, 45–49
    center of the earth, 48, 50, 172
Jesus, thirty years old, 117, 162
jewelry-making, Watchers teach, 143–44
Job
    contemporary of Abraham, 176
    contemporary of Nimrod, 176
John, Apocalypse of, 28, 262
John, apostle, 41
Jonah 1 and 2, works, 53
Jonge, M. de, 120, 136–37
Joseph, 203, 208, 216
    significance of in Armenian tradition, 203
    type of Christ, 208
Joshua
    ben Nun, xxv, 99, 232
    ascesis of, 213
    high priest, 102–3
Jubal, 114–15, 143
Jubilees, work, 46–47, 79, 164
Judah, son of Jacob, 208
judgment, last, 76–77
Kambiwros, invents mining precious metals, 175
Kamesar, A., 80, 188
Kaynan (Cainan, Kenan), 116
Kaynan, son of Arpachshad, 173
Kazazian, N., xxviii
Kedron, brook of, 48
Kelly, F., 57
Kenan, son of Enosh, 115
Kēoseyan, Y., 73
Ketura, 207
    six sons of, 207
Khzmalyan, Ara, xiv
Kim, A. Y., 117, 122

King, M., 51
kingship, Adam's, 49, 73, 86, 90–92, 96
Kister, M., 42, 77, 196
Kittel, R., 89
Kiwleserian, P., xxxi
Klein, M. L., 127
Klijn, A. J. F., 138
Kmosko, M., 13, 52, 146
Kortekaas, G. A. A., 180
Kosman, A., 97
Kowalski, A., 93
Krauss, S., 41
Kronholm, T., 138, 146
Kruisheer, D., 116
Kuehn, S., 62–63, 66, 90, 93
Kugel, J., 121
Kulik, A., 28, 31, 59, 95
Kuyumdzhieva, M., 121
La Porta, S., 35
Laban, 137, 208
Lambden, S. N., 89, 91, 96
Lamech
    Cainite, 114, 143, 154
    killed Cain, 118–19, 152
    son of Methuselah, 116
Lamsur, Shemite, 190–91
Langlois, V., 139
languages, division of, 175, 193, 195, 198, 200–201
Latins, 171
Łazaryan, V., 13, 18
leaders, nine ranks of, 33
Leah, 208
lector, ecclesiastical, 36
Leslau, W., 47, 49, 187
lesser, in titles of works, 9
Levene, A., 120
Levi, 99, 208
Leviathan, skin of, 95
Levites, 221, 224
Lewis, J. P., 163, 167
Lewy, H., 23, 94
Licht, J., 206, 212
Life of Adam and Eve, work, 15, 59, 62, 117, 175

Life of Adam, work, 46
light, 40, 42, 44, 60, 90, 97, 99
    and darkness, 42, 60, 65, 91, 122
    creation of, 40
    Edenic, 77–78, 82
    eschatological, 97
    garments of, 93, 96, 100
Lint, Th. M. van, 17, 81
Lipatov-Chicherin, N., 49, 52, 54
Lipscomb, W. Lowndes, xxvii, 53, 60, 91, 117, 122, 126, 131, 146, 150, 152–53, 165
List of 24 Prophets, work, 26
lists, xxix, xxxiv, 6, 8, 10, 39, 64, 72, 75–76, 82–83, 116, 169, 176–77, 199, 204, 206, 212, 215, 231–32
literate nations, lists of, 177, 199
Little Genesis, work, 46
liturgy
    heavenly, angelic, 12, 16, 21, 105
    Jewish, 21–22
living creatures, praise or sounds of, 11, 21, 26
Livingstone, E. A., 78
Loeff, Y., 61
Lord of Hosts, divine title, 20
Lot, 209–10
    and his daughters, 124
Lucifer, 58, 62
Lüdtke, W., 166, 191
Luibheid, Colm, 6, 13–14, 20
luminaries
    creation of, 40–41, 82
    praise of, 10
luminosity
    angelic, Edenic, eschatological, 92
    characteristic of elevated status, 89
luminous garments
    of Adam, 72–73, 85–106
    Satan loses, 95
Lupieri, E., 166–68
Macedonians, 171
Mach, M., 17
Madoyan, A., 81
magical potions, 148

magicians, competition with Moses, 221, 224–25
Magog, Japhethite, 177
Maguire, H., 90, 106
Maier, J., 21
Maimonides, 15
Małaliel, 116
Malan, S., 49–50
Malxaseancʻ, S. C., 40
Manichean Book of the Giants, work, 134
Maniton,
    astrologer and diviner, 174–75, 180, 182–83, 191
    portion of, 172, 180–81
    taught Nimrod astrology, 175, 179, 183
    Yonton, son of Noah, xxviii, 54–55, 169, 172, 178–79, 182–85, 201
manna, urn full of, 222
Manoogian, Torkom, Patriarch, xiv
Manougian, Nourhan, Patriarch, xiv
Mansfeld, J. J., 196
Fritz, J.-M., 119
Martinez, D. G., 10, 19–22, 24
Mary, Virgin, Mother of God, 41
Mastema, 164. *See also* Satan
Matʻevosyan, A.S., 176, 200
Matenadaran Institute of Ancient Manuscripts, v, xiv, 32
Mathews, E. G., 114, 116
matter, preexistent, xxx–xxxi
Mazor, L., 71, 73–74, 96, 141
McNamara, M., 15
Medians, 177
Meeks, W., 103
Megas, G. A., 51, 75, 95
Mekhitarist Fathers, Venice, 30
Melchizedek, 48, 52–54, 100
    Abraham grooms, 101
    descendant of Nimrod, 187
Mellnik, M. J., 178
men, white, symbolize angels, 92
Meribah, place, 224
Meshech, Japhethite, 177
Methuselah, 116, 152

Metzger, B. M., 199
Micah, prophet, 186, 232
Michael the Syrian, 146
    Chronography, xxviii–xxix, xxxiv, 54, 139, 156, 174
Michael, archangel, 18, 28, 31, 64, 95, 103
Milik, J. T., 134
millennarianism, 75–76
Miltenova, A., 95
Minov, S., 16, 49, 58–59, 61, 63, 94, 113, 115, 124, 131, 141, 162–63, 169, 176–77, 184–87, 198
miwṙon, xxxiii. See also charismatic oil
Mnemosyne, 14
monk, ecclesiastic rank, 37–38
Montesano, M., 51
moon, 23, 40–41, 98, 104, 197, 223
Morgan, M. A., 30
Moriah, Mount, 48
Moses, xxix, 46, 71, 100, 174, 181, 220, 223–25, 232
    chronology of, 220
    died on Mount Nebo, 224
    glory of, 92, 97–100, 105
    split the sea by incantations and staff, 221
    supplication of, 223
    taught by Jannes and Jambres, 220
Moses's host, number of feasts of the Old Testament, 224
mountain of paradise, cosmic, 140–41, 146
Movsēs Xorenacʻi, 178, 181, 186, 201, 207
manuscripts
    Bod arm f27, 31
    Bod arm g4, 31
    Chester Beatty 636, 31
    Galata 154, xxxi, 3, 204–5, 207, 209, 219
    J1171, 199
    J1925, 17
    M0605, 199
    M10200, 150, 199
    M10547, 6
    M10720, 83–84, 181
    M10725, 42, 51, 79, 199

manuscripts (*continued*)
    M1267, 5, 15, 43, 71, 78–79, 139, 191
    M187, 39
    M203, 39
    M2036, 148, 199
    M2111, 153, 197
    M2152, 6
    M2182, 82
    M2245, 82, 153
    M2679, 176, 200
    M268, 6, 19, 24
    M4618, 51, 53
    M5254, 176, 200
    M533, 169
    M537, 15
    M5523, xi
    M5960, 6
    M6420, 91
    M717, 212
    M682, xxvii, 3, 6, 13–14, 24, 57, 73, 83, 169, 203, 215
    M8494, 199
    PA56, 91
Mulder, O., 96
mule, miscegenation forbidden, 209–11
Murad, F., 20
Muradyan, G., 166
Muradyan, K., 39
Murdoch, B. O., 87, 91–92
Murray, R., 35
Muses, nine, 14
music and dance, cause debauchery, 146, 153–54
Mxitʻar Ayrivanecʻi, 15
myrrh, 227, 228
    bitter, used in embalming and soporific, 229
    with vinegar, given to Christ on cross, 229
mystery, 35, 38
Nahor, son of Terah, 174, 206, 208
nail, garments of, 91
names of the animals, corrupted, 119
naming, part of creation, 119
Naphtali, son of Jacob, 208

Narkiss, B., 17, 91
nations, seven, extirpated from land, 224
Naveh, J., 31–32
Nebo, Mount, Moses dies on, 224
Nebrovtʻ, 175. See also Nimrod
Nebuchadnezzar, 100, 233
Nersēs Šnorhali, St., 31
Nersēs, Noah's helper, 166, 168
Nersoyan, T., 24, 105
Newsom, C. A., 16–17
Nickelsburg, G. W. E., 16, 135, 143
Nicklas, T., 43
Nimrod, 179, 190
   and fire, worship, 187–89
   and Ham, switch roles, 188
   casts Abraham into fire, 186–88, 211
   descendant of Canaan, 187
   discovered Palestine center of world, 191
   fed tower builders with game, 190
   founded Edessa, 189
   founder and king of Babylon, 186, 191
   giant, 176, 186, 191
   hunter, 184–86, 189–91
   identified with Bēl and Kronos, 187, 189–90
   in Georgian tradition, 189
   in the Bible, 185–86
   initiates building of tower, 189
   instructed in wisdom by Maniton, 191
   killed by wind of tower, 187
   king of Babylon and Assyria, 186–87
   king of Canaan, 186
   leads Tower-builders, 186–87, 189
   learned astrology from Maniton, 175, 182–84
   name means rebellion, 189
   positive view of, 184
   proclaims himself a god, 175
   three eyes and horn, 176
   wore Adam's special clothes, 190
nine, perfect number, 14–15
Ninus, 186
Nineveh, named after Ninus, 186
Noah, xxxii, xxxiii, 52–54, 116

Noah (continued)
   and ark, 51, 133, 164, 178
   birth and names of sons, 162, 182
   buries Adam on Golgotha, 54–55
   children of, xxxiii, 161
   chronology of, 161–62
   daughter. See Astłik
   daughters-in-law, 182
   descendants of, ancestors of nations, 169, 177
   four sons, earth divided among, 159, 182, 184
   fourth son of, xxviii, 172, 180, 182. See also Maniton
   marries Noemzara (Neeemzara), 115, 152, 182
   pure, son of God, Sethite, ascetic virtue, 137, 160, 163
   remained celibate five hundred years, 137, 140–41, 152, 159–60, 162–63
Noyēm (Naama), daughter of Cainite Lamech, 115
oath, Watchers swear, on Mount Hermon, 135–36, 151
obsidian, as knife, 126
Odeberg, H., 22
Of Moses and Aaron, work, 99
Og, king, size of, 224
Oholiab, 223. See also Eliav
oil of anointing, xxxiii, 103, 128, 215
   ingredients and their qualities, 226–29
oil, of tree of Eden, 72
Old Adam–New Adam typology, 47, 50–51, 71, 96, 173
Olyan, S., 13
Olympus, Mount, 141
ophanim, angelic rank, 17, 26
Orion Center for the Study of the Dead Sea Scrolls, 134
Orlov, A. A., 58, 66, 89, 91, 93, 95–97, 102, 119, 145
Otros, sea, 182
Otzen, B., 100
Ovēayn, sea, Maniton goes to, 180, 183
Pahl, city, 207

Palaea Historica, work, 57, 191
Palestine, 172–73, 181, 191, 206
Palhavunis, 207
Papazian, M., 73
papyri, magical, 32
parabiblical books, Armenian, xxiii–xxvi, xxxiv
paradise. *See* Eden
Paramelle, J., 116, 162
patriarchs, burial of, 52
Paul, apostle, 38, 41
Pearson, B. A., 138, 182
Peleg, 162, 174
Penitence of Adam, work, 59, 62, 64, 72
Peoples of the Sons of Noah, work, xxxii, xxxiv, 169–78
Perezites, 224
Persians, 171–72, 181, 188
Peters, D. M., 165
Petrosyan, A., 178
Phanuel, angel, 18
pharaoh, 206, 221, 224
Philo of Tikor, *Chronography*, work, xxxiv
Phineas, stopped killing, 224
Pietersma, A., 215, 220, 225
pillars, two, legend of, 119
Piovanelli, P., 101
Pison, River, 228
Pivazyan, E., 154
plagues of Egypt, 216, 219
plants, created, 41, 78, 80
Poe, Edgar Allen, 164
Połarean, N., 91
possession, demonic, 65–66, 126
powers, angelic class, 8, 15–16, 34, 36, 38, 42
praise
  by creations, 11, 13, 19
  by day and night, 12
prayers, apotropaic, 25, 28, 30
preexistent matter, denial of, 71, 78–79
Prescott, H.F., 141
Preuschen, E., xxiii
priest, of church, 34, 36–38, 105–6

priesthood, Adam had, 49, 73, 86–87, 97, 101, 105
priestly garments, meaning of, 99, 102, 104–6
priests, resemble angels, 96
principalities, angelic class, 8, 16, 34, 36, 38
prophecy, Adam had, 49, 73, 84, 86, 96–97
prophet, angelic garb of, 104
prophets, xxxiii, 10, 28, 41, 52, 92, 97, 101, 104–5, 228, 231, 233
  praise by, 25
  twenty-four, xxxii, 231
Pseudo-Dionysius the Areopagite, *Celestial Hierarchy*, 5–6, 13, 18, 20, 22, 33, 38
Pseudo-Methodius, *Apocalypse of*, 179–80, 184–85
purification
  change of garments, 102
  of prophet and high priest, 102–3, 105
purity, postnatal, 46
Pythagoreans, 14
Qedushah. *See* thrice holy
quadrupeds, creation of, 41
Question about Archangels, work, 65
Question, in titles of Armenian works, 9
Questionnaire
  7.2, xxix
  character of, xxxiii
  date of, xxviii, 145
  literary method of, xxix, xxxiv, 9–10
  scholastic features, 125
  Scripture in, 98
  structure, xxxii
  title of, 8
  views held by, xxx
Questions and Answers from the Holy Books, work, xxxiv, 9–10, 13, 77, 119
Questions of the Queen, work, 9
Rabinowitz, L., Rabbi, 72
Rachel, 208
ram or sheep, Abel's offering, 48, 113, 123, 128–29

ram or calf, Abraham offered three men, 128–29
ram, Isaac's replacement, 48, 53, 128
Rapp, S. H., 189
raven, 163–68
　attitudes, 163
　black color, 126, 128, 164, 166
　care for young, 163–64
　cawing, 128, 163–64
　connection with evil, 165–66
　demons take form of, 126, 165
　drowned while mating, 167
　eats corpses, 166–68
　lives in desolate places, 163
　Noah sends, 162–63, 165
　qualities of, 163
　Satan or demon takes form of, 126–127, 165–66
　symbol of Satan, 162, 164, 166
　teaches Cain, 126, 165
ravens (crows)
　Abraham and, 127, 164, 210
　Satan uses, to teach humans, 126–27, 165
　symbolize enemies of Israel, 126, 166
Rebecca, 208
Rebiger, B., 12, 28, 59
Reed, A. Y., 135, 137, 153
Reemts, Ch., 49, 52
Reeves, J. C., 134–35
Reinink, G. J., 179–80
Reiterer, F. V., 43
repentance, 80, 100
Repentance of Adam and Eve, work, 53–54, 71, 116, 118, 173
reptiles, 41, 95
resurrection, 76–77
Reu, 136, 156, 174, 187, 191
Reuben, son of Jacob, 208
Reuling, H., 92
Ricks, S. D., 93, 95–96
righteous, tested in furnace, 188, 190, 211
Robbins, G. A., 39
Robinson, S. E., 13–14, 17, 22
Romans, literate, 177

Rompay, L. van, 91
Rorem, C., 6, 13–14, 20
Rose, H., 57
Rosenthal, F., 76
Rowland, C., 5, 17
Rubin, N., 97
Rudolph, K., 61
Rüger, H. P., 127
rulers, angelic class, 8, 15–16, 34, 36, 38, 42
Runia, D. T., 66, 78
Russell, J., 30, 57, 62
Russell, J. R., 30, 118, 154, 225
Sabbath, eschatological, 75–76
sacrifices of the Old Testament, list of, 223–24
sacrifices, cultic, 128, 215, 223–24
Sadaēl, Sadayēl. *See* Satan
Sadayēl, Satanayel, 57–60, 62, 64
Sałay, 173
Sałmanasar (Shalmanezer), 232
Saltair na Rann, work, 15, 48, 57
Samarios, Samiros, king. *See* Samiros
Samaritan works, 96–97, 99, 124, 155, 187, 206
Samaritans, 11
Šamatun, territory of Shem, 53
Samiros, king of Cainites, 133, 144, 175
Sammael, 59. *See also* Satan
Samuel Anecʻi, 79
Sanctus, prayer, 21, 24
Sanders, S. L., 99
Sanjian, A. K., 50
Sarah, 206, 207, 211
Sargsyan. L., xxxiii
Sariel, angel, 18
Satan, xxx, 142
　and serpent, relation of, 65–66
　angels of, 60
　brought Sethites to Cainite women and in, 149
　builder of hell, 61
　cause of evil, 65
　darkness of, 91, 96, 128
　envy or jealously of, 62–63, 65, 70, 121

Satan (*continued*)
  fall of, xiii, xxxii, 57–61, 63–66, 200
  form of, as raven, 162, 164–66
  giants will destroy, 151
  glory of, original, 60, 95
  identified as dragon or serpent, 64–66
  identified as Hellel son of Dawn, 58
  name(s) of, 57–60, 70
  owner of arable land, 123
  possesses serpent, Cain, etc., 65–66, 122
  pride of, 62, 64
  rebellion of, 57, 61–64
  role in Sethite sin, 142, 144, 148–49, 151, 153
  transformation of, 57, 95
Satanel. *See* Satan
Satran, D., 17, 101
Saul, king, 103
Sawalaneanc', T., 187, 189–90, 200
Schäfer, P., xxx, 49, 63, 66, 74, 94
Schermann, Th., 199
Schimmel, A. M., 14
Schmidt, A. B., 136, 139
Schneider, M., 96
scholasticism, Armenian, xxix, 6, 10, 125
Scholem, G. G., 22
Schopflin, K., 43
Scott, J. M., 169, 176, 181
Sea of Tiberias, work, 42
sea, creation of, 41
seals, 73, 175
Sebēos, 177
second hour of day, 12, 22
Sefer Harazim, work, 30
Seleucus, rebuilt Edessa, 189
Semazios, king of fallen Watchers, 174
Semiazos, king of Cainites, 144
Semiramis, 133
Sennacherib, destroyed Edessa, 189
serpent, xxx, 70–71, 75, 91, 95
seraphs, angelic class, 7, 11, 15–16, 18–19, 21–23, 31, 34, 36, 38, 42
serpent, possessed by, identified with Satan, 64–66

serpent, skin of, 95
Serug, 162, 174
Seth, 52, 71–72, 89, 115–18, 133, 138–39
  and Enoch, sons of, went to Mount Hermon, 151
  and Melchizedek and protoplasts' remains, 52–53
  giant, 150, 155–56
  invented writing, 119
  quest of, 72
Sethite, first king, astrologer, 145, 174
Sethites, 111, 131, 133–34
  200 or 500, 133, 136–37, 140, 142, 152–54, 160
  520, 140, 152
  abandoning celibacy, chronology of, 149
  after 200 years Cainite women made cosmetics, 152
  and Cainites, xxxii, 111, 131–33, 138–39, 146–48, 150, 156, 159
  prohibition of mixing, 138, 151–52
  beget giants, 137, 142, 148, 150–51, 156
  celibacy of, 500 or 800 years, 142, 149
  descend from mountain, join Cainites, 133, 142–44, 150, 152, 154
  giants, 140, 148–49
  inhabited mountain, 65, 131–32, 139–41, 149–51, 153–54
  men and Cainite women begat giants, 150, 154
  replace Satan, 65
  suborned, abandon oath, 142–43, 154
Sabbath Songs, work, 16–17
seven steps. *See* steps, seven
seven things existed before creation, 43, 80
seventy years
  eschatological, 27
  exile, 27
Sextus Iulius Africanus, 138
Seymour, St. J. D., 15
Shaked, Sh., 31–32
sheep, Abel's. *See* ram, Abel's

General Index   303

Shelach, 162
Shem, 52, 89, 161, 171, 173, 182, 190
   and remains of protoplasts, 52–53, 173
   portion of, 171–72, 181
Shemḥazai, demonic prince, 144–45
Shemiḥazah, chief Watcher, 135
shining faces, 92, 99, 122
Shirinian, M. E., 40
Short History of Joshua, work, 8
Short History of the Holy Forefathers, work, 8, 153, 196
short, in titles of works, 8
Sidersky, D., 127
Sihon, king, 224
Simeon, 172, 208
Simon Peter, apostle, 41
sin, angels, Watchers, xxx, 134–35, 137, 146, 148, 155, 159, 174
Sinai, Mount, 51, 98–99, 105, 141, 227, 228
Sinai, St. Catherine's Monastery, 51
Sisan, weaver, 191
six, role of, 40
skin, garments of, 93, 95
skull, Adam's, beneath Cross, 49–51, 173, 184–85
Smith, M., 10, 13
Sodom, 206
Sodomites, description of, 149–50
sons of God, 111, 131, 134–35, 139, 142–43, 148, 153, 200. *See also* Watchers
   angels, 10–12, 43, 135, 146, 186, 200–201
   Sethites, 137–38, 140, 142, 151
Speyer, W., 196
spheres, heavenly, 23, 94, 197
Spurling, H., 48, 52, 138, 140
St. Ejmiacin, Chapel, Jerusalem, 91
stars, 10, 23, 40–41, 43, 178, 180, 191
   creation of, 41
   fixed, 23, 94
stelae, pillars, 115, 119, 196
Stepʿanos Orbelean, 179, 183, 185
steps, seven
   of ascent of souls, 23

steps, seven (*continued*)
   of descent, 23
Stokes, R., 11
Stone, M. E., passim
Stone, N., 31, 166
Stordalen, T., 101–2
Story of Daniel, work, 27
Story of Terah and of Father Abraham, work, 101, 213
Stroumsa, G.G., 48–49
Struggle of Michael with Satanael, work, 95
Stuckenbruck, L., 11, 28, 134, 155
subdeacon, 36
Su-min Ri, 180, 183
Sumner, P.B., 11
sun, 23, 90, 98, 100, 103–4
   creation of, 41
Syriac language, prime role of, 119, 177, 199–200
Tʿobel, 114
Tʿurkʿ, 207
tabernacle, xxxiii, 46, 96
tabernacle, chronology of building, 222
tabernacle, dimensions of, 222
Tablets of the Law, 222
Tabor, Mount, 100, 135
Tabula Gentium, 125, 159, 169, 171–72, 175–76, 187, 206
Tal, A., 63, 99, 124–25, 187, 206
Tardieu, M., 94
Tartarus, 23
Tchekhanovets, Y., 50
Teʾezaza Sanbat, work, 47, 49, 187
Teaching of St. Gregory, work, 43, 62, 64
temple, 46–47, 71, 74, 80, 90, 96, 100–102 105, 172, 175, 233
   Adam created in, 47
Ten Commandments, 26, 221
Ten Plagues of Egypt, work, xxix, xxxiv
ten plagues, list of, 215, 220
Ten Trials of Abraham, work, xxix, xxxiv, 204, 206
ten, significance of, 14–15, 76
Tēr Nersēsean, N., 81, 177

Ter-Ghevondyan, Vahan, xiv
Terah, 174, 206, 209, 211
　idolater, 209–10
Terian, A., 50, 65, 146
Testament of Adam, work, 11–12, 14, 17, 22, 52, 146
Testament of Levi, work, xxii, 16
Testament of Seth, Syriac, work, 50, 52
Testaments of the Twelve Patriarch, 60, 136
Thackeray, H. St. J., 21
The Twelve Fridays, work, 71
Thebiad (Egypt), 229
Theodor, J., 13
thirty years, between Eve's children, 117–18, 162
thirty, age, 72, 114, 117–18, 161
Thomson, R. W., 6, 11, 18, 23, 29, 39, 43, 62, 81, 138, 145, 174–75, 177–78, 186–87, 193, 201, 207, 225
thrice holy, 11–12, 18–24
throne, divine, 5, 10–11, 21 80, 103
thrones, angelic class, 5, 7, 15–16, 34, 38, 47
Tiglath-pileser, 232
Tigris River, 172, 181
time, creation of, 42
Timotin, E., 51, 66, 77, 95, 123, 175
Tiras, Japhethite, 177–78, 181, 199
Tirayr, Archbishop, 91
Titans, 137
Titus, 233
Toepel, A., 16, 49, 63, 72, 90, 95–96, 138, 183
tongues, confusion of, 175, 195, 198, 200–201
Toorn, A. van der, 185, 187
Topchyan, A., 178–80
Torah, 80, 223
　given fifty days after Red Sea crossing, 221
Torgom, Japhethite, 178, 181
tower of Babel, xxxii–xxxiii, 175, 187, 189–91, 193–97
　10 months' journey high, 194–95

tower of Babel (continued)
　texts concerning, 174
　tradition, author's attitude to, 174
tree in garden, olive, 71–72
Tree of Sabek, work, 48, 53
tree or bush, Isaac's ram caught in, 48
trees, creation of, 41
triads, three, 14
Trishagion. See thrice holy
Tubal, Cainite, 177
Tuffin, P., 9, 46–47
Turdeanu, E., 58–60
twelve glories or boons, of Adam, 72, 82–84, 93
twelve refuse to build tower, 190
twelve tribes, 198
two floods, Enoch prophesies, 196
Ugaritic epics, 141
Ulm, Germany, 141
Uluhogian, G., 30
Urbach, E. E., 76
Uriah, architect of tabernacle, Bezalel's father, 222–23
Uriel, angel, 18
VanderKam, J. C., 16, 135, 137, 139, 143
Vardan Arewelc'i, 72, 121, 124, 139, 226
　Commentary on Genesis, 5, 15, 43, 71, 73, 78–79, 165, 191
　Historical Compilation, xxviii–xxix, xxxiv, 81, 126, 225
Vardanyan, E., 30
Vespasian, emperor, 233
vessels, luminaries in, 41
Vision of Ezekiel, Armenian, xi, 17, 29
Vogelzang, M. E., 93
Wagner, T., 18
Warren, A.L., 21
Watchers, 21, 115, 136, 138, 143–44, 153. See also sons of God
　and women, intercourse of, 135–38, 148, 159
　fall of, 131, 134–36, 146
　tradition, transmission of, 136, 146–47
Waterfield, R. 14

General Index

waters
  praise God, 13
  upper and lower, 40
Watson, W. G., 58
Wednesday, 40–41
  serpent seduced Eve, 70
Weiss, Tz., 30
Weitzmann, K., 51
Wevers, J. W., 135
wheels, 17, 26, 27. *See also* Ophannim
white garments, 90, 92, 97, 100, 103, 105–6
white, meaning of, 92
Wilkinson, J., 48, 50, 52
Williams, C. A., 100
wind, destroys tower, 187, 195
wings, six, 11
Winkler, G., 24
Winston, D., 63
Witakowski, W., 59, 66, 118, 124
Witztum, J. B., 66, 87, 126–27
world-week, 75
Wright, B. G., 17
Wright, J. E., 11
Wutz, F. X., 121
Xačʻikyan, L.Y., 73
Yadin, Y., 18
Yassif, E., 198
Yonṭon. *See* Maniton
Yovasapʻ Sebastacʻi, 210
Yovhannēs Erznkacʻi, 60, 147
Yovhannēs J̌ułayecʻi, 166
Yovhannēs Mandakuni, 64
Yovhannēs Ojnecʻi, 70
Yovhannēs Tʻlkurancʻi, 15, 81, 116, 123–124, 140, 143, 147, 156
Yovsēpʻeancʻ, S., xxiii–xxiv, xxvi–xxvii, 9, 146, 150
Zakʻaria Catholicos, 54, 58, 61
Zebulun, son of Jacob, 208
Zechariah, prophet, 27
Zeus, 14
Zilpah, 208
Zion, called mother, 46
Zion, Mount, 141

Zion, Mount (*continued*)
  Adam created on, 48
Zohrab, 201
  Bible, 20
zone, lunar, 194, 197
Zoroaster, 188
Zurawski, 145

www.ingramcontent.com/pod-product-compliance
Lightning Source LLC
Chambersburg PA
CBHW050856300426
44111CB00010B/1271